perspectives

Nutrition

# perspectives

## Nutrition

Academic Editor
**Dirk Nelson**
*Missouri Southern State College*

coursewise
publishing
inc.

Boulder • Bellevue • Dubuque • Madison

Our mission at **coursewise** is to help students make connections—linking theory to practice and the classroom to the outside world. Learners are motivated to synthesize ideas when course materials are placed in a context they recognize. By providing gateways to contemporary and enduring issues, **coursewise** publications will expand students' awareness of and context for the course subject.

For more information on **coursewise** visit us at our web site: http://www.coursewise.com

**coursewise publishing editorial staff**

Thomas Doran, ceo/publisher: Journalism/Marketing/Speech
Edgar Laube, publisher: Geography/Political Science/Psychology/Sociology
Linda Meehan Avenarius, publisher: **courselinks**
Sue Pulvermacher-Alt, publisher: Education/Health/Gender Studies
Victoria Putman, publisher: Anthropology/Philosophy/Religion
Tom Romaniak, publisher: Business/Criminal Justice/Economics

**coursewise publishing production staff**

Victoria Putman, production manager
Lori A. Blosch, permissions coordinator
Mary M. Monner, production coordinator, print/online

Cover photo: Copyright © 1997 T. Teshigawara/Panoramic Images, Chicago, IL. All Rights Reserved.

Interior design and cover design by Jeff Storm

Printed in the United States of America by **coursewise publishing,** Inc.
1379 Lodge Lane, Boulder, CO 80303

10 9 8 7 6 5 4 3 2

# from the
# Publisher

## coursewise publishing

*Sue Pulvermacher-Alt*

> *Never eat anything at one sitting that you can't lift.*
> —Miss Piggy

Fortunately, I'm a strong person.

I enjoy food and over the years have eaten a lot of it. I've learned from years of publishing in the health field that what I eat is one very important aspect of who I am and my overall health state. Along with exercise, adequate sleep, regular medical checkups, and other healthy behaviors, I need to watch what I eat. Variety and balance are essential.

Food and information are both for your consumption. We didn't package a snack with this volume (sorry, maybe next time), so we had to focus on information about food and nutrition. We want you to "eat" this volume—to consume every article and enjoy every bite. And we thought it important to offer you variety and balance in this information meal.

Some of the articles in this reader are like a big plate of spaghetti or clams in the shell—they'll take some time to get through thoroughly and cleanly. For example, a couple of articles in Section 2 are from the *Journal of Nutritional Education.* Another in Section 5 is from the *Journal of the American Dietetic Association.* These selections will challenge you. They're meaty articles full of statistics and quantitative analysis. You'll need to chew on them slowly and carefully. Take time to read the questions that precede the articles and log onto the **courselinks**™ site for Nutrition to check your answers. You'll get more out of the "meal" if you prepare well.

On the other hand, other selections are like a snack of baby carrots or a taco at the drive-up window—quick to get through, yet satisfying. Take a look at "Big Food" in Section 1 or "The Chow of Champions" in Section 3. You'll get through these in short order. You'll only need a few bites, so make sure you enjoy those few bites. Just as you should strive for variety and balance in your diet to enhance your nutritional health, we tried to offer variety and balance in our selections to enhance your nutritional understanding.

But don't stop dining with the articles. In addition, you'll find web sites that will expand your understanding of the issues surrounding nutrition. The R.E.A.L. sites you'll find throughout this *Perspectives: Nutrition* volume and at the **courselinks**™ site have been chosen because they are particularly useful sites. You, however, are the one at the table consuming this information. Read the annotations and decide if the site is worth visiting. Do the activities so you can get to know the site better. Search the **courselinks**™ site by key topic and find the information you need to be a more informed diner.

As publisher for this volume, I had the good fortune to work with Dirk Nelson as the Academic Editor. Dirk brings a cheerful, optimistic spirit and an impressive academic background to this project. He earned his bachelor's degree in exercise science and sports medicine from Montana

State University; his master's in kinesiology and exercise physiology from the University of Kansas; and his doctorate in physical education also from the University of Kansas. Dirk has taught a variety of courses, including nutrition, at the collegiate level for 11 years. He has learned the value of variety and balance in life. When he isn't teaching in the classroom or leading his department, Dirk enjoys jazz, his family, aviation, and working on his log home that sits on 15 acres of southwest Missouri prairie.

Dirk and I didn't choose the menu by ourselves. We worked with a top-notch Editorial Board. At **coursewise** we're working hard to publish **R**elevant, **E**xciting, **A**pproved, and **L**inked (what we call R.E.A.L.) learning tools. Articles and web sites are selected with these criteria in mind. Editorial Board members offered some critical feedback and posed some interesting challenges. They know their content and are a web-savvy bunch. The result is a R.E.A.L. learning tool. My thanks to Dirk and the entire Editorial Board.

Enough of my introduction to your meal of a nutrition course. It's time to dig in. After you've finished, let me know what you think. We're constantly refining the menu, and I'd welcome your feedback. Where do we need more meaty coverage? What topic areas should we put on a diet? What other R.E.A.L. sites would provide just the right spice? Different balance? More variety? It's dinnertime, so enjoy the meal and let me know how the food set with you.

Dirk Nelson is a professor and head of the department of Kinesiology at Missouri Southern State College. He received his bachelor's degree from Montana State University, and his master's and doctorate from the University of Kansas. Dr. Nelson has taught courses on nutrition, lifetime wellness, school health, and biomechanics at the collegiate level for 11 years. He and his wife Renda have two children, Alex and Emalee. When not teaching, Dr. Nelson enjoys jazz music, aviation, and working on his family's log home that sits on 15 acres of southwest Missouri prairie.

# from the
# Academic Editor

## Dirk Nelson

Mortimer Adler, a philosopher (see *Intellect: Mind over Matter; Reforming Education; Six Great Ideas; A Guidebook to Learning; How to Speak/How to Listen),* notes that all genuine learning is active, not passive. Learning involves using the mind, not just the memory. Learning is a process of discovery in which the learner is the main agent. Assuming the role of Academic Editor for *Perspectives: Nutrition* gave me the opportunity to be an active learner. The topic at hand just happens to be an issue of great interest to me and one that affects all of you—nutrition. You are what you eat.

Food can be a source of pleasure and is also associated with a number of emotions and circumstances. For example, when you do well on an exam, you may celebrate with a meal. When a relationship ends, you may soothe your depression with food. When a child is born, neighbors and friends often come with food. When a parent passes away, family members often share a meal together. Similarly, what we eat has a significant impact on athletic performance, on pregnancy outcome, and on the likelihood of chronic disease. We may consume some nutrients in excess; in other nutrients, we may be deficient. You are what you eat.

This reader is not an all-encompassing treatise on the topic of nutrition. Indeed, the goal of this work is not to discuss specific nutrients and their functions, or the digestive process, or food safety, as you may find in traditional nutrition textbooks. Instead, this reader provides contemporary information addressing a plethora of nutrition-related issues, including:

- the merits of a varied diet
- lowering your cancer risk
- diet strategies for children, athletes, pregnant women, and the elderly
- antioxidant nutrients
- weight-loss strategies

I sincerely hope that this reader poses questions, actively challenges, introduces new ideas, piques interest, links concepts from various resources, and motivates you to examine your nutrition lifestyle. Moreover, the reader will direct you to relevant experiences on the World Wide Web—a great way to facilitate active learning. However, you are responsible for discerning, evaluating, questioning, and contemplating. Subsequently, for true learning and true change, you must apply. You are what you eat.

Then you will have built a solid foundation upon which every aspect of your life is based—nutrition. YOU ARE WHAT YOU EAT!

# Editorial Board

# WiseGuide Introduction

## Critical Thinking and Bumper Stickers

The bumper sticker said: Question Authority. This is a simple directive that goes straight to the heart of critical thinking. The issue is not whether the authority is right or wrong; it's the questioning process that's important. Questioning helps you develop awareness and a clearer sense of what you think. That's critical thinking.

Critical thinking is a new label for an old approach to learning—that of challenging all ideas, hypotheses, and assumptions. In the physical and life sciences, systematic questioning and testing methods (known as the scientific method) help verify information, and objectivity is the benchmark on which all knowledge is pursued. In the social sciences, however, where the goal is to study people and their behavior, things get fuzzy. It's one thing for the chemistry experiment to work out as predicted, or for the petri dish to yield a certain result. It's quite another matter, however, in the social sciences, where the subject is ourselves. Objectivity is harder to achieve.

Although you'll hear critical thinking defined in many different ways, it really boils down to analyzing the ideas and messages that you receive. What are you being asked to think or believe? Does it make sense, objectively? Using the same facts and considerations, could you reasonably come up with a different conclusion? And, why does this matter in the first place? As the bumper sticker urged, question authority. Authority can be a textbook, a politician, a boss, a big sister, or an ad on television. Whatever the message, learning to question it appropriately is a habit that will serve you well for a lifetime. And in the meantime, thinking critically will certainly help you be course wise.

## Getting R.E.A.L.

This reader is a R.E.A.L. learning tool.™ This means that the readings and other learning aids explained here are **R**elevant, **E**xciting, **A**pproved, and **L**inked. They will help you think critically about the important issues of the course. Feedback from both instructors and students has helped us to develop some suggestions on how you can wisely use this R.E.A.L. learning tool.™

## WiseGuide Pedagogy

A wise reader is better able to be a critical reader. Therefore, we want to help you get wise about the articles in this reader. Each section of *Perspectives* has three tools to help you: the WiseGuide Intro, the WiseGuide Wrap-Up, and the Putting It in *Perspectives* review form.

## WiseGuide Intro

In the WiseGuide Intro, the Academic Editor introduces the section, gives you an overview of the topics covered, and explains why particular articles were selected and what's important about them.

Also in the WiseGuide Intro, you'll find several key points or learning objectives that highlight the most important things to remember from this section. These will help you focus your study of section topics.

At the end of the Wiseguide Intro, you'll find questions designed to stimulate critical thinking. Wise students will keep these questions in mind as they read an article (we repeat the questions at the start of the articles as a reminder). When you finish each article, check your understanding. Can you answer the questions? If not, go back and reread the article. The Academic Editor has written sample responses for many of the questions, and you'll find these online at the **courselinks**™ site for this course. More about **courselinks**™ in a minute. . . .

## WiseGuide Wrap-Up

**WiseGuide Wrap-Up**

Be course wise and develop a thorough understanding of the topics covered in this course. The WiseGuide Wrap-Up at the end of each section will help you do just that with concluding comments or summary points that repeat what's most important to understand from the section you just read.

In addition, we try to get you wired up by providing a list of select Internet resources—what we call R.E.A.L. web sites. The information at these web sites will enhance your understanding of a topic. (Remember to use your Passport and start at http://www.courselinks.com so that if any of these sites have changed, you'll have the latest link.)

## Putting It in *Perspectives* Review Form

At the end of the book is the Putting It in *Perspectives* review form. Your instructor may ask you to complete this form as an assignment or for extra credit. If nothing else, consider doing it on your own to help you critically think about the reading.

Prompts at the end of each article encourage you to complete this review form. Feel free to copy the form and use it as needed.

## The courselinks™ Site

The **courselinks**™ Passport is your ticket to a wonderful world of integrated web resources designed to help you with your course work. These resources are found at the **courselinks**™ site for your course area. This is where the readings in this book and the key topics of your course are linked to an exciting array of online learning tools. Here you will find carefully selected readings, web links, quizzes, worksheets, and more, tailored to your course and approved as R.E.A.L. learning tools.™ The ever-changing, always interesting **courselinks**™ site features a number of carefully integrated resources designed to help you be course wise. These include:

- **R.E.A.L. Sites**   At the core of a **courselinks**™ site is the list of R.E.A.L. sites. This is a select group of web sites for studying, not surfing. Like the readings in this book, these sites have been selected, reviewed, and approved by the Academic Editor and the Editorial Board. The R.E.A.L. sites are arranged by topic and are annotated with short descriptions and key words to make them easier for you to use for reference or research. With R.E.A.L. sites, you're studying approved resources within seconds—and not wasting precious time surfing unproven sites.

- **Editor's Choice**   Here you'll find updates on news related to your course, with links to the actual online sources. This is also where we'll tell you about changes to the site and about online events.

- **Course Overview**   This is a general description of the typical course in this area of study. While your instructor will provide specific course objectives, this overview helps you place the course in a generic context and offers you an additional reference point.

- **www.orksheet**   Focus your trip to a R.E.A.L. site with the www.orksheet. Each of the 10 to 15 questions will prompt you to take in the best that site has to offer. Use this tool for self-study, or if required, email it to your instructor.

- **Course Quiz**   The questions on this self-scoring quiz are related to articles in the reader, information at R.E.A.L. sites, and other course topics, and will help you pinpoint areas you need to study. Only you will know your score—it's an easy, risk-free way to keep pace!

- **Topic Key**   The Topic Key is a listing of the main topics in your course, and it correlates with the Topic Key that appears in this reader. This handy reference tool also links directly to those R.E.A.L. sites that are especially appropriate to each topic, bringing you integrated online resources within seconds!

- **Web Savvy Student Site**   If you're new to the Internet or want to brush up, stop by the Web Savvy Student site. This unique supplement is a complete **courselinks**™ site unto itself. Here, you'll find basic information on using the Internet, creating a web page, communicating on the web, and more. Quizzes and Web Savvy Worksheets test your web knowledge, and the R.E.A.L. sites listed here will further enhance your understanding of the web.

- **Student Lounge**   Drop by the Student Lounge to chat with other students taking the same course or to learn more about careers in your major. You'll find links to resources for scholarships, financial aid, internships, professional associations, and jobs. Take a look around the Student Lounge and give us your feedback. We're open to remodeling the Lounge per your suggestions.

## Building Better *Perspectives!*

Please tell us what you think of this *Perspectives* volume so we can improve the next one. Here's how you can help:

1. Visit our **coursewise** site at: http://www.coursewise.com

2. Click on *Perspectives*. Then select the Building Better *Perspectives* Form for your course.

3. Forms and instructions for submission are available online.

Basically, we want to know whether you agree or disagree that a particular reading is R.E.A.L. (**R**elevant, **E**xciting, **A**pproved, and **L**inked). You do this by indicating which articles, in your opinion, have the R.E.A.L. attributes and which ones don't. That's all there is to it. Thanks in advance for helping us build better *Perspectives*.

## Student Internships

If you enjoy evaluating these articles or would like to help us evaluate the **courselinks**™ site for this course, check out the **coursewise** Student Internship Program. For more information, visit: http://www.coursewise.com/intern.html

# Brief Contents

# Contents

# section 2

## Good Nutrition Starts Early: Nutrition for Pregnant Women and for Children

# section

# 3

# Nutrition Challenges for Adults on the Go: Sports Nutrition and Weight Management

# section

# 4

# Aging Well: Nutrition in the Later Years

# section 5

## Nutrition Choices for Your Heart and Your Immune System

# section 6

## Diets to Avoid Cancer and Diabetes Mellitus

# Topic Key

This Topic Key is an important tool for learning. It will help you integrate this reader into your course studies. Listed below, in alphabetical order, are important topics covered in this volume. Below each topic you'll find the article or articles and R.E.A.L. web site addresses relating to that topic. Note that the Topic Key might not include every topic your instructor chooses to emphasize. If you don't find the topic you're looking for in the Topic Key, check the index or the online topic key at the **courselinks**™ site.

# section

1

## Learning Objectives

After studying this section, you will know:

- the seven dietary guidelines from the U.S. Department of Agriculture and the Department of Health and Human Services.

- the possible long-term consequences of the typical American diet.

- that the most appropriate diet strategy to ensure nutrient adequacy is to eat a wide variety of foods.

- how to interpret Body Mass Index (BMI) data.

- that portion sizes in the United States are growing.

- the Dr. Dean Ornish lifestyle to reverse atherosclerosis.

- that Americans' diets are only fair or poor regarding vegetables, fruits, grains, sugars, and fats.

- that the healthiest diet is anything but fat free.

# Selecting an Adequate Diet
# You Are What You Eat

 **WiseGuide Intro**
The why, how, and what of food selection have a profound influence on your physical well-being. Nutrition (the science of food as it relates to optimal well-being) is a multidisciplinary field. Concepts from physiology, biochemistry, behavioral psychology, medicine, public health, agriculture, food technology, economics, ecology, business, and politics all affect, and are affected by, nutrition.

On a more personal level, your food selection influences your health, your productivity, your budget, indeed your life. Nutrition news is exploding, which may be a caveat. A great many new findings about a cancer-fighting vegetable, a blood cholesterol lowering fiber, an antiheart disease nutrient, butter vs. margarine, and sodium and hypertension, to name a few, are reported regularly. This information explosion may make for more confusion than understanding.

Data continue to be reported, suggesting the link between diet and chronic disease morbidity and mortality in the United States. The United States Department of Agriculture and the Department of Health and Human Services published the following seven dietary guidelines:

1. Eat a variety of foods.

2. Balance your food intake with physical activity; maintain or improve your weight.

3. Choose a diet with plenty of grain products, vegetables, and fruits.

4. Choose a diet low in fat, saturated fat, and cholesterol.

5. Choose a diet moderate in sugars.

6. Choose a diet moderate in sodium.

7. If you drink alcohol, do so in moderation.

An appropriate diet can be achieved only when the body receives proper nutrients needed for energy, physical growth, the maintenance of tissues, and the regulation of body processes. Therefore, a lifetime of sound food selection is essential for one's growth, development, productivity, and health.

Our diet has changed significantly over the past 100 years. The typical American diet of the early 1900s was rich in whole grain products. Fruits and vegetables were consumed more regularly, while sugars were not as common as today. Presently, Americans' diets are conducive to precipitating and/or exacerbating a number of chronic conditions, including heart disease, cancer, stroke, and diabetes mellitus. The dietary components which are associated with lowering the likelihood of these phenomena, including lower fat intake (particularly animal fat), sufficient fiber, and increased fruit and vegetable intake (antioxidants, phytochemicals), are more the exception than the rule.

This initial section allows you to begin to explore, to dig, to question, to challenge, and ultimately to motivate yourself toward sound eating and a more healthy, productive, and happy life. In this first section, you will discover our nation's current eating habits, you will see if it is possible to make dietary changes, and you will learn how to eat smarter.

## ? Questions ?

R1. Is the U.S. population making progress toward reaching desired dietary goals? Did all racial/ethnic groups respond similarly?

R2. What might be the long-term consequences of the typical American diet?

R3. Is your diet varied? Why or why not? Might there be any long-term consequences of your diet?

R4. Did the participants who received a self-help booklet change their nutrient intake during the twelve-month study? What would be your suggestions for eliciting diet change among a large group of Americans? Might there be problems with collecting data using a food-frequency questionnaire?

R5. Why are portion sizes in the United States growing? List and explain three strategies to reduce energy consumption.

R6. Who is Dr. Dean Ornish, and why does he advocate a very low fat diet (only 10 percent of all calories from fat)?

R7. What is capsaicin? How do endorphins play a role when eating chili peppers? What is quercetin?

Is the U.S. population making progress toward reaching desired dietary goals? Did all racial/ethnic groups respond similarly?

# U.S. Trends in Nutrient Intake

## The 1987 and 1992 National Health Interview Surveys

**Jean Norris, DrPH, RD, Lisa Harnack, DrPH, RD, Suzan Carmichael, PhD, Thandi Pouane, PhD, RN, Patsy Wakimoto, DrPH, RD, and Gladys Block, PhD**

*The authors were with the School of Public Health, University of California at Berkeley, at the time the work was conducted.*

## Abstract

### Objectives

This study examined US trends in nutrient intake, using almost identical methods and nutrient databases in two time periods.

### Methods

An extensive dietary intake questionnaire was included in supplements to the 1987 and 1992 National Health Interview Surveys. Dietary data from approximately 11,000 persons in each of those years were analyzed.

### Results

The total and saturated fat intake and the percentage of energy from fat declined among Whites and Hispanics, but only minimal changes were seen in Black Americans. The changes in fat intake were attributable principally to behavioral changes in frequency and type of fat-containing foods consumed rather than to the increased availability of leaner cuts of meat. Dietary cholesterol showed one of the largest declines of the nutrients examined. Less desirable changes were also seen. Cereal fortification played an important role in the observed changes in several micronutrients.

### Conclusions

Educational campaigns on dietary fat and cholesterol have been moderately effective, but not in all racial/ethnic groups. Future campaigns should emphasize maintaining or increasing micronutrient intake. (*Am J Public Health,* 1997;87: 740–746)

Requests for reprints or a copy of the questionnaire should be sent to Gladys Block, PhD, 419 Warren Hall, School of Public Health, University of California at Berkeley, Berkeley, CA 94720. This paper was accepted July 29, 1996.

## Introduction

Scientific evidence continues to accumulate substantiating the link between diet and a range of chronic diseases.[1] Several dietary guidelines and programs have been developed to promote health[2–8]; these include recommendations to reduce dietary fat intake to 30% of energy or less; reduce saturated fat, dietary cholesterol, and sodium intake; and increase intake of calcium, fiber, vegetables, fruits, and grain products. This study provides information on the effects of these efforts by evaluating the progress of dietary change in the US population.

The principal data on the nutrient intake of the American population come from major national surveys. Trends in nutrient intake have been reported comparing the 1977 versus the 1985 Continuing Survey of Food Intakes by Individuals[9] and the 1977/1978 versus the 1989/1990 Nationwide Food Consumption Survey,[10] and trends in fat and calorie intake have been reported comparing the 1976 through 1980 National Health and Nutrition Examination Survey (NHANES) II vs the 1988 through 1991 phase of the NHANES III.[11] Some studies have exmined changes in the intake of particular foods or food groups or of only one or two nutrients,[11,12] have examined restricted age or gender groups,[13–16] or have evaluated trends in food supply data,[17,18] but relatively few studies have examined nutrient trends in nationally representative samples.[11,12,16,19]

This study reports dietary data from the 1987 and 1992 National Health Interview Surveys (NHIS). The dietary data are based on food-frequency questionnaires, which were almost identical in both years, providing a unique opportunity to examine trends in a methodologically consistent way. Trends in estimates of usual intake of macro- and micronutrients are examined in White, Black, and Hispanic adults with data from both time periods, to determine whether Americans are making changes toward the recommended guidelines.

## Methods

The National Cancer Institute (NCI), in collaboration with the National Center for Health Statistics (NCHS) and the Census Bureau, sponsored supplements to the 1987 and 1992 NHIS surveys to provide information on behaviors, knowledge, and attitudes related to cancer prevention. A multistage cluster design was used to obtain representative samples of US households. Blacks and Hispanics were oversampled. In-home interviews were conducted by Census Bureau interviewers. The response rate was 82% for the 1987 supplement and 86% for the 1992 supplement. Interview procedures and nutrient estimates from the 1987 survey are reported elsewhere.[20,21]

The dietary data were based on food-frequency questionnaires, which were almost identical in both years. (These questionaires are available from the author.) The 1987 and 1992 questionaires contained a 59-item subset of the full-length Block questionnaire.[22,23] Food items were selected to include the most important nutrient contributors in the US diet,[24,25] and the 59-item list included foods that represented at least 80% of population intake of each of the nutrients on the NHANES II database. Nutrient estimates for this report are based on reported frequency of food intake, exclusive of vitamin supplements.

Validation studies have been conducted on the full Block/NCI questionnaire in a wide range of age, gender, income, and ethnic groups.[26–31] It produced not only a good ranking of individuals but also quite accurate estimates of mean nutrient intake. The 59-item version used in the NHIS surveys produced correlations with diet records that were almost identical to those achieved by the full-length questionnaire.[23] Previous studies showed estimates for energy and macronutrients from the 59-item version to be somewhat underestimated,[23] as would be expected when only 59 foods are asked about. Similarly, also as seen in the previous study,[23] because total energy was more underestimated than total fat with this food list, the percentage of energy from fat is expected to be somewhat overestimated. *The emphasis in this paper is on trends over time, and not on actual point estimates of levels of nutrient intake.*

Comparability between the two questionnaires was maintained with respect to editing procedures, seasonality, the food list, portion-size assumptions, and, as discussed further below, nutrient-content assumptions. Computerized edits were identical in 1987 and 1992.[32,33] Approximately 6% to 7% of questionnaires in both years had coding or consistency errors and were deleted from further analyses. Because reporting of usual intake can vary somewhat by season (A. F. Subar et al., unpublished data, 1993), analyses of 1987 data were limited to questionnaires administered in the first 6 months of the year; this maintained a time frame comparable to that of the 1992 survey, which was administered only during the first half of 1992.

The 1992 questionnaire originally contained 8 new items, which were added principally to increase the point estimates of fruit, vegetable, and mixed-dish consumption. Since we were interested in trends rather than in point estimates, nutrient estimates for this analysis were limited to the 59 foods contained in both the 1987 and the 1992 questionnaires; this maintained comparability. Some minor differences between the questionnaires in question wording, question ordering, and instructions to the respondents remained. An identical portion-size database, representing grams in a small, medium, or large portion

**Table 1**  Sample Sizes Used in This Analysis: NHIS Cancer Epidemiology Supplement, 1987 and 1992[a]

| | Black | | | | Hispanic | | | | White | | | | Total | |
| | Female | | Male | | Female | | Male | | Female | | Male | | | |
| Age, y | 1987 | 1992 | 1987 | 1992 | 1987 | 1992 | 1987 | 1992 | 1987 | 1992 | 1987 | 1992 | 1987 | 1992 |
| --- | --- | --- | --- | --- | --- | --- | --- | --- | --- | --- | --- | --- | --- | --- |
| 18–34 | 386 | 363 | 181 | 180 | 200 | 308 | 126 | 213 | 1628 | 1474 | 1318 | 1290 | | |
| 35–49 | 238 | 246 | 152 | 141 | 93 | 172 | 68 | 159 | 1181 | 1257 | 979 | 1126 | | |
| 50–64 | 127 | 144 | 84 | 75 | 70 | 83 | 45 | 65 | 872 | 791 | 640 | 646 | | |
| 65–79 | 113 | 111 | 71 | 52 | 30 | 32 | 25 | 34 | 836 | 883 | 501 | 511 | | |
| 80+ | 5 | 34 | 2 | 16 | 29 | 16 | 8 | 6 | 229 | 286 | 90 | 113 | | |
| Total | 869 | 898 | 490 | 464 | 422 | 611 | 272 | 477 | 4746 | 4691 | 3528 | 3686 | 10 327 | 10 827 |

[a]For 1987, only data from the first two quarters of the year were used, to correspond to the time period encompassed by the 1992 data.

for each of six age-sex groups for each food, was used in both years.

Nutrient estimates were calculated with the Block/NCI nutrient-content and portion-size databases and software.[22,33,34] The nutrient content of some food items available to consumers changed between 1987 and 1992. Some meats became leaner and fortification of breakfast cereals changed; these changes in the fat content of beef and pork and the fortification of cereals are reflected in the 1992 nutrient-composition database used to calculate nutrient estimates. These are the only differences between the two nutrient databases. Accordingly, most of our analyses use the 1987 nutrient-composition database for 1987 data and the 1992 nutrient-composition database for the 1992 data. However, to investigate whether changes in total nutrient intake were a function of changes in dietary practices or changes in nutrient composition, the nutrient intake was calculated in two different ways.

First, the 1987 nutrient-composition database was used to calculate nutrients for both the 1987 and the 1992 surveys. Thus, since nutrient composition of all foods is forced to be identical in the 2 years, trend information derived from this method reflects changes in food choices, such as choosing low-fat rather than whole milk, eating red meat less often, and reducing the frequency or amount of discretionary fat (e.g., butter). With the second method, nutrient estimates for the 1987 data were calculated with the 1987 nutrient datbase, and estimates for the 1992 data were calculated with the 1992 nutrient database. Trend information derived from this method reflects changes both in food choices and in the nutrient composition of red meats and breakfast cereals.

To permit generalizability to the noninstitutionalized US population, estimates were calculated with the use of sample weights and software appropriate for the complex survey design (B. V. Shah, unpublished data, 1981).

## Results

The sample sizes on which the analyses are based are shown in Table 1. Among Hispanics, the 1987 and 1992 samples differed somewhat in ethnic distribution and language of interview. The proportion of Mexican Americans increased from 43.5% to 53.9%, with proportionately fewer Puerto Ricans, Cuban Americans, and other Latin Americans. The proportion of Hispanics completing the interview entirely or mostly in English declined from 47% to 38%. Other ethnicities are not shown owing to small numbers.

Nutrient-intake estimates from the 1992 survey, and the change from 1987, are shown in Table 2 by gender and race. A negative change indicates a decline in mean intake. Trends reflected in this table represent the sum of changes in food choices and changes in the fat content of meat and fortification levels of cereals.

The percentage of energy from fat fell from 38.3 to 36.0% (a change of 6% relative to 1987). The largest changes in the percentage of fat were seen among Hispanics, whose levels were already the lowest of the three ethnic groups. The smallest changes occurred in Blacks, whose levels were the highest of the ethnic groups. Fat intake decreased in persons both above and below the poverty level, but decreases were greatest in those above poverty (data not shown).

Most of the decline in the percentage of total fat was due to a decline in fat obtained primarily

**Table 2** Mean Nutrient Intake 1992, Change from 1987 and 95% Confidence Interval of the Change, by Race and Gender: Data from the 1987 and 1992 National Health Interview Surveys

| | Black | | | | Hispanic | | | |
| | Female | | Male | | Female | | Male | |
| Nutrient | 1992 Mean | Difference (95% CI) | 1992 Mean | Difference (95% CI) | 1992 Mean | Difference (95% CI) | 1992 Mean | Difference (95% CI) |
|---|---|---|---|---|---|---|---|---|
| Energy, kcal | 1422 | −19 (−80, 42) | 2026 | −140 (−299, 19) | 1437 | −149 (−257, −41) | 2059 | −255 (−461, −49) |
| Fat, % kcal | 37.0 | −1.5 (−2.5, −0.5) | 36.4 | −1.0 (−2.1, 0.1) | 33.1 | −3.0 (−4.3, −1.7) | 32.3 | −2.8 (−4.2, −1.4) |
| Saturated fat, % kcal | 12.9 | −1.1 (−1.5, −0.7) | 12.8 | −1.0 (−1.6, −0.5) | 12.2 | −1.8 (−2.4, −1.2) | 11.8 | −1.7 (−2.4, −1.0) |
| Carbohydrate, % kcal | 46.5 | 2.1 (1.0, 3.2) | 44.4 | 1.5 (0.1, 2.9) | 49.2 | 3.0 (1.6, 4.4) | 47.9 | 3.7 (2.3, 5.0) |
| Protein, % kcal | 16.2 | 0.0 (−0.3, 0.3) | 16.1 | 0.4 (−0.2, 1.0) | 17.1 | 0.1 (−0.5, 0.7) | 16.7 | 0.2 (−0.4, 0.7) |
| Cholesterol, mg | 267 | −46 (−64, −27) | 394 | −69 (−108, −31) | 275 | −73 (−102, −44) | 424 | −80 (−132, −28) |
| Alcoholic beverages, % kcal | 1.7 | −0.3 (−0.9, 0.3) | 5.2 | −0.8 (−2.1, 0.5) | 1.7 | 0.04 (−0.5, 0.6) | 4.9 | −1.5 (−2.8, −0.3) |
| Calcium, mg | 596 | 7 (−32, 46) | 695 | −49 (−120, 22) | 736 | −41 (−105, 23) | 848 | −84 (−188, 20) |
| Carotene, mg | 2941 | 11 (−276, 298) | 4118 | −47 (−696, 602) | 2774 | −460 (−835, −85) | 3743 | −161 (−860, 538) |
| Retinol, IU | 666 | −193 (−270, −115) | 788 | −177 (−309, −46) | 574 | −292 (−409, −176) | 750 | −127 (−329, 76) |
| Fiber, g | 9.1 | 0.3 (−0.3, 0.9) | 12.1 | 0.3 (−0.8, 1.4) | 11.7 | 0.56 (−0.7, 1.8) | 15.9 | 0.67 (−1.3, 2.6) |
| Folate, μg | 230 | −1.3 (−14.6, 12.0) | 318 | 2.6 (−24.8, 30.0) | 268 | −7.3 (−27.7, 13.1) | 352 | −18.5 (−64.0, 27.0) |
| Iron, mg | 8.9 | −0.5 (−0.9, −0.0) | 12.7 | −0.8 (−1.8, 0.2) | 10.1 | −0.8 (−1.6, 0.1) | 14.2 | −1.3 (−2.8, 0.3) |
| Vitamin C, mg | 139 | 11.4 (0.9, 21.9) | 158 | 7.0 (−12.0, 26.0) | 148 | −0.1 (−15.4, 15.2) | 156 | −8.2 (−41.2, 24.8) |
| Vitamin E, αTE | 7.42 | 1.82 (1.42, 2.22) | 9.63 | 2.42 (1.59, 3.25) | 7.51 | 1.73 (1.17, 2.29) | 9.58 | 2.15 (1.40, 2.90) |

*Note.* CI = confidence interval; αTE = alpha-tocopherol equivalents.

from animal sources. Saturated fat fell 11.2% relative to 1987. Again, the smallest changes were seen among Blacks. Monounsaturated fat (oleic acid) fell by a similar amount, whereas polyunsaturated fat (linoleic acid) fell by only 3% (data not shown). Dietary cholesterol showed one of the largest declines of the nutrients examined, falling almost 20% relative to 1987. This decline was similar in magnitude among ethnic groups, but the decline was proportionately greater in Whites than in Blacks and Hispanics.

The percentage of energy from carbohydrates rose somewhat, while the percentage of energy from protein was essentially unchanged. The percentage of energy from alcoholic beverages and from sweets (data not shown) fell 7% and 4%, respectively, relative to 1987.

While the above results for fats and cholesterol indicate trends in the desired direction, other results are less impressive. Despite recommendations to increase fiber intake, mean intake rose negligibly relative to 1987 levels, except among White males, and was well below the NCI's recommendation of 25 to 35 grams. Similarly, since 1987 there has been considerable publicity on the desirability of increasing fruit and vegetable intake. However, the intake of carotene, a nutrient found

almost exclusively in fruits and vegetables, actually fell slightly over that period. Vitamin C and folate, also found in fruits and vegetables, rose only slightly, and as discussed below, this rise did not appear to be due to increased fruit and vegetable intake.

Several other nutrients did not move in the recommended direction. Calcium and iron, whose intakes are already below the recommended daily allowance in most age-sex groups according to NHANES III data,[35] fell 5.1% and 5.6%, respectively. Retinol fell 23.1%, consistent with the decline in cholesterol intake. Zinc intake was lower in 1992 (10.3 vs 9.8 mg), consistent with a shift away from

| | White | | | | | |
|---|---|---|---|---|---|---|
| | Female | | Male | | Total Population | |
| | 1992 Mean | Difference (95% CI) | 1992 Mean | Difference (95% CI) | 1992 Mean | Difference (95% CI) |
| | 1264 | −64 (−88, −40) | 1901 | −127 (−176, −78) | 1591 | −101 (−130, −72) |
| | 36.3 | −2.5 (−2.9, −2.1) | 36.4 | −2.0 (−2.4, −1.5) | 36.0 | −2.3 (−2.6, −2.0) |
| | 12.6 | −1.7 (−2.0, −1.4) | 13.0 | −1.4 (−1.7, −1.1) | 12.7 | −1.6 (−1.7, −1.5) |
| | 46.4 | 2.8 (2.4, 3.2) | 44.3 | 2.3 (1.9, 2.7) | 45.8 | 2.6 (2.3, 2.9) |
| | 16.4 | 0.0 (−0.2, 0.4) | 16.0 | 0.0 (−0.2, 0.4) | 16.3 | 0.1 (−0.0, 0.2) |
| | 190 | −53 (−59, −47) | 298 | −77 (−89, −66) | 259 | −63 (−70, −56) |
| | 2.7 | −0.0 (−0.4, 0.2) | 5.8 | −0.4 (−0.9, 0.2) | 4.0 | −0.3 (−0.6, −0.0) |
| | 688 | −32 (−53.7, −9.7) | 845 | −40 (−70, −10) | 747 | −40 (−58, −22) |
| | 2392 | −72 (−176, 32) | 3130 | −6 (−164, 152) | 2885 | −43 (−132, 46) |
| | 501 | −177 (−204, −150) | 641 | −178 (−208, −147) | 590 | −176 (−197, −158) |
| | 8.9 | 0.2 (−0.0, 0.5) | 11.3 | −0.1 (−0.4, 0.2) | 10.4 | 0.2 (−0.0, 0.5) |
| | 224 | 11.7 (6.4, 17.0) | 297 | 6.9 (−1.4, 15.2) | 263 | 6.5 (1.4, 11.6) |
| | 8.3 | −0.2 (−0.5, 0.0) | 11.8 | −0.9 (−1.2, −0.6) | 10.2 | −0.6 (−0.9, −0.3) |
| | 118 | 0.6 (−3.0, 4.2) | 130 | 1.5 (−3.1, 6.0) | 129 | 1.7 (−1.6, 5.0) |
| | 7.35 | 1.72 (1.54, 1.90) | 9.72 | 2.24 (1.97, 2.51) | 8.4 | 1.9 (1.76, 2.04) |

red meat, and riboflavin and niacin fell slightly (data not shown).

The changes in intakes presented in Table 2 reflect a combination of changes in food choices (e.g., less frequent consumption of red meat, switching to low-fat milk) and in food composition (i.e., lower fat content of red meat and changes in cereal fortification). Table 3 examines the separate effect of these two components of change. In column 1, nutrients are calculated with the use of the 1987 food-frequency responses and the 1987 nutrient-composition data. Column 3 uses the 1992 food-frequency responses but the 1987 nutrient database to calculate nutrients. Column 5 uses the 1992 food-frequency responses and the 1992 nutrient database. Thus, changes between column 1 and column 3 are due entirely to changes in food choices, since the nutrient-composition databases are identical. Changes between column 3 and column 5 are due entirely to changes in the nutrient composition of the foods consumed, since the reported food-frequency choices are identical but the databases differ in the fat content of meats and the fortification levels of cereals. Changes in estimated nutrient intake between column 1 and column 5 reflect the combination of changes in food choices and in nutrient content of the foods.

The estimates of the percentage of energy from fat fell from 38.2% in 1987 (column 1) to 36.3% in 1992 with use of the 1987 database (column 3); use of the 1992 database, with its lower fat content for meats, produced only a slight further drop, to 36.0% (column 5). That is, the largest drop was seen between column 1 and column 3, when the 1987 and 1992 data were analyzed with identical assumptions about nutrient content. Thus, it would appear that the lowering of the fat content of meat contributed relatively little to further decreases. The same pattern is seen for saturated fat, oleic acid, and cholesterol. Changes in food choices, such as a reduction in red meat or whole-milk intake, were the primary causes of the changes in total intake of fat from 1987 to 1992.

In contrast, the slight increases in vitamin C and folate intakes noted earlier are shown in Table 3 to result entirely from changes in cereal fortification. Folate intake, for example, fell from 257 µg in column 1 to 253 in column 3, which differ only in food choices and not in assumptions about nutrient content. The rise from column 3 to 263 µg in column 5, which differ only in cereal fortification and not in reported food choices, illustrates the role of fortification. Had it not been for increases in fortification of breakfast cereals with vitamin C and folate, intake of these nutrients would have been lower in 1992 than in 1987. The same was true of vitamin E, the increase being entirely due to increased fortification of breakfast cereals. Similarly, the minimal increase in fiber intake can be seen to result exclusively from increases in the fiber content of certain foods in the food supply.

**Table 3**

Comparison of Nutrient Change from 1987 to 1992 Attributable to Changes in Food Choices and to Changes in Fat Content of Meats and Fortification Levels of Cereals[a]

| | 1987 Frequency, 1987 Nutrient Values | | 1992 Frequency 1987 Nutrient Values | | 1992 Nutrient Values | |
|---|---|---|---|---|---|---|
| **Nutrient** | **Mean** | **SE** | **Mean** | **SE** | **Mean** | **SE** |
| Fat, % kcal | 38.2 | 0.1 | 36.3 | 0.1 | 36.0 | 0.1 |
| Fat, g | 72.3 | 0.5 | 65.5 | 0.4 | 64.4 | 0.4 |
| Saturated fat, g | 27.2 | 0.2 | 24.0 | 0.2 | 23.0 | 0.2 |
| Oleic acid, g | 26.3 | 0.2 | 23.8 | 0.2 | 23.3 | 0.2 |
| Cholesterol, mg | 322 | 2.8 | 270 | 2.2 | 259 | 2.1 |
| Retinol, IU | 768 | 7.8 | 678 | 6.9 | 590 | 6.5 |
| Iron, mg | 10.8 | 0.1 | 10.4 | 0.1 | 10.2 | 0.1 |
| Dietary fiber, g | 10.2 | 0.1 | 10.1 | 0.1 | 10.3 | 0.1 |
| Vitamin C, mg | 126.9 | 1.2 | 126.8 | 1.2 | 128.7 | 1.2 |
| Carotene, μg | 2928 | 36 | 2884 | 28 | 2885 | 28 |
| Vitamin E, αTE | 6.4 | 0.1 | 6.3 | 0.1 | 8.4 | 0.1 |
| Folate, μg | 257 | 2.0 | 253 | 1.6 | 263 | 1.7 |

*Note.* αTE = alpha-tocopherol equivalent.

[a]The values in the first and third columns were calculated from the different food choices reported by respondents in 1987 and 1992, but with identical nutrient content values being used for all foods on the food list, including meats and breakfast cereals; thus, the difference between these two columns arises solely as a result of differing frequency of reported consumption of meats or of breakfast cereals, or differing reported portion sizes for those foods. The values in the third and fifth columns were calculated with the use of the identical reported frequency of reported consumption or portion sizes of meats or breakfast cereals, but with different nutrient content values for meats and breakfast cereals; thus, the difference between these two columns arises solely from the change in the nutrient content values of fats in meat and fortification of breakfast cereals.

Conversely, cereal fortification with vitamin A decreased. Thus, the drop in retinol intake was due to a combination of a reduction in egg intake[18] (column 1 vs column 3) and to lower fortification of cereals with this nutrient (column 3 vs column 5).

## Discussion

A unique aspect of the present study is its ability to examine separately nutrient trends attributable to changes in food choices and those attributable to certain changes in the food supply (i.e., changes in the fat content of meat and in cereal fortification levels). This information may aid policy decisions on how to focus national nutrition efforts.

One of the chief findings of this study concerns fat intake. The drop of 2.3% in the percentage of energy from fat in absolute terms and of 6% relative to 1987 is virtually identical to the change reported from NHANES II to NHANES III[11] (which reported a reduction from 36% to 34% of energy from fat), despite major methodologic differences between the NHANES and NHIS dietary data. This is an encouraging indication that Americans are modifying the fat in their diets in line with recommendations. However, while White Americans dropped their fat intake considerably, the changes in Black men and women were modest. Similarly, while changes in cholesterol intake were substantial among Whites, they

were less so among Blacks and leave the mean intake of Black men and women above that of Whites. These relative cholesterol levels are also consistent with NHANES III.[11]

Some trends are of concern. Calcium intake appears to be flat or negative, perhaps a result of the emphasis on reducing fat intake; women may be reducing fat by reducing whole-milk intake, but not consuming a corresponding amount of low-fat milk. Negative effects on other nutrients may accompany the fat-reduction trend: the fall in iron and zinc may be related to a reduction in red-meat intake, and the fall in retinol is likely to be related to a drop in egg consumption. While we continue our educational efforts against excessive fat consumption, it may be important to increase educational and other efforts to maintain ample intakes of minerals and other micronutrients.

Recommendations have also emphasized increasing the intake of dietary fiber and of fruits and vegetables. Here again, the trends observable in the present data are not encouraging. Although fiber in particular was emphasized during the period 1987 through 1992, intake increased by just 2% in that period, and remains far below the NCI recommendations. Intake of carotene, a nutrient provided almost exclusively by fruits and vegetables, appeared to be lower in 1992 than in 1987. It is worth noting that this time period was one of increasing economic stress for many Americans; median income in constant dollars fell and the percentage of the population near or below the poverty line rose.[36] Fruits and vegetables may have been viewed as expendable luxuries by some Americans.[37,38]

Indeed, Table 3 indicates that had fortification of cereals not increased, intake of vitamin C, folate, and fiber would have decreased, and the increase in vitamin E intake was attributable entirely to the increased fortification of cereals. While educational campaigns to increase fruit and vegetable consumption should be continued and amplified, the major role of cereal fortification in maintaining adequate micronutrient intake is clear in Table 3 and cannot be overlooked. It is unlikely that vitamin and mineral supplement use would negate the observed negative trends, since, if anything, it appears that national supplement consumption *decreased* during the period 1987 through 1992.[39]

For dietary fats, in contrast to vitamins and minerals, it was changes in the population's behavior (a shift to less frequent consumption of important fat sources), rather than in the nutrient composition of foods (the decreased fat content of beef and pork), that were the principal determinants of the shifts in intake. As Table 3 shows, the major drop in fat intake was seen when the 1987 and 1992 data were analyzed using the *identical* food composition databases. When the 1992 data were analyzed with the use of the 1992 database that reflected the reduced fat content of meats, only a modest further drop in fat intake occurred.

Several limitations of these data can be noted. First, although study design and diet-assessment methodologies were nearly identical for 1987 and 1992, there were some differences that could have affected responses. For example, there were minor differences in the wording and order of the food items.

The data presented here were based on responses to a food-frequency questionnaire, the limitations of which are discussed in detail elsewhere.[40] For example, the absolute value of estimated mean intakes from food-frequency questionnaires is not precise. The questionnaire was shown, however, to reflect accurately the nutrient-intake differences between the genders,[28,29] between different age groups,[22,28,29] and between those on reduced-fat and normal-fat diets,[27] suggesting that group comparisons may be valid.

Further, a limited food list cannot include all the foods consumed by the population. Thus, it is possible, for example, that carotene intake increased but that

the increase was not reflected by the foods included on the questionnaire. The increase, however, would have had to occur through a vegetable consumption increase that was limited to foods not on the list, without a parallel increase in the major carotene sources, such as carrots and broccoli, which were on the list. Thus, while the food list limits confidence in the point estimates of mean intake, it may be a less important limitation for inferences as to trends.

A similar reservation applies to the result for fat: that the food list, because it was held constant over the two time periods, did not include new low-fat foods in the marketplace such as low-fat cheeses. This limitation affects the magnitude, but not the direction, of the observed trend. Had the list included the new foods, the percentage of energy from fat would probably have been still lower in the second time period. Despite this shortcoming, however, the instrument was able to detect a drop in the percentage of energy from fat comparable to that seen with NHANES III 24-hour recall data. Inclusion of the new low-fat foods would not change conclusions about the trend in fat intake or about the ethnic differences in those trends. Indeed, had those foods been included, the ethnic differences would probably have been still more pronounced, since it is the more affluent who are more likely to consume these more expensive reduced-fat items.

It is also possible that changes in intake occurred within food items on the questionnaire. For example, if people shifted from 1% milk to skim milk between 1987 and 1992, the concomitant decreased fat intake would not be ascertained because these two foods are both encompassed in a single item. (Note that 2% milk is a separate item.) Again, this would have affected the magnitude, but not the direction, of these findings.

It is also possible that respondents reported consuming fewer fatty foods because health messages had emphasized the desirability of lowering fat intake. Although such a response bias is possible, it would presumably be a factor in all dietary surveys. Furthermore, if it is true, we would expect to have seen increases in reported fiber intake between column 1 and column 3 of Table 3, since messages about the value of cereal fiber were prominent during that period.

We did observe an overall decrease in energy intake, which is surprising in view of increasing obesity in the United States.[41] It is possible that the major sources of energy intake changed between 1987 and 1992, and that caloric intake estimates for 1992 were lower than those for 1987 simply because the 59 food items ascertained caloric intake better in 1987. However, the relationship between obesity and caloric intake is not simple, and there is evidence that physical activity may also be decreasing, at least in certain subgroups,[42] contributing to an increase in obesity without a concomitant increase in energy intake. A decline in energy intake was also seen in Nationwide Food Consumption Survey data from 1977/1978 to 1989/1990, a pattern consistent with declining fat intake, and one that may not have been seen from NHANES II to NHANES III because of the changes in methodology between

the two NHANES surveys.[11] Indeed, it is notable that the decrease in energy is consistent with the decline in fat intake: at 9 kcal per gram of fat, three quarters of the fall in calories is directly attributable to the fall in fat. Other studies have shown that a decline in calories from fat is not necessarily compensated for by an increase in calories from other sources. Woods et al.,[43] for example, found that women who adopted a low-fat diet decreased their energy intake and maintained that reduced energy-intake level for at least 2 years.

Finally, ethnic-group comparisons may be questioned because of the limitations of the instrument. Comparisons of Blacks and Whites may be reasonably appropriate, since the "mainstream" diet is similar in both groups and the list includes the new food items of major importance to Black Americans but not to Whites. Cooking practices among Black Americans could have been a source of fat intake undetected by the questionnaire; however, for this to have altered the direction of the observed decrease in the percentage of fat, Blacks would have had to increase the use of fatty cooking practices, while at the same time reducing the use of the fatty foods and discretionary fats that are on the questionnaire.

Among Hispanics, the two surveys differed in the distribution of the Hispanic subgroups and in their language preferences. Thus, some of the trends observed among Hispanics may be the result of differences in the sampled population rather than of changes in intake over time. In addition, questions about the adequacy of

the food list for Hispanic Americans may be justified, since some foods typically consumed by this group (e.g., flour tortillas) were not included, and the applicability of some of our assumptions (e.g., about food preparation and portion size) are not well established. However, a recent examination of Hispanic Health and Nutrition Examination Surveys[44] suggested that with few exceptions, the foods important in the diets of White and Black Americans are also the important foods in Hispanic diets. It is also notable that these data for Hispanics are consistent with NHANES III data,[11] in which Hispanic adults also had the lowest value of percentage of energy from fat among the three reported ethnic groups. Thus, despite the caveats, it would appear that the data may be useful, since they provide nationally representative estimates of trends in intake among Hispanics now residing in the United States.

In summary, this study has found a decline in total and saturated fat intake in the US population, of a magnitude also observed from NHANES II to NHANES III; unequal participation by Black Americans in this beneficial change; changes in fat intake caused principally by behavioral shifts in food choices, rather than in changes in the fat content of meat; concomitant downward shifts in calcium and other minerals; absence of important changes in the desirable direction for fiber or micronutrients found in fruits and vegetables; and an important role for cereal fortification in the observed changes in several micronutrients.

# References

1. WHO Study Group. *Diet, Nutrition and the Prevention of Chronic Disease.* Geneva, Switzerland: World Health Organization; 1990.
2. National Research Council, Committee on Diet, Nutrition and Cancer. *Diet, Nutrition, and Cancer.* Washington, DC: National Academy Press; 1982.
3. National Research Council, National Academy of Sciences, Committee on Diet and Health. *Diet and Health.* Washington, DC: National Academy Press; 1989.
4. *The Surgeon General's Report on Nutrition and Health.* Washington, DC: Public Health Service; 1988. DHHS publication PHS 88-50210.
5. *Nutrition and Your Health: Dietary Guidelines for Americans.* Washington, DC: US Dept of Agriculture and US Dept of Health and Human Services; 1980.
6. *Healthy People 2000: National Health Promotion and Disease Prevention Objectives.* Washington, DC: Public Health Service, 1991. DHHS publication PHS 91-50212.
7. *Cancer Control Objectives for the Nation: 1985–2000.* Bethesda, Md: Public Health Service and National Cancer Institute; 1986. DHHS NIH 86-2880; NCI monograph No. 2.
8. *Report of the Expert Panel on Population Strategies for Blood Cholesterol Reduction.* Bethesda, Md: National Heart, Lung, and Blood Institute; 1990. NIH publication 90-3046.
9. Peterkin, BB. Women's diets: 1977 and 1985. *J Nutr Educ.* 1986; 18:251–257.
10. *Nutrition: Eating for Good Health.* Washington, DC: Dept of Agriculture; 1993. Agriculture information bulletin 685.
11. Centers for Disease Control and Prevention. Daily dietary fat and total food-energy intakes—Third National Health and Nutrition Examination Survey, Phase 1, 1988–91. *MMWR Morb Wkly Rep.* 1994;43:116–122.
12. Stephen A, Wald N. Trends in individual consumption of dietary fat in the United States, 1920–1984. *Am J Clin Nutr.* 1990;52:457–469.
13. Haines PS, Hungerford DW, Popkin BM, Guilkey DK. Eating patterns and energy and nutrient intakes of US women. *J Am Diet Assoc.* 1992;92:698–704.
14. Popkin BM, Haines PS, Patterson RE. Dietary changes in older Americans, 1977–1987. *Am J Clin Nutr.* 1992;55:823–830.
15. Albertson AM, Cala Tobelmann R, Engstrom A. Nutrient intakes of 2- to 10-year-old American children: 10-year trends. *J Am Diet Assoc.* 1992;92:1492–1496.
16. Popkin BM, Haines PS, Reidy KC. Food consumption trends of US women: patterns and determinants between 1977 and 1985. *Am J Clin Nutr.* 1989;49:1307–1319.
17. Byers T. Dietary trends in the United States. *Cancer.* 1993; 72:1015–1018.
18. Putnam JJ, Allshouse JE. *Food Consumption, Prices, and Expenditures: 1970–93.* Washington, DC: US Dept of Agriculture, Food and Consumer Economics Division; 1994. Statistical bulletin 915.
19. Federation of American Societies for Experimental Biology. *Nutrition Monitoring in the United States: An Update Report on Nutrition Monitoring.* Washington, DC: Public Health Service, 1989. DHHS publication PHS 89-1255.
20. Block G, Kessler L. *Training Viedo: Administering the Diet Questionnaire.* Bethesda, Md: National Cancer Institute; 1986.
21. Block G, Subar AF. Estimates of nutrient intake from a food frequency questionnaire: the 1987 National Health Interview Survey. *J Am Diet Assoc.* 1992;92:969–977.
22. Block G, Hartman AM, Dresser CM, et al. A data-based approach to diet questionnaire design and testing. *Am J Epidemiol.* 1986; 124:453–469.
23. Block G, Hartman AM, Naughton D. A reduced dietary questionnaire: development and validation. *Epidemiol.* 1990;1:58–64.
24. Block G, Dresser CM, Hartman AM, et al. Nutrient sources in the American diet: quantitative data from the NHANES II survey: I. vitamins and minerals. *Am J Epidemiol.* 1985;122:13–26.
25. Block G, Dresser CM, Hartman AM, et al. Nutrient sources in the American diet: quantitative data from the NHANES II survey: II. macronutrients and fats. *Am J Epidemiol.* 1985;122:27–40.
26. Sobell J, Block G, Koslowe P, et al. Validation of a retrospective questionnaire assessing diet 10–15 years ago. *Am J Epidemiol.* 1989; 130:173–187.
27. Block G, Woods M, Potosky A, et al. Validation of a self-administered diet history questionnaire using multiple diet records. *J Clin Epidemiol.* 1990;43:1327–1335.
28. Mares-Perlman JA, Klein BEK, Klein R, et al. A diet history questionnaire ranks nutrient intakes in middle-aged and older men and women similarly to multiple food records. *J Nutr.* 1993;123:489–501.
29. Block G, Thompson FE, Hartman AM, et al. Comparison of two dietary questionnaires validated against multiple dietary records collected during a 1-year period. *J Am Diet Assoc.* 1992;92:686–693.
30. Coates RJ, Eley JW, Block G, et al. An evaluation of a food frequency questionnaire for assessing dietary intake of specific carotenoids and vitamin E among low-income Black women. *Am J Epidemiol.* 1991;134: 658–671.
31. DiSogra C, Block G. WIC Dietary Assessment Validation Study. Hyattsville, Md: US Dept of Agriculture, Food and Nutrition Service; 1995.
32. Smucker R, Block G, Coyle L, et al. A dietary and risk factor questionnaire and analysis system for personal computers. *Am J Epidemiol.* 1989;129:445–449.
33. Block G, Coyle L, Smucker R, Harlan LC. *Health Habits and History Questionnaire: Diet History and Other Risk Factors.* Bethesda, Md: National Cancer Institute; 1989. Personal computer system documentation.
34. Block G, Coyle LM, Hartman AM, et al. Revision of dietary analysis software for the Health Habits and History Questionnaire. *Am J Epidemiol.* 1994;139:1190–1196.
35. Alaimo K, McDowell MA, Briefel RR, et al. Dietary intake of

vitamins, minerals, and fiber of persons ages 2 months and over in the United States: third National Health and Nutrition Examination Survey, Phase 1, 1988–91. *Adv Data Vital Health Stat.* 1995; 258. DHHS publication PHS 95-1250.

36. *Statistical Abstract of the United States.* 114th ed. Suitland, Md: Bureau of the Census; 1994.

37. Reicks M, Randall J, Haynes B. Factors affecting consumption of fruits and vegetables by low-income families. *J Am Diet Assoc.* 1994;94:1309–1311.

38. Jeffery R, French S, Raether C, Baxter J. An environmental intervention to increase fruit and salad purchases in a cafeteria. *Prev Med.* 1994;23:788–792.

39. Slesinski MJ, Subar A, Kahle L. Trends in use of vitamin and mineral supplements in the United States: the 1987 and 1992 National Health Interview Surveys. *J Am Diet Assoc.* 1995;95:921–923.

40. Briefel RR, Flegal KM, Winn DM, Loria CM, Johnson CL, Sempos CT. Assessing the nation's diet: limitations of the FFQ. *J Am Diet Assoc.* 1992;92:959–962.

41. Kuczmarski R, Flegal KM, Campbell SM, Johnson CL. Increasing prevalence of overweight among US adults. The National Health and Nutrition Examination Surveys, 1990 to 1991. *JAMA.* 1994;272:205–211.

42. Ravussin E, Lillioja S, Knowler WC, et al. Reduced rate of energy expenditure as a risk factor for body-weight gain. *New Engl J Med.* 1988;318:467–472.

43. White E, Shattuck AL, Kristal AR, et al. Maintenance of a low-fat diet—follow-up of the Women's Health Trial. *Cancer Epidemiol.* 1992;1:315–323.

44. Block G, Norris JC, Mandel RM, Di Sogra C. Sources of energy and six nutrients in diets of low-income Hispanic-American women and children: quantitative data from HHANES, 1982–1984. *J Am Diet Assoc.* 1995;95:195–208.

**Article Review Form at end of book.**

What might be the long-term consequences of the typical American diet?

# Report Card for Americans' Eating Habits

| | Excellent | Good | Fair | Poor | Comments |
|---|---|---|---|---|---|
| Vegetables | | | ✔ | | We're at the low end of the recommended 3 to 5 servings daily, with almost half coming from potatoes. We average only ⅓ of a serving of dark green and deep yellow vegetables a day—about 2 bites worth. |
| Fruits | | | ✔ | | Only 24 percent of us are eating the minimum recommended 2 servings a day. And that's only when you include apples from apple pie, etc. |
| Grains | | | ✔ | | 85 percent of our grain-based foods are refined rather than whole-grain, which contributes to a huge fiber shortfall. |
| Dairy | | | ✔ | | Two to 3 servings a day are called for. We're averaging 1½ servings daily. Women over 20 are averaging only 1 serving a day. |
| Meat, poultry, fish | | ✔ | | | Men don't exceed the 5 to 7 ounces recommended each day. Women eat 4 ounces daily. |
| Added sugars & fats | | | | ✔ | No more than 27 percent of calories are supposed to come from these sources, but we're up to 40 percent. |
| Exercise | | | ✔ | | One third of men and almost half of women "rarely" or "never" work up a sweat. |

The USDA's Agricultural Research Service is completing its tenth nationwide look at America's eating habits as part of its Continuing Survey of Food Intake by Individuals (CSFII). The "grades" for how people ate in 1994 are already in, and let's just say that if the folks at USDA were our parents, many among us would be grounded.

Yes, based on responses from almost 5,000 people across the country, the average American is now eating the minimum recommended 3 servings of vegetables a day (the advice is to have 3 to 5 servings). But more than half of the country isn't eating even that much. And 40 percent of the vegetables that *are* eaten come in the form of selections like French fries and mashed potatoes. On any given day, while 1 in 4 people eats fries, only 1 in 10 eats a dark green or deep yellow vegetable—the type with antioxidants and other substances now associated with better health and longevity.

As for fruit, the average number of servings eaten a day is 1⅔, while what's called for is 2 to 4 servings. Three out of 4 Americans fall short of the 2-servings-a-day minimum recommendation.

People also aren't doing well in dairy, grains, and other "required" categories. They are overdoing it only in the popular "elective," added sugars and fats.

Now, unless you're ahead of the "class," turn off that TV and . . . make a salad (or buy one ready-made).

 **Article Review Form at end of book.**

"Report Card for Americans' Eating Habits" reprinted with permission, TUFTS UNIVERSITY HEALTH & NUTRITION LETTER, tel: 1–800–274–7581.

Is your diet varied? Why or why not? Might there be any long-term consequences of your diet?

# Variety Makes a Better Diet

Nutritionists always say variety is one of the cornerstones of a healthful diet. But just what is variety? Ten foods a day? Twenty? Thirty? Furthermore, do more foods really translate into more nutritious eating? Researchers reporting in the *Journal of the American Dietetic Association* attempted to answer these questions by asking people about their food choices over the course of 15 days.

Their finding: people who averaged 71 to 83 foods during the 15 days as opposed to a range of 37 to 58 items ate diets much higher in vitamin C. Their eating patterns were also significantly lower in sugar and sodium and a little lower in saturated fat.

The findings are no small potatoes as far as healthful diets go. Consider, for instance, that while the current Recommended Dietary Allowance for vitamin C is 60 milligrams, many experts now recommend more on the order of 200 milligrams—just a little more than the 192 milligrams averaged by those following the most varied diets (see box). The reason for the recommendation of 200 milligrams is that vitamin C has been shown to be an antioxidant that can potentially help ward off a number of degenera-

Consumed per day . . .

|  | Vitamin C | Sodium | Sugar | Saturated Fat |
|---|---|---|---|---|
| 71-83 foods over 15 days | 192 mgs | 3231 mgs | 20 tsps | 10% of calories |
| 37–58 foods over 15 days | 137 mgs | 3946 mgs | 27 tsps | 11% of calories |

tive diseases, including cataracts and several types of cancer.

As for sodium, the limit advised by the National Academy of Sciences is 2,400 milligrams. Those in the "varied" group came in some 800 milligrams over, while those with the least variety in their diets came in 1,500 milligrams over.

The 7-teaspoon difference in sugar is significant, too, making for 112 fewer calories in the high-variety group devoted to a food that adds nothing in the way of vitamins and minerals. Likewise, 10 percent of calories coming from saturated fat in the high-variety group puts it in line with the American Heart Association's recommendation that saturated fat contribute no more than 10 percent of total calories.

## Is Your Diet Varied Enough?

Tufts researcher Katherine Tucker, PhD, uses the 37 foods listed here (on page 15) to determine whether people's diets have adequate variety—and therefore an adequate distribution of nutrients. "If you can check off 28 of these foods over the course of 3 days," she says, "you're probably doing pretty well. But if you're eating closer to 14 or 15 foods, you probably should be expanding your food universe."

A variety of foods in each category makes the diet that much better, Dr. Tucker notes. For the citrus category, for example, it is better to eat a tangerine, an orange, and half a grapefruit over 3 days than to eat 3 tangerines.

Note that there are 5 vegetable groups and 5 fruit groups but only 1 group for sweet baked goods and desserts. In other words, a Twinkie, a doughnut, and a brownie are not the kind of variety health experts are talking about when they recommend eating many different types of foods.

"Variety Makes a Better Diet" reprinted with permission, TUFTS UNIVERSITY HEALTH & NUTRITION LETTER, tel: 1–800–274–7581.

1. ❏ milk
2. ❏ yogurt
3. ❏ cheese
4. ❏ ice cream/milk-based desserts
5. ❏ other dairy
6. ❏ eggs
7. ❏ poultry
8. ❏ beef
9. ❏ pork
10. ❏ lamb, veal, game
11. ❏ fish
12. ❏ liver/organ meats
13. ❏ processed meats

14. ❏ beans and legumes
15. ❏ nuts and seeds
16. ❏ green leafy vegetables
17. ❏ orange and yellow vegetables
18. ❏ tomatoes and tomato products
19. ❏ potatoes and other root crops
20. ❏ other vegetables
21. ❏ citrus fruits
22. ❏ berries
23. ❏ melons
24. ❏ other fruit

25. ❏ fruit juices
26. ❏ white bread
27. ❏ whole wheat bread
28. ❏ cold breakfast cereals
29. ❏ hot breakfast cereals
30. ❏ rice
31. ❏ pasta
32. ❏ other grains
33. ❏ margarine, butter, and oils
34. ❏ sweet baked goods and desserts
35. ❏ salty snacks
36. ❏ soft drinks
37. ❏ candy

**Article Review Form at end of book.**

Did the participants who received a self-help booklet change their nutrient intake during the twelve-month study? What would be your suggestions for eliciting diet change among a large group of Americans? Might there be problems with collecting data using a food-frequency questionnaire?

# A Dietary Intervention in Primary Care Practice

## The eating patterns study

**Shirley A. A. Beresford, PhD, Susan J. Curry, PhD, Alan R. Kristal, DrPH, DeAnn Lazovich, PhD, MPH, Ziding Feng, PhD, and Edward H. Wagner, MD, MPH**

*Shirley A. A. Beresford and Alan R. Kristal are with the Department of Epidemiology, University of Washington, and the Fred Hutchinson Cancer Research Center, Seattle, Wash. Susan J. Curry and Edward H. Wagner are with the Department of Health Services, University of Washington and the Center for Health Studies, Seattle, Wash. DeAnn Lazovinch was with the Fred Hutchinson Cancer Research Center, Seattle, Wash., at the time of the study and is now with the School of Public Health, University of Minnesota, Minneapolis. Ziding Feng is with the Fred Hutchinson Cancer Research Center, Seattle, Wash.*

## Introduction

A high intake of dietary fat and a low intake of fiber are associated with an increased risk of serious diseases, including digestive system cancers and cardiovascular disease.[1] The scientific evidence supporting a causal relationship is not yet definitive, but there is reasonable consensus that public health interventions are now warranted.

Most dietary intervention research has targeted individuals at high risk for disease. In general, these interventions are based on intensive individual or group counseling, with goals of significant and rapid dietary behavior change.[2–6] Although such intensive interventions are effective among individuals highly motivated to change their diet, their application to the general population is relatively costly and may be less successful among comparatively healthy individuals. Only recently have studies evaluated public health approaches designed both to be accessible to a wide audience of healthy individuals, and to encourage small dietary changes in everyone, regardless of disease risk.[7–11]

Low-intensity interventions, such as self-help materials, may be an important public health strategy for changing diet. Self-help diet-change interventions have been shown to be as effective as more intensive, interpersonal interventions for the control of diabetes,[12] hypercholesterolemia,[4,13] and weight loss[14] and in promoting a very low-fat diet.[15] Further, it has been found that many people prefer self-help materials as an approach to the promotion of changes in health behavior.[16-18] The importance of these low-intensity interventions lies in their potential to affect large numbers of the population.[7] Although the resulting change in behavior may be quite small at the individual level, its impact at the population level can be quite dramatic.

This study follows a small study[19] using the health care setting to deliver the dietary intervention, conducted by one of us (S. Beresford) in North Carolina. The Eating Patterns Study is a larger randomized controlled trial in the Seattle area, to evaluate the effectiveness of self-help materials in decreasing fat and increasing fiber among individuals visiting their primary care physician.

## Methods

We conducted the study in primary care clinics of Group Health Cooperative, a large health maintenance organization in the Puget Sound area, starting in April 1990. Six clinics were recruited within the Group Health System through presentations to the leadership in the primary care network. A presentation was made in each interested clinic to recruit physician practices, and between 4 and 6 physician practice units participated from each. Within each clinic, an equal number of practices were randomized to inter-

vention and to control status. Specifically, within each clinic, all possible combinations of intervention and control practices consistent with a balanced design were enumerated, and one combination was chosen by the use of a table of random numbers. Altogether, we randomized 28 physician practice units, each consisting of 1 full-time or 2 to 3 part-time family practice physicians, to deliver either the self-help dietary intervention or no intervention (usual care) to patients with a nonacute, nonurgent doctor's visit.

## Participant Recruitment

We identified potential study participants by abstracting the names of patients who had routine appointments with participating physicians, 1 to 2 weeks prior to their scheduled visit. We requested that this list be reviewed by the physicians and that names of patients be removed of they had a cognitive impairment or were critically ill. Very few names were removed as a result of this review. We attempted to reach the remaining individuals to check their eligibility and invite them to participate in the study, provided no more than 9 patients were recruited from any one physician practice in any 1 day. Individuals who were unable to speak English, were pregnant, or were likely to leave the area within the year were excluded. Both the interviewer and the potential participant were blind to the group assignment. At the screening interview, we set up an appointment for a 45-minute telephone interview prior to the doctor's

visit with those who agreed to participate. About 21% of each group refused to make an appointment, and a further 11.2% and 9.6%, in the intervention and control groups respectively, indicated a willingness in principle to join the study but a lack of time before their appointment. A further 5.9% and 5.2%, respectively, were unavailable for the interview at the time that had been scheduled. About 75 patients per physician practice unit were recruited to the study, and a total of 2121 individuals completed the baseline interview. The effective interview rate is the product of the screening rate and the interview rate, which was 50.9% for the intervention group and 53.4% for the control group, with adjustment made for names removed from the pool when the quota per practice day had been reached (Table 1).*

## The Intervention

The intervention consisted of two components: a self-help booklet and physician endorsement. We developed the booklet, *Help Yourself: A Guide to Healthful Eating,*[20] on the basis of behavior-change principles derived from social learning theory,[21] and the dietary recommendations of the National Research Council.[1] We presented motivations for dietary change such as improving health, following the changing social norm to eat lower fat, higher fiber foods, and doing something positive for oneself. Current dietary behavior was assessed through the use of a brief self-test at the beginning of the book. We presented specific behavioral skills in

*Not included with this publication.

an easy-to-follow format, beginning by identifying current behaviors and suggesting sequential changes in small, simple steps. No external goals were included: rather, individuals were encouraged to set their own goals. We organized the materials around meals (i.e., breakfast, lunch, dinner) and, for each eating pattern (e.g., bacon and eggs for breakfast), displayed both small (e.g., eggs with Canadian bacon) and large (e.g., poached egg with fruit) changes toward a low-fat/high-fiber diet. We included self-assessment questionnaires and sections for recording short- and long- term goals. Finally, we included sections on eating out, shopping, and social activities.

Physicians randomized to the intervention were asked to introduce the booklet to the subject in a standardized fashion, taking less than 3 minutes, and received training for this either individually or as a group. The purpose of the physician endorsement of dietary change was to add a motivational element to the self-help booklet. Just prior to the participant's appointment, a self-help booklet and a script to introduce it were placed in the patient's medical chart. The physician introduced the booklet to the participant at a convenient time during the encounter. After the visit, the physician recorded the disposition of the intervention on a tracking form. About 2 weeks later, a reminder letter signed by the physician was sent to participants who had received the intervention.

## Evaluation Measures

As described above, we conducted baseline telephone interviews with study participants after physician randomization,

but before their scheduled visit. We completed follow-up interviews at 3 and 12 months after randomization. The main outcome measures were change in fat and fiber intake from baseline (from a food-frequency questionnaire) and change from baseline in scales that measure dietary habits related to reducing fat or increasing fiber (from the fat- and fiber-related diet behavior questionnaire). We also measured stage of change in adopting a low-fat and high-fiber diet, autonomy in meal preparation, and descriptive demographic and medical information. The main diet-related measures are described below.

### Food-Frequency Questionnaire

We developed a food-frequency questionnaire based on a previously validated instrument[22] that was extensively modified both for ease of telephone administration and to be sensitive to fat-modified foods and food-preparation methods. This questionnaire consisted of 94 food items or food groups, with 13 introductory questions and 2 summary questions used to refine nutrient calculations. Frequency responses allowed participants to specify number of times per day, week, or month. At the beginning of each section, interviewers explicitly asked about portion sizes in relation to a specified medium portion size. Particular attention was paid in the wording of the interview to elicit portion size for those foods contributing a large amount of fat or fiber to the diet. We used verbal cues such as comparisons with the size of a slice of bread for meats and fish. The nutrient database, from the University of Minnesota Nutrition Coordinating Center's Nutrient Data

System and algorithms for analyzing this food-frequency questionnaire are described in detail elsewhere.[23] Some respondents to a food-frequency questionnaire tend to exaggerate the frequency of consumption of food items and some respondents underestimate the frequency. To correct for systematic underreporting or overreporting of foods, we expressed fat intake in terms of the percentage of energy from fat and fiber in terms of grams of fiber per 1000 kilocalories.

### Fat- and Fiber-Related Behavior Questionnaire

This questionnaire, modified for telephone interview and expanded from a previously validated self-administered instrument,[24] consisted of 41 items that assessed food choices made in the last month. The items provided information on five factors related to selecting low-fat diets and three factors related to selecting diets high in fiber. Item responses were usually, sometimes, or rarely/never, and were coded 1, 2, and 3, respectively. Responses were rescaled so that an item in the fat score correlated positively with the percentage of energy obtained from fat, and an item in the fiber score correlated positively with fiber intake. The summary fat-related and fiber-related diet-behavior scores were the means of their related factors. Detailed results on the validity and reliability of the fat- and fiber-related behavior questionnaire have been published.[25] The correlation of the fat score with the percentage of energy obtained from fat from this questionnaire was 0.53, and between the fiber score and grams of fiber per 1000 kcal was 0.49.

### Stage of Change

Using a construct based on the transtheoretical model of change,[26] we measured participants' readiness to adopt new dietary behavior. This measure has been validated.[27] According to this model, we expected greater dietary behavior change among respondents in the action or maintenance stage of readiness for behavior change than among those just contemplating change. We classified respondents along a continuum—precontemplation, contemplation, decision, action, and maintenance—related to reducing fat. A similar set of questions measured stage of change for increasing fiber.

### Autonomy in Meal Preparation

We defined autonomy as the extent to which a participant had control over his or her diet via responsibility in planning, shopping, and preparing meals. Each item had responses of little or none, about half, and all or most. Participants with all or most responsibility for all three were defined as having complete autonomy. To explore the hypothesis[9] that this group made larger changes, we compared changes in those who had complete autonomy with changes in those who had partial or no autonomy at baseline.

### Plasma Cholesterol

At the time of the clinic visit, for both intervention and control groups, a study laboratory technician collected 5 mL of blood using venipuncture techniques. Blood was centrifuged, frozen, and analyzed for total plasma cholesterol in batches containing vials from both intervention and control patients.

### Social Desirability

We included a measure of social desirability trait at baseline because we were concerned that the self-report of dietary intake might be biased in the intervention group at follow-up. We hypothesized that intervention participants would be better able to discern what answers would reflect desirable dietary behavior and that those with the trait of high social desirability would show a larger intervention effect than those with a low social desirability trait. This line of reasoning is supported by studies suggesting that social approval needs may influence the reporting of socially desirable foods.[28] We classified individuals into low and high social desirability using the median value.

### Statistical Analysis

We analyzed results using a mixed linear model[29] in which the design effects were clinic, arm (intervention or control), and physician practice (nested in clinic and arm). Because the unit of randomization was the physician practice (within clinic), the clinic effects and the physician practice effects were treated as random effects in the model. This model acknowledges that the intervention effects vary among clinic and physician practices and thus allows the results of this trial to be generalized to the population of similar clinics and physician practices. The main covariates in the model were baseline dietary intake or behavior and age and gender. Adjustments for other characteristics did not affect the results that we present. For two a priori hypotheses, we evaluated interaction effects, namely, whether there were differences in intervention effects depending on respondents' baseline values of stage of change and autonomy. Because the unit of randomization was physician practice within clinic, we repeated the main analyses for the percentage of energy obtained from fat using group means. We calculated intervention and control means within each clinic by averaging the appropriate practice means and compared them using both a nonparametric signed rank test and a $t$ test on the six within-clinic differences.

## Results

### Characteristics of Participants

Baseline characteristics for intervention and control groups were similar: 24% of the intervention group and 27% of the control group were aged 65 years and over; 69% and 67%, respectively, were female; 92% and 90%, respectively, were White; 75% and 71%, respectively, had at least some college education; and 27% and 29%, respectively, had family income below $25,000 per year. Of the participants, 86% completed the 1-year follow-up; the loss to follow-up was similar in the intervention and control groups. Participants who dropped out of the study were younger, less likely to be White, and more likely to have lower family income than those who completed follow-up. They also had slightly higher fat intake and lower fiber intake.

Table 2 gives the baseline values for nutrient intake and fat- and fiber-related diet-behavior scores for the intervention and control groups. The groups were very similar in all measures, with

**Table 2** Nutrient Intake and Fat- and Fiber-Related Diet-Behavior Scale Scores at Baseline, among Those Completing 1-Year Follow-Up in the Eating Patterns Study, Seattle, 1990 to 1992

| | Mean[a] (SE of Mean) | | | | | |
|---|---|---|---|---|---|---|
| | Fat, g | Fat, % Energy | Fiber, g | Fiber, g/1000 kcal | Fat Score | Fiber Score |
| Full group | | | | | | |
|   Intervention (n = 859) | 71 (2) | 37.6 (0.3) | 14.9 (0.2) | 10 (0.1) | 1.95 (0.006) | 1.85 (0.01) |
|   Control (n = 959) | 70 (2) | 37.5 (0.3) | 15.3 (0.2) | 10 (0.1) | 1.95 (0.006) | 1.85 (0.01) |
| Complete autonomy | | | | | | |
|   Intervention (n = 501) | 69 (3) | 37.3 (0.4) | 14.9 (0.3) | 10 (0.2) | 1.95 (0.01) | 1.84 (0.02) |
|   Control (n = 536) | 67 (3) | 36.8 (0.3) | 15.4 (0.2) | 10 (0.2) | 1.95 (0.01) | 1.85 (0.02) |
| Partial or no autonomy | | | | | | |
|   Intervention (n = 357) | 73 (3) | 38.0 (0.4) | 14.9 (0.3) | 9.9 (0.2) | 1.95 (0.01) | 1.85 (0.02) |
|   Control (n = 423) | 73 (3) | 38.3 (0.4) | 14.9 (0.3) | 9.7 (0.2) | 1.94 (0.01) | 1.84 (0.02) |
| Action or maintenance stage | | | | | | |
|   Intervention (n = 632) | 64 (2) | 36.2 (0.3) | 13.3 (0.2)[b] | 11 (0.2)[b] | 1.87 (0.012) | 1.95 (0.019) |
|   Control (n = 679) | 65 (2) | 36.1 (0.3) | 13.4 (0.2)[c] | 11 (0.2)[c] | 1.88 (0.012) | 1.96 (0.019) |
| Earlier stage | | | | | | |
|   Intervention (n = 226) | 91 (4) | 41.4 (0.5) | 16.4 (0.2)[d] | 8.9 (0.2)[d] | 2.18 (0.020) | 1.72 (0.020) |
|   Control (n = 279) | 81 (4) | 40.9 (0.4) | 16.8 (0.2)[e] | 8.9 (0.2) | 2.15 (0.018) | 1.73 (0.019) |

[a]Adjusted for clinic and practice effects, age, and gender.
[b]Staged for fiber change; n = 461.
[c]Staged for fiber change; n = 512.
[d]n = 397.
[e]n = 445.

the exception of a higher baseline intake of fiber in grams in the control group. The control group also had higher calorie intake, so that the fiber intake per 1000 kcal was identical in the two groups. This table also gives the baseline values by autonomy and stage of change. As expected, the highest fat intakes were reported by participants in precontemplation, contemplation, or preparation stages of change. Indeed, with the exception of fiber in grams, those at an early stage of readiness for change had a less healthy diet. Individuals at an early stage of readiness for fiber change consumed more calories, somewhat more fiber in grams, but less fiber per 1000 kcal.

## Dietary Outcomes

According to our clinic documentation, 95% of intervention subjects who kept their appointment received the booklet. Regardless of whether or not they received the booklet, participants who kept their doctor's appointment were included in the analysis. Table 3 gives the changes from baseline in percentage of energy obtained from fat, fiber (grams per 1000 kcal), summary fat score, and summary fiber score at both the 3- and 12-month follow-ups. Both groups reduced their fat intake (percentage of energy from fat), but at both 3 and 12 months, changes were significantly larger in the intervention group. The intervention effects and their associ-

ated 95% confidence intervals (CI) were −1.04 (95% CI = −1.67, −0.41) and −1.20 (95% CI = −1.68, −0.73), respectively, as shown in Table 3. The corresponding differential change in fat score was −0.046 (95% CI = −0.074, −0.018) at 3 months, and −0.044 (95% CI = −0.073, −0.016) at 12 months. Both groups increased their fiber by 3 months, but the control group did not appear to sustain the increase to 12 months. Although the intervention group increased their fiber intake more than the control group at both 3 and 12 months, the differences were not statistically significant. The intervention effect in g/1000 kcal was 0.14 (95% CI = −0.35, 0.64) at 3 months and 0.32 (95% CI = −0.06, 0.70) at

**Table 3** Changes from Baseline in Nutrient Intake and Fat- and Fiber-Related Diet-Behavior Scale Scores, and Intervention Effects at 3- and 12-Month Follow-Up in the Eating Patterns Study, Seattle, 1990 to 1992

| | Fat, % Energy | Fiber, g/1000 kcal | Fat Score | Fiber Score |
|---|---|---|---|---|
| **3-month follow-up** | | | | |
| Intervention group (n = 896) | | | | |
| Mean change | −1.52 | 0.50 | −0.085 | 0.062 |
| 95% CI | (−1.98, −1.06) | (0.14, 0.86) | (−0.105, −0.065) | (0.039, 0.085) |
| Control group (n = 990) | | | | |
| Mean change | −0.48 | 0.36 | −0.039 | 0.024 |
| 95% CI | (−0.91, −0.05) | (0.02, 0.70) | (−0.058, −0.020) | (0.003, 0.046) |
| Intervention effect | | | | |
| Mean effect | −1.04 | 0.14 | −0.046 | 0.038 |
| 95% CI | (−1.67, −0.41)** | (−0.35, 0.64) | (−0.074, −0.018)** | (0.006, 0.069)* |
| **12-month follow-up** | | | | |
| Intervention group (n = 859) | | | | |
| Mean change | −1.54 | 0.55 | −0.084 | 0.046 |
| 95% CI | (−1.88, −1.19) | (0.27, 0.83) | (−0.105, −0.063) | (0.028, 0.064) |
| Control group (n = 959) | | | | |
| Mean change | −0.34 | 0.22 | −0.040 | 0.011 |
| 95% CI | (−0.66, −0.01) | (−0.03, 0.49) | (−0.059, −0.020) | (−0.007, 0.028) |
| Intervention effect | | | | |
| Mean effect | −1.20 | 0.32 | −0.044 | 0.036 |
| 95% CI | (−1.68, −0.73)** | (−0.06, 0.70) | (−0.073, −0.016)** | (0.011, 0.061)* |

*Note.* Data are adjusted for clinic and practice effects, baseline value, age and gender. CI = confidence interval.
*$P < .05$; **$P < .01$.

12 months. On the other hand, the fiber score from the fat- and fiber-related behavior questionnaire increased in both groups, with a significantly larger increase in the intervention group at both 3- and 12-month follow-up. The differential change was 0.038 (95% CI = 0.006, 0.069) at 3 months, and 0.036 (95% CI = 0.011, 0.061) at 12 months. When we repeated the analyses for percentage of energy from fat using differences in group means, we found the mean decrease in fat in the intervention group was larger than in the control group within all six clinics. The nonparametric signed rank test yielded $P = .031$. The corresponding $t$ test on 5 $df$ was 7.29, ($P = .00076$).

## The Role of Autonomy

Table 4 presents results by autonomy and stage of change at baseline, giving only the differential change (the intervention effect) between intervention and control groups. The intervention effects within the subgroup with complete autonomy were statistically significant for both fat measures at 3 and 12 months, but for fiber only at the 12-month follow-up and only for fiber score. At 3 months for percentage of energy obtained from fat and fiber intake, and at 12 months for all measures, the intervention effects appeared to be higher among those with complete autonomy for shopping, planning, and preparing meals than among those with partial or no autonomy, but the interaction effect was statistically significant only for percentage of energy obtained from fat at 12 months ($P = .019$).

## The Role of Stage of Change

Intervention and control participants in the action or maintenance stage demonstrated a larger

| | Fat, % Energy | Fiber, g/1000 kcal | Fat Score | Fiber Score |
|---|---|---|---|---|
| **Table 4** Intervention Effects at 3 and 12 Months, by Autonomy and Stage of Dietary Change at Baseline, in the Eating Patterns Study, Seattle, 1990 to 1992 | | | | |
| | | 3-month follow-up | | |
| **Autonomy** | | | | |
| Complete | | | | |
| Mean effect | −1.28 | 0.24 | −0.044 | 0.034 |
| 95% CI | (−2.13, −0.44)* | (−0.42, 0.89) | (−0.081, −0.007)* | (−0.007, 0.076) |
| Partial or none | | | | |
| Mean effect | −0.74 | 0.02 | −0.049 | 0.042 |
| 95% CI | (−1.69, 0.22) | (−0.71, 0.76) | (−0.090, −0.007)* | (−0.005, 0.089) |
| **Stage of dietary change** | | | | |
| Action or maintenance | | | | |
| Mean effect | −1.13 | 0.10 | −0.035 | 0.041 |
| 95% CI | (−1.80, −0.46)** | (−0.59, 0.80) | (−0.065, −0.005)* | (−0.003, 0.085) |
| Earlier stage | | | | |
| Mean effect | −0.69 | 0.18 | −0.067 | 0.034 |
| 95% CI | (−1.77, 0.38) | (−0.54, 0.90) | (−0.115, −0.020)* | (−0.011, 0.079) |
| **Autonomy** | | 12-month follow-up | | |
| Complete | | | | |
| Mean effect | −1.85 | 0.44 | −0.046 | 0.045 |
| 95% CI | (−2.50, −1.20)***† | (−0.07, 0.95) | (−0.083, −0.009)* | (−0.012, 0.078)* |
| Partial or none | | | | |
| Mean effect | −0.37 | 0.17 | −0.042 | 0.024 |
| 95% CI | (−1.10, 0.36) | (−0.41, 0.75) | (−0.084, −0.000)* | (−0.014, 0.061) |
| **Stage of dietary change** | | | | |
| Action or maintenance | | | | |
| Mean effect | −1.28 | 0.33 | −0.034 | 0.048 |
| 95% CI | (−1.88, −0.68)** | (−0.16, 0.83) | (−0.063, −0.005)* | (−0.013, 0.083)* |
| Earlier stage | | | | |
| Mean effect | −0.90 | 0.27 | −0.067 | 0.021 |
| 95% CI | (−1.86, 0.07) | (−0.25, 0.79) | (−0.113, −0.020)* | (−0.016, 0.058) |

*Note.* Data are adjusted for clinic and practice effects, baseline value, age and gender. CI = confidence interval.

*P for intervention effects < .05; **P for intervention effects < .01; ***P for intervention effects < .001; †P for interaction = .019.

change in percentage of energy obtained from fat and in fat score than those in the earlier stages. Further, the intervention effect for percentage of energy obtained from fat appeared to be larger in the subgroup at the action or maintenance stage at both 3 and 12 months. The intervention effect for fat score, although significant for both stage groups at each follow-up, appeared somewhat smaller among those in the action or maintenance stage, owing to the large changes made in the control group. The differential change in fiber g/1000 kcal was small at both 3 and 12 months and varied little by stage of readiness for fiber change. The intervention effect for fiber score appeared stronger in the subgroup at the action or maintenance stage and was significant at 12 months (P < .05). None of the interactions by subgroup of stage of change were statistically significant.

## Plasma Cholesterol and Body Mass Index

Over the 12-month follow-up period, both groups decreased their total cholesterol levels by a similar and small amount (approximately 3.5 mg/dL). There was no change in either group in body mass index, as calculated from self-reported height and weight.

## Social Desirability

We found that the intervention effect for percentage of energy obtained from fat was larger (but not significantly so) among those with a low social desirability trait (–1.7%; $P < .01$) compared with those with a high social desirability trait (–1.0%; $P < .01$), contrary to expectation. Similar results were found for fat score and fiber score, favoring those with a low social desirability trait. These results strengthen the inference that the observed effect of the intervention reflected true dietary change and not bias.

## Discussion

We found that a low-intensity nutrition intervention delivered by a physician resulted in healthful dietary changes in fat and fiber consumption, as measured by the percentage of energy obtained from fat, fat score, and fiber score. The effect of the intervention was evident at both 3 and 12 months postintervention. Indeed, the effect was somewhat stronger for fat as percentage energy at 1-year follow-up. The intervention effect as assessed by fiber per 1000 kcal at 12 months was significant only at $P = .09$. The trend toward improved time with self-help intervention is consistent with interventions on other health behaviors such as smoking cessation.[30]

## Consistency with Other Studies

The findings from this study are consistent with other studies in health care settings that have used a low-intensity, public health ap-proach. Only three studies have been published that evaluated a low-intensity dietary intervention in a health care setting. Baron et al.[19] randomized 368 patients attending a general medical practice in Britain to receive either a self-help booklet with individual counseling from a nurse or no intervention. They found significant and sustained changes associated with the intervention in some dietary behavior at 1 year. Beresford et al.[9] randomized 242 individuals to receive either a set of self-help materials, introduced in 5 minutes by a nurse, or no intervention. At 3 months, there was a small differential reduction in fat intake associated with the intervention, which was statistically significant when the analysis was restricted to persons with some responsibility for meal preparation. Campbell et al.[31] randomized 558 adult patients attending family practice clinics to receive one of the following: a packet of tailored nutritional information, a packet of nontailored nutritional information, and no information. Although the food-frequency questionnaire they used contained only 28 items, and no adjustment was made for calories, they found that the tailored intervention was associated with a significant differential reduction in total fat consumption of 9 g per day at 4 months' follow-up.

## Limitations

The findings from this study are all based on self-report. Although we included plasma total cholesterol as an objective measure, the amount of dietary change in this study was too small to affect it. Self-report is obviously liable to exaggeration and misrepresentation in ways that might be influenced by the intervention. Our examination of the effect of social desirability was one way we tried to test the robustness of our self-report findings. That a similar decrease in fat intake was reported in the intervention groups with high and low social desirability, whereas the control group with high social desirability, reported larger changes than the control group with low social desirability gave us confidence in the self-report of the intervention group. We also checked the consistency of the finding using different measures of dietary fat change and within subgroups of respondents chosen in advance. All these investigations are consistent with the finding of a true dietary fat change. The evidence is less strong for fiber change.

The generalizability of this study has some obvious limitations. Although the study was designed to be an effectiveness study, only people able to be contacted by telephone and agreeing to be interviewed within a week before their clinic visit were included. Thus, busy people were underrepresented in this study. In addition, individuals with no primary care physician or with no nonurgent visits to their doctor were excluded by virtue of the study design.

## Contrast with More Intensive Interventions

Although the efficacy of the low-intensity intervention of the Eating Patterns Study is much smaller than some intensive dietary fat interventions (The Women's Health Trial intensive group intervention was associated with a reduction of 16% in energy obtained from fat at 12 months[6]), the cost of the intervention in both provider and participant time is substantially less. Our low-intensity intervention required between 1 and 3 minutes of clinician time, followed by discretionary time on the part of participants, using self-help materials at their own convenience. In contrast, the intensive intervention of the Women's Health Trail calls for 18 scheduled group sessions, each lasting 1 hour, supplemented with review of written materials by participants at their own convenience.[32]

## Importance of Public Health Interventions

While the full generalizability of this intervention is still to be established, a low-intensity dietary intervention could have important public health implications when applied at the population level, because of its potential to reach and involve large numbers of the population. The public health model, or population strategy, consists of shifting the entire distribution of a risk factor, including the mean, down. The diminution in risk for a given individual is typically small and may not even be clinically important. Nevertheless, because the entire distribution is affected, the impact on morbidity and mortality can be substantial. This is the prevention paradox, explained so lucidly by Sir Geoffrey Rose.[33,34] A 1% reduction in dietary calories from fat made populationwide could result in about 10,000 deaths saved in the United States in a year, on the basis of models fit from aggregate data and shown to be consistent with data from observational studies of cancers of the colon, breast, and prostate.[35] Both Rose[33] and Hitt[36] have argued for a combined approach to prevention, comprising both the public health approach and the high-risk strategy, familiar

to clinicians, in which intensive resources are concentrated on individuals at the extreme high end of the distribution.

## Conclusions

We demonstrated that this low-intensity intervention was effective and could be incorporated into routine delivery of primary care. The Eating Patterns Study confirmed the approach of the North Carolina study[9] in a very different setting, using the participant's own physician and a shorter introduction. It further demonstrated the durability of the intervention to 1 year. We conclude that this kind of low-intensity intervention based on public health and sound behavioral change principles is efficacious for use in primary care practice.

## Acknowledgments

This research was supported by the National Cancer Institute, R01 CA 49643.

We are grateful to the physicians, nurses, and staff of Group Health Cooperative of Puget Sound who helped us with the study, and to the many interviewers, programmers, and research assistants who were members of the study team. We extend special thanks to the enrollees of Group Health Cooperative who participated, without whom this study would not have been possible.

## References

1. National Research Council. Committee on Diet and Health. *Diet and Health: Implications for Reducing Chronic Disease Risk.* Washington, DC: National Academy Press, 1989.
2. Hjermann I. Intervention on smoking and eating habits in healthy men carrying high risk for coronary heart disease: the Oslo Study. *Acta Med Scand.* 1981;651 (suppl):281–284.
3. Neaton JD, Broste S. Cohen L. Fishman EL, Kjelsberg MO, Schoenberger J. The multiple risk factor intervention trial (MR-FIT) VII: a comparison of risk factor changes between the two study groups. *Prev Med.* 1981;10:519–543.
4. Mojonnier MH, Hall Y, Berkson DM, et al. Experience in changing food habits of hyperlipidemic men and women. *J Am Diet Assoc.* 1980;77:140–150.
5. Menotti A. An Italian preventive trial of coronary heart disease: the Rome project of coronary heart disease prevention. *Prog Biochem Pharmacol.* 1983;19:230–244.
6. Insull W. Henderson MM, Prentice RL, et al. Results of a randomized feasibility study of a low-fat diet. *Arch Intern Med.* 1990;150:421–427.
7. Finnegan JR, Rooney B, Viswanath K, et al. Process evaluation of a home-based program to reduce diet-related cancer risk: the "WIN At Home Series." *Health Educ Q.* 1992;19:233–248.
8. Potter J, Graves K, Finnegan J. et al. The Cancer and Dietary Intervention Project: a community-based intervention to reduce nutrition-related cancer risk. *Health Educ Res.* 1990; 5:489–503.
9. Beresford SAA, Farmer EMZ, Feingold L, Graves KL, Sumner SK, Baker RM. Evaluation of a self-help dietary intervention in a primary care setting. *Am J Public Health.* 1992;82:79–84.
10. Stern MP, Farquhar JW, Maccoby N, Russell SH. Results of a two-year health education campaign on dietary behavior: the Stanford Three Community Study. *Circulation.* 1976;54:826–833.
11. Murray DM, Luepker RV, Pirie PL, et al. Systematic risk factor screening and education: a community-wide approach to prevention of coronary heart disease. *Prev Med.* 1986;15:661–672.
12. Tani GS, Hankin JH. A self-learning unit for patients with diabetes. *J Am Diet Assoc.* 1971;58:331–335.
13. Crouch M, Sallis JF, Farquhar JW, et al. Personal and mediated health counseling for sustained dietary reduction of hypercholesterolemia. *Prev Med.* 1986;15:282–291.
14. Behn S. Lane DS. A self-teaching weight control manual: method for

increasing compliance and reducing obesity. *Patient Educ Counseling.* 1983;5:63–67.

15. Schapira DV, Kumar NB, Lyman GH, Baile WF. The effect of duration of intervention and locus of control on dietary change. *Am J Prev Med.* 1991;73:341–347.

16. Lefebvre RC, Linnan L, Sundarum S, Ronan A. Counseling strategies for blood cholesterol screening programs: recommendations for practice. *Patient Educ Counseling.* 1990;16:97–108.

17. Jackson C, Cinkleby MA, Flora JA, Fortmann SP. Use of educational resources for cardiovascular risk reduction in the Stanford Five-City Project. *Am J Prev Med.* 1991; 7:82–88.

18. Allen SS, Froberg D. McCarthy P, Myers S, Hunninghake DB. Preferences and opinions of consumers vs. dietitians on cholesterol education materials. *J Am Diet Assoc.* 1991;91:604–606.

19. Baron J. Gleason R, Crowe B. Mann J. Preliminary trial of the effect of general practice based nutritional advice. *Br J Gen Pract.* 1990; 40:137–141.

20. Curry S. Burrows B. Beresford SAA, et al. *Help Yourself: A Guide to Healthful Eating.* Seattle, Wash: University of Washington; 1990.

21. Bandura A. *Social Learning Theory.* Englewood Cliffs, NJ: Prentice-Hall, 1977.

22. Block G. Hartman AM, Dresser CM, Carroll MD, Gannon J. Gardner L. A data-based approach to diet questionnaire design and testing. *Am J Epidemiol.* 1986; 124:453.

23. Kristal AR, Shattuck AL, Williams A. Food frequency questionnaires for diet intervention research. In: *Proceedings of the 17th National Nutrient Databank Conference; June 7–10, 1992. Baltimore, MD.* Washington, DC: International Life Sciences Institute, 1994, 116–125.

24. Kristal AR, Shattuck AL, Henn, HI. Patterns of dietary behavior associated with electing diets low in fat: reliability and validity of a behavioral approach to dietary assessment. *J Am Diet Assoc.* 1990;90:214–220.

25. Kristal AR, Beresford SAA, Lazovitch D. Assessing change in diet intervention research. *Am J Clin Nutr.* 1994:59(suppl):185S–189S.

26. Prochaska JO, DiClemente CC. Stages and processes of self-change in smoking: toward an integrative model of change. *J Consult Clin Psychol.* 1983;51:390–395.

27. Curry SJ, Kristal AR, Bowen DJ. An application of the stage model of behavior change to dietary fat reduction. *Health Educ Res.* 1992; 7:97–105.

28. Worsley A, Baghurst KI, Leitch DR. Social desirability response bias and dietary inventory responses. *Hum Nutr: Appl Nutr.* 1984; 38:29–35.

29. Searle SS. Casella G, McCulloch CE. *Variance Components.* New York, NY: Wiley; 1992.

30. Curry S. Self-help interventions for smoking cessation. *J Consult Clin Psychol.* 1993;61:790–803.

31. Campbell MK, De Vellis BM, Strecher VJ, Ammerman AS, De Vellis RF, Sandler RS. Improving dietary behavior: the effectiveness of tailored messages in primary care settings. *Am J Public Health.* 1994;84:783–787.

32. Henderson M, Kushi L, Thompson D. et al. Feasibility of a randomized trial of a low-fat diet for the prevention of breast cancer: dietary compliance in the Women's Health Trial Vanguard Study. *Prev Med.* 1990;19:115–133.

33. Rose G. Future of disease prevention: British perspective on the US preventive services task force guidelines. *J Gen Intern Med.* 1990; 5(suppl):S128–S132.

34. Rose G. Sick individuals and sick populations. *Int J Epidemiol.* 1985; 14:32–38.

35. Prentice RL, Sheppard L. Dietary fat and cancer: consistency of the epidemiologic data, and disease prevention that may follow from a practical reduction in fat consumption. *Cancer Causes Control.* 1990;1:81–97.

36. Hitt C. Nutrition and risk reduction. In: Faver MM, Reinhardt AM, eds. *Promoting Health through Risk Reeducation,* New York NY: Macmillan: 1982;168–185.

 **Article Review Form at end of book.**

Why are portion sizes in the United States growing? List and explain three strategies to reduce energy consumption.

# Big Food

## The newest diet downfall

Think you're getting more for your money when you buy a supercombo or a Macho meal? You're getting more all right—more calories and more fat!

**Julia Califano**

*Pssst.*

Don't look now, but some people out there are trying to make you fat. If you don't believe it, just stop by a major chain restaurant for breakfast. You could order a healthful bowl of whole—grain cereal with fresh fruit and low-fat milk. But for half the price, you can get a platter of eggs, home fries, bacon and sausage, plus a side of pancakes.

In an effort to appeal to Americans' appetite for value— and their belief that bigger is always better—the food industry is offering more food for less money than ever before. The result? Portion sizes are raging out of control. And it's not only happening in restaurants. Giant servings have invaded fast-food franchises, concession stands, convenience stores, even your own kitchen.

This is no small matter. Many experts cite megaportions, along with lack of exercise, as a major reason why the average adult weighs 8 pounds more today than she did a decade ago and why, according to a Harris poll, a staggering 74 percent of Americans are overweight.

## It's a Bird. It's a Plane. No, It's a Burger.

It was bad enough when Mom pushed food on you. Now an entire industry is doing it. Virtually every fast-food chain entices you to "supersize" your meal (i.e., tack on a large order of fries and a soft drink) for just a few extra pennies. Meanwhile, most of these establishments have added jumbo-size items, packed with ever-higher ratios of fat, to their already nutritionally dubious lineups. Case in point: Soon after dropping its reduced-fat McLean Deluxe, McDonald's introduced its biggest burger yet—the Arch Deluxe (with 570 calories, it out-ranks the Big Mac). At the same time Pizza Hut, inventor of the cheese-stuffed crust, rolled out its triple-decker pizza—a pie that manages to cram one and a half days' worth of fat into four slices. And Del Taco created the Macho meal, which gives you the option of adding a large bag of fries and a 44-ounce drink to your order for a paltry 49 cents.

But huge portions are not limited to fast-food chains. Go to the movies and just try to order a small popcorn and soda. The clerk will eye you with curiosity and ask, "Don't you want to try a supercombo?" Concession stands at sports stadiums urge you to indulge in jumbo chili dogs and nachos deluxe. And most sit-down restaurants serve portions that are two to four times as much as you should be eating, according to Jayne Hurley, senior nutritionist at the Center for Science in the Public Interest, a consumer group based in Washington, D.C.

## The biggest foods in America

- Olive Garden's Lasagna Classico Dinner: After downing its 1,010 calories, you should probably skip dessert—not to mention breakfast and lunch tomorrow.
- Quincy's Family Steakhouse's 14-ounce T-bone: This entrée breaks the size barrier with 1,610 calories and the fat equivalent of 12 tablespoons of lard.

- Hardee's Big Country Breakfast with sausage: At 1,000 calories, you'll "eat up" more than half of the day's entire calorie allotment.
- Long John Silver's Two-Piece Fish and More Dinner: There's something fishy about a meal that packs as much fat as eight Hostess cream-filled cupcakes.
- Subway's 12-inch Spicy Italian Sub: This tub of a sub delivers 1,043 calories and more fat than four Snickers bars.

Packaged-food manufacturers have also jumped on the big-food bandwagon. Nabisco recently introduced a version of a Fig Newton cookie that's nearly twice the size of the original.

Most disturbing of all, however, is the fact that giant food has muscled its way into the American psyche. Even when we prepare food at home (where we *can* control the portion size), we overdo it. "Consumers are so used to being served large portions that a normal one looks skimpy by comparison," says Kris Clark, Ph.D., director of sports nutrition at Pennsylvania State University in University Park. "When I show clients the size of a recommended serving of pasta—half a cup—their jaws drop in horror. Most people are eating six times that much."

What's more, chronic exposure to oversize food fosters the idea that we should eat not until we feel satisfied but until we're filled to the gills. "Most of us no longer know the difference between feeling satiated and feeling stuffed," says Nadine Pazder, out-patient dietitian at the Morton Plant Hospital in Clearwater, Fla., and a spokesperson for the American Dietetic Association.

## Hey! What's the Big Idea?

You can blame this national feeding frenzy in large part on the economy. Competition in the food-service industry has dramatically increased in recent years, says Wendy Webster, a spokesperson for the National Restaurant Association. Unprecedented numbers of fast-food and full-service restaurant chains are vying for your food dollars. And what better way to win customers than to offer a good deal? "Value is a persuasive selling tool right now," Webster explains. "People are tentative about spending money, and everyone is looking for a bargain."

Another factor: Beef prices are at a five-year low in the United States, which makes it possible for McDonald's to offer two Big Macs for less than $2, and if that's not enough, the chain is test-marketing a triple cheeseburger that contains—count 'em—three beef patties.

But big food also has a lot of psychological appeal. It fits right in with this country's love affair with living large, Pazder notes. "The mentality in America is that

bigger is better," she explains. "We like big cars, big buildings, big boats—so why should it be any different with food?"

## A Crash Course in Sensible Portion Control

What's a hungry person to do? For starters, you don't have to avoid restaurants or hide out in a closet clutching a bag of carrot sticks. Indeed, experts say that simply becoming aware of the problem is half the battle. The next is to gain some perspective on portion size. Nutritionists recommend you use the United States Department of Agriculture (USDA) Food Guide Pyramid as a general guide (see "How Big Is a Portion?" p. 28). You can also try these defensive strategies.

*At home:* Measure out the recommended serving size (listed on the label) of the foods you frequently eat so you'll know what the proper portion looks like, Pazder advises. You may discover that your virtuous bowl of low-fat granola contains three servings instead of one, that you're getting three times as many calories as you thought.

*At special events:* If you're going somewhere—to a baseball game or a movie, say—where your food options will be limited, eat at home beforehand, or bring along a healthful snack, suggests Robyn DeBell, owner of Sound Bites, a nutrition consulting company in Phoenix.

*At restaurants:* If you eat out twice a week or more, you can no longer afford to think of doing so as an opportunity to throw your careful calorie counting to the

## How Big Is a Portion?

**Your palm = 3 oz meat**

**Your fist = I cup rice**

**Your thumb = I oz cheese**

In the land of big food, getting a grip on exactly how much equals a serving can be a challenge. Fortunately, there are some quick ways to recognize what's okay and what's out of control. Take a look at these photos, *left*.* Commit them to memory and you'll have a convenient guide to portion control no matter where you are. (Now *that's* handy.)

*Refers to the proportions at the top of this column. The photos are not included in this publication.

How many servings of foods should you eat each day? It's smart to follow the USDA Food Guide Pyramid (stick to the lower numbers if you want to lose weight). Here's what the pyramid recommends:

- **Grains:** six to II servings daily. A single portion equals one slice of bread; half of a small bagel (don't be fooled: A gargantuan New York City bagel translates to five or six helpings!); or half a cup of cooked rice, pasta or hot cereal.
- **Vegetables:** three to five servings daily. A cup of raw, leafy greens or half a cup of vegetables (cooked or raw) counts as one portion.

- **Fruits:** two to four servings daily. One medium apple, banana or orange equals a serving; so does half a cup of raw, cooked or canned fruit.
- **Dairy:** two to three servings daily. A standard portion is I cup of milk or yogurt, or 1½ to 2 ounces of cheese.
- **Meat:** Have no more than two or three servings daily (fewer is better). Two to 3 ounces of cooked lean beef, poultry or fish equals one helping.
- **Fats:** Limit high-fat condiments, such as mayonnaise, some salad dressings and cooking oils, to I tablespoon per meal.

---

wind and indulge in a nutritionally incorrect meal. Instead:

1. **Shrink the portion.** Request a lunch-size serving of an entrée, an appetizer instead of a main course, or a child's portion, advises Barbara Day, a health and nutrition educator in Louisville, Ky. Or ask the waiter to halve your meal in the kitchen, and take the uneaten part home in a doggie bag.

2. **Slow down.** Savor each bite to avoid overeating. It takes at least 20 minutes for the brain to register that your stomach is full, DeBell explains.

3. **Become fast-food savvy.** Despite all the big new offerings, you can still find sensible options at the fast-food counter. Avoid words like *deluxe, giant, super, mega, macho* and *feed bag.* Finally, if you're not the moderate type, plan for your indulgence. If you know you're going to have a Big Mac for dinner, bank calories by cutting back at breakfast and lunch.

No matter where you're dining, remember that a value-added meal may sound like a good idea at the time, but in terms of your overall health and well-

being, it's no bargain. "Eating huge quantities of unhealthy food over time raises your risk of heart disease, cancer, diabetes and other debilitating illnesses—and the cost of treating these conditions far outweighs the few pennies you may have saved," notes Hurley. So the next time a server starts giving you the hard sell on a supercolossal, you'd-be-an-idiot-to-pass-it-up deal, just say no (thank you).

 **Article Review Form at end of book.**

Who is Dr. Dean Ornish, and why does he advocate a very low fat diet (only 10 percent of all calories from fat)?

# Welcome Fat Back into Your Kitchen

For years you've been avoiding it like the plague. But study after study from around the world shows that the healthiest diet is anything but fat-free.

## Michael Mason

*Michael Mason has been a staff writer at the magazine since 1992.*

Hard to believe, but there was a time when comfort food was actually comforting. American tables were plumped high with cheese omelettes and sizzling steaks and pies wreathed in whipped cream. At Sunday dinner, as tureens of gravy collided with great floes of sour cream, we looked across at one another with satisfaction, not alarm. This was the cuisine of affluence. And warning us away from it, scientists found, was like shooting us from prosperity itself.

But warn us, scientists have—about fat and heart disease, fat and cancer, fat and obesity. Ten years ago only 16 percent of consumers fretted about the fat in their diets, according to the Food Marketing Institute. By 1995 that figure had risen to 65 percent. The average American now gets 33 percent of her calories from fat, down from 40 percent in 1977. In the grocery store nutrition labels incriminate rich foods like striped

jerseys once marked convicts. The shelves are awash in supposedly virtuous alternatives: fat-free cookies, low-fat chips, reduced-fat ice cream. And in what may prove to be the crescendo to this fat-free symphony, the Food and Drug Administration recently approved olestra for use in snacks as a non-fat fat—an "artifat," perhaps.

All of this might seem a triumph of intellect over appetite. But one hefty flaw mars the victory: The official advice to cut back on all fat is not well supported by science. While it's clearly a good idea to eat less saturated fat, researchers have never found much evidence that limiting the other two kinds—polyunsaturated, such as corn oil, and monounsaturated, like olive oil—will make a bit of difference in how healthy you are.

This contrarian bit of wisdom comes to light, ironically, amid an effort to squelch fat intake still further. Even as diet docs like Dean Ornish and John McDougall promote meals of only 10 percent of calories from fat, researchers announce that the cui-

sine of deprivation may not be much better for us than the rich food of affluence. There is, they say, a middle ground.

Strange how the nutritional pendulum swings. Before fat, we worried about salt. Before salt, sugar. None of these items has been completely exonerated, of course. But sooner or later each mealtime villain serves its time in exile and is welcomed, blinking and dazed, into the light of the kitchen. See the saucer of olive oil at your favorite restaurant? The canola-singed popcorn at the movie theater? Some oily foods are inching back to respectability. That they ever fell out of favor is a lesson in good intentions gone south.

YOU MAY REMEMBER former senator George McGovern for one spectacular belly flop of a presidential bid. Many scientists remember him for something else: Throughout much of the seventies McGovern chaired a congressional committee investigating the links between what we eat and our rates of heart disease and cancer. In 1977 the committee issued a report,

# Five Foods That Made a Comeback

Sometimes it seems as if all nutrition findings are grim: Enjoy eating and die, the studies suggest. But just as often there's great news from research labs—only it never gets as much ink or airtime. Here are some former bad guys that have received pardons since 1987.

## Sugar

**then** A predictable trigger of hyperactivity in children and a prime cause of tooth decay.

**NOW** Just one of many respectable sweeteners.

**WHAT CHANGED** The link between sugar and hyperactivity turned out to be mostly in parents' heads. In one study researchers fitted a group of preschoolers with activity meters, which recorded lots of squirming but no extra fidgeting among those who'd eaten a sugary goody. In another, parents were asked to note the activity levels of a bunch of children, half of whom, the researchers explained, had just gulped a big dose of sugar. (Actually, none had.) The parents were more likely to say that the kids they believed had eaten sugar were acting up. Meanwhile, other studies showed that sticky "natural" foods such as raisins, fruit rolls, and even bread are more likely to promote cavities than candy or soft drinks.

**THE CAVEAT** Sugar delivers no vitamins or minerals—and can add inches to the waistline of anyone with a sweet tooth.

## Shrimp

**THEN** A cholesterol-rich food, best shunned by people worried about heart disease.

**NOW** A food so low in saturated fat that it's even suggested for people with high blood cholesterol.

**WHAT CHANGED** Scientists found that the cholesterol in animal products is less harmful than the saturated fat. What's more, studies showed eating shrimp doesn't worsen the ratio of bad cholesterol to good in the blood.

**THE CAVEAT** Shrimp cooked in butter or cream wins no prizes. Try it grilled, broiled, or stir-fried.

## Avocados

**THEN** A vegetable that's as fatty as cream cheese or ground beef.

**NOW** An ideal stand-in for meat and cheese in a sandwich, burrito, or salad.

**WHAT CHANGED** As studies rolled in on the pros and cons of various fats and oils, the "cut back on all fat" cry gave way to findings that avocados and other foods rich in monounsaturated fats are actually good for you.

**THE CAVEAT** Avocados are high in calories. Dunk ten chips in a bowl of guacamole and you might as well eat a whole plate of french fries.

## Salt

**THEN** Once the archvillain of the American diet; a known cause of high blood pressure, stroke, and heart disease.

**NOW** A seasoning that's fine to shake onto your chicken, beans, and salad.

**WHAT CHANGED** First many researchers tried to show that sodium-avoiders live longer. No such luck. Then experts found that heart patients who cut back on salt were actually *more* likely to die than those who didn't. Meanwhile, others chimed in that a mere fourth of our sodium comes from salt added at the table or during cooking (the rest comes from chips, cheese, and other packaged foods). Eventually many health experts began to feel uneasy demanding that Americans who already fill their meals with fresh produce (low in sodium, rich in potassium and magnesium) avoid the saltshaker.

**THE CAVEAT** Recent studies suggest that women who eat lots of salty foods lose more bone as they age.

## Alcohol

**THEN** An addictive but accepted drug.

**NOW** A traditional beverage proven to prevent heart attacks.

**WHAT CHANGED** Study after study confirmed that regular, moderate drinkers die of heart disease less often than nondrinkers. Alcohol raises good cholesterol levels and slows blood clotting in arteries. Last year even the government said it's fine to have a drink or two a day. Beer, wine, and hard liquor appear to be equally good for your arteries, experts say.

**THE CAVEAT** Alcohol is still a potentially dangerous drug, one linked to liver disease as well as cancers of the mouth, throat, esophagus, and breast.

---

*Dietary Goals for the United States,* that, in ways its authors could never have foreseen, changed how we think about our meals.

After examining virtually all nutritional research from the late fifties to mid-seventies, McGovern's committee concluded that dietary cholesterol and saturated fats, mostly from meat and dairy products, were contributing to the huge numbers of heart attacks among Americans and perhaps to the cancer epidemic as well. It was the first time any branch of the government acknowledged the rising tide of scientific research indicating that saturated fats raise blood levels of artery-clogging cholesterol. Naturally, *Dietary Goals* recommended some changes at the kitchen table. Americans should eat more fruits and vegetables, fewer high-fat dairy products, and less meat. Simple advice; anyone could have understood it.

Some understood all too well. The meat, dairy, and egg industries launched an immediate counteroffensive. "The beef and pork people went bonkers, and they pressured the senators to change the report," says Patricia Hausman, a nutritionist who has written about the controversy. "Some of the committee members were just flabbergasted because they'd been dealing with top doctors with impeccable credentials and they didn't realize that their recommendations would be controversial." Hausman recalls one hearing in which McGovern told eminent researcher Jeremiah Stamler: "Livestock producers are going to start raising cain about this committee telling people to eat less beef."

Responding to intense lobbying by the likes of the National Cattlemen's Association and the United Egg Producers, members of McGovern's committee convinced the chairman to hold another set of hearings wherein the virtues of meat and eggs were loudly extolled. The committee then released a second edition of *Dietary Goals,* and suddenly the advice was muddier: "Decrease consumption of animal fat, and choose meats, poultry, and fish which will reduce saturated fat intake." In the foreword, committee member Bob Dole of Kansas expressed relief that the report no longer advised Americans to eat less "nutritious protein food" like beef. Like Kansas beef.

And there it was: Because saturated fat and cholesterol had in essence their own political lobbies, McGovern's committee actually denounced nothing—not red meat, not eggs, not whole milk. Instead, the report stressed general guidelines about fat and cholesterol consumption. Fat of all types shouldn't account for more than 30 percent of our calories, said the committee, and saturated fat only 10 percent; cholesterol should be limited to 300 milligrams daily. Over the years vari-

ations on this theme became standard in government pronouncements and publications. Yet it was almost as if the surgeon general had warned us to limit "smoke intake" without specifically barring cigarettes.

Not surprisingly, people found it difficult to translate the advice into action. Until nutrition labels started to appear a few years ago, it wasn't clear which foods contained hazardous amounts of saturated fat and cholesterol. In real life eating less saturated fat meant cutting back on red meat, butter, and whole milk; less cholesterol meant cutting back on eggs. But government officials were rarely that direct. "Total fat has always been a euphemism for 'eat less meat and dairy,' " says Marion Nestle, a nutrition expert at New York University.

There was another complication: The same research that fingered cholesterol and saturated fat as dietary demons had also found that some of the healthiest people in the world regularly ate meals that were dripping with fat. This apparent contradiction never made headlines, never triggered senate hearings. Had anyone paid more attention, America's kitchens—hell, its hospitals—might be very different places.

AMONG THE FIRST skirmishes in the war on fat was a study in the late sixties by Ancel Keys, a legendary epidemiologist at the University of Minnesota. Keys compared the diets, cholesterol levels, and life expectancies of 16 groups of men in seven countries and found that people were living longest in Greece, specifically rural Crete,

where cancer was rare and the rate of heart disease was a tenth of that in the United States. The Greeks' blood levels of cholesterol, not coincidentally, were low.

The secret? Keys pointed to local eating habits. Mediterranean societies lived on fresh fruits and vegetables; pastas, breads, and other grains; and beans and nuts. People rarely touched meat, milk, and eggs. Even more interesting to Keys, the Mediterranean menu didn't skimp on fat. Some villagers got as much as 40 percent of their calories from fat, mostly olive oil. Before heading out to the fields Greek farmers were chugging *glasses* of it for breakfast. But the fat in olive oil is mostly monounsaturated. It didn't raise their cholesterol levels, Keys found, and it didn't jeopardize their health. Keys's research helped indict dietary cholesterol and saturated fat, but the notion that other types of fat might benefit the heart failed to catch on.

Why? At the time scientists didn't feel comfortable describing a rich diet as healthy. For one thing, animal studies were suggesting that polyunsaturated fats might cause cancer. "The heart disease experts always knew the problem was saturated fat," says Nancy Ernst, nutrition coordinator of the Heart, Lung, and Blood Institute. "But they went along with the advice on total fat mostly because of the worries about cancer." Researchers also suspected that food fats were contributing to Americans' ever-expanding waistlines. Worried about both cancer and obesity, experts by and large supported the notion that people should eat less fat in general.

**It's not fat itself that causes flabby thighs and love handles, say most researchers. It's calories.**

Yet research hasn't borne out the connection between polyunsaturated fats and human cancer, and obesity specialists have mostly concluded that there is no relationship between fat intake per se and flabby thighs. It's the calories that matter, not the fat. The last decade provides ample proof. Even as Americans cut back on fat, increasing numbers gained weight, a trend driven partly by our assumption that we can eat all we want as long as it's low in fat.

"Recommendations about low-fat diets have only caused people to eat more sugar and more calories," says Frank Sacks, a researcher at the Harvard School of Public Health. "For our society there's good evidence that a moderate-fat diet would be healthier than a low-fat diet."

The desire for rich foods, hardwired into our brains, is no evolutionary accident. We hunger for ice cream and buttery sauces because our bodies need fat. All fats provide energy, maintain cell membranes and blood vessels, transmit nerve impulses, and produce essential hormones. But among the 20-odd fatty acids, scientists have found several whose powers may explain how a higher-fat diet could actually fight disease.

Fish, for instance, is oily, but experts now know it's chock-ablock with polyunsaturated omega-3 fats, which seem to protect the heart by making particular blood cells less likely to clump together and gum up the works. Nuts get three-quarters of their calories from fat, yet because they contain alpha-linolenic acid, which converts to omega-3 fats in the body, nut-lovers tend to have low cholesterol levels. So a diet of pasta and olive oil may be loaded with fat, but it's not likely to send your cholesterol rocketing. For some people, such a diet might even raise good (high-density lipoprotein) cholesterol and lower heart disease risk.

"The monounsaturates and polyunsaturates are not harmful," says Sacks. "In fact, they're probably beneficial."

The message has been difficult to hear above the clamor of fat phobics. But that's changing. A story in this magazine seven years ago spread the word about the so-called French paradox: Although they eat and drink like medieval kings, the French have a lower heart disease rate than Americans do. They drink far more red wine, researchers found, which seems to help protect their hearts.

But that explanation only sidestepped the larger issue. As Keys noted long ago, the French weren't the only heart-healthy tribe in the region. To the south, Mediterranean populations also thrived on luscious meals. Every oil-quaffing, long-lived farmer effectively refuted America's official advice that fatty diets were always, inevitably, dangerous.

Since then Mediterranean cookbooks and prepackaged pasta offerings have flowed like ouzo at a Greek wedding. An enjoyable change, but the challenge now is more formidable than just stocking up on olives and vermicelli at a gourmet deli. Somehow we must build new eating habits around moderate indulgence in the kinds of fats the body needs.

For most of us, that means selecting more foods that go well with olive and canola oils: fish, lean poultry, vegetables, salads, breads. It means meat need not be the entrée; pasta or a rice dish can occupy the place of honor instead. Also given minor roles are buttered biscuits, pastries, and the like. Obviously, this heart-friendly fare isn't the comfort food of the past. These meals require more planning and preparation, which take time—but hey, so does recovering from a heart attack. A better diet is worth the effort.

It feels strange, doesn't it, this notion of embracing fat? Just when we'd found the discipline to deny ourselves, the will to appease the whiny guilt-pilgrims lurking inside each American, scientists have started to favor palatability over puritanism. What they are offering, amazingly, is just what this nation, so inured to abundance, has always claimed to want: a chance to live off the fat of the land.

 **Article Review Form at end of book.**

What is capsaicin? How do endorphins play a role when eating chili peppers? What is quercetin?

# Why Hot Is Healthy

Not feeling up to snuff? Try putting some spice in your life.

## Dorothy Foltz-Gray

I eat hot chile peppers on Fridays in dark restaurants that specialize in nachos and icy beer. I'm happy, very hungry, and I scoop up chips heaped with nature's fire, delighted that the heap is dauntingly large. A couple of good friends are with me, a fortunate intimacy because between bites all of us are snuffling like crybabies.

Although we don't know it, we're reaping one of the benefits of eating hot foods, specifically chile peppers, the fruit that's been spicing palates for thousands of years—ever since Latin American Indians began cultivating chiles to eat, to soothe toothaches, and to treat upper respiratory disorders. Ancient Mayans used chiles to calm asthma and coughs, and they're still considered standard therapy in India and Mexico. Medical textbooks in Asia and Europe frequently mention chiles and other hot spices as cold treatments.

Chiles are nature's decongestant, a fiery, albeit temporary, way to relieve stuffy sinuses and help clear congested lungs. We dive into a bowlful of hot salsa, and within seconds we're dabbing our running noses, tearing eyes, and sweating brows. The waterworks are on.

These hot gems trigger a sudden release of watery fluids in the nose and throat. The secretions help thin respiratory mucus so it's easier to expel, and they aid digestion. Chiles also stimulate mucus glands deep in the nasal passages. As we know all too well, when we have an allergy, cold, or sinus infection, our sinuses can't drain and we can't breathe through our noses. Chiles rescue us—without the side effects of stupefying decongestant drugs—by prompting nasal glands to release fluid that helps drain clogged sinuses, says Bruce Scott, a head and neck surgeon in Louisville, Kentucky.

The whole reaction begins with capsaicin, the chemical in hot peppers that blasts the mouth. "Under normal eating circumstances—say, if we bite into a mild cracker—our response is to salivate," explains George Philip, who studied peppers while an allergist at Johns Hopkins Asthma and Allergy Center in Baltimore. "But capsaicin stimulates not only the nerve fibers that control saliva but neighboring fibers as well, the ones that control our nasal glands." And the very process that clears sinuses can also relieve the pain and pressure that comes with a stuffy head.

Not that you're hungry anymore, but the next time you have a cold or a toothache you may be cheered to know that eating chiles can also soothe mouth pain. That's because capsaicin, after its initial burn, has a numbing effect.

Capsaicin fires our mouths with heat, or more accurately pain. (The chemical also prompts a lot of people to sweat, though tests have shown that body temperature doesn't actually rise.) What's going on? Capsaicin ignores the mouth's taste buds, and instead stimulates nearby nerve cells that send pain messages to the brain via a neurotransmitter called substance P. But it provokes such a strong response that after

## Bell Peppers: For Fighting Disease, They're Better Red Than Green

Research reveals some compelling reasons to choose ripe red bell peppers over their bright green siblings: Reds have twice the vitamin C and nine times the beta-carotene of green bells, which are picked before they ripen.

The antioxidants vitamin C and beta-carotene, it now appears, work best to prevent disease when eaten together. Antioxidants help rid the body of molecules called free radicals, which invade healthy cells and attack crucial parts of the molecular machinery to steal electrons. The resulting mutations can lead to cancer, heart disease, and other ills.

For years scientists thought that any of the key antioxidants—vitamin E, vitamin C, or beta-carotene—could battle these scavengers. But when smokers taking beta-carotene supplements actually showed a heightened risk of lung cancer, researchers began scrambling for an explanation.

A recent study by chemists in Great Britain offers intriguing clues. It seems it takes a chain reaction involving all three antioxidants to vanquish free radicals. Vitamin E launches the defense by giving up an electron to the free radicals, thereby preventing damage to cells. This, however, turns vitamin E into a potential free radical itself. Not to worry: The damaged vitamin E molecule gets repaired by beta-carotene, then the beta-carotene is fixed by vitamin C—when there is enough of it around in the bloodstream and tissues. Because vitamin C is soluble in water, its radicals wash safely out of the body.

"Nutrients act in a certain combination and a certain order," says Paul Lachance, a food scientist at Rutgers University in New Brunswick, New Jersey. "You can't separate antioxidants from one another and expect a positive result."

Alas, red bell peppers have no vitamin E, but two good sources of the nutrient are fresh, raw spinach and sunflower seeds. A hearty salad with all these ingredients will pack a powerful antioxidant punch. For an appetizer, try red bell peppers roasted under a broiler until black, skinned and seeded, then marinated in olive oil.

Or take the advice of Jean Andrews, a Texas botanist and author of some great books on the history and lore of peppers. She eats red bell pepper slices right off the cutting board—nature's own anticancer snack. "The reds are sweeter and more flavorful," says Andrews. "Nothing else tastes quite like them."

—Alex Gramling

---

several bites the cells' supply of substance P gives out like ammunition at the Alamo. You're numb—so numb you don't even feel other kinds of pain. In fact, capsaicin has been used as a painkiller for sore gums.

If you eat jalapeños daily, however, something else happens: The mouth's nerve cells that send pain signals are dulled forever. "The cells effectively say, 'I don't like this. Let me pull in the gate,'" says Philip. The chiles no longer taste so hot, and you no longer sweat when you eat them.

Few people in North America ever eat enough chiles to become blasé about their heat. True, Americans have made salsa more popular than ketchup, but it's the mild dip we're buying. So when we do bite into an incendiary jalapeño, we haul out the hankies and scream for water. (Try milk or bread instead; capsaicin's oily resin isn't water soluble.)

If chile peppers provoke so much pain, why don't we throw down the fork after the first bite? Some scientists believe that endorphins, the neurochemicals associated with runner's high, kick in to overcome the discomfort triggered when we chomp chiles, spurring us on to eat more and more. In fact, Andrew Weil, the physician who studies alternative medicine, speculates that this rush is precisely what pepper lovers are after.

Ah, if only all pleasures had such salutary side effects. "Chile peppers are truly a way to eat low-fat food and get fiber, beta-carotene, and vitamin C," says Ann Bock, a professor of human nutrition at New Mexico State University in Las Cruces. A half cup of chopped chile supplies more than twice the vitamin C of an orange; and the redder (which is to say riper) a pepper gets, the higher its dose of beta-carotene.

Chiles are also steeped in quercetin, a phytochemical shown to lower cancer risk in lab animals. Spicy leftovers last longer, too. Capsaicin is a natural antibiotic, slowing down bacteria's growth, another reason why the refrigerator-deprived Aztecs prized chiles' fire.

So what's the downside? Amazingly, there isn't one. The more researchers examine chiles, the fewer concerns they have. Our grandparents were convinced spicy foods caused stomach ulcers, but a 1988 study buried that old wives' tale. When doctors at Baylor College of Medicine in Houston compared the stomach-irritating effects of bland food, food loaded with chiles, and food mixed with aspirin, only the aspirin-laced snacks inflamed the gastric lining.

"Spicy food doesn't harm the stomach," says David Y. Graham, lead author of the study and chief of digestive diseases at the

Veterans Administration Medical Center in Houston. "At least not to the extent that you can see the damage. Even if you had ulcers and ate chiles, they wouldn't hurt or help." The slight irritation chiles do bring might even protect the stomach from further irritation, Graham says. In animal studies the stomach lining responds to mild irritants by replacing its cells, in essence becoming tougher and more resilient.

What's more, population studies showing higher rates of stomach cancer among people who eat lots of chiles have not held up under scrutiny. A 1990 study in Mexico City found that heavy pepper eaters were more likely to develop stomach cancer. But follow-up interviews revealed that these self-described heavy eaters downed the same number of chiles each week as light chile eaters. The cancer link vanished.

One recent study on rats did suggest that chiles may lessen absorption of calcium. But no one yet knows if that's true in humans, and Southern Hemisphere populations that eat scads of chiles don't have high rates of osteoporosis.

Evidence of chiles' appeal, however, is indisputable. And you needn't have the sniffles to benefit. If you do find yourself clogged up by summer allergies or a cold, sure, cut up a jalapeño into a steamy bowl of chicken soup; you'll soon be clearheadedly spooning your way to a kind of tropical paradise. But even on your best days, you can use chiles to spice up healthful dishes.

Looking for a cheap thrill? Try mincing a habanero—the hottest of the hot, 40 times hotter than the jalapeños—and sprinkling it into a pot of bean soup.

If that seems extreme, look for the large, mild, broad-shouldered peppers such as anaheims (readily available canned as "whole green chiles") and poblanos (now sold fresh in many groceries).

Roasted under a broiler till blackened uniformly, then peeled gently under a stream of cold water, poblanos are great for stuffing. Some people fill them simply with cooked rice and sautéed vegetables, then bake them. Another good stuffing is picadillo: Sauté ground turkey breast, diced onions, bell peppers, and apples with some raisins and chopped almonds. Spoon the mixture into roasted poblano or canned whole chiles, cover, and bake or microwave till hot. Serve with a meatless tomato sauce.

Or try sautéing a chopped jalapeño, an onion, some garlic, and a green bell pepper in a pot. Add a cup of uncooked rice, two cups of water, and a dash of cumin. Twenty minutes later stir in two fistfuls of chopped raw spinach and a bit of fresh cilantro. I dare you to stop eating.

 **Article Review Form at end of book.**

# WiseGuide Wrap-Up

- Regardless of gender, age, race, or activity level, by following the seven Dietary Guidelines from the U.S. Department of Agriculture and the Department of Health and Human Services you can have a sound diet.

- Choosing to consume a wide variety of meat products, dairy foods, breads and grains, fruits, and vegetables is the best strategy to receive all nutrients essential for physiologic function.

- You can reduce the likelihood of getting many chronic diseases (heart disease, cancer, diabetes mellitus) by making prudent diet choices.

## R.E.A.L. Sites

This list provides a print preview of typical **coursewise** R.E.A.L. sites. (There are over 100 such sites at the **courselinks**™ site.) The danger in printing URLs is that web sites can change overnight. As we went to press, these sites were functional using the URLs provided. If you come across one that isn't, please let us know via email to: webmaster@coursewise.com. Use your Passport to access the most current list of R.E.A.L. sites at the **courselinks**™ site.

**Site name:** U.S. Department of Agriculture's Food and Nutrition Information Center

**URL:** http://www.nalusda.gov/fnic/

**Why is it R.E.A.L.?** This is an agricultural network center for the U.S. Department of Agriculture (USDA). Topics presented include other publications, as well as databases on nutrition education, Women, Infants and Children (WIC), and healthy school meals.

**Activities:** (1)Describe the mission of the USDA's School Meals Initiative for Healthy Children. (2)What is WIC and what are the merits of WIC?

**Site name:** The American Dietetic Association

**URL:** http://www.eatright.org

**Why is it R.E.A.L.?** The Gateway to Nutrition provides a number of links to help you develop sound food selection skills.

**Activities:** (1)What was the "tip of the day" from the ADA? Did you heed this advice today? Why or why not? (2)Browse the "latest nutrition topics." Summarize three of these and present them to the class.

**Site name:** Wellness Web

**URL:** http://www.wellweb.com

**Why is it R.E.A.L.?** This page provides links to hospitals, news groups, online forums, and other resources for nutrition information.

**Activities:** (1)What does this site say about having desserts? (2)Summarize the information on "what Americans should eat to stay healthy."

**Site name:** Healthwise at Columbia University

**URL:** http://www.columbia.edu/cu/healthwise

**Why is it R.E.A.L.?** This is the Health Education and Wellness program of the Columbia University Health Service. You can post an anonymous health-related question, and the response will come from Columbia Health Services in New York City. Previously posted questions and answers are organized by topic.

**Activities:** Ask a nutrition-related question to this service and present your question and response to the class.

# section 2

# Good Nutrition Starts Early
## Nutrition for Pregnant Women and for Children

 **WiseGuide Intro**

While in your mother's womb and during the first few years of life, you grew and developed at a rate greater than at any other time. Nutrition can clearly affect pregnancy outcome and lactation performance. Unfortunately, a number of pregnant women in the United States receive inadequate (if any) prenatal care. Consequently, the infant mortality rate in our nation is higher than that in twenty-three other industrialized countries. How does that make you feel?

## Learning Objectives

After studying this section, you will know:

- nutrient needs that may increase during pregnancy, and food choices to meet this demand.

- the outcomes of fetal alcohol syndrome (FAS).

- how folate affects the likelihood of neural tube defects.

- the rate of physical growth in infancy vs. childhood vs. adolescence and how diet affects this.

- strategies for parents to help ensure food consumption.

- the rationale for initiating a healthy diet early in life.

- the role of snacks in a child's diet.

- practical strategies to improve food selection and physical activity among children.

- that many behaviors, such as physical inactivity or a poor diet, that put adults at risk for chronic disease are established in childhood.

As we grow from infants to adolescents to adults, our nutrient and calorie needs change. Infants need a concentrated source of energy to meet the high rate of growth. The most effective time to establish appropriate diet is during the childhood years.

Pregnancy affects nutrient demands. The need for iron, folate, magnesium, and zinc increases substantially during pregnancy. However, these nutrient needs are to be met with but a modest (300 kcal per day) increase in energy intake. Moreover, this energy increase should occur during the second and third trimesters only. Therefore, soon-to-be mothers should not eat "ad libitum." Contrary, nutrient-dense food selection is vitally important to the mother as well as the child.

Nutrition can affect (positively or negatively) a child's growth and development. An infant is growing at a very rapid rate. Concomitantly, the infant's needs for essential nutrients are higher (based on weight) than they will be at any other time in childhood. During toddlerhood, this rate of growth slows substantially and, consequently, the relative amount of food required lessens. The adolescent growth spurt occurs in conjunction with the individual finding his or her own identity. Therefore, diet strategies for this group should be based on these physical and emotional changes.

Diet inadequacies may be associated with growth retardation, increased heart disease risk, overweightness, iron deficiency anemia, and increased susceptibility to infection. Therefore, it should be obvious what the role of sound diet is in promoting health and preventing illnesses among infants, children, and adolescents.

The following section will teach you the importance of sound nutrition during pregnancy, the nutritional status of our nation's children, and how sound nutrition education can affect a child's risk for chronic disease.

R8. What might happen if the pregnant woman gains too much weight during pregnancy? How about if the woman gains too little weight? Discuss suggestions on how to curb alcohol intake during pregnancy and the concept of fetal alcohol syndrome (FAS). List some diet strategies to deal with "morning sickness." What is the significance of each of the following nutrients to a pregnant woman and her child: iron, folate, vitamin $B^{12}$, calcium?

R9. List some foods that are good sources of folate. Explain anencephaly and spina bifida. How does folate play a role in these phenomena? How much folate should a pregnant woman consume? Explain the folate fortification requirements effective January 1, 1998.

R10. Using Body Mass Index (BMI), what is happening to the prevalence of obesity among adolescents? During this time period (1976 to 1990), what has happened to energy intake? What has happened to physical activity levels? Limiting total fat intake to less than 30 percent of total calorie intake has been advocated by a number of health organizations. What were the results from the School Nutrition Dietary Assessment Study (SNDA) of 1992 in this regard? Are there differences in fat consumption among children of different races? Why? Explain the phenomenon of iron deficiency anemia. Fruits and vegetables are excellent sources of the antioxidant nutrients, which may be protective in terms of cancer and coronary heart disease. Are our children consuming enough fruits and vegetables? Are our children receiving enough calcium? What might be the consequences of this? What might be some possible solutions to this?

R11. Were there differences in nutrient intake across states, across gender, across race? If so, what were the differences? Summarize the CATCH strategies to improve food selection and physical activity. What is the trend regarding percentage of calories from fat? How is this trend explained?

R12. Describe the idea of the USDA's Team Nutrition Program.

R13. Did changes in the school lunch menu reduce the fat content yet maintain the caloric content in the foods served? Did nutrition knowledge, skills, and attitudes of students improve? Did the students' physical fitness improve?

What might happen if the pregnant woman gains too much weight during pregnancy? How about if the woman gains too little weight? Discuss suggestions on how to curb alcohol intake during pregnancy and the concept of fetal alcohol syndrome (FAS). List some diet strategies to deal with "morning sickness." What is the significance of each of the following nutrients to a pregnant woman and her child: iron, folate, vitamin B$_{12}$, calcium?

# Nutrition During Pregnancy

## A Gift for Your Baby

**Barbara P. McLaurin, Ph.D., R.D., L.D.,**

*Human Nutrition Specialist; Mississippi Cooperative Extension Service; Mississippi State University*

Wouldn't you like to give your unborn baby a special gift? You can! One of the most important things you can do for your baby before he or she is born is just to eat a healthy diet. From the moment you conceive, you should start taking care of your baby, but it's never too late to start. Your baby will be more dependent on you now than any other time in life.

## Weight Gain

### Amount of Weight Gain

Gaining the right amount of weight when you are pregnant is important. It is one measure of the healthy growth of your baby, especially after the first three months of pregnancy. Your weight gain also affects your baby's birth weight—and studies have shown that babies with birth weights in the range of 5½ to 9 pounds tend to be healthier.

The number of pounds you should gain while you are pregnant depends on your weight before pregnancy and your height.

Studies show that shorter women should gain near the lower end of the range; black women and very young women should gain close to the upper end of the range. The recommended gain for women who are carrying twins is 35 to 45 pounds.

A word of WARNING! Pregnancy is not the time to diet to lose weight. Gaining too little weight during pregnancy may produce a baby too small at birth. Gaining too much weight during pregnancy can cause problems such as high blood pressure, diabetes, and a difficult delivery. It can also result in very large babies (more than 9 pounds), who are more likely to have health problems than smaller babies.

### Rate of Weight Gain

During your first 3 months of pregnancy, you will usually gain 2 to 4 pounds. When your baby begins to grow fast, you gain about one pound per week (more if you are underweight, less if you are overweight). Small differences in this rate are not important.

### Recommended Total Weight Gain

|  | Pounds |
|---|---|
| Women who are underweight for height* | 28–40 |
| Women who are normal weight for height* | 25–35 |
| Women who are overweight for height* | 15–25 |

*Before pregnancy

"Nutrition During Pregnancy: A Gift for Your Baby," by Barbara P. McLaurin, Ph.D., R.D., L.D., Human Nutrition Specialist; Mississippi Cooperative Extension Service:, Mississippi State University.

Mild swelling during the last 3 months of pregnancy is normal. If your legs, ankles, or feet become puffy, put your feet on a stool or chair for a while. A large, sudden weight gain accompanied by swelling of your hands and face is not normal, however, and needs medical attention quickly. (If you gain less than 2 pounds per month after the first 3 months, you should tell your doctor.)

## Recommended Calorie Levels

To meet your extra food needs for a healthy weight gain, you need to add an average of 300 extra calories per day to your diet after the first 3 months of pregnancy. (If your exercise habits change during pregnancy, you may need to make adjustments.)

Add these extra calories with extra servings of milk, lowfat cheese, lean meats, poultry, fish, leafy and dark green vegetables, dried beans and peas, fruits, whole grain, and enriched breads and cereals. (See *Table 1.**)

Don't eat lots of cookies, candies, cakes, chips, soft drinks, and fats such as butter, margarine, gravy, fried foods, salad dressings, and mayonnaise. These high-calorie foods provide very little nourishment for you and your baby.

## Other Nutrient Needs

Your needs for almost all nutrients (vitamins and minerals) are greater when you are pregnant. Nutrients are important in your own body's growth, your baby's, and later for breast-feeding.

The amount of iron and folate in your diet is important, so eat foods containing these nutrients often.

*Not included in this publication.

**Iron** is a mineral that carries oxygen to your baby. You need more iron than you normally do for the baby, and it is hard to get enough from foods alone. Your doctor will probably recommend an iron supplement while you are pregnant. Taking an iron supplement between meals or at bedtime on an empty stomach helps to increase its absorption. It is also important to eat iron-rich foods daily. (See *Table 2* for iron-rich foods.**)

**Folate** (Folacin, or Folic Acid) is a B vitamin that helps your body make red blood cells and genes. The amount of folate you need more than doubles when you are pregnant.

Eating various foods that contain folate is the best way to get enough. (Good food sources of folate are listed in *Table 2.**)

The iron in meat, fish, and poultry is more readily absorbed by the body than the iron in plant foods. To increase iron absorption, eat plant foods with meat or with foods that contain vitamin C. Some good sources of vitamin C are oranges, grapefruits, tangerines, strawberries, potatoes, and bell pepper.

## Multi-vitamin and Mineral Supplements

Although vitamin and mineral supplements are common, extra servings of healthy foods are the best sources for most women. Also, supplements may not contain all the essential nutrients supplied by healthy foods, which are less likely to cause unhealthy nutrient interactions.

Taking too many vitamin or mineral supplements can harm your unborn baby. More than 150 percent of the Recommended Daily Allowance (RDA) shown on the label is considered too much. Most damage occurs during the first 3 months when you may not know that you are pregnant.

However, you may need a multi-vitamin and mineral supplement if these conditions apply to you:

- You have a poor diet, lacking in any of the basic food groups.

- You are pregnant with more than one baby.

- You smoke, drink alcohol, or use drugs (more about this follows).

Talk to your doctor about supplements.

## Special Nutrient Needs in Special Circumstances

- Vitamin $B_{12}$ supplements may be needed if you are a "complete vegetarian" that is—you eat no animal foods.

- Calcium supplements may be needed if you are under age 25, especially if you do not drink enough milk. (Take calcium supplements at meal times, so they do not inhibit the absorption of iron supplements.)

**Caution:** Take supplements only with the advice of your doctor!

## Making Nutrition Part of Your Life During Pregnancy

Choose foods that you enjoy and like. Do not try to force yourself to eat foods that you dislike.

Be realistic and plan meals that will fit into your lifestyle. If you are always rushing in the morning, try to plan some simple but nourishing meals that can be eaten in a hurry. A bran muffin, a glass of milk, and an orange is one suggestion.

**Table 3** Some Ideas for Snacks

**Vegetable Snacks**

Raw vegetables such as carrots, cauliflower, broccoli, green pepper, green beans, snow peas, and mushrooms. Eat them alone or with cheese or yogurt dips. Tomato juice or mixed vegetable juice.

**Fruit Snacks**

Sliced or whole fresh, canned, or dried fruit. Eat plain or with cottage cheese, ricotta cheese, or yogurt with cinnamon.

**Milk Snacks**

Milk fruit shakes, yogurt with fresh fruit, cheese and crackers, cottage cheese and fruit, custard, pudding.

**Breads and Crackers**

Eat plain or with cheese or peanut butter. Try a variety of quick breads and muffins with whole grain and/or fruits and vegetables (for example, pumpkin, cranberry, nut, or whole wheat bread and oatmeal, apple, blueberry, corn, or bran muffins); whole grain cereal with milk and fresh fruit.

**Meat, Fish, Poultry, and Egg Group and Alternates**

Turkey or roast beef sandwich, beef stew, chicken, hard-boiled or deviled egg. Use a nuts and seed mix, peanut butter with crackers, and split pea or lentil soup as meat alternates.

It is also a good idea to plan ahead so you don't just grab what's there when you are hungry. Pregnancy is not the time to snack on a bag of chips and a soft drink. Try some cheese, fruit, and crackers for a quick snack away from home.

To meet all your needs, eat at least three meals a day and possibly two or three snacks. Let your appetite be your guide. *Table 3* lists some suggested snack foods during pregnancy. Remember, any nutritious food is appropriate for a snack.

## Alcohol and Caffeine

### What about Alcohol?

We know that drinking alcoholic beverages can be dangerous to unborn babies. Yet many women continue to drink wine, beer, or liquor during pregnancy.

More than 50 percent of the babies born to alcoholic mothers have what is known as "fetal alcohol syndrome" (FAS). Their infants have birth defects, mental retardation, and reduced growth rates.

Even if alcohol intake does not cause full-blown FAS, it is associated with miscarriage, low birth weight, and learning disorders.

No safe level of alcohol consumption has been established for pregnant women. Some studies show that as few as one or two drinks per day may be harmful to the developing fetus. Both the Food and Drug Administration (FDA) and the U.S. Surgeon General have recommended that pregnant women avoid drinking any alcohol during pregnancy. Damage may occur during the first 3 months before a woman knows she is pregnant. Avoid alcohol if you are even considering pregnancy.

### What about Caffeine?

Caffeine is a stimulant found in coffee, tea, colas, other soft drinks, chocolate, cocoa, and some drugs. Whether a pregnant woman should avoid caffeine is still open to question.

Pregnant women who choose to consume foods and drinks con-taining caffeine should do so in moderation. Use all drugs only on the advice of your doctor.

## Common Problems During Pregnancy

### Nausea or Vomiting

Nausea ("morning sickness") can occur at any time of the day, but it is often most troublesome when you get up in the morning. The problem is usually mild and often goes away after the first 3 months of pregnancy. You can stop or re-duce your nausea and vomiting if you take these precautions:

- Eat a few crackers, a handful of dry cereal, or a piece of dry toast or bread before you get out of bed in the morning. Put these within easy reach the night before.

- Get up slowly in the morning. Avoid sudden movements.

- Eat five or six small meals a day. Never go for long periods without food. Try not to get hungry.

- Drink fluids, including soups, between meals rather than with them.

- Drink a small amount of apple juice, grape juice, or a carbonated beverage if you feel nauseated between meals.

- Avoid greasy and fried foods and other foods that upset your stomach, such as greasy or highly seasoned foods.

- Open windows or use the exhaust fan to get rid of odors when you cook.

- Have plenty of fresh air in the room while you are sleeping.

## Constipation

During pregnancy, your digestive system relaxes so that your body can absorb more nutrients. This relaxation can cause constipation. During your last 3 months of pregnancy, your uterus will apply pressure to the large intestine, aggravating the problem. These suggestions may help:

- Eat more raw fruits and vegetables, including skins, dried fruits, stewed prunes and apricots, and prune juice.

- Eat whole grain cereals, such as oatmeal or brown rice and whole wheat breads. Sprinkle wheat germ or bran on cereal, or have a bran muffin.

- Eat more dried beans and peas.

- Drink more liquids. Include water, milk, fruit juices, and soups.

- Eat meals at regular times.

- Exercise regularly.

## Heartburn

Especially in late pregnancy, your uterus will push up on your stomach. After you eat, swallowed food can be forced back up. This causes a "burning" feeling called heartburn.

Eating five to six small meals a day, rather than two or three large ones, often relieves this discomfort. Avoid fatty, fried, and spicy foods.

## Hemorrhoids

Some women already have hemorrhoids and others develop them during the last 3 months of pregnancy. The reason is the weight of the baby. The suggestions for relieving constipation also help hemorrhoids.

## Cravings

Some women crave non-food items, such as clay, dirt, or starch when they are pregnant. Try not to eat these because they do not provide nutrients that you and your baby need. They may also block the nutrients from foods that you do eat.

## References

American Red Cross. *Better Eating for Better Health: Participant's Guide. I'm Pregnant: What Should I Eat?* Washington, D.C.: American Red Cross, 1984.

IOM. (Institute of Medicine). Food and Nutrition Board. *Nutrition During Pregnancy, Executive Summary.* Report of the Subcommittee on Nutritional Status and Weight Gain During Pregnancy and the Subcommittee on Dietary Intake and Nutrient Supplements during Pregnancy. Washington, D.C.: National Academy Press, 1990.

NRC. (National Research Council). Food and Nutrition Board. *Recommended Dietary Allowances.* 10th rev. ed. Washington, D.C.: National Academy Press, 1989.

 **Article Review Form at end of book.**

List some foods that are good sources of folate. Explain anencephaly and spina bifida. How does folate play a role in these phenomena? How much folate should a pregnant woman consume? Explain the folate fortification requirements effective January 1, 1998.

# How Folate Can Help Prevent Birth Defects

## Paula Kurtzweil

*Paula Kurtzweil is a member of FDA's public affairs staff.*

If you plan to have children some day, here's important information for the future mother-to-be: Think folate now.

Folate is a B vitamin found in a variety of foods and added to many vitamin and mineral supplements as folic acid, a synthetic form of folate. Folate is needed both before and in the first weeks of pregnancy and can help reduce the risk of certain serious and common birth defects called neural tube defects, which affect the brain and spinal cord.

The tricky part is that neural tube defects can occur in an embryo before a woman realizes she's pregnant. That's why it's important for all women of childbearing age (15 to 45) to include folate in their diets: If they get pregnant, it reduces the chance of the baby having a birth defect of the brain or spinal cord.

"Adequate folate should be eaten daily and throughout the childbearing years," said Elizabeth Yetley, Ph.D., a registered dietitian and director of FDA's Office of Special Nutritionals.

There are several ways to do this:

- Eat fruits, dark-green leafy vegetables, dried beans and peas, and other foods that are natural sources of folate.

- Eat folic acid-fortified breakfast cereals.

- Take a vitamin supplement containing folic acid.

Folate's potential to reduce the risk of neural tube defects is so important that the Food and Drug Administration is requiring that by 1998, food manufacturers fortify enriched grain products with folic acid. This will give women another way to get sufficient folate: by eating fortified breads and other grains.

Nutrition information on food and dietary supplement labels can help women determine whether they are getting enough folate, which is 400 micrograms (0.4 milligrams) a day before pregnancy and 800 micrograms a day during pregnancy.

## Neural Tube Birth Defects

The technical names of the two major neural tube birth defects reduced by adequate folate intake are anencephaly and spina bifida. Babies with anencephaly do not develop a brain and are stillborn or die shortly after birth. Those with spina bifida have a defect of the spinal column that can result in varying degrees of handicap, from mild and hardly noticeable cases of scoliosis (a sideways bending of the spine) to paralysis and bladder or bowel incontinence. With proper medical treatment, most babies born with spina bifida can survive to adulthood. But they may require leg braces, crutches, and other devices to help them walk, and they may have learning disabilities. About 30 percent have slight to severe mental retardation.

The National Centers for Disease Control and Prevention estimate that about 2,500 infants with spina bifida and anencephaly are born each year in the United States.

"How Folate Can Help Prevent Birth Defects" by Paula Kurtzweil as appeared in FDA CONSUMER Magazine, September 1996, pp. 7–10.

Other maternal factors also may contribute to the development of neural tube defects. These include:

- family history of neural tube defects
- prior neural tube defect-affected pregnancy
- use of certain antiseizure medications
- severe overweight
- hot tub use in early pregnancy
- fever during early pregnancy
- diabetes.

Any woman concerned about these factors should consult her doctor.

## Folate Link

Scientists first suggested a link between neural tube birth defects and diet in the 1950s. The incidence of these conditions has always been higher in low socioeconomic groups in which women may have poorer diets. Also, babies conceived in the winter and early spring are more likely to be born with spina bifida, perhaps because the mother's diet lacks fresh fruits and vegetables—which are good sources of folate—during the early weeks of pregnancy.

In 1991, British researchers found that 72 percent of women who had one pregnancy with a neural tube birth defect had a lower risk of having another child with this birth defect when they took prescription doses of folic acid before and during early pregnancy.

Another study looked at folic acid intake in Hungarian women. The evidence indicated that mothers who had never given birth to babies with neural tube defects

## Some Good Sources of Folate

| Food | Serving Size | Amount (Micrograms) | % Daily Value* |
|---|---|---|---|
| Chicken liver | 3.5 oz | 770 | 193 |
| Breakfast cereals | ½ to 1½ cup | 100 to 400 | 25 to 100 |
| Braised beef liver | 3.5 oz | 217 | 54 |
| Lentils, cooked | ½ cup | 180 | 45 |
| Chickpeas | ½ cup | 141 | 35 |
| Asparagus | ½ cup | 132 | 33 |
| Spinach, cooked | ½ cup | 131 | 33 |
| Black beans | ½ cup | 128 | 32 |
| Burrito with beans | 2 | 118 | 30 |
| Kidney beans | ½ cup | 115 | 29 |
| Baked beans with pork | 1 cup | 92 | 23 |
| Lima beans | ½ cup | 78 | 20 |
| Tomato juice | 1 cup | 48 | 12 |
| Brussels sprouts | ½ cup | 47 | 12 |
| Orange | 1 medium | 47 | 12 |
| Broccoli, cooked | ½ cup | 39 | 10 |
| Fast-food French fries | large order | 38 | 10 |
| Wheat germ | 2 tbsp | 38 | 10 |
| Fortified white bread | 1 slice | 38 | 10 |

\* Based on Daily Value for folate of 400 micrograms
(Source: *Food Values of Portions Commonly Used*, 16th edition)

and who took a multivitamin and mineral supplement with folic acid had less risk in subsequent pregnancies for having babies with neural tube defects than women given a placebo.

These studies led the U.S. Public Health Service in September 1992 to recommend that all women of childbearing age capable of becoming pregnant consume 0.4 mg of folate daily to reduce their risk of having a pregnancy affected with spina bifida or other neural tube defects.

That corresponds to FDA's Daily Value for folic acid, which is 400 micrograms for nonpregnant women, as well as children 4 and older and adult men. For pregnant women, the Daily Value jumps to 800 micrograms. Daily Values are dietary reference numbers used on the Nutrition Facts panel on food labels to show the amounts of various nutrients in a serving of food.

Many women between 19 and 50 get only 200 micrograms of folate a day, according to the U.S. Department of Agriculture.

## Folate Sources

Folate occurs naturally in a variety of foods, including liver; dark-green leafy vegetables such as collards, turnip greens, and Romaine lettuce; broccoli and asparagus; citrus fruits and juices; whole-grain products; wheat germ; and dried beans and peas, such as pinto, navy and lima beans, and chickpeas and black-eyed peas.

Under FDA's folic acid fortification program, the agency is requiring manufacturers to add from 0.43 mg to 1.4 mg of folic acid per pound of product to enriched flour, bread, rolls and buns, farina, corn grits, cornmeal, rice, and noodle products. A serving of each product will provide about 10 percent of the Daily Value for folic acid. Whole-grain products do not have to be enriched because they contain natural folate. Some of the natural folate in non-whole-grain products is lost in the process of refining whole grains.

The fortification regulations become effective Jan. 1, 1998, although manufacturers may begin folic acid fortification immediately, as long as they adhere to the regulations.

Folate also can be obtained from dietary supplements, such as folic acid tablets and multivitamins with folic acid, and from fortified breakfast cereals.

A study reported in the March 9, 1996, issue of *The Lancet,* suggested that folic acid, the synthetic form of folate, may be better absorbed than folate found naturally in foods. Christine Lewis, Ph.D., a registered dietitian and special assistant in FDA's Office of Special Nutritionals, said, "This is a complex and poorly understood issue, and more data are needed."

## Finding Foods with Folate

Certain information on food and dietary supplement labels can help women spot foods containing substantial amounts of folate. Some labels may claim that the product is "high in folate or folic acid," which means a serving of the food provides 20 percent or more of the Daily Value for folic acid. Or the label may say the food is a "good source" of folate, which means a serving of the food provides 10 to 19 percent of the Daily Value for folic acid. The exact amount will be given in the label's Nutrition Facts panel.

Some food and dietary supplement labels may carry a longer claim that says adequate folate intake may reduce the risk of neural tube birth defects. Products carrying this claim must:

- provide 10 percent or more of the Daily Value for folic acid per serving

- not contain more than 100 percent of the Daily Value for vitamins A and D per serving because high intakes of these vitamins are associated with other birth defects

- carry a caution on the label about excess folic acid intake, if a serving of food provides more than 100 percent of the Daily Value for folic acid. FDA has set 1 mg (or 1,000 micrograms) of folate daily as the maximum safe level. There are limited data on the safety of consuming more than 1 mg daily, and there may be a risk for people with low amounts of vitamin $B_{12}$ in their bodies—for example, older people with malabsorption problems, and people on certain anticancer drugs or drugs for epilepsy whose effectiveness can diminish when taken with high intakes of folate.

- list on the label's Nutrition or Supplement Facts panel the amount by weight in micrograms and the % Daily Value of folate per serving of the product. This information, which appears toward the bottom of the panel, along with the listing of other vitamins and minerals, can be used to compare folate levels in various foods and supplements.

Optional information may appear with the health claim to let consumers know about other risks associated with neural tube birth defects, when to consult a doctor, other foods that are good sources of folate, and other important messages about neural tube defects.

## Other Considerations

The claim about folate cannot imply that adequate folate intake alone will ensure a healthy baby, since so many factors can affect a pregnancy.

Women should bear this in mind when contemplating pregnancy, advises Jeanne Latham, a registered dietitian and consumer safety officer in FDA's Office of Special Nutritionals. "Folate can make a significant contribution," she said, "but it's no guarantee of a healthy baby."

Genetics plays a role, as do other healthful prenatal practices, such as eating an all-around good diet. But unlike genetics, diet is a risk factor women can modify to their—and their baby's—advantage, said Jeanne Rader, Ph.D., director of the division of science and applied technology in FDA's Office of Food Labeling.

"Folic acid is one of many nutrients needed in a healthy diet for women of childbearing age," she said. "A well-balanced diet with a variety of foods can provide all those nutrients, including adequate amounts of folate."

Women have options for reaching the folate intake goal: They can get the necessary nutrients and calories both before and during pregnancy by eating a well-balanced diet, keeping in mind folate-rich foods, nutrition experts say. Folic acid-fortified grain products, including breakfast cereals, will help, too. Dietary supplements are another source of folate. Any one or a combination of these options for ensuring adequate folate can help assure women of childbearing age that, if they become pregnant, their babies will be off to a healthy start.

 **Article Review Form at end of book.**

Using Body Mass Index (BMI), what is happening to the prevalence of obesity among adolescents? During this time period (1976 to 1980), what has happened to energy intake? What has happened to physical activity levels? Limiting total fat intake to less than 30 percent of total calorie intake has been advocated by a number of health organizations. What were the results from the School Nutrition Dietary Assessment Study (SNDA) of 1992 in this regard? Are there differences in fat consumption among children of different races? Why? Explain the phenomenon of iron deficiency anemia. Fruits and vegetables are excellent sources of the antioxidant nutrients, which may be protective in terms of cancer and coronary heart disease. Are our children consuming enough fruits and vegetables? Are our children receiving enough calcium? What might be the consequences of this? What might be some possible solutions to this?

# Nutritional Status of Children

## What Do We Know?

**R. Sue McPherson, Deanna H. Montgomery, and Milton Z. Nichaman**

*University of Texas–Houston Health Science Center, School of Public Health, Houston, Texas 77030*

## Executive Summary

Optimal nutritional intake during childhood for prevention of chronic disease in adulthood is not clearly defined, because of a lack of information regarding the relationship of nutrient intake in childhood to the later development of chronic diseases. Thus, criteria for nutritional intake in children are based on data regarding associations of foods and nutrients with chronic diseases that have been seen among adults. Using this current body of knowledge, an evaluation of the limited data regarding the nutritional status of children and adolescents indicates that certain age and/or gender subgroups may be at increased risk of developing chronic diseases later in life, if their current nutritional intake practices are continued.

While there are extensive data on children's intakes of some nutrients, such as calories, fat, and calcium, there is limited information available on dietary intake of many other foods and nutrients among children. Much work remains to be done to adequately evaluate children's nutritional intake patterns. It is essential that new and more accurate methods of dietary assessment be developed to effectively and comprehensively monitor children's dietary intake and nutrition behaviors, knowledge, and attitudes, and to utilize the information gleaned from these monitoring systems to provide effective and cost-efficient ways to evaluate dietary recommendations, implement nutrition interventions, and guide food distribution services.

## Introduction

What do we know about the nutritional intake and status of children today? How will this information affect the nation, both today and in the future? This paper presents background information from government- and industry-sponsored national surveys, as well as from the scientific literature. It addresses the nutritional status of American children today as it relates to their current health and their risk of developing chronic diseases later in life. It was evident during this review that there are many gaps in the available data, particularly in relation to age-specific and ethnic subgroups of the population. Filling these gaps will require a major organizational effort and collaboration between government, university, and industry researchers. Obtaining this missing information is crucial to the future health of America, as a growing body of literature supports the tracking of physiologic and behavioral risk factors from childhood to adulthood.[1–11]

This discussion will focus on the nutritional status of children over the age of 2 years and nonpregnant adolescents, since there are common nutritional goals and guidelines for these age groups.[12-15] Information regarding fat and fruit and vegetable intake will be highlighted, because of the priority given to these nutrients and foods in the Year 2000 Health Objectives for the Nation.[13] Similarly, data regarding the prevalence of obesity will be presented, as a decrease in obesity is one of the major goals of all recommendations for children and adolescents.[13] The development of obesity can be attributed to two major factors: excessive energy intake and lack of physical exercise.[16,17] It is unfortunate, however, that few data are available on physical activity in children. We therefore recommend that practical and valid methods be developed for assessing physical activity in children and that the use of these methods be implemented in surveys of nutritional status.

This paper also describes the prevalence of restricted intakes of energy, iron, fruits, vegetables, fiber, and calcium, and of excessive intakes of energy, total fat, and sodium in children. These topics are relevant because of the evidence supporting the relationship of these foods and nutrients to growth retardation, iron-deficiency anemia, and the possible development of cardiovascular disease, cancer, diabetes, and osteoporosis in adults. [12, 18–26] We acknowledge that, in addition to the effects of adverse nutritional status on biologic parameters, inadequate dietary intake can lead to hunger—a situation that is difficult to define scientifically, and for which there are few, or no, valid data. We also highlight what is known about children's awareness of the risk factors for developing chronic diseases, and their knowledge of the role that foods and nutrients play in determining these risk factors.

Adverse nutritional status includes both overnutrition and undernutrition. For the purposes of this presentation, overnutrition is defined as excessive food and nutrient intake as it relates to the development of obesity and the risk of cardiovascular disease, cancer, and diabetes in adulthood. Undernutrition is defined as restricted intake of iron, energy, fruits, vegetables, dietary fiber, and calcium as it relates to the occurrence of anemia, growth retardation, and subsequent risk for the development of cardiovascular disease, cancer, and osteoporosis in adults.

## Overnutrition

### Energy Intake

An imbalance of energy intake (food consumption) and energy output (physical activity and the energy costs of metabolic processes) can result in conditions of overweight or obesity, and underweight, or growth retardation, in children. All available evidence suggests that overweight is a much more prevalent condition among American children than is underweight. The importance of obesity stems from its known association with hypertension, diabetes, and dyslipidemias in adults.[18,19] In children, obesity has been shown to continue into young adulthood and is important for that reason, if for no other.[11, 16,17,27–29] In order to understand obesity in childhood, it is necessary to evaluate several parameters, including energy intake, physical activity, and body size.[16]

Although children today are heavier than they were in the past, a review of the data on children 2 to 10 years old indicates that energy intake has remained constant during the last decade.[30] Intake of dietary fat has also remained quite stable over this 10-year period, at about 65 grams per day.[30] Data from the Nationwide Food Consumption Survey (NFCS) 1977–78 and 1987–88 confirm these findings; children today are consuming no more energy or fat than children in previous years. [31] In fact, there is a suggestion of a downward trend in fat consumption over the past 10 years among children in all age groups. According to data form Phase I of the Third National Health & Nutrition Examination Survey (NHANES III 1988–91), daily mean energy intakes among children are as follows: 1591 kcal among 3 to 5 years olds; 1897 kcal among 6 to 11 year olds; 2218 kcal among 12 to 15 year olds; and 2533 kcal among 16 to 19 year olds.[32] Unpublished data from the Continuing Survey of Food Intakes by Individuals (CSFII) 1989–91 indicate similar energy intakes: 1458–1473 kcal among 3 to 5 year olds; 1832–1891 kcal among 6 to 11 year olds and 1748–2459 kcal among 12 to 19 year olds.[33]

The data regarding physical activity among children are difficult to interpret. We do not have data on trends in physical activity among children. Thus, we do not know whether current assessments of physical activity among most children or a sharp decrease among a subset of children who are especially sedentary. According to the President's Council on Physical Fitness and Sports (PCPFS), only 36% of school-aged children are enrolled in daily physical education classes.[34] Assessment of fitness levels on the PCPFS test indicates that fitness Study (NCYFS) II found that 97% of children in grades 1 to 4 participate in physical education classes three times per week. The 1984 NCYFS reported that 63% of 10th to 12th graders participated in physical activity classes three or more times a week.[35] These results suggest that physical activity patterns progressively decreased as children age. The 1991 Youth Risk Behavior Survey (YRBS) found that only 45% of girls and 53% of boys in high school participated regularly in physical education classes. Of those, only 75% of the girls and 85% of the boys actually exercised for at least 20 minutes per class.[36]

Using body mass index (BMI) as the measure of body size, data from national surveys suggest that the prevalence of obesity among adolescents is rising. A comparison of data from NHANES II 1976–80 with that of NHANES III 1988–91 showed an increase of approximately 5% in the prevalence of overweight adolescents 12 to 19 years old. Data from NHANES II 1976–80 indicated that 15% of adolescent girls and 16% of adolescent boys were overweight. Data from NHANES III 1988–91 indicated that those figures had increased to 22% for girls and 20% for boys.[37] The data indicating that children's energy intake has remained constant while their physical activity levels are possibly declining may help explain the increase in the incidence of obesity.

Based on data from the National Health Examination Survey (NHES) and the NHANES I and II surveys, Gortmaker and colleagues[38] reported that, between 1963 and 1980, the prevalence of obesity, based on triceps skinfold measurements greater than the 85th percentile, increased in both girls and boys and in blacks and whites 6 to 11 years old and 12 to 17 years old. The changes that occurred over the three measurement periods were all statistically significant and of major public health importance. It is noteworthy that the levels of obesity in black boys at all time periods and in both age groups were lower than those in white boys. Data from the YRBS, conducted in 1990 by the Centers for Disease Control (CDC), showed that approximately 20% of adolescents reported that they were slightly overweight, and 2–4% reported that they were very overweight.[39]

In summary, the available data indicate that the prevalence of overweight and obesity, together with low levels of physical exercise, represent major nutritional concerns in American children today.

## Fat Intake

Intake of total fat in the United States has been a public health concern over the last 20 years, largely because of the association between excessive fat intake and the subsequent development of chronic diseases, such as cardiovascular disease, diabetes, and certain cancers.[12,18–20,39,40] An excessive intake of fat, especially saturated fat, has been found to increase blood lipid levels, a major risk factor for cardiovascular disease.[12] The development of cardiovascular disease begins early in life; in fact, plaque formation has been noted in the arteries of children and young adults.[1,41] Since fat contains more kcal per gram than protein or carbohydrate, excessive fat intake can contribute to high energy intakes that, along with physical inactivity, can lead to an increased risk of obesity.[19,28,40]

Limiting total fat intake to 20% or less of total kcal has been a hallmark of many national dietary recommendations, including the Dietary Guidelines for Americans,[42] the National Cholesterol Education Program Recommendations for Children and Adolescents,[12] and the Year 2000 Health Objectives for the Nation.[13] In the United States, total fat intake among children has decreased during the past 2 decades.[32,43] In data from NHANES I (1971–1975), the mean percent of calories from total fat was 37% for children 6 to 11 years old.[44] Other national surveys conducted during the late 1970s and 1980s reported mean fat intakes ranging from 35.1%[32] to 40.6%.[45] The most recent national survey data from CSFII 1989–91 and

NHANES III 1988–91 indicate that the mean total fat intake of children 2 to 19 years old was 33–34% of total kcal.[32,33] In the NHANES III 1988-91 survey, non-Hispanic black children 6 to 19 years old consumed a diet that was high in fat (36.1% of calories from fat) than that consumed by non-Hispanic white children (33.7% and Mexican-American children (34.7%).[32] Although national survey data indicate that the overall percentage of calories from fat has decreased among children, only about 23% of children 2 to 5 years old had intakes below 30% of calories from fat.[46] The percentage of children with intakes at or below 30% of calories from fat was even lower among those 6 to 11 years old (16%) and among children 12 to 19 years old (15%).[46]

The School Nutrition Dietary Assessment Study (SNDA) 1992[43] reported that the mean percent of calories from total fat was 34% for children in grades 1 through 12. Higher fat intakes were reported in the General Mills Dietary Intake Study 1990–92 for children 11 to 18 years old, with both boys and girls averaging 37% of calories from fat.[47] Furthermore, in this study, only 11% of children 2 to 10 years old had intakes at or less than 30% of calories from fat.[47]

Several factors could contribute to the decreased percentage of calories from fat in children's diets, including an increased prevalence of reduced-fat foods in the marketplace, increased consumption of other foods high in carbohydrate or protein, secular trends toward lower fat consumption in the general population, and methodological differences between studies.[46] Although it appears that total fat consumption is decreasing among children, their average intake still

exceeds current recommendation.[12,42] These recommendations have been criticized recently because of the possible negative effects of lower fat consumption on child growth and development.[48] There is, however, a growing body of evidence that children consuming diets of 30% of calories or less from fat can be adequately nourished.[33,49,50]

Excessive intake of saturated fat has been more closely associated with the development of cardiovascular disease than has an excessive intake of total fat.[51] Because of this relationship, current dietary recommendations suggest an intake of less than 10% of calories form saturated fat.[12,13,42] Mean intake of saturated fat for children 6 to 11 years old was 14% of total calories in NHANES I 1971–75 and 13% of total calories in NHANES II 1976–80. More recent data from national surveys show intakes of saturated fat for children 3 to 19 years old ranging from 12.2% to 14.0%.[32,43,46,47] Boys tend to have higher intakes of saturated fat than girls.[32,46] Less than 10% of children 2 to 19 years old currently derive 10% or less of their calories from saturated fat.[32,47]

Children's intake of saturated fat has decreased somewhat over the last 20 years, but not to the same extent as that of total fat. Higher-fat dairy products and meat, poultry, and fish products are the major contributors of saturated fat to children's diets,[52,53] with baked goods, such as cookies, cakes, and pies, also providing a significant share of saturated fat intake.[53] The National School Lunch Progarm (NSLP) and School Breakfast Program (SBP) also may have contributed to the higher intakes of saturated fat than children who did not eat school lunch or breakfast.[43] It

should be noted that nutritionists and administrators of child nutrition programs in the United States are currently aware of the problems associated with the NSLP and SBP.[54,55] Recently, proposed changes in these programs throughout the Healthy Meals for Healthy Americans Act of 1994 will hopefully remedy this situation.[56]

## Sodium Intake

Based on estimates form NHANES III 1988-91, approximately 25% of adults in the United States have hypertension.[57] Since high blood pressure can contribute to the development of stroke, coronary heart disease, congestive heart failure, and renal insufficiency,[58,59] public health nutrition policies must address strategies for prevention of this condition.[46]

Although the occurrence of hypertension in childhood is rare and not correlated with sodium intake, it has been shown that a decrease in sodium consumption among adults is an effective, population-based public health approach to the reduction of hypertension.[57,60,61] It is know that mean sodium intake in the United States far exceeds the minimum biological requirements.[14] Moderation of sodium intake is recommended by the Dietary Guidelines for Americans, Year 2000 Health Objectives for the Nation, and the National High Blood Pressure Education Program.[13,42,62] A daily intake of no more than 6 grams of sodium chloride (approximately 2300–2400 mg sodium) is typically recommended.[57–62]

Sodium intake has increased during the last 20 years, from approximately 2400 mg per day, as reported by NHANES I 1971–75, to 2998 mg per day, as reported by HNANES III 1988–91.[63] According to national surveys, sodium intake increases through adolescence and then decreases in adulthood.[32,33] Mean sodium intake correlates with mean energy consumption and is highest among teenagers and young adults.[64] Racial differences in sodium consumption among children also exist: reports from NHANES III 1988–91 indicate that, for children 1 to 19 years old, sodium intake is consistently higher among non-Hispanic black children than it is among non-Hispanic white and Mexican-American children.[63]

Major contributors to sodium intake in children 14 to 16 years old include grain products (25% of daily intake), mixed dishes (20%), and processed meats (17%).[64] Children participating in the NSLP and SBP consumed more sodium than children who did not eat school meals.[43]

Sodium intake is difficult to quantify, and the methodology is not always consistent (i.e., whether to include drinking water, salt added at the table, medications, etc.), contributing to the widely varying ranges of sodium intake reported. Nevertheless, most surveys indicate that mean sodium intakes of children are higher than recommended.

## Undernutrition
### Energy Intake

Since the incidence of obesity and overweight in children and adolescents seems to be increasing, energy intakes in the United States, on the whole, would appear to be adequate. Nevertheless, energy restriction in children may be problematic for certain populations, such as young children from minority subgroups, children of low socioeconomic status, homeless children, and children with disabilities.[13,65] Restricted energy intake has been found to stem from a chronic marginal deficiency of food quantity, which has been identified more recently as a form of food insecurity.[66] Inadequate energy intake, which may result in hunger, cannot be adequately addressed in this framework, because there is no clear definition of the problem, nor are there any data to describe the magnitude of the health consequences of hunger in the United States.

Because children experience rapid growth rates that make them vulnerable to undernutrition, longitudinal growth data have been used as one measure of the adequacy of a child's diet.[13,67] Growth retardation in a population can be defined as an overall prevalence of more than 5% of children below the fifth percentile of height for age, as compared to the National Center for Health Statistics' reference data from NHANES I 1971–75.[13] In 1988, the prevalence of growth retardation exceeded 5% for several subgroups of children, including low-income Hispanic children, low-income black children, and low-income Asian-Pacific Island children.[46] Growth retardation prevalence rates varied from 13% for low-income Hispanic children less than 1 year old to 15% for low-income Asian/Pacific Island children 2 to 4 years old.[13]

However, data from 1992[46] indicate that the prevalence of underweight is decreasing among most of these subgroups of children. Population subgroups 5 years old and younger that met or exceeded the Year 2000 goals (10% prevalence of growth retardation) included low-income black, white, Hispanic, and American Indian/Pacific Island children. Low-income Asian/Pacific Island children did not meet the objective of a 10% or less prevalence of growth retardation, although the incidence of short stature has decreased steadily in this subgroup since 1988.[46]

Little is known about growth retardation in other special populations, such as homeless children or children with disabilities. Since the scattered data that exist suggest that food insecurity, and therefore energy restriction, occurs frequently in these populations, additional efforts should be made to ensure that theses children are adequately surveyed along with other low-income subgroups. In these populations, it is also necessary to distinguish growth retardation as a result of dietary insufficiency from other causes, such as neglect.

### Iron Intake

Iron-deficiency anemia is the condition in which the amount of iron in the body is less than that required for normal formation of hemoglobin and other functional iron-containing compounds.[18] Iron-deficiency anemia is defined by a hemoglobin concentration that is two standard deviations below the mean for normal individuals of the same age and sex.[19] This deficiency results in a decrease in iron stores and would be expected to impair iron-dependent physiologic functions. Iron-deficiency anemia is by far the most prevalent disease related to under-nutrition among children today and has been shown to be associated with low birth weight[21] and retardation of longitudinal growth and weight gain. It may also contribute to scholastic underachievement and behavioral disturbances in children.[16,68]

In a 1993 report, The Institute of Medicine reviewed the subject of iron-deficiency anemia and provided recommendations for iron intake in children. Iron-deficiency anemia was defined as anemia associated with laboratory evidence of iron depletion, based on one or more of the following test results: low serum ferritin or transferrin saturation, or an elevation in erythrocyte protoporphyrin levels. Based on this definition, the prevalence of iron-deficiency anemia ranged from 9.3% among children 1 to 2 years old to 3.9% among children 3 to 10 years old.[69] Among older children, the prevalence was 4.1% among boys and 2.8% among girls 11 to 14 years old and 0.6% among boys and 7.2% among girls 15 to 19 years old. Results from the CDC Pediatric Surveillance System indicate that iron-deficiency anemia among infants and preschool-aged children decreased from over 10% in the 1970s to 3% in the late 1980s.[70,71] Unpublished data from NHANES III 1988–91 showed that the prevalence of iron-deficiency anemia, based on both low hemoglobin and transferrin saturation level, was 3% in both black and white children 1 to 5 years old.[21] These results, taken together, suggest that the high prevalence of iron deficiency, with and without anemia, seen in young children in the 1970s has significantly decreased to approximately 3%, based on the most current data available. However, further analysis of NHANES III 1988–91 and Hispanic HANES data will provide important information about the prevalence of iron-deficiency anemia in high-risk subgroups of the population. Adolescent girls appear to be at continued risk for iron deficiency.

## Fruit and Vegetable Intake

Data in the epidemiologic literature indicate that higher intakes of fruits and vegetables are consistently, although not universally, associated with a lower risk of cancer at most physiologic sites.[23] It has also been suggested that the antioxidant vitamins found in fruits and vegetables reduce the risk of coronary heart disease.[72,73] The existing evidence provides strong support for a protective effect of a diet rich in fruits and vegetables, without identifying the specific vitamins, minerals, or nutrients responsible for the effects.[23,25,74]

Very few children and adolescents consume five servings of fruits and vegetables per day, as recommended for optimal health and prevention of cardiovascular disease and cancer. According to results from the 1991 YRBS, only 13% of high school students reported consumption of five or more fruits and vegetables on the day preceding the survey.[36] Boys were more likely to consume five servings of fruits and vegetables (15%) than were girls (10%), and whites (14%) were more likely to do so than blacks (7%) or Hispanics (10%).[36,75]

In the 1993 YRBS, it was found that 33–46% of high school students consumed no fruit or fruit juice on the day preceding the survey. The older the high school student, the lower the prevalence of consumption of either fruit or fruit juice. Among ethnic groups, 55% of black students consumed no fruit on the previous day, as compared to 40% of the white students and 43% of the Hispanic students.[76] Consumption of vegetables on the day before the YRBS was even lower that that of fruits. Fifty-two to 55% of high school students ate no cooked vegetables on the day

preceding the survey. The highest prevalence of no reported intake of vegetables on the day before the survey was 66% among Hispanics, followed by 60% among blacks and 51% among whites.[76] Aggregated data on total fruit and vegetable consumption on the day before the survey are not yet available.

Estimates of fruit and vegetable consumption among younger children is available from surveys conducted by the Market Research Corporation of America in conjunction with the Dole Food Company. In this nationally representative sample of children 6 to 12 years old, average consumption of fruits and vegetables per day was only 2.5 servings.[77]

State and local surveys of fruit and vegetable consumption also have found that intake of fruits and vegetables among children was consistently less than the recommended five servings per day. In California, a combined mail and telephone survey found that children 9 to 11 years old consumed an average of 3.4 servings of fruits and vegetables per day.[78] The higher consumption of fruits and vegetables found in this survey may be the result of sampling errors and low response rates. Specifically, the sample studied may have been more motivated and interested than the general population it was intended to represent. In a 3-year observational study of Latino children in New York City beginning when they were 4 years old, the mean number of servings of fruits and vegetables consumed per day was 2.8, with no gender differences in consumption patterns.[78] In summary, all of the available data support that, on average, children consume only about half of the recommended number of servings of fruits and vegetables per day.

## Restricted Fiber Intake

Evidence from available studies suggests that there is an inverse relationship between dietary fiber intake and both colon cancer and coronary heart disease mortality.[14,19] Presently, however, there are no accepted guidelines for optimal fiber intake in children. The Dietary Guidelines for Americans suggest six servings of grain products per day, but do not specify the amount of fiber to consume.[42] In May of 1994, it was proposed that the minimum daily intake of dietary fiber for children 3 to 18 years old be the equivalent of their age plus 5 grams.[80] Using this guideline, recommended fiber intake would range from 8 grams per day among children 3 years old to about 23 grams per day among children 18 years old. This proposed recommendation is consistent with the National Cancer Institute's recommendation of 20 to 35 grams of fiber per day for adults.[81] Action should be taken by pediatric nutrition groups to determine the validity of the proposed dietary fiber recommendation and to develop a consensus statement that facilitates evaluation of children's fiber intake.

Dietary fiber intakes among children studied in CSFII 1989-91 and in Phase I of NHANES III 1988–91 were as follows: 10–11 grams among children 3 to 5 years old; 12–13 grams among children 6 to 11 years old; and 12–16 grams among children 12 to 19 years old.[33,63] Mexican-American children consistently consumed higher amounts of fiber across all age groups than did non-Hispanic white or non-Hispanic black children. Dietary fiber intake was about 7 grams per day among 2- to 10-year-old children in a national sample of 4000 households surveyed by the Marketing Research Corporation of America.[30] In the General Mills Dietary Intake Study 1990–92, girls 11 to 18 years old consumed 10 grams of fiber per day, and boys in the same age group consumed 13 grams per day.[47] In summary, for almost all children, with the possible exception of the very younger age groups, current dietary fiber intake is well below the suggested recommendation made by Nicklas et al.[80]

## Calcium Intake

Children need adequate calcium in their diets for adequate linear growth and to achieve peak bone mass, which reduces the risk of developing osteoporosis as an adult.[18,82,83] Inadequate calcium consumption has also been associated with the development of other adult chronic diseases, such as colon cancer and hypertension.[26,84]

Calcium requirements vary throughout the lifetime in accordance with growth patterns, pregnancy and lactation, and stage of adult life. The Recommended Dietary Allowances (RDA) for calcium are 800 mg for children 1 to 5 years old, 800 to 1200 mg for children 6 to 10 years old, and 1200 to 1500 mg for children 11 to 24 years old.[14] The CSFII 1989–91 found that 90% or more of children 1 to 5 years old consumed 100% of the RDA for calcium.[33] Only 86% of girls and 95% of boys 12 to 19 years old consumed 100% of the RDA for calcium. Income- and age-specific data are not available from CSFII 1989-91. Data from NHANES III 1988-91 support the fact that, on average, children over 11 years of age do not consume the recommended amounts of calcium. Mean intake of calcium was 855 mg among 3 to 5 years olds, 938 mg among 6 to 11 year olds, 971 mg among 12 to 15 year olds, and 1050 mg among 16 to 19 year olds.[63] Girls across all ages and non-Hispanic blacks consistently reported lower calcium intake than did their counterparts. Reports using the General Mills Dietary Intake Study data indicated that children 2 to 10 years old have a mean calcium intake of 938 mg per day, which exceeds the RDA for children 1 to 5 year old and is at the low end of the RDA for children 6 to 10 years old.[30] Additional data from the General Mills Dietary Intake Study found that 95% of 11- to 18-year-old girls and 79% of 11- to 18-year old boys age 11 to 18 consumed less than the RDA for calcium. This review of current intake data makes it very apparent that calcium intake needs to be increased among children more than 6 years old.[26]

---

## Awareness

### Knowledge of the Link Between Nutrition and Health

Although there is very little data available, evidence indicates that children do understand the link between nutrition and health.[85] In a recent survey, virtually all (94%) of the children 9 to 15 years old, and 65% of the children 6 to 9 years old, recognized that diet can affect future health.[86] Almost three-quarters of high school students in the United States are aware of the relationship between eating fatty foods and cardiovascular disease, while fewer than 20% are aware of the relationship between dietary fiber and colon cancer.[87] While over 90% of 10th- and 12th-grade students recognized that eating fiber is good for your health, only about half (49%) of 3rd graders did so.[88]

In a recent survey in Michigan, students in grades, 5, 8, and 11 were aware of the health risks associated with underweight, but less familiar with the risk associated with excess weight.[89] In general, 5th-grade students were less aware of relationships between weight and cardiovascular disease, causes of overweight, and risks of underweight than were 8th and 11th graders. Children, especially older children and adolescents, seem to be familiar with overall relationships between nutrition and health, but are less aware of some specific nutrition/health interactions.

## Knowledge of Food Sources of Nutrients

Children are familiar with food grouping schemes and most of the Dietary Guidelines for Americans.[86,89,90] More than 90% of children are aware of the importance of fruits, vegetables, and high-fiber foods in the diet.[85,86] Children and adolescents in Michigan were not familiar with the USDA Food Guide Pyramid,[89] probably because of its recent introduction and use. Overall, students in Michigan gave "the importance of learning about nutrition" a score of 6.8 out of a possible 10, with 10 indicating that students "strongly agree" that "learning about nutrition is important." Younger children participating in the same survey agreed more strongly that learning about nutrition was important. Fifth graders rated learning about nutrition more positively than did 11th graders (7.7 vs. 5.9). Nationwide, two-thirds of 6- to 9-year-old children claimed that nutrition is very important to them.[86] Children reported receiving nutrition information most often in school (95%), from parents (86%), and from doctors or nurses (73%).[85]

Elementary students are fairly confident about their nutrition knowledge. Approximately two-thirds of 5th-grade students in Michigan rated their nutrition knowledge as "excellent" or "very good."[86] Older children were not as confident. Fifty-seven percent of 8th graders and 52% of 11th graders rated their nutrition knowledge as "not very good."[86] Although children are aware of the importance of limiting fat consumption, most do not have adequate knowledge of which foods are high in fat.[88,89] Children also have difficulty identifying foods that are high in fiber and cholesterol.[88,89] For example, fewer than half of the children in grades 1 to 8 were aware that beans contain fiber.[88]

In 1993, nearly 1200 students in grades 3 to 6 were surveyed about their snacking habits by Louis Harris and Associates for Bozell Public Relations.[91] Over half of the students surveyed thought fruit pies and fruit-flavored snacks were good for you (62% and 55%, respectively). Both fruit pies and fruit-flavored snacks were rated higher on a scale of foods that were "good for you to eat" than were peanut butter and jelly sandwiches, pizza, and pretzels.

Nutrition knowledge is essential, but does not always impact behavior or attitudes toward foods.[92] Although children are aware of the relationships between dietary intake and health, translation of this knowledge into actual behavior is still incomplete. Emphasis needs to be placed on understanding the barriers to this practice of behavioral change to facilitate children's transfer of knowledge into practice.

## Recommendations

**Develop new and more accurate methods to assess nutritional status in children.** Current methods of assessment need to be refined and standardized so that measurements of dietary intake (both in terms of nutrients and foods), food behaviors, and physical activity are valid, reliable, and simple to administer. Better methods of dietary assessment would ensure that trends noted in the data are factual and are not artifacts of the data collection procedure. A national nutrient database that includes a comprehensive listing of foods and nutrient information should be developed. This database should contain nutrient values for cultural and regional varieties of foods. It should also include nutrient data from food manufacturers. Finally, the database should be structured in a way that allows new products to be quickly added as they enter the marketplace.

**Monitor dietary intake, energy expenditure, and nutrition behavior, attitudes, and knowledge among children.** Gaps in our knowledge of children's dietary intake and energy expenditure in physical activity need to be addressed through the use of current and new surveillance tools proposed in the National Nutrition Monitoring Act of 1990, and through coordination with current nutrition monitoring systems, such as NHANES and CSFII. Sampling strategies that provide data on the general population, high-risk subgroups, and groups within states are necessary to examine regional and cultural differences in dietary habits.

**Use information from monitoring systems to evaluate dietary recommendations and guide food assistance and nutrition education programs.** A national nutrition monitoring system should provide data to examine the link between health status in children and disease risk in adulthood. In addition, a comprehensive surveillance system can furnish information for developing and revising national dietary recommendations for children. A system to coordinate data from these current and proposed monitoring systems should be developed so that the information is readily available for planning and implementing food distribution services and nutrition education programs. More information is needed on dietary patterns and food choices so that nutrient requirements can be translated into food recommendations for the public. Better data about children's dietary behaviors, knowledge, and attitudes would provide the impetus to design nutrition interventions that can effectively influence children's food choices.

From the available data, we know that children's diets are far from optimal. We must have the coordination of monitoring tools and systems in order to provide timely and relevant data to fill the gaps in our knowledge about children's diets and to monitor trends in food consumption and nutrient intakes. By knowing about children's diets, we can direct our limited resources to where they can achieve the most good, and set the stage for the growth and development of healthy children who become healthy adults.

## Acknowledgments

The authors gratefully acknowledge the comments of the reviewers: Ronette Briefel, Dr. P.H., R.D. (National Center for Health Statistics, Centers for Disease Control and Prevention, DHHS), Jeanne Goldberg, Ph.D. (Tufts University, Eileen Kennedy, Ph.D., R.D. (United States Department of Agriculture), Kathleen McMahon, Ph.D., R.D. (Education Public Relations Worldwide), Linda Meyers, Ph.D. (Office of Disease Prevention and Health Promotion, DHHS), Elizabeth Pivonka, Ph.D., R.D. (Produce Marketing Association), Kathy Wiemer, M.S., R.D. (General Mills Inc.), and Margo Wootan, D.Sc. (Center for Science in the Public Interest).

## References

1. Enos WF, Beyer JC, Holmes RH. Pathogenesis of coronary disease in American soldiers killed in Korea. JAMA 1955;158:912–4.
2. McNamara JJ, Molot MA, Stremple JF, Catting RT. Coronary artery disease in combat casualties in Vietnam. JAMA 1971;216:1185–7.
3. Perry CL, Klepp K-I, Sillers C. Community-wide strategies for cardiovascular health: the Minnesota Heart Health Program youth program. Health Educ Res Theory Pract 1989;4:87–101.
4. Perry CL, Stone EJ, Parcel GS, et al. School-based cardiovascular health promotion: the Child and Adolescent Trial for Cardiovascular Health (CATCH). J Sch Health 1990;60:406–13.
5. Neaton JD, Wentworth D. Serum cholesterol, blood pressure, cigarette smoking and death from coronary heart disease. Arch Intern Med 1992;152:56–64.
6. Porkka KV, Viikari JSA, Akerblom HK. Tracking of serum HDL-cholesterol and other lipids in children and adolescents: the Cardiovascular Risk in Young Finns Study. Prev Med 1991;20:713–24.
7. Clark, WR, Schott HG, Leaverton PE, et al. Tracking of blood lipids and blood pressure in school age children. The Muscatine Study, Circulation 1978;58:626–34.
8. Pagnan A, Ambrosio GB, Vincenzi M. et al. Precursors of atherosclerosis in children: the Cittadella Study. Follow-up and tracking of total serum cholesterol, triglycerides, and blood glucose. Prev Med 1982;11:381–90.
9. Orchard TJ, Donahue RP, Kuller LH, Hodge PN, Drash AL. Cholesterol screening in childhood: does it predict adult hypercholesterolemia? The Beaver County experience. J Pediatr 1983;103:687–91.
10. Laurer RM, Lee J. Clarke WR. Factors affecting the relationship between childhood and adult cholesterol levels: the Muscatine Study Pediatrics 1988;82:309–18.
11. Kelder SH, Perry CL, Klepp K-1, Lytle LA. Longitudinal tracking of adolescent smoking, physical activity, and food choice behaviors. Am J Public Health 1994;84:1121–6.
12. National Cholesterol Education Program. Report of the Expert Panel on Blood Cholesterol Levels in Children and Adolescents. NIH Pub. No. 91–2732. Bethesda, MD: US Department of Health and Human Services, Public Health Service. National Institutes of Health, National Heart, Lung, and Blood Institute, 1991.
13. US Department of Health and Human Services. Public Health Service. Healthy people 2000: national health promotion and disease prevention objectives. DHHS Pub No. 91–50212. Washington, DC: US Government Printing Office, 1991.
14. National Research Council, Commission on Life Sciences, Food and Nutrition Board. Recommended Dietary Allowances, 10th Ed. Washington, DC: National Academy Press, 1989.
15. American Academy of Pediatrics, Committee on Nutrition. Statement on cholesterol. Pediatrics 1992;90:469–73.
16. Schlicker SA, Borra ST, Regan C. The weight and fitness status of United States children. Nutr Rev 1994;52:11–7.
17. Kolata G. Obese children: a growing problem. Science 1986;232:20–1.
18. National Research Council, Food and Nutrition Board. Diet and health: implications for reducing chronic disease risk. Washington, DC: National Academy Press, 1989.
19. Public Health Service. The surgeon general's report on nutrition and health. DHHS Pub. No. (PHS) 88–50210, Washington, DC: US Department of Health and Human Services, Public Health Service, 1989.
20. Diet, nutrition and the prevention of chronic diseases: a report of the WHO Study Group on diet, nutrition and prevention of communicable diseases. Nutr Rev 1991; 49:291–301.
21. Institute of Medicine, Food and Nutrition Board. Iron deficiency anemia: recommended guidelines

for prevention, detection, and management among US children and women of childbearing age. In: Earl R. Woteki CE, eds. Washington, DC: National Academy Press, 1993:1–10, 75–79.

22. Kritchevsky D. Antioxidant vitamins in the prevention of cardiovascular disease. Nutr Today 1992;27:30–3.

23. Steinmetz KA, Potter JD. Vegetables, fruit and cancer. Part 1, epidemiology. Cancer Causes Control 1991;2:325–57.

24. Steinberg D. Antioxidants in the prevention of human atherosclerosis. Circulation 1992;85:2338–44.

25. Block G, Patterson B, Subar A. Fruit, vegetables, and cancer prevention: a review of the epidemiologic evidence. Nutr Cancer 1992;18:1–29.

26. Looker AC, Briefel RR, McDowell MA. Calcium intake in the United States. Optimal Calcium Intake: NIH Consensus Development Conference, Bethesda, MD, June 6–8, 1994.

27. Guo SS, Roche AF, Chumlea WC, Gardner JD, Siervogel RM. The predictive value of childhood body mass index values for overweight at age 35 y. Am J Clin Nutr 1994;59:810–9.

28. Must A, Jacques PF, Dallal GE, Bajema CL. Dietz WH. Long-term morbidity and mortality of overweight adolescents. N Engl J Med 1992;327:1350–5.

29. Casey VA, Dwyer JT, Coleman KA, Valadian I. Body mass index from childhood to middle age: a 50 year follow-up. Am J Clin Nutr 1992;56:14–8.

30. Albertson AM, Tobelmann RC, Engstron A, Asp EH. Nutrient intakes of 2 to 10 year old children: 10-year trends. J Am Diet Assoc 1992;92:1492–6.

31. Gazzaniga JM, Burns TL. Relationship between diet composition and body fatness, with adjustment for resting energy expenditure and physical activity in pre-adolescents. Am J Clin Nutr 1993;58:21–8.

32. McDowell MA, Briefel RR, Alaimo K, et al. Energy and macronutrient intakes of persons ages 2 months and over in the United States: Third National Health and Nutrition Examination Survey, Phase 1, 1988–91. Advance Data 1994;255:1–25.

33. US Department of Agriculture. Continuing Survey of Food Intakes by Individuals 1989–91. Unpublished data, 1994.

34. US Department of Health and Human Services. 1985 President's Council on Physical Fitness and Sports Youth Fitness Survey. Washington, DC: US Government Printing Office, 1986.

35. Ross JG, Pate RR. The National Children and Youth Fitness Study II: a summary of findings. J Phys Edu Recr Dance 1987;58:51–6.

36. Morbidity and Mortality Weekly Report. Participation in school physical education and selected dietary patterns among high school students—United States, 1991. 1992;41(33).

37. Morbidity and Mortality Weekly Report. Prevalence of overweight among adolescents—United States, 1994. 1994;43(44).

38. Gortmaker SL, Dietz WH, Sobol AM, Wehler CA. Increasing pediatric obesity in the United States. Am J Dis Child 1987;141:535–40.

39. Serdula MK, Collins E, Williamson DF, Anda RF, Pamuk E, Byers T. Weight control practices of US adolescents and adults. Ann Intern Med 1993;119:667–71.

40. Rolls BJ, Shide DJ. The influence of dietary fat on food intake and body weight. Nutr Rev 1992;50:283–90.

41. Strong JP, Newman WP, Freedman DS, Gard Pd, Tracy RE, Solberg LA. Atherosclerotic disease in children and young adults: relationship to cardiovascular risk factors. In: Berenson GE, ed. Causation of cardiovascular risk factors in children: perspectives on cardiovascular risk in early life. New York: Raven Press, 1986:27–41.

42. US Department of Agriculture, US Department of Health and Human Services. Nutrition and your health: Dietary Guidelines for Americans. 3rd Ed. home and Garden Bulletin No. 232. Washington, DC: US Government Printing Office, 1990.

43. Devaney B, Gordon A, Burghardt J. The School Nutrition Dietary Assessment Study: dietary intakes of program participants and nonparticipants. Washington, DC: US Department of Agriculture, Food and Nutrition Service, 1993.

44. Braitman LE, Adlin EV, Stanton JL. Obesity and calorie intake: the National Health and Nutrition Examination Survey of 1971–1975 (NHANES I). J. Chronic Dis 1985;38:727–32.

45. Pao EM, Mickle SJ. Problem nutrients in the United States. Food Tech 1981;35:58–69.

46. Lewis CJ, Crane NT, Moore BJ, Hubbard VS. Healthy people 2000: report on the 1994 Nutrition Progress Review. Nutrition Today 1994;29:6–14.

47. General Mills Dietary Intake Study 1900–92. Unpublished data, 1994.

48. Joint Working Group of the Canadian Pediatric Society and Health Canada. Nutrition recommendations update. Dietary fat and children. Ottawa, ON: Ministry of National Health and Welfare, 1993.

49. McPherson RS, Nichaman MZ, Kohl HW, Reed DB, Labarthe DR. Intake and food sources of dietary fat among schoolchildren in The Woodlands, Texas. Pediatrics 1990;86:520–6.

50. Nicklas TA, Webber LS, Koschak ML, Berenson GS. Nutrient adequacy of low fat intakes for children: the Bogalusa Heart Study. Pediatrics 1992;89:221–8.

51. Barr SL, Ramakrishnan R, Johnson C, Holleran S, Dell RB, Ginsberg HN. Reducing total dietary fat without reducing saturated fatty acids does not significantly lower total plasma cholesterol concentrations in normal males. Am J Clin Nutr 1992;55:675–81.

52. US Department of Agriculture. Nationwide Food Consumption Survey. Continuing Survey of Food Intakes of Individuals. Women 19–50 and their children 1–5 years, 4 days, 1986. Report No. 86–3. Hyattsville, MD: Nutrition Monitoring Division, Human Nutrition Information Service, 1988.

53. Park YK, Yetley EA. Trend changes in use and current intakes of tropical oils in the United States. Am J Clin Nutr 1990;51:738–48.

54. Sneed J, Gregoire MB, Cline TJ. Nutrition, integrity: increasing the focus on nutrition in child nutrition programs. Top Clin Nutr 1994;9(4):30–6.

55. Position of ADA, SNE, and ASFSA: school based nutrition programs and services. J Am Diet Assoc 1995;95:367–9.

56. New "Healthy Meals" legislation promises improved child nutrition programs, but GOP contact may dismantle progress. J Am Diet Assoc 1995;95:14.

57. National High Blood Pressure Education Program. The Fifth Report of the Joint National

Committee on Detection, Evaluation, and Treatment of High Blood Pressure. Washington, DC: National Institutes of Health, 1993.

58. MacMahon S, Peto R, Cutler J, Collin R. Blood pressure, stroke, and coronary heart disease. Part 1, prolonged differences in blood pressure: prospective observational studies corrected for the regression dilution bias, Lancet 1990;335:765–74.

59. Whelton PK, Klag MJ. Hypertension as a risk factor for renal disease. Review of clinical and epidemiological evidence. Hypertension 1989;13(Suppl): 119–27.

60. Law MR, Frost CD, Wald NJ. By how much does dietary salt reduction lower blood pressure? Part III, analysis of data from trials of salt reduction. Br J Med 1991;302:819–24.

61. Cutler JA, Follmann D, Elliott P, Suh I. An overview of randomized trials of sodium reduction and blood pressure. Hypertension 1991;17(Suppl):127–33.

62. National High Blood Pressure Education Program. Working Group Report on Primary Prevention of Hypertension. NIH Pub. No. 93-2669. Bethesda, MD: US Department of Health and Human Services, Public Health Service, National Institute of Health, National Heart, Lung and Blood Institute, 1993.

63. Alaimo K, McDowell MA, Briefel RR, et al. Dietary intake of vitamins, minerals, and fiber of persons ages 2 months and over in the United States: Third National Health and Nutrition Examination Survey, Phase I, 1988–91. Advance Data 1994;258:1–27.

64. Briefel R, Alaimo K, Wright J, McDowell M. Dietary sources of salt and sodium. Presentation at the NHLBI Workshop on Implementing Recommendations for Dietary Salt Reduction, Rockville, MD: August 25–26, 1994.

65. Kerr GR, Lee ES, Lorimor RJ, Mueller WH, Lam MM-K. Height distributions of US children: associations with race, poverty status and parental size. Growth 1982;46:135–49.

66. Campbell CC. Food insecurity: a nutritional outcome or a predictor variable? J Nutr 1991;121:408–15.

67. Allen LH. Functional indicators and outcomes of undernutrition. J Nutr 1990;120:924–32.

68. Shils ME, Olson JA, Shike M. Modern nutrition in health and disease.Vol 1. Philadelphia, PA: Lea & Febiger, 1994.

69. Life Sciences Research Office. Assessment of the iron nutritional status of the US population based on the data collected in the Second National Health and Nutrition Examination Survey, 1976–1980. In Pilch SM, Senti FR, eds. Bethesda, MD: Federation of American Societies for Experimental Biology, 1984:19–53.

70. Yip R, Binkin NJ, Fleshood L, Trowbridge FL. Declining prevalence of anemia among low-income children in the United States. JAMA 1987:258:1619–23.

71. Yip R, Walsh KM, Goldfarb MG, Binkin NJ. Declining prevalence of anemia in childhood in a middle-class setting: a pediatric success tory? Pediatrics 1987;80:330–4.

72. Esterbauer H, Puhl H, Dieber-Rotheneder M, Waeg G, Rabl H. Effect of antioxidants on oxidative modification of LDL. Ann Med 1991;23:573–81.

73. Gey KF. The antioxidant hypothesis of cardiovascular disease: epidemiology and mechanisms. Cardiovasc Dysfunction 1990;18:1041–5.

74. 5-A-Day for Better Health, Bethesda, MD: National Cancer Institute, RFA No. CA–92–17, 1992.

75. Morbidity and Mortality Weekly Report. Selected tobacco-use behaviors and dietary patterns among high school students - United States, 1991. 1992:41(24).

76. Morbidity and Mortality Weekly Report. Youth Risk Behavior Survey, 1993 National Survey. In press.

77. Market Research Corporation of America. National Menu Census, Chicago, IL: MRCA, 1993.

78. California Department of Health Services. The California Dietary Practices Survey of Children, Ages 9 to 11 Years: Focus on Fruits and Vegetables, Sacramento, CA: CDHS, 1993.

79. Basch CE, Zybert P, Shea S. 5-A-Day: Dietary behavior and the fruit and vegetable intake of Latino children. Am J Public Health 1994;84:814–8.

80. Nicklas TA. Dietary fiber in childhood proposal for a recommended intake. The Digest, American Dietetic Association, 1994.

81. National Cancer Institute. National Institute of Health, Public Health Service. US Department of Health and Human Services. Diet, nutrition and cancer prevention: a guide to food choices. NIH Pub. No. 87–2878. Washington, DC: US Government Printing Office, 1987.

82. Bronner F. Calcium and osteoporosis. Am J Clin Nutr 1994;60:831–6.

83. Nieves JW, Golden AL, Siris E. Kelsey JL, Linsay R. Teenage and current calcium intake are related to bone mineral density of the hip and forearm in women aged 30–39. Am J Epidemiol 1995;8:342–51.

84. Reusser ME, McCarron DA. Micronutrient effects on blood pressure. Nutr Rev 1994;52:367–75.

85. International Food Information Council and The American Dietetic Association. How are kids making food choices? Princeton, NJ: The Gallup Organization, 1991.

86. International Food Information Council. Kids make the nutritional grade. YOUTH Research Surveys, June 1992. Washington, DC: IFIC.

87. American School Health Association. The National Adolescent Student Health Survey: a report on the health of America's youth. Oakland,CA: Third Party Publishing Co., 1989.

88. Resnicow K, Reinhardt J. What do children know about fat, fiber, and cholesterol? A survey of 5,116 primary and secondary school students. J Nutr Educ 1991;23:65–71.

89. Murphy AS, Youatt JP, Hoerr SL, Sawyer CA, Andrews SL. Nutrition education needs and learning preferences of Michigan students in grades 5, 8, and 11. J Sch Health 1994;64:273–8.

90. Foley CS, Vaden AG, Newell GK, Dayton AD. Establishing the need for nutrition education: Part III, elementary students' nutrition knowledge, attitudes, and practices. J Am Diet Assoc 1983;83:564–8.

91. Bozell Public Relations. Kids and afternoon snacks. New York: Louis Harris & Associates, 1994.

92. Contento IR. Children's dietary knowledge, skills, and attitudes: Measurement issues. J Sch Health 1991;61:208–11.

 **Article Review Form at end of book.**

Were there differences in nutrient intake across states, across gender, across race? If so, what were the differences? Summarize the CATCH strategies to improve food selection and physical activity. What is the trend regarding percentage of calories from fat? How is this trend explained?

# Nutrient Intakes of Third Graders

## Results from the child and adolescent trial for cardiovascular health (CATCH) baseline survey

**Leslie A. Lytle,[1] Mary Kay Ebzery,[2] Theresa Nicklas,[3] Deanna Montgomery,[4] Michelle Zive,[5] Marguerite Evans,[6] Patricia Snyder,[1] Milton Nichaman,[4] Steven H. Kelder,[4] Debra Reed,[7] Ellen Busch,[5] and Paul Mitchell[8]**

[1]School of Public Health, Division of Epidemiology, University of Minnesota, Minneapolis, Minnesota 55454; [2]Frances Stern Nutrition Center, New England Medical Center Hospital, Boston, Massachusetts 02111; [3]School of Public Health and Tropical Medicine, Tulane University, New Orleans, Louisiana 70112;

[4]School of Public Health, Center for Health Promotion Research and Development, University of Texas Health Science Center, Houston, Texas 77225; [5]Department of Pediatrics, Community Pediatrics Division, University of California, San Diego, San Diego, La Jolla, California 92093-0927; [6]Division of Epidemiology and Clinical Applications, National Heart, Lung, and Blood Institute, Bethesda, Maryland 20892; [7]School of Human Ecology, Louisiana State University, Baton Rouge, Louisiana 70803-4300; [8]New England Research Institute, Inc., Watertown, Massachusetts 02172

## Abstract

The purpose of this article is to report on baseline intakes of 1874 third-grade children representing a subsample of the Child and Adolescent Trial for Cardiovascular Health (CATCH) cohort. Intakes were assessed using a single, food record-assisted, 24-hour recall. The sample is unique in that it is drawn from four states and includes students from various ethnic backgrounds. Nutrients of interest include total energy, sodium, dietary cholesterol, and percent of energy from total fat and saturated fat. At baseline, third-grade students were consuming above nationally recommended levels of energy from fat, saturated fat, and sodium. The CATCH findings show a mean energy intake of 2031 kcal with significant differences by sex. Significant differences by site were seen for percent of energy from total fat, saturated fat, and dietary cholesterol. Children from Minnesota consumed the lowest proportion of energy from total fat and saturated fat while children from Texas had the highest proportion of energy from total fat and saturated fat. Intake of dietary cholesterol was lowest in Minnesota and highest in Louisiana. Nutrient differences by ethnic group were seen only for energy, with African Americans having the highest energy intake and Hispanics having the lowest energy intake. The number of meals consumed from school food service significantly influenced children's nutrient intake; children consuming two meals from school food service had significantly greater intakes of energy, saturated fat, and dietary cholesterol compared to students consuming one or no meals from school food service. The results are compared to other national nutritional surveys of children. (JNE 28:338–347, 1996)

## Introduction

Children's diets exceed national recommendations for intake of total fat, saturated fat, and sodium[1-5] and contribute to the presence of precursors of cardiovascular disease risk in youth.[6,7] There is a continuing need to monitor trends in children's dietary intake and to learn more about differences in intake by geographic location and by racial or ethnic group.

The Child and Adolescent Trial for Cardiovascular Health (CATCH) was a multicenter trial in 96 schools in California, Louisiana, Minnesota, and Texas to reduce cardiovascular disease risk factors in youth. CATCH evaluated classroom-based curricula, a family program, and school environment modifications aimed at reducing fat and sodium consumption and increasing physical activity in a cohort of children as they advanced from third to fifth grade. Eat Smart, the CATCH cafeteria intervention program, was designed to reduce total fat, saturated fat, and sodium in meals offered to children at school.[8,9] CATCH classroom curricula taught students to engage in behaviors and skills for choosing healthful foods and increasing physical activity. Teachers were trained to use goal setting, role modeling, and skill building. To improve physical education, teachers were given instruction on how to increase students' enjoyment of and participation in moderate-to-vigorous activity. The foodservice intervention helped school foodservice staff plan healthier menus and prepare meals with less total fat, saturated fat, and sodium. Additionally, the classroom intervention for fifth graders focused on avoiding tobacco use, including how to resist social pressure to start smoking. Schools were also given guidance on how to establish smoke-free policies. CATCH used family fun nights and activities for students to do at home to involve parents. The details of the CATCH intervention and research design are described elsewhere.[10-12]

The purpose of this article is to report on baseline intakes of selected nutrients of 1874 third-grade children representing a subsample of the CATCH cohort. Nutrients of interest include those nutrients targeted by the intervention: intake of sodium and proportion of energy from total and saturated fat. In addition, the overall composition of the diet (energy from fat, carbohydrate, and protein), total energy intake, and dietary cholesterol are reported. Mean nutrient intakes are examined by site, ethnicity, sex, and the number of meals children report eating from school food service. In addition, findings from CATCH are compared with other youth-based national nutritional surveys.

## Methods

### Subjects

The subsample of the total CATCH cohort to be involved in the collection of 24-hour recalls was determined by randomly selecting 2826 third-grade students across the four sites. To augment the sample, 660 additional students who had consented to participate in CATCH were selected from a randomly ordered list of remaining students at each school. A total of 3486 students were eligible to participate, of which 268 were dropped since they were later determined to be noncohort (no blood cholesterol was available), leaving a sample of 3218. Dietary recalls were collected from 1920 consenting children, representing 60% of the children selected to participate in the substudy and 38% of the total CATCH cohort. There were slightly higher participation rates in Minnesota (64.4%) as compared to California (54.6%), Louisiana (58.3%), and Texas (61.9%). Nonparticipation by those students selected for the substudy was due to failure to bring in a signed consent form (26%), failure to bring in a completed food record (7%), and absenteeism on the day of the recall or food record administration (7%). Although there were no differ-

**Table 1** Participation in CATCH Baseline 24-Hour Recalls

| Site | Number of Recalls | Participants (%) | | | | |
| --- | --- | --- | --- | --- | --- | --- |
| | | Males | Caucasian | African American | Hispanic | Other |
| California | 452 | 47 | 71 | 7 | 15 | 7 |
| Louisiana | 443 | 52 | 71 | 27 | 1 | 1 |
| Minnesota | 494 | 52 | 91 | 2 | 2 | 5 |
| Texas | 485 | 48 | 44 | 13 | 42 | 1 |
| Total | 1874 | 50 | 69 | 12 | 15 | 4 |

ences by sex between participating and nonparticipating students, a smaller proportion of African Americans (53.8%) participated compared to Caucasians (61.4%), Hispanics (58.3%), and children from other ethnic groups combined (58.8%). Data collection occurred during the fall of 1991. Human subjects' approval for data collection was obtained from the Committee on Human Subjects in Research at each participating institution. Procedural details and results of the baseline risk factor screening have been published elsewhere.[13]

Forty-six cases were eliminated from the final analysis based on the presence of unverified nutrient outliers. Nutrient values for energy, total fat, saturated fat, sodium, and cholesterol were compared to portions commonly eaten by children.[14] Those values greater than the 99th percentile (without documented verification during data collection of unusual amounts consumed) were flagged as unverified outliers and these recalls were eliminated from the analyses. Sixty-seven students classified as other than Caucasian, African America, or Hispanic were not included in the mixed-model analysis of variance (ANOVA) evaluating statistical differences by site, sex, ethnicity, and number

of meals consumed from school meals because of the small sample size.

Table 1 presents participation rates and sample characteristics. The ethnic group and sex distributions of 24-hour recall subjects are similar to the distribution in the total CATCH cohort.[13]

## Dietary Assessment Method

A food record-assisted 24-hour recall was used to assess children's diets. This diet assessment methodology was validated during the pilot phase of CATCH using observation at school and at home as the criterion measure to validate children's self-report of their previous day's intake.[15] On Day 1, CATCH staff instructed groups of children on how to keep a food record. Children were asked to list all foods they took "at least one sip or one bite of" from that morning until bedtime. On Day 2, those children returning a food record were individually asked to recall the food eaten in the last 24 hours, using the food record as a memory aid. Children were asked to estimate portion sizes with the help of three-dimensional food models, measuring utensils, and tableware. Information on salt used in food

preparation or at the table was not obtained. The information was directly entered by a CATCH staff person into a laptop computer using the Nutrition Data System (NDS) (Version 2.2, 1990, Nutrition Coordinating Center, University of Minnesota, Minneapolis, MN). These 24-hour dietary recalls were administered via a one-on-one interview between individual children and a CATCH staff person.

Centralized training for the dietary data collection was conducted at New England Research Institutes, the study's coordinating center, and included training on using the NDS and study-specific protocols. Site nutritionists and interviewers were certified after successfully completing training and certification exercises. Quality control was maintained by having a senior nutritionist at each site observe and provide feedback to each interviewer using a standardized checklist targeting important elements of the protocol. Quality control observations were conducted at least three times over the course of the baseline measurement period for each data collector. In addition, quality control site visits were conducted by personnel from the study's coordinating center to ensure that study protocols were being followed.

## Use of School Meal Information in NDS and in Data Analysis

CATCH nutritionists collected information on school menus, recipes, and vendor products in order to assess changes in school food service resulting from the Eat Smart cafeteria intervention.[9,16] These school-specific data were used in the analysis of 24-hour recalls for children who reported eating a school-prepared meal. For example, if a child consumed pizza served at school lunch, specific vendor product or recipe information for pizza served at that school was used in analyzing the child's nutrient intake. This was accomplished by customizing the NDS software to allow school recipe and vendor product identification numbers and proportions eaten to be included in the nutrient summary files. Foodservice nutrient data were linked with 24-hour recall summary files for children who reported eating a school meal. All foodservice data were sent to the University of Minnesota's Nutrition Coordinating Center for central coding, data entry, and nutrient calculation.

It was important to be able to identify school-prepared foods and integrate this information into the 24-hour recalls for several reasons. First, a large percentage of 8- to 9-year-old children consume school-prepared meals, which may contribute as much as 50% to 60% of total daily nutrient intakes.[1] Yet, it may be difficult to determine what school meals consist of with respect to their nutrient components unless items are specified precisely.[17] Second, since fat and sodium modifications were expected for the 56 CATCH intervention schools participating in Eat Smart,[9] the inclusion of school-specific meal information instead of generic recipes and ingredients was essential for characterizing differences in eating patterns between children in intervention and control schools.

## Statistical Analysis

Mixed-model ANOVA was used to investigate the influence of site, ethnic group, sex, and the number of meals received from school food services on mean levels of nutrient intake at baseline. The child's school was included in each model as a random effect, nested within site and treatment group, to account for any between-school variation occurring within treatment groups and between sites. The treatment group was included in the models as a fixed effect.

The sample included in the mixed-model ANOVA includes those 1807 students classified as Caucasian, African American, or Hispanic. Students from other ethnic groups were not included in these analyses due to the small number of students thus classified.

Dependent variables included total energy (kcal), percent of energy from total fat, protein, carbohydrate, saturated fat, monounsaturated fat, and polyunsaturated fat, as well as total dietary cholesterol (mg) and sodium (mg). CATCH site (df = 3), sex (df = 1), and ethnic group (df = 2) were included as fixed independent effects, in addition to an interaction term for sex and ethnic group. The number of meals received from school food service was never more than two, so this was entered into the models as a class-level, fixed effect.

Means obtained from the mixed-model ANOVA were adjusted for all factors entered in the model, including site, treatment group, number of meals received from school food services, ethnic group, sex, and the interaction of ethnic group and sex. The data were analyzed using the Statistical Analysis System.[18]

## Results

Mean energy and selected nutrient intakes by site and sex are presented in Table 2. The adjusted mean intake for all sites combined was 2031 kcal, with 33% of energy from fat, 15% from protein, and 54% from carbohydrates. The proportion of energy from saturated fat was 12.7% and the mean intake of dietary cholesterol and sodium was 220 mg and 2972 mg, respectively.

Significant differences were found by site for all nutrients except total energy, sodium, and percent of energy from protein. The percent of energy from fat ranged from 31% in Minnesota to 34% in Texas. Minnesota children consumed more energy from carbohydrate (56%) while children from Texas consumed the least amount of energy from carbohydrate ( 52%). Minnesota children consumed the least amount of energy from saturated fat (11.9%) and monounsaturated fat (14.%) while Texas children consumed the greatest proportion of energy from saturated fat (13.4%) and monounsaturated fat (12.5%). Louisiana children consumed more energy from polyunsaturated fat (6.2%) and more dietary cholesterol (238 mg) compared to children from Minnesota (5.3% energy from polyunsaturated fat and 198 mg from dietary cholesterol). When sodium intake is represented per 1000 kcal (data not shown), there is a significant difference by site (p < .05), with

**Table 2** Selected Nutrient Levels by Site and Sex

| Subgroup (n) | Energy (kcal) | % Energy from Fat | % Energy from Protein | % Energy from Carbohydrate | % Energy from SFA | % Energy from MFA | % Energy from PFA | Cholesterol (mg) | Sodium (mg) |
|---|---|---|---|---|---|---|---|---|---|
| All (1874)[a] | 2031 (674) | 32.6 (7.0) | 14.7 (3.5) | 53.9 (8.5) | 12.7 (3.5) | 11.9 (3.0) | 5.7 (2.4) | 220 (150) | 2972 (1248) |
| California (419)[b] | 2007 (39) | 31.9 (0.4) | 14.9 (0.2) | 54.5 (0.5) | 12.6 (0.2) | 11.5 (0.2) | 5.5 (0.2) | 218 (9) | 2820 (75) |
| Louisiana (440)[b] | 2018 (40) | 33.8 (0.4) | 14.3 (0.2) | 52.8 (0.5) | 12.8 (0.2) | 12.4 (0.2) | 6.2 (0.2) | 238 (9) | 3085 (9) |
| Minnesota (468)[b] | 2124 (39) | 30.8 (0.4) | 14.8 (0.2) | 55.7 (0.5) | 11.9 (0.2) | 11.4 (0.2) | 5.3 (0.2) | 198 (9) | 3035 (74) |
| Texas (480)[b] | 1983 (40) | 34.2 (0.4) | 14.8 (0.2) | 52.4 (0.5) | 13.4 (0.2) | 12.5 (0.2) | 5.8 (0.2) | 231 (9) | 2954 (76) |
| Significance Level | $p < .07$ | $p < .0001$ | $p > .35$ | $p < .0001$ | $p < .0001$ | $p < .0001$ | $p < .006$ | $p < .02$ | $p < .08$ |
| Males (899)[b] | 2106 (24) | 32.7 (0.2) | 14.8 (0.1) | 53.8 (0.3) | 12.8 (0.1) | 12.0 (0.1) | 5.6 (0.1) | 228 (6) | 3059 (46) |
| Females (908)[b] | 1961 (24) | 32.7 (0.2) | 14.6 (0.1) | 53.9 (0.3) | 12.6 (0.1) | 11.8 (0.1) | 5.8 (0.1) | 214 (6) | 2892 (46) |
| Significance Level | $p < .003$ | $p > .75$ | $p > .15$ | $p > .40$ | $p > .35$ | $p > .20$ | $p < .05$ | $p < .003$ | $p > .10$ |

[a]Unadjusted mean (standard deviation); n = 1874.

[b]Adjusted mean (standard error): site means adjusted for sex, sex means for site. All means additionally adjusted for ethnicity, treatment group, and number of meals received from school food service. Sample includes only those students identified as Caucasian, African American, or Hispanic; n = 1807.

SFA = saturated fat; MFA = monounsaturated fat; PFA = polyunsaturated fat.

Louisiana children consuming the most sodium (1535 mg per 1000 kcal) and California children consuming the least sodium (1428 mg per 1000 kcal). Data on sodium intake are limited by the lack of information on children's salting practices and salting that may have occurred during meal preparation in the home.

Differences in intake by sex are evident, with males consuming more total energy ($p < .003$), less energy from polyunsaturated fat ($p < .05$), and more dietary cholesterol ($p < .003$) than females. However, when cholesterol intake is adjusted for total energy, the difference between sexes disappears.

Nutrient comparisons of adjusted means by ethnic group and by ethnicity and sex interaction are shown in Table 3. Significant differences by ethnicity are seen only for energy. African-American children consumed the most energy (2106 kcal) while Hispanic children had lower energy intakes (1937 kcal). No significant ethnicity and sex interactions were seen except when dietary cholesterol was adjusted for total energy.

African-American females consumed the least amount of dietary cholesterol (98 mg per 1000 kcal) while Hispanic males consumed the greatest amount of dietary cholesterol (118 mg per 1000 kcal).

The majority of children (63%) consumed one meal from school food service, usually lunch, while 14% and 23% received two meals or no meals, respectively. The number of meals consumed from school food service had a significant effect on adjusted mean nutrient intake for all nutrients except proportion of energy from fat, monounsaturated fat, and total sodium (Table 4). Children who ate two meals from school food service consumed significantly more total energy, a higher proportion of energy from saturated fat, and more dietary cholesterol as compared to children who ate no meals from school food service. Students who consumed no meals from school food service had a higher intake of energy from carbohydrate and polyunsaturated fat. Children consuming one meal from school food service had the highest intake of energy from protein while

students consuming no meals from school have the lowest intake of protein.

# Discussion

We are unable to characterize an individual's diet or the nutritional adequacy of school meals from a single 24-hour recall or a single assessment of a school lunch due to intraindividual variation in what is consumed and in meals offered. However, pooling multiple single 24-hour recalls or pooling multiple school meals to derive a group mean allows us to consider intergroup variation. These CATCH baseline data combined over 1800 dietary recalls and examined differences by site, sex, and ethnicity. The differences that are seen between groups (e.g., energy from fat for Minnesota children equalled 31% as compared to 34% of energy from fat for children from Texas) may have little biological importance if considered at the individual level for a single day but have important implications when considering disease risk in populations.[22]

**Table 3** Selected Nutrient Levels by Sex and Ethnicity

| Race/Sex | *Energy (kcal) | % Energy from Fat | % Energy from Protein | % Energy from Carbohydrate | % Energy from SFA | % Energy from MFA | % Energy from PFA | Cholesterol (mg) | Sodium (mg) |
|---|---|---|---|---|---|---|---|---|---|
| **Caucasian[a]** | | | | | | | | | |
| Males (n = 664) | 2122 (29)[a] | 32.7 (0.3) | 14.8 (0.2) | 53.8 (0.4) | 12.8 (0.1) | 12.0 (0.1) | 5.6 (0.1) | 223 (6) | 3110 (54) |
| Females (n = 633) | 1964 (29) | 32.8 (0.3) | 14.7 (0.2) | 53.7 (0.4) | 12.6 (0.1) | 11.9 (0.1) | 5.9 (0.1) | 217 (6) | 2916 (55) |
| Total (n = 1297) | 2043 (22) | 32.7 (0.2) | 14.7 (0.1) | 53.8 (0.3) | 12.7 (0.1) | 11.9 (0.1) | 5.7 (0.1) | 220 (5) | 3013 (42) |
| **African American[a]** | | | | | | | | | |
| Males (n = 100) | 2141 (70) | 32.3 (0.7) | 14.7 (0.4) | 54.2 (0.9) | 12.4 (0.4) | 12.1 (0.3) | 5.4 (0.2) | 254 (16) | 2976 (131) |
| Females (n = 126) | 2072 (62) | 31.9 (0.6) | 14.3 (0.3) | 55.0 (0.8) | 12.0 (0.3) | 11.8 (0.3) | 5.8 (0.2) | 204 (14) | 3017 (117) |
| Total (n = 226) | 2106 (49) | 32.1 (0.5) | 14.5 (0.3) | 54.6 (0.6) | 12.2 (0.2) | 11.9 (0.2) | 5.6 (0.2) | 229 (11) | 2996 (92) |
| **Hispanic[a]** | | | | | | | | | |
| Males (n = 135) | 2009 (63) | 33.0 (0.6) | 14.8 (0.3) | 53.3 (0.8) | 12.9 (0.3) | 12.2 (0.3) | 5.5 (0.2) | 223 (14) | 2895 (118) |
| Females (n = 149) | 1865 (60) | 32.9 (0.6) | 14.4 (0.3) | 54.0 (0.8) | 13.0 (0.3) | 11.9 (0.3) | 5.7 (0.2) | 207 (13) | 2690 (112) |
| Total (n = 284) | 1937 (47) | 33.0 (0.5) | 14.6 (0.2) | 53.6 (0.6) | 12.9 (0.2) | 12.0 (0.2) | 5.6 (0.2) | 220 (11) | 2793 (88) |
| **Other[b]** | | | | | | | | | |
| Males (n = 34) | 2104 (841) | 32.0 (7.0) | 15.2 (3.0) | 53.8 (8.0) | 13.3 (3.6) | 11.0 (3.1) | 5.2 (2.7) | 253 (166) | 3055 (1390) |
| Females (n = 33) | 1903 (661) | 30.9 (6.9) | 16.1 (5.5) | 53.8 (9.3) | 12.1 (3.4) | 11.1 (2.9) | 5.4 (3.9) | 200 (111) | 2806 (1127) |
| Total (n = 67) | 2005 (759) | 31.5 (6.9) | 15.6 (4.4) | 53.8 (8.6) | 12.7 (3.5) | 11.0 (3.0) | 5.3 (3.3) | 227 (143) | 2932 (1264) |

*Adjusted means (comparing Caucasian, African-American, and Hispanic students) are significantly different (p < .04).
[a]Adjusted means (standard error). Means adjusted for site, sex, treatment group, and number of meals received from school food service; n = 1807.
[b]Unadjusted mean (standard deviation); n = 67.
SFA = saturated fat; MFA = monounsaturated fat; PFA = polyunsaturated fat.

These CATCH baseline data, combined with results from other national nutrition surveys of youth, provide an additional point marking the trends in children's nutrient intakes. A summary of dietary studies in children, the methodology used for diet assessment, and nutrient comparisons across these studies is presented in Tables 5 and 6.

The studies compared span 20 years of nutritional survey information on children ranging in age from 6 to 11. The most common assessment method was a single 24-hour recall.

Energy intakes across the nine reviewed studies ranged from 1728 kcal in the Dietary Intervention Study in Children (DISC; a study of children with elevated LDL-cholesterol levels)[2] to 2220 kcal in the School Nutrition Dietary Assessment (SNDA) Study.[19] No trend or change in the pattern of energy intake over time was obvious.

A trend toward lower percent of energy from fat is evident across these studies. The CATCH baseline findings are consistent with the findings from the SNDA study,[19] DISC,[2] and NHANES III.[5] These studies, conducted between 1988 and 1993, using very similar methodology for data collection and similar nutrient databases, showed average energy from fat to be between 33% and 34% of calories. Earlier studies carried out between 1971 and 1988,[3,4,20,21] in which similar methodology for data collection was used (24-hour recall in-person interviews), show the proportion of energy from fat between 36% and 37%.

The trend toward lower fat intakes over time could be due to a variety of factors, including the increase of available lower fat foods in the marketplace, secular trends toward lower fat con-

sumption in the population, an increase in reporting bias, or methodological differences in 24-hour recall protocol between studies. From an epidemiologic viewpoint, the reduction of fat in children's diets (assuming it represents a real reduction and not an artifact of assessment methodology) from 38%[3] to 34% of total energy seen in this study and other studies,[5,19] represents a factor that may have an important impact on the incidence of heart disease. The maintenance of this lower fat eating pattern into and throughout adult life needs to be studied in order to evaluate the full importance of this finding. Moreover, it is yet to be determined if children's fat intake can be reduced to meet the national recommendation of no more than 30% of energy from total fat without compromising intake of other important nutrients.[22]

**Table 4** Selected Nutrient Levels by Number of Meals Consumed from School Food Service

| Number of School Meals Consumed | Energy (kcal) | % Energy from Fat | % Energy from Protein | % Energy from Carbohydrate | % Energy from SFA | % Energy from MFA | % Energy from PFA | Cholesterol (mg) | Sodium (mg) |
|---|---|---|---|---|---|---|---|---|---|
| Zero meals* from school (n = 420) | 1991 (36) | 32.2 (0.4) | 14.2 (0.2) | 55.1 (0.4) | 11.9 (0.2) | 12.0 (0.2) | 6.0 (0.1) | 203 (8) | 2891 (67) |
| One meal* from school (n = 1126) | 2014 (22) | 32.6 (0.2) | 14.9 (0.1) | 53.6 (0.3) | 12.8 (0.1) | 11.9 (0.1) | 5.6 (0.1) | 224 (5) | 2969 (43) |
| Two meals* from school (n = 261) | 2180 (47) | 33.6 (0.5) | 14.6 (0.2) | 52.8 (0.6) | 13.5 (0.2) | 12.0 (0.2) | 5.8 (0.2) | 235 (10) | 3133 (88) |
| p value | p < .003 | p < .08 | p < .003 | p < .005 | p < .0001 | p > .80 | p < .001 | p < .03 | p < .10 |

*Adjusted mean (standard errors). Means adjusted for site, treatment group, ethnicity, sex, ethnicity × sex. Sample includes only those students identified as Caucasian, African American, or Hispanic; n = 1807.
SFA = saturated fat; MFA = monounsaturated fat; PFA = polyunsaturated fat.

While the proportion of energy from total fat appears to be declining, the proportion of energy from saturated fat has remained fairly stable (13–14% of energy) and exceeds national recommendations for saturated fat (no more than 10% of energy).[22] Eating pattern messages for children need to encourage consumption of foods lower in saturated fat as well as foods lower in total fat. Concrete food examples should be used rather than generic messages to "choose a diet low in fat, saturated fat, and cholesterol."[23] Qualitative work by Lytle et al.[24] indicates that children, even at the sixth-grade level, do not understand what saturated fat is and cannot name foods that are high or low in saturated fats. Effective messages to affect eating behavior change targeted at children should explicitly identify and encourage consumption of foods that are low in saturated fat, such as skim milk and low-fat cheeses. Children should also be encouraged to increase their consumption of meatless meals.

Energy from protein has remained fairly stable across studies, providing about 15% of total energy. The decrease in energy from fat appears to have been accompanied by an increase in energy intake from carbohydrate. Carbohydrate intake, expressed as percent of total energy, increased from 47% to 50% in studies conducted prior to 1987 to 52% to 54% in the studies conducted since 1988.

The intake of dietary cholesterol has been variable across studies and time, ranging from 195 mg in the DISC study[2] to 314 mg in NHANES I.[20] Most often, mean intake of cholesterol is within the national recommendation of no more than 300 mg per day.

Mean sodium values from CATCH baseline results were consistent with other values in the literature (see Table 6), with the exception of those from the SNDA,[19] where sodium intake exceeded 3 grams per day. Sodium intake in CATCH might be underestimated since children could not report on salt added to foods during meal preparation at home and were not asked to estimate the amount of salt added to foods at the table. Pilot work showed that children were not able to estimate the amount of salt they added to foods at the table; therefore, dietary recalls did not probe for that information. In all of the studies reviewed, sodium intake exceeded dietary recommendations.

These CATCH baseline findings examining the nutrient contribution of school food service are an important replication of SNDA study findings.[19] As in the SNDA, children eating two meals from school food service consumed significantly more energy from saturated fat and more total energy as compared to children eating no meals from school food service. While SNDA showed significant differences in the percent of energy from total fat and sodium based on school meals consumed, the CATCH baseline results revealed a similar pattern but no significant differences (p > .10). In general, however, the CATCH data support the SNDA findings that children eating school meals consume more fat, saturated fat, cholesterol, and sodium than children not participating in the school lunch or breakfast programs. New recommendations from USDA regarding foods offered via school meal service are likely to positively impact fat and saturated fat content of school meals nationwide. It is also important to note that CATCH data suggest that students who consume two meals

| Survey | Dates of Data Collection | Number of Subjects/Sex | Age Range (Mean Age) | Method of Diet Assessment | Data Source (Release Date) |
|---|---|---|---|---|---|
| NHANES I USDHHS, 1983[20] | 1971–1974 | 2057 1026 males 1031 females | 6–11 | 24-hr recall in-person interview | USDA Handbook 8 (1972) |
| NHANES II USDHHS, 1989[4] | 1976–1980 | 1725 885 males 840 females | 6–11 | 24-hr recall in-person interview | USDA Handbook 8 (Revised) (1972) |
| USDA NFCS Thompson et al., 1986[21] | 1977–1978 | 4107 | 6–11 | 24-hr recall 2-day food records | USDA HNIS National Nutrient Databank (1980) |
| USDA NFCS Wright et al., 1990[3] | 1987–1988 | 10172 4476 males 5696 females | 6–11 | 24-hr recall 2-day food records | USDA HNIS National Nutrient Databank (1992) |
| NGHS baseline Crawford et al., 1995[27] | 1987–1988 | 2149 females 1104 Caucasian 1045 African American | 9–10 | 3-day food record | University of Minnesota/NCC Version 19 |
| NHANES III McDowell et al., 1994[5] Alaimo et al., 1994[26] | 1988–1991 | 1745 868 males 877 females | 6–11 | 24-hr recall in-person interview | USDA NFCS 1994 (1993) |
| DISC Van Horn et al., 1993[2] | 1990–1993 | 652 356 males 296 females | 8–11 (9.6) | 3 24-hr recalls: 1 in-person, 2 telephone interviews | University of Minnesota/NCC Version 20 |
| SNDA Devaney et al., 1993[19] | 1992 | 1383 | 6–10 | 24-hr recall in-person interview | University of Minnesota/NCC Version 20 |
| CATCH baseline Lytle et al. | 1991–1992 | 1874 933 males 941 females | (8.7) | 24-hr recall in-person interview | University of Minnesota/NCC Version 19 |

HNIS = Human Nutrition Information Service; NCC = Nutrition Coordinating Center.

from school lunch have significantly higher intakes of calcium, phosphorus, and potassium as compared to students not participating in school foodservice programs.

Physiologic risk factors for chronic disease appear to differ by ethnic group;[25] however, nutritional intake by ethnicity has been examined in only a few surveys of children. The CATCH results allowed comparison of nutrient intake by ethnicity, sex, and site. Few significant differences in dietary intake were observed by ethnicity or sex. Energy intake was most influenced by sex and ethnicity, with males and African Americans consuming the most energy. Hispanic children had the lowest energy intake but consumed more energy from saturated fat than other racial groups. African-American children consumed the most sodium and Hispanic females consumed the least sodium.

Comparisons of nutrient intake by non-Hispanic white, non-Hispanic black, and Mexican-American children were reported in the NHANES III data. These results are not directly comparable to CATCH results since ethnic and racial groupings are slightly different between the studies, results of nutrient intake from CATCH are adjusted, and children aged 6

**Table 6** Comparison of United States Nutritional Surveys of Children: Mean Nutrient Intakes

| Survey | Energy (kcal) | % Energy from Fat | % Energy from Protein | % Energy from Carbohydrate | % Energy from SFA | % Energy from MFA | % Energy from PFA | Cholesterol (mg) | Sodium (mg) |
|---|---|---|---|---|---|---|---|---|---|
| NHANES I USDHHS, 1983[20] | 2045 | 37 | 15 | 49 | 14[a] | 13[a] | 4[a] | 314 | 2393 |
| NHANES II USDHHS, 1989[4] | 1960 | 36 | 15 | 50 | 13[a] | 13[a] | 4[a] | 278 | 2716 |
| USDA NFCS Thompson et al., 1986[21] | 1876 | 38 | 16 | 47 | NA | NA | NA | NA | NA |
| USDA NFCS Wright et al., 1990[3] | 1883 Male | 36 Male | 16 Male | 50 Male | 14 Male | 13 Male | 6 Male | 272 Male | 2988 Male |
| | 1680 Female | 35 Female | 15 Female | 51 Female | 13 Female | 13 Female | 6 Female | 239 Female | 2692 Female |
| NGHS baseline Crawford et al., 1995[27] | 1803 White | 35 White | 14 White | 52 White | 13 White | 13 White | 6 White | 247 White | NA |
| | 1858 Black | 37 Black | 14 Black | 50 Black | 13 Black | 14 Black | 7 Black | 215 Black | |
| NHANES III McDowell et al., 1994[5] Alaimo et al., 1994[26] | 1897 | 34 | 14 | 53 | 13 | 13 | 6 | 225 | 2996 |
| DISC Van Horn et al., 1993[2] | 1759 Intervention | 33 Intervention | 15 Intervention | 52 Intervention | 13 Intervention | 13 Intervention | 6 Intervention | 209 Intervention | NA |
| | 1728 Control | 13 Control | 15 Control | 53 Control | 13 Control | 13 Control | 6 Control | 195 Control | |
| SNDA Devaney et al., 1993[19] | 2220[b] | 34 | 15[b] | 53 | 13 | NA | NA | 270 | 4076 |
| CATCH baseline Lytle et al. | 2031 | 33 | 15 | 54 | 13 | 12 | 6 | 220 | 2972 |

[a]Value calculated from available information; [b]value approximated; originally reported as percent of RDA.

SFA = saturated fat; MFA = monounsaturated fat; PFA = polyunsaturated fat.

NA = data not available.

to 11 are grouped together in NHANES III. Data from NHANES III[5,26] do not report if mean differences in nutrient levels between groups are significantly different. Nevertheless, results reported from CATCH and NHANES III are similar across racial/ethnic groups. In NHANES III and CATCH, energy intake was highest in blacks and lowest in Mexican Americans. Comparable with CATCH, data show that Mexican Americans and non-Hispanic white children in NHANES III consumed more energy from saturated fat (12.9%) as compared to non-Hispanic black children (12.6%). As in CATCH, sodium consumption was found to be highest in non-Hispanic black children (3222 mg) and lowest in Mexican-American children (2922 mg). The National Growth and Health Study (NGHS)[27] also shows data by white and black. As in CATCH and NHANES III, energy intake was higher in black girls as compared to white girls. However, energy from saturated fat was equal between black and white girls.

Site differences were significant for most nutrients, suggesting that geographic location has an important influence on eating patterns among children. Regional foods or norms related to food-related behavior appear to influence what is consumed above and beyond the racial or ethnic mix in an area. The findings regarding racial/ethnic and site differences suggest that intervention efforts to alter the diet of America's children should consider regional eating patterns and the influence of race and ethnic groups when formulating messages to modify eating patterns.

An examination of the vitamin and mineral intakes of the CATCH baseline sample is beyond the scope of this article due to space constraints. In brief, group mean levels of vitamin and mineral intakes were similar to those found in NHANES III and met the RDA.[26] Changes in the nutrient density of vitamin and mineral intake occurring concomitantly with efforts to reduce dietary fat will be examined in follow-up studies of CATCH.

Differences in socioeconomic status (SES) by site were not investigated and may be an important factor in explaining site differences. Children were relied upon for the vast majority of information obtained; interviewing parents to determine SES was not feasible.

## Conclusions

CATCH's large sample and the inclusion of both sexes and three racial groups in four states adds to our understanding of children's dietary intake. In addition, the results of the study are an important confirmation of the SNDA study in which the effect of school meals on children's nutritional intakes was also evaluated. However, as in most studies assessing dietary intake, there are several limitations. The methodology used cannot adequately assess the long-term dietary intake of individual children; only group comparisons and mean nutrient intakes can be made.[28] Using a single 24-hour recall, a "snapshot" of children's intake is provided,

allowing group comparisons across site, ethnic group, sex, and participation in school meals. The actual nutritional health of these children cannot be ascertained without multiple days of intake information that assesses both intra- and interindividual variation of intake.

The use of self-report to assess children's diets may result in inherent problems with memory, problems estimating portion size, and the possibility of response bias—all sources of potential error. The validation of the methodology, using observation as the reference standard,[15] provides us with some confidence in the quality of the assessment method. Using actual school food-service recipe information also adds to our confidence in the data collected. Another limitation is that no data on weekend intake are available; there is evidence to suggest that weekend intakes may differ from weekday intakes.[21] Lack of information on students' SES is a constraint of this study.

While the results of CATCH add to the literature by presenting nutrient information on Caucasians, African Americans, and Hispanics, other subpopulations need to be studied to complete the picture of dietary intakes of American children. The CATCH baseline sample, which included 67 students classified as "other," was not large enough to include in analyses involving statistical comparisons. More information is needed on the nutritional intake of Asian and Native-American children. In addition, another subgroup of children being increasingly recognized and warranting nutritional surveillance is children living in poverty. It is estimated that, in 1990, nearly 11 million American children were living in poverty, an

increase of 14% over the previous decade.[29] Future population surveys of children need to focus on the nutritional status of these children.

## Acknowledgment

The authors would like to thank Henry Feldman of the New England Research Institutes for his valuable assistance in data analysis and presentation.

## References

1. Burghardt J, Gordon A, Chapman N, Gleason P, Fraker T. The School Nutrition Dietary Assessment Study: school food service, meals offered, and dietary intakes. Princeton, NJ: Mathematica Policy Research, 1993.
2. Van Horn LV, Stumbo P, Moag-Stahlberg A, et al. The Dietary Intervention Study in Children (DISC): dietary assessment methods for 8- to 10-year-olds. J Am Diet Assoc 1993;93:1396–1403.
3. Wright HS, Guthrie HS, Wang MQ, Bernardo V. The 1987–88 Nationwide Food Consumption Survey: an update on the nutrient intake of respondents. Nutr Today 1990;May/June:21–7.
4. U.S. Department of Health and Human Services. Federation of American Societies for Experimental Biology. Life Sciences Research Office. Nutrition monitoring in the United States—an update report on nutrition monitoring. NHANES II. PHS publication 89-1255. Hyattsville, MD: Public Health Service, 1989.
5. McDowell MA, Briefel RR, Alaimo K, et al. Energy and macronutrient intakes of persons ages 2 months and over in the United States. Third National Health and Nutrition Examination Survey, Phase 1, 1988–91. Advance Data 1994;255:1–24.
6. Webber LS, Srinivassan SR, Wattigney W, Berenson GS. Tracking of serum lipids and lipoproteins from childhood to adulthood—The Bogalusa Heart Study. Am J Epidemiol 1991;133:884–99.
7. Strasser T. Prevention in children of major cardiovascular disease of

adults. In: Falkner F, ed. Prevention in childhood of major cardiovascular disease in adults. Geneva: World Health Organization, 1980: 71–158.

8. Nicklas TA, Webber LS, Srinivassan SR, Berenson G. Secular trends in dietary intakes and cardiovascular risk factor of 10-year-old children: The Bogalusa Heart Study (1973–1988). Am J Clin Nutr 1993;57:930–7.

9. Nicklas TA, Stone E, Montgomery D, et al. Meeting the dietary goals for school meals by the year 2000: The CATCH Eat Smart School Nutrition Program. J Health Educ 1994;25:299–307.

10. Perry CL, Stone EJ, Parcel GS, et al. School-based cardiovascular health promotion: The Child and Adolescent Trial for Cardiovascular Health (CATCH). J Sch Health 1990;60:406–13.

11. Perry CL, Parcel GS, Stone EJ, et al. The Child and Adolescent Trial for Cardiovascular Health (CATCH): overview of the intervention program and evaluation methods. Cardiovasc Risk Factors 1992;2 (1): 36–44.

12. Zucker DM, Lakatos E, Webber LS, et al. Statistical design of the Child and Adolescent Trial for Cardiovascular Health (CATCH): implications of cluster randomization. Controlled Clin Trials 1995;16:96–118.

13. Webber LS, Osganian V, Luepker RV, et al. Cardiovascular risk factors among third grade children in four regions of the United States: the CATCH study. Am J Epidemiol 1995;141:428–39.

14. Pao EM, Fleming KH, Guenther PM, Mickle SJ. Foods commonly eaten by individuals: amount per day and per eating occasion. HERR No. 44. Hyattsville, MD: U.S. Department of Agriculture, Human Nutrition Information Service, 1982.

15. Lytle LA, Nichaman MZ, Obarzanek E, et al. Validation of 24-hour recalls assisted by food records in third-grade children. J Am Diet Assoc 1993;93:1431–6.

16. Ebzery MK, Montgomery DH, Evans MA, et al. School meal data collection and documentation methods in a multisite study. Sch Food Serv Res Rev 1996; in press.

17. Nicklas TA, Forcier JE, Webber LS, Berenson GS. School lunch assessment to improve accuracy of 24-hour dietary recall for children. J Am Diet Assoc 1991;91:711–3.

18. SAS Institute, Inc. SAS/STAT software: changes and enhancements, Release 6.07.SAS Technical Report P-229. Cary, NC: SAS Institute, 1992.

19. Devaney B, Gordon A, Burghardt J. The School Nutrition Dietary Assessment Study: dietary intakes of program participants and nonparticipants. Princeton, NJ: Mathematica Policy Research, 1993.

20. U.S. Department of Health and Human Services, Carroll MD, Abraham S, Dresser CM. Dietary intake source data: United States, 1971–1974 NHANES I. Vital and health statistics, Series 11, No. 231, PHS publication 83-1681. Hyattsville, MD: Public Health Service, 1983.

21. Thompson FE, Larkin FA, Brown MB. Weekend–weekday differences in reported dietary intakes: The Nationwide Food Consumption Survey, 1977–1978. Nutr Res 1986;6:647–62.

22. National Research Council. Diet and health: implications for reducing chronic disease risk. Washington, DC: National Academy Press, 1989.

23. U.S. Department of Health and Human Services. Nutrition and your health: Dietary Guidelines for Americans. 3rd Ed. HG Bulletin No. 232. Washington, DC: USDA, 1990.

24. Lytle LA, Eldridge A, Kotz K, Piper J, Williams S. Children's responses to dietary recommendations: a qualitative study. Final report to the Minnesota Department of Education, St. Paul, MN, July 1993.

25. Dennison BA. Screening for hyperlipidemia in children and adolescents. In: Filer JL Jr, Lauer RM, Luepker RV, eds. Prevention of atherosclerosis and hypertension beginning in youth. Philadelphia: Lea & Febiger, 1994: 73–87.

26. Alaimo K, McDowell MA, Briefel RR, et al. Dietary intake of vitamins, minerals, and fiber of persons ages 2 months and over in the United States: Third National Health and Nutrition Examination Survey, Phase 1, 1988–91. Advance Data 1994;258:1–28.

27. Crawford PB, Obarzanek E, Schreiber GB, et al. The effects of race, household income and parental education on nutrient intakes of 9- and 10-year-old girls: NHLBI Growth and Health Study. Ann Epidemiol 1995;5:360–8.

28. Beaton G, Milner J, Corey P, et al. Sources of variance in 24-hour dietary recall data: implications for nutrition study design and interpretation. Am J Clin Nutr 1979;32:2546–59.

29. Troccoli KB. Eat to learn, learn to eat: the link between nutrition and learning in children. National Health/Education Consortium Occasional Paper #7. National Commission to Prevent Infant Mortality, 1993.

 **Article Review Form at end of book.**

Describe the idea of the USDA's Team Nutrition Program.

# Let's Eat! What's for Lunch?

Kids spill the beans about their favorite school lunches . . .and some of their answers may surprise you.

## Jodie Shield, RD

*Jodie Shield, RD, of Kildeer, Illinois, encourages her three kids to eat—rather than trade—their school lunches.*

Last year my kids begged me to let them buy their lunch at school. After getting over my initial sense of rejection, I did a little research and agreed to give it a try. I was happy to learn that the National School Lunch Program (NSLP) had undergone a nutrition makeover and that "mystery" meat and other high-fat foods had been removed from the menu.

I also learned that a new federal program, the School Meals Initiative for Healthy Children, had been launched in the fall of 1996 and was largely responsible for these changes. The program mandates that schools participating in the NSLP follow standard nutritional guidelines and serve lunches that are consistent with the Dietary Guidelines for Americans.

In order to meet the guidelines, schools are required to:

- add more fruits, vegetables, and grains to their menus;

- create more-balanced menus, using foods from each of the five food groups;

- reduce fat content in lunches by using less beef, offering vegetarian entrees, and serving fewer fried foods;

- introduce more ethnic entrees to increase variety.

To help schools implement the initiative, the U.S. Department of Agriculture established a program called Team Nutrition, in which food-service professionals, registered dietitians, and other nutrition experts help schools revamp their school lunches by providing recipes, training, and assistance to food-service staff and nutrition education to students. More than 20,000 schools have already signed up with Team Nutrition, and more schools are likely to join as the program and grant monies are expanded.

Jim Cole, manager of economic research at the American School Food Service Association, says more students are now participating in the NSLP. First of all, kids are interested in eating healthier foods, such as the ever-popular salad bar, he says. Second, they enjoy having a wider variety of options available to them. And third, schools are finally serving foods that are popular with kids, such as pizza and tacos.

## Lunch: To Buy or to Bag?

Whether your child opts to buy his lunch or to take it, there's no question that noontime eating is important for kids. "Lunch helps supply up to one-third of the calories and nutrients children need to grow properly, and it may improve their concentration during the school day—and thus increase their ability to learn," according to Susan Baker, MD, FAAP, professor of pediatrics at the Medical

University of South Carolina, in Charleston.

If you're torn between letting your child brown-bag or purchase a school lunch, here are a few things to consider.

**With brown-bagging, you can:**

- Control the types of food provided. This is particularly helpful if your child has a food intolerance or allergy.

- Eliminate waste, because you're in charge of portion sizes.

- Cater to your child's individual likes and dislikes.

**With the school-lunch program, you can:**

- Avoid early morning hassles and delays about what to pack for lunch.

- Provide your child with more varied options, including foods that are difficult to pack.

- Potentially save money, because a school lunch is cost-effective.

## Think Before You Pack

Both school and brown-bag lunches have the potential to be nutritious. But a survey conducted for the Quaker Oats Company found that one out of four kids trades or throws away part of his lunch. To ensure that your child's lunch makes it into his stomach and not someone else's, try the following:

- Get a copy of the weekly school menus in advance, and go over the choices with your child.

- Volunteer to be a lunchroom helper, and see firsthand what your child is eating.

- Introduce yourself to the school food-service personnel, and share your thoughts about the school lunches.

- Invest in lunch equipment, such as insulated bags and thermoses.

- Get your kids actively involved with lunch planning, and let them pack their own lunch.

- Include treats like cookies, chips, and candy in your child's lunch occasionally. But be sure to pack a small amount; otherwise your child may fill up on the treats and skip the rest of his lunch.

- Slip something special in your child's lunch every now and then, such as a sticker, a family photo, or a cute handwritten note.

This school year my kids are going to enjoy the best of both worlds: a hot school lunch on mornings when we're pressed for time and a special homemade lunch when they need a little extra TLC.

 **Article Review Form at end of book.**

## The 4 HOTTEST School Lunches

According to the American School Food Service Association's online monthly survey, food-service directors throughout the country report their most popular selling lunches to be:

1 Pizza (It's so popular, it's almost as if there is no second or third place.)

2 Tacos

3 Chicken nuggets/patties

4 Hamburgers

Although these school lunches may sound like high-fat fast foods, they are healthier than typical fast-food options. Because of the new School Meals Initiative for Healthy Children, pizza and tacos are made with reduced-fat cheese. The chicken nuggets and patties are baked rather than fried. And the hamburgers are made with lean beef.

Did changes in the school lunch menu reduce the fat content yet maintain the caloric content in the foods served? Did nutrition knowledge, skills, and attitudes of students improve? Did the students' physical fitness improve?

# Reducing Elementary School Children's Risks for Chronic Diseases through School Lunch Modifications, Nutrition Education, and Physical Activity Interventions

Kari Jo Harris,[1] Adrienne Paine-Andrews,[1] Kimber P. Richter,[1] Rhonda K. Lewis,[1] Judy A. Johnston,[2] Vickie James,[2] Lori Henke,[2] and Stephen B. Fawcett[1]

[1]Department of Human Development and Family Life, University of Kansas, Lawrence, Kansas 66045; [2]Kansas LEAN, Wichita, Kansas, 67202

## Abstract

Many behaviors, such as physical inactivity or a poor diet, that put adults at risk for chronic diseases are established in childhood. This manuscript describes the outcomes of a comprehensive school health project, the Kansas LEAN School Intervention Project. The Kansas LEAN School Intervention Project in Salina and Dighton had four components, three of which were school based: (a) modified school lunches, (b) enhanced nutrition education, and (c) increased opportunities for physical activity. The fourth component, actions taken by a community partnership, is described elsewhere. Data from two case studies were used to address three primary evaluation questions: (a) did changes in the school lunch menu reduce the fat content yet maintain calories in meals served? (b) did nutrition knowledge, skills, and attitudes of students improve? and (c) did students' physical fitness improve? The findings suggest that the project was successful in reducing the fat content in school lunches in both communities from baseline levels of approximately 38% calories from fat to the target goal of 30% calories from fat during the 1993–94 school year. The schools also maintained adequate calories for students in this age group. Students' knowledge, skills, and behaviors related to nutrition as well as their physical fitness improved in both Kansas communities. The strengths and limitations of this strategy of making healthy choices easy choices through school-based intervention are discussed. (*JNE* 29: 196–202)

## Introduction

Heart disease is the leading cause of death in the United States.[1] Poor diets and physical inactivity, which are risk factors for cardiovascular diseases, are established early in life.[2-4] Research suggests that approximately 50% of children have at least one modifiable risk factor for coronary heart disease by age 12.[5] Schools are an important channel for prevention programs. Approximately 60% of school children in the U.S. participate in school lunch programs and these students receive more than one-third of the Recommended Dietary Allowances for food energy and key nutrients at school.[6] Schools also have the capacity to disseminate nutrition education and promote physical activity, reaching large numbers of children.

Several school- and community-based health initiatives have successfully reduced risk factors for chronic diseases among youth. These have used a variety of strategies, including modifying school lunches,[7-10] increasing physical activity,[9-12] providing nutritional education,[13-15] and implementing mass media campaigns.[14,16,17] Few studies, however, have examined the impact of multiple components of a school

intervention within the context of a community partnership to reduce risks for chronic diseases.

This paper describes the evaluation of three components of a comprehensive school health intervention designed to change the environment to affect health-related behavior and outcome by (1) modifying school lunches, (2) enhancing nutrition education, and (3) increasing opportunities for physical activity. Community changes introduced by establishing a community partnership to support the changes are described elsewhere.[18] First, we describe the context and collaborators of the project. Second, we describe the major components of the Kansas LEAN School Intervention Project. Third, we describe the measurement system and results for the key evaluation questions. Last, we discuss the challenges and opportunities of designing and evaluating comprehensive school interventions.

## Methods

Kansas LEAN,[19] a program of the Kansas Department of Health and Environment, Bureau of Chronic Disease and Health Promotion and the Kansas Health Foundation, designed and facilitated the implementation of the Kansas LEAN School Intervention Project. The Kansas Health Foundation provided funding over 2 years ago to design and pilot test the project. The Kansas LEAN Director, a registered dietitian, provided project oversight and direction. Two registered dietitians worked on site for approximately 20 to 30 hours per week assisting foodservice staff, classroom teachers, and physical education (PE) teachers in conducting nutritional analysis of menus, modifying menus, implementing

enhanced nutrition education in classrooms, and enhancing fitness activities. The Work Group on Health Promotion and Community Development at the University of Kansas (KU Work Group) provided technical assistance and evaluated the project.

## Communities and Schools

The communities of Salina and Dighton, and their respective school districts, agreed to implement the program. The two communities were selected to represent two different-sized communities and school districts in Kansas. Salina (population 42,300) is relatively urban with over 6000 students in 15 schools in the district. Cooks prepared school meals for the district in four centralized kitchens. By contrast, Dighton (population 1400) is a rural, geographically isolated community with an economy based on farming and ranching. The school district served 400 students and meals were prepared at one central kitchen. In Salina, all 4th graders in one elementary school (N = 74) received the intervention; 4th-grade students (N = 62) in two other schools in Salina served as a comparison group. In Dighton, all 5th graders (N = 34) participated in the intervention. Since there was only one elementary school in Dighton, a comparison group of 5th graders was not available. PE teachers in both schools, 4th-grade teachers in Salina, and 5th-grade teachers in Dighton agreed to participate in designing and implementing the project.

## School-Based Components

Table 1 outlines the three school-based components implemented by each community. The implementation of each component var-

| Table 1 | School-Based Components and Elements of the Kansas LEAN School Intervention Project to Reduce Children's Risks for Chronic Diseases. |
|---|---|

| Components | Elements |
|---|---|
| Modify school lunch | (a) Recording nutritional content of menu items (e.g., or measuring or weighting and recording ingredients) |
| | (b) Determining nutritional content of products (e.g., requesting dietary information from food vendors) |
| | (c) Receiving feedback (before and after modifications) on the percent calories from fat and calories in menu items and menu combinations |
| | (d) Modifying food preparation techniques (e, g., rinsing cooked ground beef in hot water before serving) |
| | (e) Modifying recipe ingredients (e.g., substituting nonfat yogurt for mayonnaise in salads, dips, dressings, and tarter sauce) |
| | (f) Modifying products ordered from vendors (e.g., lower fat fish sticks) |
| | (g) Changing menu combinations to reduce percent calories from fat in overall weekly menus |
| | (h) Locating or assisting vendors to develop new products (e. g., developing product with higher percentage of wheat flour) |
| Provide nutrition education | (a) Assisting teachers and administrators to integrate the American Cancer Society's Changing the Course (CTC) into health units or core subject (e.g., math, English) |
| | (b) Providing training for teachers on nutrition and using CTC (CTC included individual worksheets, food tasting, small-group activities, field trips, and class discussion) |
| | (c) Arranging for coordinators, community volunteers, or food service employees to serve as role models and provide general assistance |
| | (d) Facilitating field trips and special activities (e.g., supermarket tours, lunch at McDonald's) |
| | (e) Providing incentives for teachers to implement the curriculum (e.g., $100 for classroom materials) |
| Increase physical activity | (a) Installing physical fitness stations in each classroom, which consisted of individual workbooks (e.g., readings on fitness, songs about nutrition) and optional physical fitness activites (e.g., stretching, sitting, and reaching) |
| | (b) Initiating a noncompetitive incentive system based on students' personal goals (e.g., students earned class parties for using the fitness stations) |
| | (c) Training of PE teachers in how to increase the amount of time students engaged in cardiovascular fitness activities |
| | (d) Providing lesson plans for PE teachers with enhanced variety and intensity of physical activity (e.g., games, music, and dance) |

ied between the two communities and is briefly described below.

## School Lunch

Changing school lunches to reduce dietary fat while maintaining both adequate calories and food acceptability was one of the primary goals of this project. The director of Kansas LEAN and two on-site coordinators providing training, technical assistance, and direct support to foodservice professionals in the school districts. Coordinators used workshops, one-on-one training, coaching, and modeling to train foodservice workers. The training was informal and collaborative, and changes were made gradually as foodservice staff became comfortable with new food preparation techniques and products. Foodservice staff made many recommendations that were incorporated into routine kitchen practices. To maintain acceptability of the new foods served, potential food products and recipes were evaluated with food tasting panels consisting of students, parents, foodservice staff, and teachers.

The foodservice programs in Salina and Dighton differed in size, location, and experience of foodservice professionals. Assistance provided to the two programs differed to respond to the unique challenges and opportunities in each community. For example, training in Dighton focused on food preparation techniques to lower fat because nearly all menu items were prepared from scratch. By contrast, food served in the Salina district was purchased frozen from vendors, prepared in central kitchens, and delivered to school cafeterias. Accordingly, training in Salina focused on ordering from vendors and locating or assisting vendors in the development of new products.

## Nutrition Education

Project coordinators collaborated with elementary school teachers and school administrators to implement the American Cancer Society's (ACS) nutrition education program, *Changing the Course* (CTC).[20] The goals of the curriculum were for students to eat a variety of fruits and vegetables, more high-fiber foods, and fewer higher fat foods. The curriculum focused on teaching healthy food choices, rather than labeling food as "good" or "bad." The curriculum was behaviorally oriented and activity based. The ACS provided teachers with the CTC Upper Elementary curriculum and teachers' handbooks.

## Physical Activity

Each community enhanced opportunities for physical activity by installing classroom fitness stations and modifying PE classes to increase the proportion of time spent on cardiovascular fitness activities.

## Evaluating the School-Based Components of the Partnerships

Evaluators and project staff designed the evaluation system to examine outcomes of the project and to facilitate continuous improvements of the project's efforts. There were several key evaluation questions of interest to the staff and leadership of the community partnerships. Questions related to the school components included (a) did changes in the school lunch menu reduce the fat content and calories in food served? (b) did

nutrition knowledge, skills, and attitudes of students improve? and (c) did the physical fitness of students improve? To address these key questions, the evaluation system used three measurement instruments: (a) menu analysis, (b) a review of foodservice records, and (c) student surveys on nutrition and fitness. In addition, evaluators used a measure of community change[21] to track implementation of innovations in nutrition education, school lunch, and PE; community change data are reported elsewhere.[18] The measures, methods for data collection, feedback system, and statistical analysis are described in the sections below.

## Menu Analysis

School foodservice menus were analyzed using Nutritionist IV,[22] a computerized menu analysis program that used an extensive database of nutrients for specified foods. Menus were analyzed in several stages: (1) local foodservice employees recorded foods included in each recipe by weighing or measuring quantities, (2) the dietitian entering the data contacted local foodservice employees to clarify quantity or ingredient information, as necessary, (3) foods for each recipe were entered into Nutritionist IV, (4) printouts of the nutrients for each recipe and menu combinations were sent back to foodservice employees, (5) foodservice employees modified the menus to reduce dietary fat and maintain calories, and (6) steps 1 and 5 were repeated until percent of calories from fat and total fat were within target. Prepared products were entered into the database using manufacturer's nutritional analysis data. A registered dietitian conducted an analysis of recipes and menus for all menu

combinations during baseline (3 months in Dighton and 5 months in Salina) and after menu changes (7 months in Dighton and 8 months in Salina).

## Review of Foodservice Records

Archival records were reviewed, including school attendance, meals served in the lunch program, food costs, and personnel expenses. Where possible, data from the records were used to calculate the cost and percentage of students participating in the school lunch program.

## Student Surveys

Surveys were used to assess students knowledge, skills, and attitudes related to nutrition and students' physical fitness. Surveys were administered to students before and after the intervention was implemented. Paper and pencil assessments developed to accompany the CTC Lower (66-item) and Upper Elementary (53-item) curricula were used to assess the effectiveness of the nutrition education curriculum in Salina (Lower) and Dighton (Upper). Teachers administered the assessments, which took about 45 minutes to complete, during school hours. The assessment included items related to knowledge (e.g., "It is a good idea to eat a variety of foods each day"), skills (e.g., "Identify high fat foods"), and attitudes (e.g., "All people like the same food"). A formative evaluation of the CTC curriculum[23] reported that the test items were written at age-appropriate levels and that teachers were highly satisfied with the curriculum. Researchers who conducted this evaluation also used review of experts to establish that the assessment had high content validity and calculated Cronbach's alpha reliability coefficients, which were .79 and .92 on the upper and lower upper elementary assessment, respectively.[23]

The Amateur Athletic Union (AAU) physical fitness assessment[24] was used to assess the impact of increased opportunities for physical activity on students' fitness. Project staff and a fitness expert trained the PE teachers to administer the assessment, a behavioral observation designed to measure students' strength, muscular endurance, circulorespiratory endurance, and flexibility. Students demonstrated their fitness in five required events (such as pull-ups and endurance runs) and six to seven optional events (such as long jumps and sprints). Students' performance levels were categorized based on age and national AAU fitness standards.[24] Attainment and Outstanding levels from the AAU corresponded to the 45th and 80th percentile of sample scores.

### Feedback

The intervention model called for regular reports on all key measures, including (a) menu analyses; (b) students' nutrition knowledge, skills, and attitudes; and (c) students' fitness. Regular feedback on menu revisions was delayed until late in the project because of the amount of training involved in getting the menu reporting and data entry systems in place. Students' levels of nutrition knowledge, skills, and attitudes as well as fitness were graphed and fed back to project staff after assessments were administered.

### Design and Statistical Analysis.

An interrupted time-series analysis[25] was used to analyze data on nutritional content of menus over

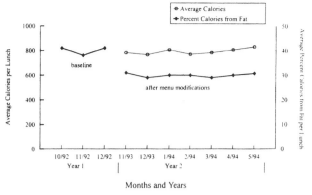

**Figure 1.** Trends in fat and calorie count in school lunches for Dighton.

time in Dighton and Salina. Individual level data on students' knowledge of nutrition and levels of physical fitness were assessed using pretest–post-test group designs[25] with a comparison school in Salina and replications of findings in Dighton. Statistical tests, performed using SPSS for Windows,[26] were used to conduct statistical analysis of individual level data. A two-tailed dependent t-test[27] was used to examine the differences before and after the intervention was implemented for (a) nutrition knowledge in Dighton and (b) a fitness indicator in Salina. Effect sizes were analyzed using the d statistic.[28] The McNemar Change Test[29] was used to test differences in fitness scores in Dighton. An f ratio[28] was used to analyze differences in nutrition knowledge between students who received the intervention and those who did not. An $R^2$ proportion was used to measure the strength of association between the variables.

## Results

This section describes the findings organized under several key evaluation questions about the school-based components of the partnerships.

## Did Changes in the School Lunch Menu Reduce the Fat Content and Maintain Calories in Foods Served?

After the intervention was implemented, the fat content of school lunches was reduced to target levels while maintaining or increasing total calories in both sites. Figure 1 shows daily average of calories and percent calories from fat in the school lunch menus served during the 1993–94 school year and percent calories from fat during baseline for the project in Dighton. Baseline levels of percent calories from fat were calculated using menu data from the first 3 months of the grant period (October–December 1992). Mean percent calories from fat fell from baseline levels of 40% to the target level of 30% during the 1993–94 school year. After menu modifications, total calories ranged from 767 kcal to 830 kcal, which is above the target level of 750 kcal.

Figure 2 shows trends in average daily caloric and fat content of the Salina school lunch program. Mean percent calories from fat decreased from baseline levels of 38% to the target level of 30% after menus were modified. Mean calories per month increased from baseline levels of 738 kcal to 821

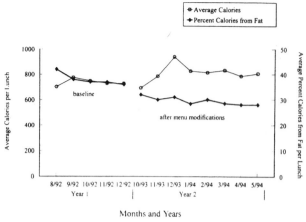

**Figure 2.** Trends in fat and calorie count in school lunches for Salina.

kcal in the second year of the project.

Reviews of foodservice records showed that participation in the school lunch program remained relatively constant in the two communities as the menus changed. The accounting system in Salina did not separate expenses in a way that allowed researchers to calculate the cost per meal. Data on the cost of the lunch program were available for Dighton and showed that the cost increased less than 5%. This may be due to economic inflation and an increased number of portions consumed by each student (e.g., more students going back for "seconds"), and not to higher costs of lower fat menus.

## Did Nutrition Knowledge, Skills, and Attitudes of Students Improve?

The percentage of youth who answered the nutrition knowledge, skills, and attitude questions correctly or favorably increased significantly from pretest to post-test in Dighton. In Salina, intervention students' scores were significantly higher when compared to students who did not receive the curriculum in Salina. In

Dighton, intervention students' performance on the Upper Elementary Assessment increased from pretest (71%) to post-test (84%), and the increase was maintained at a 1-year follow-up (83%). Changes from pretest to post-test were statistically significant (t[33] = –6.64, p < .0001) with a very large effect size (d statistic = 6.9). These findings were replicated with 5th graders receiving the same curriculum in the following year; their knowledge increased from pretest (68%) to post-test (83%). In addition, the lower performance scores (66%) of 5th graders (who had not received the curriculum) at the end of the previous year suggested that the findings were due to the curriculum rather than maturation.

Fourth-grade students who received nutrition education in Salina scored higher at post-test on the Lower Elementary Assessment (82%) than students who did not receive the enhanced nutrition education (74% and 72%). Difference between these scores is statistically significant (F[2,133] = 20.179, p <.0001) with a large proportion of variability due to differences between groups (R² = .2328).

## Did Youth Physical Fitness Improve?

Analysis of the fitness data suggests that fitness levels of the intervention students increased from pretest to post-test and, in Salina, intervention students were more fit than similar students who did not participate in the project. The percentage of Dighton students experiencing the intervention who performed at or above the AAU Fitness Attainment level increased from pretest (18%) to post-test (29%). These differences, however, were not statistically significant (p = .29). The small number of intervention students may not have provided enough power to detect any potential statistical significance.

The AAU Fitness Assessment was modified slightly in Salina. In the "Endurance Run" event, students ran 1 mile rather than the standard ¾ of a mile. Overall performance awards, therefore, could not be determined for students in Salina. The endurance run event was selected for analysis because it is a measure of circulorespiratory endurance and is the event that is most closely linked to reduced risks of cardiovascular diseases. In Salina, compared to same-grade students in comparison schools, intervention students showed a larger reduction in the amount of time taken to complete the mile run from pretest to post-test. Girls in the intervention group reduced their average time by 1.21 minutes while girls in the comparison group reduced their average time by only 0.32 minutes. Boys in the intervention group reduced their average time by 1.76 minutes while boys in the comparison group reduced their average time by 0.64 minutes. The differences between comparison and intervention students' performance changes from pretest to post-test were statistically significant for both girls (t[48] = 2.60, p = 0.12) and boys (t[59] = 2.19, p = .033).

## Discussion

This manuscript describes two case studies of the school-based components of the Kansas LEAN School Health Project. The results suggest that the projects in Salina and Dighton facilitated important changes in the school to reduce youth risks for chronic diseases. Each community facilitated changes of the school lunch menus, including adopting new food products, revising recipes, and developing new menus. These changes resulted in reduced fat and maintained calories in school lunch menus without negatively influencing costs or participation. Further, nutrition knowledge, skills, and attitudes as well as physical fitness improved among participating students in both schools.

There were several challenges to evaluating the school-based components of these partnerships. First, without randomized control groups, conclusions about the strength of the intervention's effects are limited. Other events, such as the national interest in diet and exercise, could have contributed to the effects. However, attempts were made to control for such confounding variables, such as using comparison schools in Salina and comparison groups in Dighton, for the nutrition education and fitness assessments. No data from control or comparison groups were available for changes in the school lunches. Although comparison groups would have helped rule out other possible explanations of the observed effects, establishing a con-

trol group was not seen as feasible given the complexity of conducting nutrient analysis.

Second, a strength of the AAU Physical Fitness Assessment is the reliance on direct observation of students' fitness rather than self-reports. However, one drawback is that students may not consistently perform to the best of their ability in single assessments may not accurately assess their fitness. The assessment is time consuming, prohibiting multiple administration in this community demonstration.

Third, this study assessed changes in students' knowledge, skills, and behavior related to nutrition using assessments developed and tested by other researchers. Since the assessments were not pilot tested locally, our understanding of the findings may be limited. In addition, to maintain consistency across multiple testing of intervention students in Salina, the Lower Elementary assessment was used to assess 4th graders, who were beyond the recommended age range for this assessment.

Fourth, the accuracy of the nutritional analysis was not systematically verified by laboratory studies. Further, the measurement system was intentionally reactive: documenting the fat content of foods served was intended to draw attention to foods' nutritional content and prompt kitchen staff to modify menus. In addition, as a result of multiple computer-related problems, summarized nutrition information was not available to project staff until after the project was completed; foodservice staff made menu and recipe revisions without complete and ongoing information on the fat content of menus. Overall, however, nutrient analysis data collected over a 2-

year period strongly suggest that the project successfully met its goals for revisions in school lunches. Finally, data on the actual consumption of school lunches are not available. Plate waste studies were attempted but abandoned due to large variability in consumption and a lack of staff time and resources to conduct frequent plate waste studies. However, taste testing and sampling were conducted with students and foodservice staff to help assess the palatability and the likelihood of consumption of the school lunches.

Despite these limitations, the findings from this multiple case study contribute substantially to our understanding of nutrition, education, physical activity opportunities, and changes in food served during school lunch to reduce children's risks for chronic diseases. The data suggest that the major components of the intervention were implemented, and positive changes in nutrition knowledge and physical fitness were found among participants. Further, increasing opportunities for healthier school lunches increases the likelihood that children might consume fewer calories from fat when in school.

Future research is warranted to extend understanding about and improve methods for reducing children's risks for chronic diseases. First, future research should attempt to identify comparison communities. Second, future research should attempt multiple assessments of physical fitness and food consumption. The Kansas LEAN School Intervention Project is being replicated in six communities in Kansas. These applications of the school and community components should help to extend our understanding of the strengths and challenges of such interventions that have the mission of reducing risks for chronic diseases among children.

The overarching strategy of the Kansas LEAN School Intervention Project is to change the environmental context for children's health-related behaviors. By modifying school lunches, the opportunities for selecting (and potentially eating) lower fat foods is enhanced. By enhancing students' knowledge and skills through behaviorally based nutrition education, selections of healthy food choices may be improved. By increasing opportunities for school-linked physical activity, children are more likely to engage in those behaviors associated with fitness. Rather than blame children (or their parents or teachers) for engaging in health risks, this approach demonstrates how environmental changes may improve health behavior. In so doing, it illustrates a fundamental tenant of public health: make healthy choices easy choices.

## Acknowledgments

This project was made possible by the concern and effort of people in the communities of Dighton and Salina, Kansas. Teachers, administrators, foodservice personnel in Dighton and Salina Unified School Districts, and youth and parents were instrumental in making this project a success.

## References

1. Rosenberg HM, Ventura SJ, Maurer JD, Heuser RL, Freedman MA. Births and deaths: United States, 1995. Monthly Vital Statistics Report, Hyattsville, MD: National Center for Health Statistics, 1996:45(3) Suppl 2.
2. Jenkins CD. Epidemiology of cardiovascular diseases. J Consult Clin Psychol 1988;56:324–32.
3. Blackburn H. Population strategies of cardiovascular disease prevention: scientific base, rationale and public health implications. Ann Med 1989; 21:157–62.
4. Newman WP III, Freedman DS, Voors AW, et al. Relation of serum lipoprotein levels and systolic blood pressure to early atherosclerosis. N Engl J Med 1986; 314:138–44.
5. Williams CL, Carter BJ, Wynder EL. Prevalence of selected cardiovascular and cancer risk factors in a pediatric population: The "Know Your Body" Project, New York, Prev Med 1981; 10:235–50.
6. Burghardt J, Gordon A, Chapman N, Gleason P, Fraker T. The school nutrition dietary assessment study: school food service, meals offered, and dietary intakes. Alexandria, VA: Department of Agriculture, 1993.
7. Ellison CR, Capper AL, Goldberg RJ, Witschi JC, Stare IJ. The environmental component: changing school food service to promote cardiovascular health. Health Educ Q 1989;16:285–97.
8. Hunter SM, Johnson CC, Little-Christian SS, et al. Heart Smart: a multifaceted cardiovascular risk reduction program for grade school students. Am J Health Promotion 1990;4:352–60.
9. Perry CL, Klepp KI, Shultz JM. Primary prevention of cardiovascular disease: community-wide strategies for youth. J Consult Clin Psychol 1988;56:358–64.
10. Simons-Morton B, Parcel GS, O'Hara NM. Implementing organizational changes to promote healthful diet and physical activity at school. Health Educ Q 1988; 15:115–30.
11. Killen JD, Robinson TN, Telch MJ, et al. The Stanford Adolescent Heart Health Program. Health Educ Q 1989;16:263–82.
12. Parcel GS, Simons-Morton B, O'Hara NM, Baranowski T, Wilson B. School promotion of healthful diet and physical activity: impact on learning outcomes and self-reported behavior. Health Educ Q 1989;16:181–99.
13. Crow R, Blackburn H, Jacobs DR, et al. Population strategies to enhance physical activity: The Minnesota Heart Health Program. Acta Med Scand 1986;711:93–112.
14. King AC, Saylor KE, Foster S, et al. Promoting dietary change in adolescents: a school-based approach for modifying and maintaining healthful behavior. Am J Prev Med 1988;4:68–74.
15. Perry CL, Mullis RM, Maile MC. Modifying the eating behavior of young children. J Sch Health 1985;55:399–402.

 **Article Review Form at end of book.**

# WiseGuide Wrap-Up

- Although a pregnant woman is eating for two, her energy intake need not increase during the first trimester. Daily caloric consumption should increase by about 300 kilocalories for the final two trimesters of pregnancy.

- Folate (one of the B-complex vitamins) plays a crucial role in DNA synthesis, metabolism of various amino acids, and cell division. Deficient folate intake by a pregnant woman increases the likelihood for neural tube defects in the child.

- Excess body weight is becoming more prevalent among our nation's youth. This phenomenon is most likely due to a lack of physical activity.

- Diet inadequacies during childhood may lead to growth retardation, increased risk of heart disease, dental caries, overweightness, iron deficiency anemia, and increased susceptibility to infections.

## R.E.A.L. Sites

This list provides a print preview of typical **coursewise** R.E.A.L. sites. (There are over 100 such sites at the **courselinks**™ site.) The danger in printing URLs is that web sites can change overnight. As we went to press, these sites were functional using the URLs provided. If you come across one that isn't, please let us know via email to: webmaster@coursewise.com. Use your Passport to access the most current list of R.E.A.L. sites at the **courselinks**™ site.

**Site name:** Baylor College of Medicine Children's Nutrition Research Center

**URL:** http://www.bcm.tmc.edu/cnrc/

**Why is it R.E.A.L.?** Easy links to additional sites of interest. The page also explains the latest research being done at the center.

**Activities:** Review a recent issue of the center's newsletter. Summarize your findings and present them to the class.

**Site name:** Nutrition During Pregnancy and Lactation

**URL:** http://www.public.health.wa.gov.au/hp3056.htm

**Why is it R.E.A.L.?** The Health Department of Western Australia home page allows for easy access to information regarding weight gain, pregnancy planning, morning sickness, caffeine use, and the "Golden Rules" during pregnancy.

**Activities:** Summarize the nutrients that are needed in larger amounts during pregnancy. What are appropriate food sources for these nutrients?

**Site name:** New York Online Access to Health

**URL:** http://www.noah.cuny.edu/pregnancy/march_of_dimes/pre_preg.plan/eatingis.html

**Why is it R.E.A.L.?** The March of Dimes explains the role of nutrition during pregnancy and addresses issues, including weight gain for the woman, guidelines for food choices, and substances to avoid.

**Activities:** (1)Describe how much weight a woman should gain during pregnancy. (2)Elucidate guidelines for daily food choices during pregnancy.

**Site name:** Information for Women Who Are Pregnant

**URL:** http://vm.cfsan.fda.gov/~dms/wh-preg.html

**Why it is R.E.A.L.?** This page has valid information and allows you to easily select articles that cover all aspects of nutrition during pregnancy.

**Activities:** (1)How does folate play a role in reducing the likelihood of neural tube defects? (2)What form of vitamin A acts as a teratogen (an agent associated with causing birth defects) if it is consumed in excess?

# section 3

## Learning Objectives

After studying this section, you will know:

- who should carbohydrate load and the positive merits of this.

- the importance of hydration for athletes.

- sound strategies for designing a diet for athletes.

- that some sports-nutrition myths have become sports-nutrition gospel.

- that athletes who consume excessive amounts of carbohydrates may fall below recommended amounts for other nutrients.

- the principal causes of overweightness.

- sound activity and diet choices for weight loss and management.

- possible consequences of overweightness.

# Nutrition Challenges for Adults on the Go
## Sports Nutrition and Weight Management

 **WiseGuide Intro**

Possibly due to pressure for success (winning, scholarships, a new multiyear contract), athletes will pursue just about any avenue to enhance performance. A change in training, a technique modification, a new game strategy, a mental image of success, and diet modifications are a few of the steps which may be of help to the athlete.

However, there is no single diet to enhance athletes' performances. Different sports, different athletes necessitate individualizing one's diet. Regardless of the sport or the athlete, sound fundamental diet strategies must be followed.

Several years ago, a very successful university track and field coach insisted that his athletes' pre-meet meals consist of the largest plate of mashed potatoes they could consume. These potatoes, however, were bathed with honey! Mashed potatoes and honey! Why might this be successful? The potatoes would be a great source of complex carbohydrate (starch); thus, these athletes were carbohydrate loading. Complex carbohydrate is often recommended, particularly for endurance athletes. The honey (simple carbohydrate) would have a quick, yet short-acting effect on one's blood glucose. The coach felt strongly about this practice. Physiologically, did it help? Possibly some of the athletes would benefit from this (10,000 meter run), but certainly not all (shot put). However, if the coach were able to convince the athletes that this concoction would help their performance, it likely did just that! (By the way, mashed potatoes and honey are actually pretty tasty together!) Carbohydrate loading may have merit for individuals who compete in activities which last longer than one hour. Sports of shorter duration require nothing more than a well-balanced diet, with about 60 percent of the calories coming from carbohydrate (7 gm carbohydrate per kg of body weight).

The majority of research indicates that active individuals, including competitive athletes, should simply consume a diet which is prudent even for a sedentary person. Proper nutrition for athletes is sound nutrition for all, the possible exception to this similarity being that athletes are likely to consume more of the same foods to maintain (or increase) body weight during training.

This concept may be a "tough pill to swallow" for athletes. Consider the variety of nutrition centers with advertised supplements to improve your golf game, gain muscle, feel better, etc. But the fact of the issue is that, by eating a wide variety of foods, and by being cognizant of caloric balance, athletes will be well on their way to optimizing their performance. The best source of all the nutrients essential to human performance is not a convenient supplement but, rather food.

It is estimated, that 30 percent of all Americans are overweight. Concomitantly, the number of dollars spent on weight-loss products and procedures is climbing. For the consumer, unfortunately, many of these services are not successful in the long term (low-calorie dieting has a two-year success rate of 2 to 5 percent.

Pills, diets, creams, and surgeries are some of the techniques Americans use in an attempt to lose unwanted pounds. Regardless of the lifestyle incorporated for weight management, the body must experience a relative decrease in energy intake and a relative increase in energy output. Moreover, these lifestyle changes should not occur abruptly. Consider that it may have taken several years for an individual to become overweight. Similarly, it may take a long time of appropriate nutrition and exercise to manage one's weight.

## Questions

R14. Describe the concept of carbohydrate loading.

R15. How might eating red meat, which contains little, if any, carbohydrate, once or twice a week improve endurance performance?

R16. According to Judy Nelson, the nutrition coordinator for the U.S. Olympic Committee, how much protein do athletes in training need? Is she an advocate for vitamins, minerals, herbs, and other ergogenic (energy-yielding) aids? Why or why not? Describe Mujaahid Maynard's strategy to lose weight. How might this routine affect his performance?

R17. The article describes a weight-loss study in which volunteers were placed in one of three groups: diet only, exercise only, or a combination of diet and exercise. Which one was most successful in the long term? What might be other benefits of exercise?

Describe the concept of carbohydrate loading.

# Are You Going To Swallow That?

Somewhere along the line, certain sports-nutrition myths have become sports-nutrition gospel. Here, the truth about eating right for exercise.

## Julie Walsh

*Freelance writer Julie Walsh is a registered dietitian who covers sports and nutrition issues.*

When it comes to sports nutrition, everyone is an expert. But don't be too quick to take just anybody's advice on the subject. Much of what you hear—from trainers, workout partners and many top athletes—is based on anecdotal information or half-truths rather than sound scientific research. To set the record straight, *Women's Sports + Fitness* asked some leading sports nutritionists to put six locker-room myths to rest.

## Myth No. 1: *Thinner is better.*

Although body weight does affect performance, percentage of body fat affects it more. Some athletic women may not like what the bathroom scale says, even though their body fat is plenty low; that's because muscle weighs a lot more than fat. For women, a healthy range of body fat is considered to be 18 to 25 percent.

Many athletes—particularly runners, gymnasts and body-builders—have a much lower percentage, but this can lead to serious medical problems. Once their body fat drops below 17 percent, women experience a greater incidence of halted or erratic periods, which can lead to permanent bone loss and other problems. Regardless of what activities you participate in, there's an optimal level of body fat *for you*, and trying to become any leaner than that will provide no additional benefits.

"Starving yourself to maintain a weight you or your coach thinks is ideal can backfire," explains Ellen Coleman, M.P.H., R.D., a nutrition consultant at the SportClinic in Riverside, California. "When you get thinner than your body wants to be, you lose muscle mass and disrupt estrogen levels, which eventually weakens your bones. Injuries and colds and other illnesses may result." Sports nutritionist Jackie Berning, Ph.D., R.D., who works with U.S. Swimming, agrees. "I've seen athletes lose five to ten pounds and suffer in terms of performance. They were tired and lacked the energy and stamina to train effectively."

## Myth No. 2: *Vitamins provide energy.*

It's estimated that more than 80 percent of all athletes pop nutritional supplements on a regular basis. Why? "For all the wrong reasons," Coleman says. Many active women think that vitamins enhance energy or that exercise increases their need for particular vitamins or minerals. The truth is, vitamins help the body process fuel, but they don't *provide* energy in any way. Only nutrients that furnish calories (carbohydrates, protein and fat) supply energy. And athletes' vitamin requirements aren't significantly higher than sedentary individuals'. A healthy, well-balanced diet will provide you with all the vitamins and minerals you need.

Many athletes, however—especially those who shun meat, poultry, fish and dairy products—tend to be short on certain vitamins and minerals, including calcium, iron, magnesium and zinc. If you adhere to a vegetarian diet or don't eat well-balanced meals most of the time, a multivitamin-and-mineral supplement can act as nutritional insurance. Remember, megadoses aren't nec-

Food Facts

## The Truth About Pasta

Pasta and other starchy carbohydrates are to endurance athletes as gasoline is to an automobile. Just as a car can't go anywhere without gas, an athlete won't be able to perform optimally without carbs. At least that's what the experts have always said—but lately some people are uttering words to the contrary.

Several months ago, an article published in *The New York Times* declared that pasta makes people fat. It went on to explain that one-quarter of all Americans are "insulin resistant," a term meaning that they cannot easily process the sugar in carbohydrates. As a result, some of the sugar is stored as fat, which increases insulin-resistance and leads to weight gain. More recently, Barry Sears, Ph.D., a former MIT researcher, argued in his book *The Zone* (HarperCollins, 1995) that a high-carbohydrate diet can actually impair athletic performance. He too thinks that carbs can cause weight gain.

So are we to believe that pasta, the ubiquitous training food, is bad for us? It's worth noting that the response of the nutrition experts to the *Times* article was so acrimonious that the paper printed a retraction of sorts, conceding that the article had been misleading and that many people succeed in losing weight on a high-carbohydrate diet. As for Sears' theories, "I don't think you'll find a lot of scientific support for what he has to say," comments Nancy Clark, M.S., R.D., the director of nutrition at SportsMedicine Brookline in Brookline, Massachusetts. "Muscles *need* carbohydrates for optimal performance."

Certainly anyone who eats vats of pasta—or of any food for that matter—will probably gain weight; carbohydrates contain calories (four per gram), and they add up. But a high-carbohydrate diet with a moderate calorie count shouldn't do you in. Even if you're insulin-resistant, says Clark, a diet that's 60 percent carbohydrates, 15 percent protein and 25 percent fat is still your best bet.

—Janet Lee

essary (or, in some cases, even safe), and supplements shouldn't take the place of healthy eating.

## Myth No. 3: Carbo-loading means a pre-competition pasta dinner.

Carbohydrate-loading is a technique that tricks your muscles and liver into overstuffing themselves with carbohydrates (in the form of glycogen), so that you'll have more fuel available during an endurance event. If your idea of applying this method is pigging out on high-carb foods the evening before a race, you may wind up feeling bloated and sick when it's time to compete. Effective use of this technique involves a weeklong, two-phase regimen of tapered-off exercise and increased carbohydrate intake. To really do it right, ask a registered dietitian who specializes in sports nutrition to help you plan a diet and training schedule.

When your goal is simply to make the most of your diet the day before an endurance endeavor, Coleman suggests substituting five to six small, carbohydrate-rich meals for your usual fare. "You'll be likely to get more carbohydrates into your body with several small meals," she explains. At dinner, don't stuff yourself; instead, eat a generous portion of pasta or another high-carb entree, then have a light snack before bedtime. You should also get into the habit of eating a good meal a few hours before the gun goes off.

## Myth No. 4: If you exercise enough, you can eat whatever you want.

Although regular exercise enables you to take in more calories without gaining weight than you would otherwise, it's still fairly easy for even active women to put on body fat. And if you don't eat a well-balanced diet, you may lack the energy you need to keep active.

Fat- and sugar-rich foods like ice cream, cake and cookies can be a problem because they're calorie-heavy and easy to binge on, so that you can find yourself downing hundreds of calories in no time at all. To burn off the 750 calories in a cup and a half of super-premium ice cream, you'd have to do intensive exercise like running or cycling for an hour or more. A training diet should emphasize the complex carbohydrates found in fruits, vegetables and grain-based foods, as well as lean meat and low-fat dairy products.

## Myth No. 5: Caffeinated and alcoholic beverages cause dehydration.

True, caffeine and alcohol are both mild diuretics that stimulate the kidneys to excrete fluid. But this doesn't mean that drinking a can of Coke or beer will cause you to lose more liquid than you consume. If your body needs fluid, it will retain some of whatever you drink.

Although it's best to concentrate on water and other non-caffeinated and nonalcoholic beverages, an occasional alcoholic drink is okay and a cup or two of coffee in the morning isn't going to harm you.

## Myth No. 6: *Dietary fat should be avoided like the plague.*

By now it seems fairly clear that fat in the diet can lead to heart disease and certain cancers. But athletes shouldn't eschew fat altogether. Your body must have a certain amount of it (10 to 15 percent of total calories) to get the essential fatty acids that aid in synthesizing hormones, maintaining the immune system, and absorbing vitamins A, D, E and K, plus beta carotene. A meal containing some fat will also make you feel fuller than a carbs-only meal.

Of course, some fats are better for you than others, says Kristine Clark, Ph.D., R.D., director of sports nutrition at Penn State University. Limit your intake of saturated fats (the kind that raise blood cholesterol) to less than 10 percent of your total calories per day.

 **Article Review Form at end of book.**

How might eating red meat, which contains little, if any, carbohydrate, once or twice a week improve endurance performance?

# Fuel for the Flame

Do Olympic athletes live on pasta? Steaks? Protein shakes? Here, the inside nutrition story.

## Julie Walsh

*Julie Walsh, M.S., R.D., writes frequently about nutrition for WS+F.*

Recently we asked gold-medal hopefuls to give us the dish. "So," we said expectantly, "tried any special superpower diets lately? Any hot new nutrition trends you care to share with us non-Olympic athletes?"

The answers were surprising: There wasn't a single report of wacky, extreme or outrageously alternative eating behavior in the lot. "That's because the hottest new dietary trend is . . . no trend at all," says Ann C. Grandjean, Ed.D., R.D., the director of the International Center for Sports Nutrition and a consultant to many national teams. "Olympic athletes tend not to do trends; it's one of the things that separate them from other athletes. Their diets generally contain adequate carbohydrates and calories and are fairly well balanced."

Okay, but they must be doing something to ensure that they're appropriately fueled for action come the Games. Turns out that many competitors have had to tweak their eating and hydrating

habits a bit to prepare for Atlanta. Here's the scoop on what's on their training tables, plus a few dietary tidbits from some of American's top contenders.

## U.S. Soccer's Slip-Up

Until recently, some members of the U.S. Women's Soccer Team have had a little problem: too many carbohydrates and not enough protein in their diets. According to Kris Clark, Ph.D., R.D., a nutritional consultant to the Olympic soccer and field-hockey teams, several of the athletes were taking the high-carb message to extremes and getting 70 percent or more of their calories from pasta, bagels and other starches. As a result, they were falling below the RDA for protein and other micronutrients. "Meat and other protein foods are not only good sources of iron," Clark points out, "but also providers of B-complex vitamins, manganese and zinc."

The benefits of those vitamins and minerals range from anemia prevention and improved energy metabolism to proper immune-system function. (For instance, some research has linked

athletes' zinc-deficient diets with an increased risk of injury. Although nobody really knows why, it may have something to do with the role zinc plays in the repair and healing process.) In addition, protein is essential to the building and repair of muscle tissue—a message that the team, says member Julie Foudy, has taken to heart. "Clark made us realize that protein is the most important nutrient for our muscles. So a lot of us are eating more lean meat, chicken, fish or eggs and drinking more milk."

## The Two-and-a-Half-Hour Rule

Gymnasts didn't used to be known as chowhounds, but that was before the two-and-a-half-hour rule. This "law," laid down by Dan Benardot, Ph.D., R.D., the National Team nutritionist for USA Gymnastics, stipulates that all members of the team should eat something—it can be a snack or a very small meal—every two-and-a-half to three hours, from the time they wake up to the time they go to bed. (The U.S. Track and Field athletes have been advised to eat small, frequent meals too.)

"Fuel for the flame" by Julie Walsh from WOMEN'S SPORTS AND FITNESS, July/August 1996. Reprinted by permission.

The only off-limits edibles on the gymnasts' list are fried foods, processed meats such as bologna and salami, and fats like margarine, butter and oil if they aren't already cooked into food. Consuming small quantities of food throughout the day, Benardot reasons, helps the athletes keep their energy up. It also tends to boost their metabolic rates so that they can eat more—and, not coincidentally, get in more vitamins, minerals and fiber—while maintaining the same low level of body fat.

## Battling Dehydration

One of the biggest challenges competitors will face in Atlanta is keeping hydrated in the midst of all that heat and humidity. "It's a major concern for all the athletes, whether they compete indoors or outdoors, or in short or long events," says Judy Nelson, M.S., who's the U.S. Olympic Committee's nutrition coordinator and who, along with other experts at the USOC, developed a 14-minute video on hydration that's been made available to all U.S. Olympic athletes.

The makers of PowerAde, the official sports drink of the Olympic Games, have also created a video (as well as print literature) on dehydration prevention.

Although competitors can bring their own drinks to the Games, the terms of sponsorship make it certain that PowerAde will be the only sports beverage served at Olympic venues or "officially" allowed in the dining hall.

In the meantime, plenty of athletes are trying to develop good imbibing habits. Gymnasts aren't considered "dressed" for practice or competition unless they have a full water bottle in hand. Kris Clark has instructed the soccer and field-hockey team members to drink 64 ounces of water daily, at least 32 ounces before noon and 32 before lights-out—and that's not including all the other fluids they may guzzle on or off the field. "Sixty-four ounces is a goal that they can remember," Clark says, "and it forces them to carry water with them to sip on all day long." Drinking that much, though, can be a challenge. "Since I'm not a big water-drinker, it's one of the hardest things for me to do," admits Foudy. "I was feeling bloated all the time at first, but it's getting easier now. And I know it will make a difference in Atlanta."

## Who's Eating What

What other goals have Olympic athletes set for themselves? Ruthie Matthes, at press time a top con-

tender for a spot on the U.S. Mountain Biking squad, has been trying to pay closer attention to what she eats away from home so that she can achieve a lighter race weight. If she makes it to the Games, she'll be packing dried pineapple and plenty of Malt-Nut PowerBars.

Besides upping their protein intake, members of U.S. Women's Soccer are trying to get through at least five servings of vegetables and four servings of fruit a day. "After just a couple of weeks, we already feel better and have more energy," Foudy reports. Swimmer Janet Evans has also made some crucial adjustments in her diet. "A year ago I had no energy, and my swimming was pathetic," she recalls. "I later found out that I was severely anemic. I hadn't been eating any red meat because I thought it was bad for athletes. Since then I've had steak or a hamburger twice a week. Now my iron levels are fine, and I have more energy." Also on her to-do nutrition list: Stay away from too many sweets, and keep hydrating. Now those are guidelines that even those of us without a ticket to Atlanta would be wise to follow.

 **Article Review Form at end of book.**

According to Judy Nelson, the nutrition coordinator for the U.S. Olympic Committee, how much protein do athletes in training need? Is she an advocate for vitamins, minerals, herbs, and other ergogenic (energy-yielding) aids? Why or why not? Describe Mujaahid Maynard's strategy to lose weight. How might this routine affect his performance?

# The Chow of Champions

For Olympians on the fast track, fast food is just a fond memory. Setting the training table is no longer a picnic but a fiercely disciplined science. Sports nutrition is more complex than when Korbut fueled on caviar.

The Olympic year was 1968; the place, Mexico City. On the night before opening ceremonies—the eve of perhaps the most important two weeks in his life—U.S. high jumper, Dick Fosbury, 21, was, frankly, partying. In fact, partying hard with two teammates, javelin thrower Gary Stenlund and swimmer Cynthia Goyette, plus pal Donna De Varona (a swimming gold medalist in '64 turned ABC sports announcer). The four hopped into Stenlund's VW bus and made their way out of the city to the ancient pyramids of Teotihuacán guided by the glow of the Olympic torch, enthroned there for its dramatic descent to the stadium the next morning. "We stayed out there all night," recalls Fosbury. "People were cooking soup over campfires and yelling, 'Hey, Gringo! Come have some soup!' We shared their food and drank beer and crashed out in the van or slept in the pyramids— I don't really remember. The next morning, we got caught in this in-

credible traffic jam and missed the opening ceremony. But that night at the pyramids, I'll always remember it. It was wonderful."

Back then, the Olympics really were anything-goes *games* rather than winning-is-the-only-thing *game plans* with seven-figure commercial contracts at stake. Wine and Mexican beer were on tap in the Olympic Village (alcohol is not served there any longer), and despite his night of carousing, Fosbury went on to take the gold. But today eating, like every other aspect of preparation, requires phenomenal dedication. Many U.S. teams and even some individual athletes have their own nutritionists.

Dominique Moceanu, 14, a California-born daughter of Rumanian immigrants, is mending from a mid-June stress fracture of her leg but still hopes to fulfill the great expectations predicted for her: America's first gymnastics gold since Mary Lou Retton in '84. She works uncom-

plainingly under the rigid eight-hour-a-day regimen of Bela Karolyi, 53, who trained Retton and (before coming over from Rumania himself) Nadia Comaneci. On the day of a competition, Karolyi allows his entrants a lunch of a four-ounce chicken breast and half cups of steamed broccoli and white rice—spartan gruel compared with the caviar (preferably red) Olga Korbut stoked up on in the early '70s. "This was a Russian trade secret," says Korbut. "Caviar is very high protein. Every morning, I ate a big bowl of it, lots and lots of caviar." But her coach, Renald Kynch, did put her on a one-step program to kick another craving. One day, he presented her with a huge cake and told her to eat that—and nothing else—for the next three days. The reprogramming worked—it was years before Korbut could even nibble cake again.

At the other end of the scale, weightlifter Mark Henry, of Silsbee, Texas, has been under the expert supervision since high school of two kinesiology professors from the University of Texas at Austin: Terry Todd, 58, a national weightlifting champ in the '60s, and his wife, Jan Todd, 44, a

## Moceanu's Morsels

Having trained most of her life, Dominique Moceanu says she hasn't developed standard teenage food cravings, although every few months she might indulge in pizza or a Snickers. Her daily diet, roughly 1,300 calories, begins with a fruit muffin. She generally lunches on grilled chicken breast, steamed veggies (with a dollop of ketchup), rice, fruit, o.j. and lots of water. Dinner is usually two cups of cereal (Apple Jacks or Corn Pops) and 2 percent milk. Fruit suffices for snacks. For her birthday, Mom bakes a special treat: chocolate marble cake with strawberries.

## Oh, Henry!

Mark Henry's daily diet in Texas—more than 5,000 calories—would put a lumberjack on antacid. Breakfast is pancakes with butter and syrup, an omelet, bacon, o.j. and milk. For lunch and dinner he feasts on barbecued ribs, roast chicken, beans, broccoli with cheese sauce, Caesar salad and blueberry cobbler à la mode. His before-bed snack is a cheeseburger. A teetotaler, he quaffs Big Red, a sweet local soft drink. Vegetables are usually served southern style: drenched in bacon fat. Amazingly, Henry (who avoids vitamins, drugs and supplements) has normal blood pressure and cholesterol, thanks to intense workouts and a naturally efficient metabolism.

former world-record holder in powerlifting. Eight weeks before Atlanta, they took Henry to their island redoubt off the coast of Nova Scotia to eat organic produce from their own garden, their own fresh catch of the day plus locally bred organic beef. The ambience, explains Terry Todd, is "nutritionally healthier than Texas."

When these and other Olympic athletes recite their vital stats, they include percentage of body fat, cholesterol levels and daily consumption (in precise grams) of protein and fat. "Eating is like a chore," says wrestler Matt Ghaffari, 34, of Colorado Springs, who is fed five or six balanced meals a day, all high in protein and carbs. So far, Ghaffari has gained 36 pounds to reach the 286-pound maximum for the heavyweight class, while reducing his body fat from 27 percent to 19.5 percent. He also scarfs down 30 vitamins and supplements a day at a monthly cost of $180 and is dubbed Mr. Pharmacy by teammates.

Marathoner Anne Marie Lauck, 27, of Marietta, Ga., says that for long-distance runners, monitoring body fat is far more important than counting calories because a single superfluous pound of fat (instead of muscle) can add fat minutes to her time. Lauck, who stands 5'6½", reports that her weight (fluctuating between 107 and 112) contains only about 8 percent fat, compared with about 20 percent for the average woman of her size and age.

Angel Martino of Americus, Ga., at 29 the oldest member of the women's swimming team, shudders when she recalls the diet of her rookie days, which included scads of Big Macs, milk shakes and fries. Now under the tutelage of her husband, Mike, 30, an exercise physiologist, she breakfasts at dawn with a mix of cottage cheese, nuts and green apples, and lunches on tuna sandwiches (with low-fat mayo on whole wheat). Dinner is chicken or fish and vegetables. Martino confesses that as much as she longs for a medal, she also dreams of the time when it's all over: "I'm going to have chocolate chip cookies every single day for the rest of my life."

For athletes competing in specific weight classes, hell is the few weeks preceding the weigh-in, generally held the day before the opening match. Mujaahid Maynard, 25, of Colorado Springs, wrestles in the 105.5-pound division, although at 5'6", his normal weight is 132 pounds. During the season, he drops easily to 123 and then skimps, taking in only a protein shake for lunch, a mini-dinner and jugs of water and juice. When he reaches 116, Maynard really cuts back: to just a daily small chicken breast and rice or noodles and only enough water to replace lost fluids. Finally, during the day between making the official weight and his bout, Maynard rehydrates like crazy and gorges on pasta in four meals a night, sometimes setting an alarm at 2 A.M. so he won't miss a chance to rebound to his fighting weight of 118-120 pounds. "I know this isn't healthy, letting your weight bounce up and down," he admits. "But it's a temporary thing."

Needless to say, eating disorders can be a serious problem for jocks. Judo contender Liliko Ogasawara, 24, of San Jose, binged and purged for years. "I felt like crap," she recalls. "I looked very pale. I'd walk around like a zombie." In extremis after trying every other technique to make weight, she would move on to "systematic spitting." "You'd chew gum to get your saliva going, and then you'd try to fill a cup. It's really gross. But you can move a good half pound that way." In '92 she so depleted herself that she lost in the U.S. team trials; then after another athlete suffering from eating difficulties went into convulsions at the start of the competition, Ogasawara was shocked into modifying her habits. This year, on a rounded regimen and moving up 11 pounds to the 145-pound class, Ogasawara has a good shot at judo gold.

Judy Nelson, 52, who has a master's degree in nutrition from Cal State, Long Beach, is nutritional coordinator for the U.S. Olympic Committee based at Colorado Springs and serves teams training throughout the country. She doesn't have authority to enforce a dietary routine but reports some success by encouraging athletes to keep a food journal: They detail what they ate, how they felt and how they performed and then study the entries for patterns. Most athletes in training need 1.2 to 2 grams of protein per kilogram of their body weight, Nelson says. The number of calories depends on the individual and the sport, from a minimum of 1,200 to 1,400 to as much as 7,000 for weightlifters. "The more muscle you have, the more calories you need," she says. Although her office shelves are full of high-protein drinks and energy-boosting supplements, Nelson says she isn't a big fan of these products (most were given to her by visiting sales reps).

"There's just this notion among a lot of athletes that they want to take a lot of supplements—some magic bullet—vitamins, minerals, herbs and other ergogenic aids that, most of the time, don't have any [proven] effect," she says.

Athletes have to be especially careful about what they consume just before the main event. Even Adam Saathoff, 21, of Hereford, Ariz., who needn't follow a strict diet training for his nonaerobic sport of moving-target shooting, has to fast the last 12 hours before shouldering his rifle, because "you don't want to be up there burping." Lisa Leslie, 24, of Inglewood, Calif., abstains from some foods "because they have things that could make us test positive for drugs," like poppy seeds, which could falsely suggest opium use. The star, slam-dunking 6'5" center on the U.S. women's basketball team is actually underweight at 170 pounds and scarfs down extra carbs before games for energy. But, after Atlanta, she faces another world

of eating extremes in her other career: On the fashion runway since age 10 (she hit six feet in sixth grade), Leslie has just signed a modeling contract with New York City's prestigious Wilhelmina agency. Leslie hopes she will not be asked to stop lifting weights, which she calls both "the key to our success on the court" and a regimen for all-around fitness and firm (though not unfeminine) good looks.

While today's athletes are better tuned nutritionally, they could still learn from stars of yore like Steve Fraser, 38, head coach now of the Greco-Roman wrestling team. "If you're not enjoying something, you're not going to do that great," says Fraser, a gold medalist at 198 pounds in Los Angeles. But he doesn't necessarily endorse the old Fosbury approach. "Only when you're coaching," jokes Fraser, "is beer good."

 **Article Review Form at end of book.**

This article describes a weight-loss study in which volunteers were placed in one of three groups: diet only, exercise only, or a combination of diet and exercise. Which one was most successful in the long term? What might be other benefits of exercise?

# The Best Way to Lose Weight

Think dieting and working out will banish your extra pounds for good? Think again.

**Daryn Eller**

When Cynthia Brown was chosen to take part in a weight-loss study at Baylor College of Medicine in Houston, she thought she'd hit pay dirt. The structured program seemed to be just what she needed to help her lose about 70 of the 180 pounds she was carrying on her diminutive 5-foot-2 frame.

What's more, Brown was among the women and men asked to adopt a combination of diet and exercise; the other volunteers were placed in diet-only or exercise-only groups. And we're talking full-fledged diet, complete with calorie-counters, kitchen scales, diet journals, even plastic models of foods so the participants could learn proper portion sizes. Brown was actually thrilled by the rigor. "Of the three approaches, I figured diet and exercise would have to work best," recalls the 44-year-old school psychologist.

She certainly had the math on her side. Dieting reduces the number of calories you take in;

exercise burns some your body has stored; so do both at once and you earn double the pound-paring benefit. The combo approach also counteracts one of the unfortunate consequences of dieting: a creeping metabolic rate. When a body suddenly gets much less food than it's used to, it starts burning calories more slowly in order to conserve energy. That makes shedding pounds harder. But exercise speeds up metabolism, so if you diet and work out together, your metabolic rate is pretty much back at square one.

It wasn't surprising, then, that people in the diet-and-exercise group initially came out ahead. Following a diet of 1,200 calories daily and exercising three to five times a week, they lost an average of 20 pounds over one year. Those in the diet-only group dropped 15; the exercisers shed just six.

But something strange happened in the second year of the study. By the end of that period members of the exercise-only group had pulled ahead of the pack—not by suddenly dropping untold pounds but by keeping off

what they had lost. The combination group had regained 15 pounds; the dieters, 13. But the exercisers put back less than a pound. What was going on?

Dieting is just too difficult, says Ken Goodrick, an assistant professor of medicine at Baylor's Behavioral Medicine Research Center and one of the study leaders. "It's like asking people to breathe through a straw. They can do it for a while, but pretty soon they're going to be gasping for air."

For dieters that usually means ending up frustrated, unhappy, and even more inclined to overindulge. Brown could write the book on that scenario. It wasn't that she found the 1,200 calories too restrictive, but at times she still needed to comfort herself with food. "I would feel nervous at a party, and I'd tend to eat more. Then I'd think, Oh no, I've blown it, and that anxiety would make me want to eat even more." Ultimately, Brown gained back all the weight she'd lost in the first year of the study and then some.

Even worse, this so-called dieters' depression can end up undermining everything in its wake, which is probably why the diet-and-exercise group barely kept up with the exercisers. "Many people got so frustrated they just gave up the whole package," Goodrick says.

Granted, exercise alone is a slow way to lose weight. Forty-five minutes of walking burns only around 200 calories, which you can reinstate in a minute with half a piece of apple pie. But the benefits it confers—more energy, less stress, a boost in self-esteem—often make people happier with their bodies and less concerned about the number on the scale.

For people who fervently want to shed pounds, Goodrick believes that just trying to eat healthfully accomplishes more than going on a diet. There may even be a physiological basis for his theory. According to researchers at the West Virginia University School of Medicine who recently completed a study of exercise and weight loss, vigorous exercise can actually dampen a person's preference for high-fat foods.

Goodrick's latest study, which began last September and is called MOVE (Motivating the Overweight to Value Exercise), has no formal eating plan. Rather, the researchers provided women with an exercise regimen as well as guidelines for lightening up the fat in their meals. The strategy already seems to be working for some of the volunteers.

Linda Thompson, a 48-year-old payroll personnel manager, no longer even thinks of low-fat eating as dieting. Best of all, she says, the study has helped her integrate good eating habits with regular exercise. Since becoming one of Goodrick's guinea pigs she visits the gym three or four times a week, where she hits the stationary bike for 20 minutes, lifts weights for 15, then finishes up with 30 minutes on the treadmill. After six months of sticking to this routine, she's lost about 50 pounds.

"I was surprised to find that exercise can be enjoyable," says Thompson. "And it's not because of the weight I've lost. I feel good. That's what's so important."

Brown, too, has had a change of heart since her experience in the earlier Baylor study. "I learned the truth: that there's a difference between losing weight and keeping it off." But now that she's hooked on exercise and healthy eating, she doesn't really care what she weighs.

 **Article Review Form at end of book.**

- Likely, the best diet for competitive athletes whose activity lasts less than one hour is simply a well-balanced approach, consuming a wide variety of foods, with about 60 percent of the calories coming from carbohydrate (7 gm carbohydrate per kg of body weight).

- Regarding maintenance of body temperature, getting nutrients to active muscles, and ultimate sports performance, ensuring adequate fluid intake may be the most crucial diet practice.

- It is estimated that 30 percent of all Americans are overweight, and we are spending an increasing amount of money on weight-loss strategies.

## R.E.A.L. Sites

This list provides a print preview of typical **coursewise** R.E.A.L. sites. (There are over 100 such sites at the **courselinks**™ site.) The danger in printing URLs is that web sites can change overnight. As we went to press, these sites were functional using the URLs provided. If you come across one that isn't, please let us know via email to: webmaster@coursewise.com. Use your Passport to access the most current list of R.E.A.L. sites at the **courselinks**™ site.

**Site name:** American Dietetic Association
**URL:** http://www.eatright.org/afitperform.html
**Why is it R.E.A.L.?** This page elucidates the position of the American Dietetic Association and the Canadian Dietetic Association regarding diet for physical fitness and athletics. The article addresses current strategies to assess body composition, energy requirements, and nutrient needs for active people.
**Activities:** (1) What does this page suggest in terms of maximizing muscle glycogen storage in preparation for a competition of long duration (greater than 90 minutes)? (2) What are some appropriate ideas for protein consumption?

**Site name:** Nutrition Knowledge: Answers to the Top Ten Questions
**URL:** http://www.physsportsmed.com/issues/oct_96/top_ten.htm
**Why is it R.E.A.L.?** The Nutrition Advisor is a regular part of this monthly journal. Sound nutrition strategies are discussed and diet controversies are clarified by well-qualified professionals in the field.
**Activities:** (1) Find out how Nancy Clark, M.S., R.D., responds to commonly asked questions on sports nutrition. (2) Can you do a web search and find different answers to these same questions? Where were these found? Whom do you agree with?

**Site name:** Nutritional Science 421 Sports Nutrition Web Page
**URL:** http://instruct1.cit.cornell.edu/Courses/ns421/NS421.html
**Why is it R.E.A.L.?** This is an informative page that addresses nearly every issue concerning sports nutrition.
**Activities:** (1) What are some signs of dehydration (hypohydration)? (2) List the possible consequences of consuming excess protein. (3) Assume that you are counseling an endurance athlete. Use the information found on this page and develop a week-long diet for your subject. Do the same for a body builder. Were your suggestions different? Why or why not?

# section 4

## Aging Well
## Nutrition in the Later Years

 **WiseGuide Intro**

Data presented by two researchers, Bellow and Breslow, noted the following lifestyle habits that have a significant impact on one's health status:

1. Always eat breakfast.
2. Eat three regularly scheduled meals per day (no snacking).
3. Exercise regularly.
4. Maintain healthy body weight.
5. Receive seven to eight hours of sleep per night.
6. Don't smoke.
7. Consume alcohol only in moderation.

Older individuals who practiced all of these habits had a health status similar to that of subjects thirty years younger who practiced few or none.

By the year 2000, there will be 4 million more Americans over the age of sixty-five than there were in 1990 (see *Healthy People 2000: A Midcourse Review and 1995 Revisions*). We are experiencing the aging of America. This phenomenon will pose a challenge to all components of our nation's health care system. What kind of economic burden will this cause? What should be the role of preventive medicine for this group? How do poverty, social isolation, medication, decline in sensory perception, and health status influence diet? Each of these issues needs to be addressed for the sake of our elderly.

This group has much to offer younger members of society. Wisdom, knowledge, skills, perspective, and patience come only from experience. We owe a great deal to our elderly colleagues. Research is continuing into the physiologic changes and requirements that occur as a result of the aging process. The least society can do is to develop nutrition education, recommendations, and strategies to meet the needs of our elderly.

## Learning Objectives

After studying this section, you will know:

- the effect of fiber on blood lipids.

- common nutrient deficiencies among the elderly.

- which vitamins, if taken in excess, may be harmful.

- that vitamins from foods and vitamins from supplements are absorbed equally well and perform the same duties once inside your body.

- that significant weight loss associated with Alzheimer's disease increases the risk of infection.

- risk factors for osteoporosis.

- the nutrients critical to the structural integrity of bone.

## ? Questions ?

**R18.** Define the following: (a) fiber, (b) lignan, (c) alpha-linolenic acid, and (d) X-cellent choice.

**R19.** Some people may assume that, if a little is good, more must be better. Is that necessarily true regarding vitamins?

**R20.** What causes weight loss resulting from Alzheimer's disease? What are some practical strategies to help ensure energy intake? Does the thought of Alzheimer's disease concern you?

**R21.** What is the principal function of vitamin D?

Define the following: (a) fiber, (b) lignan, (c) alpha-linolenic acid, and (d) X-cellent choice.

# Top Seed

## With its healing powers, flax is the next nutritional star

**Holly McCord, RD, with Linda Rao**

*Sources: Stephen C. Cunnane, PhD, associate professor, department of nutritional sciences, University of Toronto, Ontario;* **Barry Hall,** *Flax Council of Canada, Winnipeg, Manitoba;* **Kenneth Setchell, PhD,** *professor of pediatrics, and director, clinical mass spectrometry center, Children's Hospital Medical Center, Cincinnati, OH;* **Lilian U. Thompson, PhD,** *professor, department of nutritional sciences, University of Toronto, Ontario.*

A field of flax in full purple bloom? Irresistible! A bag of little flaxseeds in a health food store? Until now, a very tough sell. But that's about to change. Shoppers in the new millennium may see flaxseed as an important new superfood. Stocked inside this lowly seed are two impressive compounds looking more and more like foes of heart attacks, breast and colon cancer, arthritis, severe menstrual cramps—even depression. What's mind-boggling is that flaxseed has more of these two compounds—lignans and alpha-linolenic acid—than any other food . . . by far!

In fact, top flaxseed researcher Stephen Cunnane, PhD, of the University of Toronto, told

us, "There's nobody who won't benefit from adding flaxseed to his or her diet." If you're clueless about how to do that—like most everybody—read on. Flaxseed is a winner you'll want on your team.

### Just the Flax, Ma'am

Every fall Canadian flax farmers, the world's top producers, harvest hard, shiny flaxseeds—usually brown but sometimes gold—shaped like diminutive sesame seeds. What's inside each seed could be better health, spelled F-L-A-X:

### "F" Is for Fiber

It's amazing how much fiber a little flax contains. Just ¼ cup of ground flaxseed delivers 6 grams of fiber, as much fiber as 1½ cups of cooked oatmeal! Studies prove that when flaxseed is added to the diet, harmful LDL cholesterol drops, while good HDL cholesterol stays put, probably due to all that fiber (including the soluble kind). Regularity improves, as well.

And most Americans need more fiber. We average less than 15 g. a day, about half the amount

health authorities recommend to help reduce the risk of colon cancer, heart disease, high blood pressure and diabetes.

### "L" Is for Lignans

Here's where the flaxseed story starts racking up major points. Lignans are tantalizing plant-based compounds that can shrink existing breast- and colon-cancer tumors and stop new ones from getting started—at least in test-tube and animal studies. And flaxseed has staggering lignan levels. Many plant foods have some lignans, but flaxseed has at least 75 times more than any other. To get the lignans that are in just ¼ cup of flaxseed, you'd need to eat about 60 cups of fresh broccoli—or 100 slices of whole-wheat bread.

The discovery of flaxseed as a lignan storehouse came by sheer chance, says Kenneth Setchell, PhD, Children's Hospital Medical Center, Cincinnati. In a study in 1978, he and his colleagues unexpectedly found lignan levels in one patient several hundred times higher than had ever been seen before. The patient, it turned out, baked his own bread . . . and always added flaxseed.

Currently under way at the University of Toronto is the first study testing lignans against cancer in humans. One hundred women with breast cancer will eat a daily muffin with 25 g. of flaxseed to see if it might reduce the growth of their tumors between the time of diagnosis and surgery, according to Lilian Thompson, PhD, who leads the study. Important: Muffins are not a substitute for medical treatment. If you have breast cancer, seek or continue conventional care.

## "A" Is for Alpha-linolenic Acid

Back in January, we reported on mounting evidence that eating more omega-3 fats helps ward off fatal heart attacks, autoimmune diseases like rheumatoid arthritis, severe menstrual cramps and maybe even depression. Many researchers told us modern diets—even healthy ones—are routinely deficient in omega-3s.

Once again, flaxseed turns out to be a mega-source, this time for the plant version of omega-3 . . . called alpha-linolenic acid. The oil in flaxseed is about 50% alpha-linolenic acid. Canola and walnut oils, the next highest sources, have about 10%. But most foods have far less. It would take 25 cups of peanut butter, for example, to get the alph-linolenic acid is just ¼ cup of ground flaxseed. Although the animal version of omega-3 fat, found in fish oil, packs the most punch, research confirms that alpha-linolenic acid confers omega-3 benefits, too. So, if you're a vegetarian or you don't eat fish regularly, says Dr. Cunnane, flaxseed is your best omega-3 bet.

**But will I like it? In blind taste tests among 90 college students, muffins and cookies with ground flaxseed in the recipe won out over plain muffins and cookies. . . for flavor, tenderness ond color!** *(Journal of the American Dietetic Association,* **August 1996)**

### *Prevention's* Flaxseed Muffins

Our Test Kitchen staff created this recipe to deliver 25 g. flaxseed per muffin, the amount currently being tested against breast cancer.

1¼ c. flour

3 c. ground flaxseed*

1 tbsp. baking powder

⅓ c. to ½ c. light molasses

¾ c. skim milk

2 tbsp. canola oil

½ c. egg substitute

Preheat oven to 350° F.

Whisk together flour, flaxseed and baking powder. In a separate bowl, stir together remaining (wet) ingredients. Stir into dry ingredients until just moistened.

Pour into 2¾ inch muffin pan coated with vegetable spray. Bake until done, about 18 minutes. Can be frozen for use as needed. Makes 12 muffins.

Per muffin: 196 calories, 12.4 g. fat, 110 mg. sodium, 8.4 g. fiber, 25 g. flaxseed.

**Note:** We know this muffin is higher in fat than what we usually recommend. However, nearly half the fat is alpha-linolenic acid—the plain version of omega-3, which is sorely missing in most diets. We think it's worth finding room for this muffin in your daily low-fat plan.

*Sold in natural-food stores.

To get the most omega-3s, look for flaxseed oil in natural-food stores. But to get the entire flax arsenal . . . look for products that deliver the entire flaxseed. Note: You can use flaxseed, but not flaxseed oil, for baking; under sustained heat, flaxseed oil (added as a separate ingredient) oxidizes and should not be consumed. (To learn more about flaxseed oil, see "The Fat You Need," January 1997.)

## "X" Is for Excellent Move

Should you consider adding flaxseed to your diet? "Absolutely," says Dr. Setchell. In terms of safety, flaxseed has been consumed since the Stone Age—a rather venerable track record. Ironically, most flaxseed is used today to make an inedible product—linseed oil, a component of paints and varnishes. (The word *linseed* by itself is simply an alternate word for *flaxseed*.) Linseed oil is oil that's been chemically extracted from flaxseeds and denatured—oxidized—which makes it unfit for human consumption.

## Overcoming 'Fear of Flax'

"O.K., but how does this stuff taste?" you must be thinking. The verdict: Pleasantly nutty. To get health benefits, researchers estimate you need anywhere from 6 to 25 g. a day (in ground flaxseed, that works out to 1 level measuring tablespoon up to ¼ cup). Note: Because a few people are highly allergic to flax, start by using less than ¼ teaspoon a day, increasing gradually if no reactions occur.

Adding flax to your diet is easy:

## No-Bake Flax Snacks

This recipe delivers 4 g. flaxseed and 1 g. fiber with just 50 calories, 2 g. fat and 8 mg. sodium per spicy, chewy cookie.

¾ c. ground flaxseed*

3 tbsp. oat flour*

1½ tsp. cinnamon

1½ tsp. cloves

2 tbsp. peanut butter

½ c. rice syrup*

Combine first 4 ingredients in a small mixing bowl.

Add peanut butter and rice syrup and knead mixture thoroughly by hand.

Tear pieces off and roll them between your hands into 1-inch balls.

Place balls on waxed paper.

Dust very lightly with powdered sugar, if desired.

Serve immediately or chill for future use. (Makes about 24 1-inch balls.)

*Sold in natural-food stores.
(Recipe reprinted with permission from *Flax for Life,* by Jade Beutler, copyright Jade Beutler 1996, Progressive Health Publishing.)

## Try a Sprinkle a Day

At natural-food stores, look for preground flaxseed (it's like cornmeal in consistency) with vitamins C and E added to stabilize it against oxidation. Sometimes small amounts of vitamin $B_6$ and zinc are added, too; flax researchers aren't convinced these are necessary. Sprinkle 1 or more tablespoons in hot or cold cereal, yogurt, soup or fruit juice. (Allow for extra calories and fat: Each tablespoon contains 25 calories, 2.5 g. fat.) Once a package of preground flaxseed is opened, keep it refrigerated; try to use within 6 months.

If you prefer to buy whole flaxseed, for maximum health benefits it should be ground in a coffee grinder or food processor— any whole seeds not crushed by your teeth in chewing will pass through you undigested. Use freshly ground flaxseed promptly.

## Make Your Own Treats

Recipes for cookies or muffins using ground flaxseed are found on p. 84 and below.*

## Buy Flax Foods Ready-Made

In the United States, flaxseed is turning up at natural-food stores and in some Midwestern supermarkets, in breads and other products. In parts of Canada, flaxseed breads and breakfast cereals can also be found in supermarkets, bagel shops and restaurants.

And finally, for some freshly baked flaxseed breads, muffins and rolls delivered to your door by UPS, call Natural Ovens of Manitowoc, WI, at 1–800–772–0730, Central Time between 9 a.m. and 5 p.m.

*See recipes on this page and previous page.

 **Article Review Form at end of book.**

Some people may assume that, if a little is good, more must be better. Is that necessarily true regarding vitamins?

# New Reasons to Take Vitamins—

## Even if you feel fine

The latest research shows that supplements can lower your risk of many ills, including cancer. But do you know which ones—and what dosages—will keep you healthy?

### Liz Applegate, Ph.D.

*Nutritionist Liz Applegate, Ph.D., is the author of* Power Foods.

Every other day, it seems, a new study comes out touting the ways vitamins, minerals, and other supplements can prevent life-threatening diseases, birth defects, even aging. But too often, follow-up reports refute earlier claims and warn us that these same vitamins and minerals may even be dangerous.

Given all the hype, it's easy to be confused. But finally, nutritionists have pinpointed which supplements you really need to stay healthy.

**Q. My life is so hectic that I tend to snack at weird times and rarely sit down to real meals. But I feel fine, so do I really need to take vitamins?**
**A.** Between missing meals and grabbing food on the go, chances are you're falling short on any number of the recommended 13 vitamins and 22 minerals. So, for

nutritional insurance, it would be wise to take a multi-vitamin with 100 to 150 percent of the RDA (recommended dietary allowances) for vitamins and the minerals iron, zinc, and copper.

Keep in mind, too, that scientists may be nudging up the RDA for several nutrients. Studies show, for instance, that people who get two to three times the RDA for vitamin C have lower risks for age-related diseases like cancer and cataracts.

Along with a multivitamin, eating five fruits and veggies a day, along with 6 to 11 servings of grains and 2 to 3 servings each of protein and dairy products, is a must. Food contains disease-fighting chemicals you won't find in a vitamin pill. But even if you do have a well-balanced diet, it's smart to take a multi, since it's tough to consume just the right combination of foods to get every necessary nutrient.

**Q. I have small bones, so I take a calcium supplement and drink calcium-fortified orange juice. Is**

**that enough calcium to ward off osteoporosis?**
**A.** Unlike most women—an estimated 70 percent of whom don't meet their calcium requirements—you probably do get enough. (Women ages 25 to 50 need at least 800 to 1,000 mg of this mineral daily, 1,500 mg if they're pregnant or nursing.) It's possible to meet your calcium needs through diet alone, especially by consuming milk (one glass contains 300 mg) and other dairy products (200 mg in an ounce and a half of cheese). If you're not getting that, take a supplement.

But to ward off osteoporosis, you should also maintain a low-sodium diet (no more than 2,400 mg a day, since excess sodium may cause calcium to exit through your urine). Other ways to avoid calcium loss: Limit protein (five to six ounces of meat a day, max) and avoid excessive intake of the mineral phosphorous (found in colas and other processed foods). Weight-bearing exercise (walking, weight training) is also important.

"New reasons to take vitamins—even if you feel fine" by Liz Applegate as appeared in REDBOOK, April 1997. Reprinted by permission of the author.

**Q. I used to take lots of vitamins, but then I started reading reports of excess vitamins being harmful. Now what do I do?**
**A.** When taken in excess, the fat-soluble vitamins A, D, E, and K get trapped or stored in fatty tissue and organs. Vitamins A and D are especially toxic, causing liver damage and bone deformities when taken in amounts just five times the RDA.

By contrast, excess water-soluble vitamins (B vitamins and C) exit your body in your urine. Still, use them with caution. Vitamin $B_6$ can cause severe nerve damage when consumed in extreme excess (100 times the RDA of 2 mg).

The safety of beta carotene supplements is also in question; recent reports suggest they may increase the risk of lung cancer in smokers. Still, scientists agree we should make sure our diet is loaded with food-based sources of beta carotene and other antioxidants (agents that destroy "free radical" molecules, which cause damage that may leave the body more susceptible to cancer, cardiovascular disease, arthritis, and signs of aging). So eat plenty of foods rich in vitamins C (citrus fruits), E (oils, nuts), and beta carotene (carrots, apricots).

**Q. I'm always wiping my kids' snotty noses. Can vitamin C protect me from their colds?**
**A.** The best protection against colds for you (and your children) is frequent hand-washing to prevent the spread of viruses (it's also a deterrent against harmful bacteria). Vitamin C supplements

fail as a *preventive* measure. But taking a 250-mg vitamin C tablet at the first sign of cold or flu or loading up on vitamin C–rich foods will help lessen the symptoms and may get you back on your feet sooner.

You may also have heard about a recent study that found that zinc can help prevent colds. However, 80 percent of the study participants experienced side effects, such as nausea. What's more, excess amounts of zinc can interfere with the body's absorption of copper.

**Q. A friend of mine swears by "organic" vitamins. Should I?**
**A.** Synthetic vitamins (made in a test tube) and natural (derived from plants and animals) are absorbed equally well and perform the same duties once inside your body—with one exception. Natural vitamin E, or *d-alpha tocopherol*, is slightly more potent than the synthetic version, *dl-alpha tocopherol*. But labeling rules for vitamin E take this difference into account.

**Q. I'm under a lot of stress lately at work and home. Can "stress formula" vitamins help?**
**A.** As you know, stress can wreak havoc on your body—from headaches and back pain to skin flare-ups and yeast infections. But unfortunately, "stress formula" vitamins (which usually consist of mega-doses of B vitamins) provide little ammunition against these reactions. Nor during periods of stress do you need *more* vitamins than what a multivitamin or well-balanced diet would provide.

**Q. Now that beauty products are packed with vitamins, would it be even better to take these vitamins orally?**
**A.** Many cosmetic companies are actually selling oral vitamin supplements with promises of healthier skin, hair, and nails. Most contain the antioxidant vitamins C and E, beta carotene, and biotin, a B vitamin.

So far, the reviews are mixed as to whether these products have any impact. Vitamin C is necessary for the production of collagen, which keeps the skin from sagging and wrinkling. And some studies have shown that biotin, in amounts about eight times the RDA, may help strengthen brittle nails. But the research is sketchy, and many dermatologists aren't buying any of it. What's more, if you're taking a multivitamin, adding on a "beauty" pill could push you into the "excess" category for some vitamins.

**Q. I don't eat much red meat, so I take extra iron. But lately I'm hearing that too much iron causes heart disease. Now what do I do?**
**A.** Some researchers believe that excess iron levels play a part in the development of heart disease and even cancer. But that's mostly for men and postmenopausal women, who need less iron. If you don't get much iron in your diet, a multivitamin with iron is a good idea. Look for one with no more than 18 mg of iron; higher amounts cause constipation and reduce the absorption of zinc.

**Q. Sometimes I hear you should take supplements with food; sometimes without it. Which is it?**
**A.** Take both your multivitamin/mineral pill and calcium supplements at meals—that's when your intestinal tract is geared up for digestion and absorption. But since high doses of calcium can hamper the absorption of iron, don't take them at the *same* meal. And avoid coffee, tea, or wine when you take your multi; all contain tannins, substances that block absorption of minerals like iron or zinc. Also, many prescription medications may interfere with vitamin and mineral absorption, so check with your pharmacist.

 **Article Review Form at end of book.**

What causes weight loss resulting from Alzheimer's disease? What are some practical strategies to help ensure energy intake? Does the thought of Alzheimer's disease concern you?

# Weight Loss Resulting from Alzheimer's Disease

## Peggy K. Yen

*Peggy K. Yen, RD, LD, MPH is a nutrition consultant with Cardiovascular Health and Nutrition Services, Division of Community and Public Health Services, Maryland Department of Health and Mental Hygiene, in Baltimore.*

Significant weight loss occurs more than twice as often among older adults with Alzheimer's disease (AD) as among cognitively normal elders. Elders who later had development of AD were also twice as likely to have lost weight in the 20 years before diagnosis as were older adults who did not have development of AD. Does AD increase metabolic rate to such an extent that it causes elders to lose weight? Or is it the agitation, wandering, and poor dietary intake characteristic of these patients that causes negative calorie balance?

## What Causes Weight Loss?

Published studies show no increased energy expenditure associated with AD. The most reasonable explanation for the weight loss common in patients with AD is limited intake caused by distractibility, chewing and swallowing problems, and poor feeding techniques, combined with increased energy expenditure from wandering and restlessness. Note that, although patients with AD as a group weigh less than cognitively normal elders, some patients with AD experience periods of weight gain and have food cravings for sweets that cause them to overeat these foods. A 1990 survey of caregivers described instances where patients with AD ate sugar and jelly from a spoon to satisfy their cravings.[1] As many as 20% of patients with AD fall into this category, causing caregivers to restrict their intake of sweet foods to ensure adequate nutrition.[1]

**Creativity in devising ways to stimulate eating will pay off in better intake for patients.**

## Can Weight Loss Be Prevented?

It is difficult to maintain adequate calorie intake in a patient with dementia, but several reports show that it can be done with good nursing care and ongoing nutrition assessment and planning. In one nursing facility, the four most important factors for maintenance of good nutrition status in patients with AD were skillful feeding techniques, appropriate consistency of the food served, providing adequate time for eating, and taking advantage of peak cognitive time.[2] Peak cognitive time in patients with AD is usually morning through midday, making breakfast and lunch an opportune time to maximize calorie and nutrient intake.

The importance of medical nutrition therapy is demonstrated by a report on a small group of patients with dementia. Over a 3-day observation period, as much as 29% of the calories and 41% of the protein consumed by patients with Alzheimer's-type dementia was supplied by nutrition supplements such as beverages and puddings consumed at meals. Techniques that staff used to overcome resistance to eating, aside from patience and a generous amount of time, were reassuring touches on hands and arms, soft singing, and cheerful talk.

The appearance of food on the plate influences the intake of patients with AD. Covered foods go unnoticed, so foods must be unwrapped and put in the patient's field of vision. Too many choices on the tray can be confusing, so place only necessary items on the tray or table. Decorative items, such as garnishes or flowers, may be accidentally eaten or at the very least distract attention from eating. Finger foods are useful for patients who have difficulty using utensils. Exercise care that the elder with AD is not prone to bolting food without chewing, because this presents an obvious choking hazard.

Modeling the desired behavior for the older adult with AD can be an effective tool for boosting food intake. Put your hand over the patient's to guide and initiate eating. Seat other patients with them who demonstrate the desired eating behavior. Say "ahh" to cue opening the mouth. Creativity in devising ways to stimulate eating will pay off in better intake for patients.

## Monitoring Intake

The most important factor in assuring adequate intake of nutrients and calories is constant monitoring of food intake and weight. Weigh patients at least monthly; more often if weight loss occurs. Food records must be kept when significant weight loss occurs to determine the scope of intervention and potential nutrient deficits. Staff observation of meals can reveal problem areas. AD varies in its effects on elders. Caregivers should not assume that specific management steps will be equally effective in all patients. Individual assessment is essential.

## How Many Calories Are Needed?

Calorie levels of up to 34 kcal/kg of body weight have been used to maintain weight in elderly patients with AD. For a 120-pound woman, this represents about 1850 kcal a day. A 150-pound woman would need 2300 kcal, a substantial amount in a person who may have difficulty eating more than two meals a day. Other reports show that free-living, older patients with AD weighed less than their cognitively normal counterparts when men consumed an average of 30 kcal/kg and women consumed about 25 kcal/kg. The calorie level for weight maintenence in older patients with AD can be estimated at approximately 30 to 35 kcal/kg body weight as a rule of thumb, with adjustments for individual need. One author suggested an extra 200 kcal per day to prevent weight loss.

Weight loss and the resulting poor nutritional status of older adults with AD increases the risk of infection, the primary cause of death in patients with AD. In spite of this fact, there is some intriguing evidence that patients with dementia may have a lower incidence of certain diseases, such as cardiovascular disease and hypertension, which may prove to be an unsought benefit of lower weight.

## References

1. Mungus D. Dietary preference for sweet food in patients with dementia. J Am Geriatr Soc 1990; 38:999-1007.
2. Suski NS, Neilsen CC. Factors affecting food intake of women with Alzheimer's type dementia in long-term-care. JADA 1989;89: 1770-3.

 **Article Review Form at end of book.**

What is the principal function of vitamin D?

# Vitamin D and Bone Health[1,2]

## Michael F. Holick[3]

*Vitamin D, Skin and Bone Research Laboratory, Endocrinology Section, Department of Medicine, Boston University Medical Center, Boston, MA 02118*

**Abstract** Vitamin D plays an essential role in maintaining a healthy mineralized skeleton for most land vertebrates including humans. Sunlight causes the photoproduction of vitamin $D_3$ in the skin. Once formed, vitamin $D_3$ is metabolized sequentially in the liver and kidney to 1,25-dihydroxyvitamin D. The major biological function of 1,25-dihydroxyvitamin D is to keep the serum calcium and phosphorus concentrations within the normal range to maintain essential cellular functions and to promote mineralization of the skeleton. Most foods do not contain any vitamin D. Foods fortified with vitamin D have a variable amount present and cannot be depended on as a sole source of vitamin D nutrition. Exposure to sunlight provides most humans with their vitamin D requirement. Aging, sunscreen use and the change in the zenith angle of the sun can dramatically affect the cutaneous production of vitamin $D_3$. Vitamin D insufficiency and vitamin D deficiency is now being recognized as a major cause of metabolic bone disease in the elderly. Vitamin D deficiency not only causes osteomalacia but can exacerbate osteoporosis. It is generally accepted that an increase in calcium intake to 1000–1500 mg/d along with an adequate source of vitamin D of at least 400 IU/d is important for maintaining good bone health. J. Nutr. 126: 1159S–1164S, 1996.

**Indexing Key Words:**
• *vitamin D* • *1,25-dihydroxyvitamin D* • *osteoporosis* • *calcium*

[1]Presented as part of the Symposium: "Nutritional Advances in Human Bone Metabolism" given at the Experimental Biology '95 meeting, Atlanta, GA, on April 11, 1995. This symposium was sponsored by the American Institute of Nutrition and supported in part by the National Dairy Council. Guest editor for the symposium publication was John J. B. Anderson, University of North Carolina, Chapel Hill, NC.

[2]Supported by NIH grants AG 04390, RR 00533 and AR 36963.

[3]To whom correspondence should be addressed: Boston University School of Medicine, 80 East Concord Street (M-1013), Boston, MA 02118.

Approximately 400 million years ago as vertebrates ventured from the oceans onto land, they were confronted with a very significant crisis. In their ocean environment, which contained a high calcium content, they utilized this divalent cation for a variety of cellular and metabolic processes. In addition, this divalent cation was a major component of the skeleton that provided its ridged structure. However, on land the environment was deficient in calcium and, as a result, these early vertebrate life forms needed to develop a mechanism(s) to utilize and process the scarce amounts of calcium in their environment to maintain essential cellular and metabolic activities. In addition, they required large amounts of calcium to mineralize their skeleton. For most ocean dwelling animals, the calcium could be easily extracted by specific calcium transport mechanisms in the gills. Once on land, a new strategy developed whereby the intestine evolved to efficiently absorb what little calcium was present in the diet. For reasons that are unknown, an intimate relationship between sunlight and vitamin D evolved to play a critical role in regulating the efficiency of dietary calcium absorption and to maintain a mineralized skeleton.

## Photosynthesis of Vitamin D₃ in the Skin

There is evidence the earliest phytoplankton species that existed in the Sargasso Sea for over 750 million years produced a 5,7-diene sterol (ergosterol; provitamin $D_2$) that, when exposed to sunlight, was converted to vitamin $D_2$ (ergocalciferol) (Holick 1989). Whether this photosynthetic process played any significant role in calcium metabolism in these early life forms is unknown. However, some later time in evolution, exposure of the skin of land vertebrates to sunlight resulted in the photosynthesis of the calcium regulating secosteroid vitamin D.

7-Dehydrocholesterol (provitamin $D_3$, 7-DHC)[4] is the immediate precursor for cholesterol biosynthesis in most tissues in the body. In the skin, 7-DHC serves an additional function. 7-Dehydrocholesterol is photolabile and when exposed to high energy ultraviolet B (290–315 nm) radiation from sunlight, this cholesterol precursor is converted to previtamin $D_3$ (precholecalciferol) (Fig. 1)* (Holick 1994). Once formed, previtamin $D_3$ is efficiently converted to vitamin $D_3$ (cholecalciferol) by a membrane enhanced process (Tian et al. 1993). As vitamin $D_3$ is being formed, its conformation is altered, resulting in it selectively ex-

[4]Abbreviations used: 1,25(OH)₂D, 1,25 dihydroxyvitamin D; 7-DHC, 7-dehydrocholesterol; PTH, parathyroid hormone; VDR, vitamin D receptors.

iting the plasma membrane of the skin cell into the extracellular space where it eventually enters the circulation and it is bound to the vitamin D-binding protein.

## Metabolism and Biological Activity of Vitamin D for Calcium Metabolism

Once vitamin $D_3$ is made in the skin or vitamin $D_2$ and vitamin D are ingested from the diet, the vitamin D (vitamin D without a subscript represents either vitamin $D_2$ or $D_3$) is transported to the liver where it is metabolized to its major circulating form, 25-hydroxyvitamin D (25-hydroxycholecalciferol and 25-hydroxyergocalciferol; 25-OH-D) (Darwish and DeLuca 1993, Holick 1995). 25-OH-D is biologically inert on calcium metabolism at physiological concentrations and requires a further hydroxylation in the kidney to form its biologically active metabolite, 1,25-dihydroxyvitamin D [1,25-dihydroxycholecalciferol and 1,25-dihydroxyergocalciferol; 1,25(OH)₂D] (Fig. 1).*

The major biological function of vitamin D is to maintain the serum calcium in the normal physiological range to preserve neuromuscular and cellular functions. 1,25(OH)₂D maintains the blood calcium in the normal range by enhancing the efficiency of intestinal calcium absorption and by increasing the mobilization of stem cells to become osteoclasts that, in turn, mobilize calcium stores from bone (Darwish and DeLuca 1993, Holick 1994, Holick 1995) (Fig. 1)*. A decrease in the blood-ionized calcium concentration stimulates the parathyroid glands to increase the synthesis

and secretion of parathyroid hormone (PTH), which, in turn, increases tubular reabsorption of calcium in the kidney and enhances the production of 1,25(OH)₂D (Fig. 1).* PTH and 1,25(OH)₂D act in concert to mobilize monocytic stem cells to become osteoclasts, thereby increasing calcium removal from the bone(s). 1,25(OH)₂D independently increases the efficiency of intestinal calcium absorption. The net effect is to raise serum-ionized calcium concentrations that negatively feedback regulates synthesis and secretion of PTH from the parathyroid glands (Fig. 1)*. 1,25(OH)₂D also independently interacts with the vitamin D receptor in the parathyroid glands and results in an inhibition of the transcription of the PTH gene (Holick 1994). Thus, 1,25(OH)₂D plays a critical role in maintaining the blood calcium in the normal range.

## Biological Function of Vitamin D in Bone

It is well known that vitamin D deficiency is associated with rickets in children and osteomalacia in adults (Demay 1995, Goldring et al. 1995, Krane and Holick 1994). Before the epiphyseal plates close, vitamin D deficiency causes a disorganization and hypertrophy of the chondrocytes at the mineralization front as well as a mineralization defect (Fig. 2),* resulting in the short stature and bony deformities that are characteristic of vitamin D deficiency rickets. Osteomalacia, on the other hand, occurs after the epiphyseal plates close; therefore, this disease of adults is more subtle. There is a

*Not included in this publication.

mineralization defect in the skeleton resulting in poor mineralization of the collagen matrix (osteoid) (Goldring et al. 1995, Krane and Holick 1994). Although this does not cause bony deformities, it can cause severe osteopenia (a decrease in the opacity of the skeleton as seen by x-ray) that results in increased risk of skeletal fractures (Aaron et al. 1974, Chalmers et al. 1967, Kavookjian et al. 1990, Sokoloff 1978). In addition, some patients with osteomalacia complain of localized or generalized unrelenting deep bone pain.

It is still not clear exactly what role $1,25(OH)_2D$ has on the bone mineralization process. Osteoblasts, which are responsible for laying down the collagen and protein matrix in the skeleton, possess receptors for vitamin D (VDR). $1,25(OH)_2D_3$ stimulates the synthesis of noncollagenous proteins such as osteocalcin, osteopontin and osteonectin, increases alkaline phosphatase activity and decreases collagen synthesis (Demay et al. 1989, Chang et al. 1994).

There are several studies to support the hypothesis that the principal function of vitamin D in mineralizing bone is through its action on maintaining an adequate calcium $\times$ phosphorus product in the circulation and extracellular fluid space. When vitamin D-deficient rats were infused with high calcium and high phosphorus for several days, it was found that the bones had little evidence of rickets (Holick 1995). Similarly, when vitamin D-deficient rats were fed a high calcium, high phosphorus diet, histologic studies of the skeleton did not reveal any skeletal abnormalities consistent with either osteomalacia or rickets (Holtrop et al. 1986) (Fig. 2).* When a child with severe rickets caused by the rare hereditary disease, vitamin D-dependent rickets Type II [also known as hereditary resistance to $1,25(OH)_2D$, which caused by a genetic defect in the VDR], was infused with calcium for 7 mo, her skeleton began to mineralize normally (Balsan et al. 1986). Therefore, all evidence suggests that the principal function of vitamin D for maintaining a healthy mineralized skeleton is to ensure that the blood and extracellular concentrations of calcium and phosphorus are adequate for the deposition of calcium hydroxyapatite in the bone matrix that had been laid down by the osteoblasts. There is little evidence to suggest that vitamin D plays a direct role in the bone mineralization process.

## Importance of Vitamin D for Bone Health

Vitamin D plays a critically important role in the development, growth and mineralization of the skeleton during its formative years. Vitamin D performs an equally essential role in maintaining a healthy mineralized skeleton for adults of all ages. Vitamin D deficiency in children results in the bone-deforming disease rickets (Demay 1995, Goldring et al. 1995, Holick 1995, Krane and Holick 1994). In adults, vitamin D insufficiency and vitamin D deficiency has a more subtle effect on the skeleton. As the body becomes vitamin D insufficient, the efficiency of intestinal calcium absorption decreases from ~30–50% to no more than 15%. This results in a decrease in the ionized calcium concentration in the blood, which signals the calcium sensor in the parathyroid glands resulting in an increase in the synthesis and secretion of PTH. PTH not only tries to conserve calcium by increasing renal tubular reabsorption of calcium but also plays an active role in mobilizing stem cells to become active calcium resorbing osteoclasts (Fig. 1).* PTH also increases tubular excretion of phosphorus causing hypophosphatemia. The net effect of vitamin D insufficiency and vitamin D deficiency is a normal serum calcium, elevated PTH and alkaline phosphatase and a low or low normal phosphorus. The hallmark for vitamin D insufficiency and vitamin D deficiency is low normal (between 10 and 20 ng/ml) and low or undetectable (<10 ng/ml) 25-OH-D, respectively, in the blood. The secondary hyperparathyroidism and low calcium $\times$ phosphorus product is thought to be responsible for the increase in unmineralized osteoid, which is the hallmark for rickets and osteomalacia. In addition, the increase in serum PTH causing increased osteoclastic activity results in calcium wasting from the bone, which exacerbates osteoporosis in older adults.

There are several studies that demonstrated an increase in calcium intake of 800–1000 mg/d with supplementation of ≥400–800 units of vitamin D daily will decrease the risk of vertebral and nonvertebral fractures and increase bone mineral density (Chapuy et al. 1992, Dawson-Hughes et al. 1990, Dawson-Hughes et al. 1991, Lips et al. 1988). It has been recognized for over two decades that vitamin D deficiency is associated with increased risk of hip fracture (Aaron et al. 1974, Chalmers et al. 1967, Kavookjian et al. 1990, Sokoloff

*Not included in this publication.

1978). It has been reported in several European studies, as well as a study in Boston, that up to 40% of patients who were admitted for an acute hip fracture were vitamin D deficient (Aaron et al. 1974, Kavookjian et al. 1990). During winter when the sunlight loses its ability to produce vitamin $D_3$ in the skin, there is a more marked loss of bone mineral density of the hip and spine that is related to a decrease in circulating levels of 25-OH-D and an increase in PTH concentrations (Dawson-Hughes et al. 1991, Rosen et al. 1994) (Fig. 3).*

## Sources of Vitamin D

Vitamin D is very rare in unfortified foods. Vitamin D in varying amounts is present in the flesh of fatty fish and oils of fish including cod and tuna liver oil (Holick 1989, Holick 1994). Several foods are fortified with vitamin D including milk, some cereals and some bread products. There is preliminary evidence to suggest that meats from poultry, pork and beef contain small amounts of vitamin D that probably comes from the vitamin D that was fortified in the animal feed (Thompson and Plouffe 1993). Although milk is considered to be the major food source of vitamin D, three separate studies have shown that <20% of milk samples evaluated from all sections of the United States and in western Canada contained the amount of vitamin D stated on the label (Chen et al. 1993, Holick et al. 1992, Tanner et al. 1988). In addition, 14% of skim milk samples contained no detectable vitamin D (Holick et al. 1992). Multivitamin preparations that we evaluated contained at least the amount of vitamin D stated on the label and often contained up to 150% as

much, which is important for a good shelf life (Holick 1994).

The major source of vitamin D for most humans is casual exposure to sunlight. It is estimated that upwards of 80–90% of the body's requirement for vitamin D comes from this source (Holick 1994). There are several factors that can affect the cutaneous synthesis of vitamin $D_3$. Anything that limits the amount of solar ultraviolet B (UVB) photons to reach the skin's surface and penetrate into the viable epidermis can significantly affect this vital photosynthetic process. Melanin, which is a natural sunscreen, clothing and topically applied sunscreens absorb UVB photons and, therefore, can significantly diminish the synthesis of vitamin $D_3$ (Holick 1994, Matsuoka et al. 1987). The topical application of a sunscreen with a sun protection factor of 8 can almost completely eliminate the cutaneous production of vitamin $D_3$ (Matsuoka et al. 1987) and cause vitamin D deficiency (Matsuoka et al. 1988). Season, latitude and time of day can significantly affect the cutaneous production of vitamin $D_3$. When the zenith angle of the sun is so oblique (such as during the winter and at far southern and northern latitudes), the UVB photons are efficiently absorbed in the earth's ozone layer, resulting in little or no production of vitamin $D_3$ in the skin. In Boston between the months of November and February, exposure to sunlight for up to 5 h does not result in any significant production of vitamin $D_3$ in the skin (Webb et al. 1989). Aging causes a marked reduction in the cutaneous stores of 7-dehydrocholesterol, resulting in a marked reduction in the production of vitamin $D_3$. By the age of

70 y, the skin's ability to produce vitamin $D_3$ is only 30% as efficient as when the individual was a young adult (Holick et al. 1989).

The skin has a large capacity to produce vitamin $D_3$. For a young adult a whole body exposure to one minimal erythemal dose of sunlight can raise the blood levels of vitamin $D_3$ to a level comparable with taking an oral dose of vitamin $D_2$ of between 10,000 and 25,000 IU (Holick 1994). When the elderly were asked to sit on a verandah during the spring, summer and fall in New Zealand for 15 or 30 min a day, Reid et al. (1985) demonstrated that there was a substantial increase in circulating concentrations of 25-OH-D (Fig. 4A).* Furthermore, despite the age-related decrease in the cutaneous production of vitamin $D_3$, people over the age of 60 y still benefit from limited exposure to sunlight. There was a modest seasonal increase in 25-OH-D in the summer even in adults over 60 y of age (Lund and Sorensen 1979, McKenna et al. 1985, Webb et al. 1990) (Fig. 4B).*

It is reasonable for adults over the age of 50 to obtain their vitamin D requirement by being exposed to suberythemal doses of sunlight. I have recommended for adults in Boston that exposure of hands, face and arms two to three times a week to suberythemal doses of sunlight (~5–15 min/d, depending on the skin's sensitivity to sunlight) is adequate to provide sufficient amounts of vitamin $D_3$. Because excess vitamin $D_3$ that is produced in the skin is stored in the body fat, vitamin D is available during the winter when the sun is incapable of producing vitamin $D_3$ in the skin. Because a topical application of a sunscreen

*Not included in this publication.

can essentially prevent the production of vitamin $D_3$ in the skin, people who wish to stay outdoors for long periods of time should only expose their skin to suberythemal amounts of sunlight and then topically apply a sunscreen with a sun protection factor of 15 or greater to prevent the consequences of chronic excessive exposure to sunlight. For children and young adults, they should wear a sunscreen at all times to help prevent skin damage and skin cancer. Because children and young adults will not always wear a sunscreen over all sun exposed areas, they are still able to produce enough vitamin $D_3$ from sun exposure to satisfy their body's requirement. A multivitamin that contains 400 IU of vitamin D is an excellent source of the vitamin and will help maintain circulating concentrations of 25-OH-D. However, in the absence of sunlight, a multivitamin may not be adequate to maintain a normal vitamin D status (Holick 1994). There is mounting evidence that in the absence of sunlight the body may need 600–800 IU of vitamin D (Chapuy et al. 1992, Dawson-Hughes et al. 1991, Holick 1994). Although milk, some cereals and bread may contain some vitamin D, they cannot be depended on as a sole source of vitamin D. People should not take more than one multivitamin pill that contain vitamin D because of concern for vitamin A intoxication (a multivitamin pill usually contains 10,000 units of vitamin A). For patients who are vitamin D insufficient or vitamin D deficient, I usually treat them once a week with 50,000 IU of vitamin $D_2$ for 8 wk. The serum 25-OH-D usually increases from 15 ng/ml to 25–40 ng/ml. This treatment will maintain a normal

vitamin D status for 2–4 mo. Therefore, an adequate source of calcium in combination with vitamin D from sunlight and/or a multivitamin containing vitamin D and exercise ultimately results in good bone health.

## Literature Cited

Aaron, J. E., Gallagher, J. C., Anderson, J., Stasiak, L., Longton, E., Nordin, B. & Nicholson, M. (1974) Frequency of osteomalacia and osteoporosis in fractures of the proximal femur. Lancet (vol. i): 230–233.

Balsan, S., Garabedian, M., Lavchet, M. (1986) Long-term nocturnal calcium infusions can cure rickets and promote normal mineralization in hereditary resistance to 1,25-dihydroxyvitamin $D_3$. J. Clin. Invest. 77: 1661–1667.

Chalmers, J., Conacher, D. H., Gardner, D. L. & Scott, P. J. (1967) Osteomalacia—a common disease in elderly women. J. Bone Joint Surg. (Br) 403–423.

Chang, P. L., Ridal, A. L. & Prince, C. W. (1994) Calcitriol regulation of osteopontin expression in mouse epidermal cells. Endocrinology 135: 863–869.

Chapuy, M. C., Arlot, M., Duboeuf, F., Brun, J., Crouzet, B., Arnaud, S., Delmas, P. & Meuner, P. (1992) Vitamin $D_3$ and calcium to prevent hip fractures in elderly women. N. Engl. J. Med. 327: 1637–1642.

Chen, T. C., Heath, H. III & Holick, M. F. (1993) An update on the vitamin D content of fortified milk from the United States and Canada. N. Engl. J. Med. 329: 1507.

Darwish, H. & DeLuca, H. F. (1993) Vitamin D-regulated gene expression. Crit. Rev. Eukaryotic Gene Express 3: 89–116.

Dawson-Hughes, B., Dallal, G. E., Krall, E. A., Harris, S., Sokoll, L. J. & Falconer, G. (1991) Effect of vitamin D supplementation on wintertime and overall bone loss in healthy postmenopausal women. Ann. Intern. Med. 115: 505–512.

Dawson-Hughes, B., Dallai, G. E., Krall, E. A., Sadowksi, L., Sahyoun, N. & Tannenbaum, S. (1990) A controlled trial of the effect of calcium supplementation on bone density in postmenopausal women. N. Engl. J. Med. 323: 878–883.

Demay, M. B. (1995) Hereditary defects in vitamin D metabolism and

vitamin D receptor defects. In: Endocrinology (DeGroot, L. J., Besser, M., Burger, H. G., Jameson, J. L., Loriaux, D. L., Marshall, J. C., Odell, W. D., Potts, J. T., Jr. & Rubenstein, A. H., eds.; Cahil, G. F., Jr., Martini, L., Nelson, D. H., consulting eds.), vol. 2, 3rd ed., pp. 1173–1178. W. B. Saunders (Harcourt Brace), Philadelphia, PA.

Demay, M. B., Roth, D. A. & Kronenberg, H. M. (1989) Regions of the rat osteocalcin gene which mediate the effect of 1,25-dihydroxyvitamin $D_3$ on gene transcription. J. Biol. Chem. 264: 2279–2282.

Goldring, S. R., S. M. Krane & Avioli, L. V. (1995) Disorders of calcification: osteomalacia and rickets. In: Endocrinology (DeGroot, L. J., Cahil, G. F., Jr., Martini, L., Nelson, D. H., eds.), vol. 2, 3rd ed., pp. 1204–1227. W. B. Saunders (Harcourt Brace), Philadelphia, PA.

Holick, M. F. (1989) Phylogenetic and evolutionary aspects of vitamin D from phytoplankton to humans. In: Vertebrate Endocrinology: Fundamentals and Biomedical Implications (Pang, P. K. T. & Schreibman, M. P., eds.), vol. 3, pp. 7–43. Academic Press (Harcourt Brace Jovanovich), Orlando, FL.

Holick, M. F. McCollum Award Lecture (1994) Vitamin D: new horizons for the 21st century. Am. J. Clin. Nutr. 60: 619–630.

Holick, M. F. (1995) Vitamin D: photobiology, metabolism, and clinical Applications. In: Endocrinology (DeGroot, L. J., Besser, M., Burger, H. G., Jameson, J. L., Loriaux, D. L., Marshall, J. C., Odell, W. D., Potts, J. T., Jr. & Rubenstein, A. H., eds.) 3rd edition, pp. 990–1013. W. B. Saunders, Philadelphia, PA.

Holick, M. F., Matsuoka, L. Y. & Wortsman, J. (1989) Age, Vitamin D, and solar ultraviolet. Lancet, Nov. 4: 1104–1105.

Holick, M. F., Shao, Q., Liu, W. W. & Chen, T. C. (1992) The vitamin D Content of fortified milk and infant formula. N. Engl. J. Med. 326: 1178–1181.

Holtrop, M. E., Cox, K. A., Carnes, D. L. & Holick, M. F. (1986) Effects of serum calcium and phosphorus on skeletal mineralization in vitamin D-deficient rats. Am. J. Physiol. 251: E234–E250.

Kavookjian, H., Whitelaw, G., Lin, S. & Holick, M. F. (1990) Role of vitamin D deficiency in the level of age-associated fractures in patients treated at an inner city hospital. Ortho. Pediactr. Trans. 14: 580 (abs.).

Krane, S. M. & Holick, M. F. (1994) Metabolic bone disease. In: Harrison's Principles of Internal Medicine (Isselbacher, K. J., Braunwald, E., Wilson, J. D., Martin, J. B., Fauci, A. S. & Kasper, D. L., eds.), 13th ed., pp. 2172–2183. McGraw-Hill, New York, NY.

Lips, P., Wiersinga, A., van Ginkel, F. C., Jongen, M. J. M., Netelenbos, C. & Hackeng, W. H. L. (1988) The effect of vitamin D supplementation on vitamin D status and parathyroid function in elderly subjects. J. Clin. Endocrinol. Metab. 67: 644–650.

Lund, B. & Sorensen, O. H. (1979) Measurement of 25-hydroxyvitamin D in serum and its relation to sunshine, age and vitamin D intake in the Danish population. Scand. J. Clin. Lab. Invest. 39: 23–30.

Matsuoka, L. Y., Ide, L., Wortsman, J., MacLaughlin, J. & Holick, M. F. (1987) Sunscreens suppress cutaneous vitamin $D_3$ synthesis. J. Clin. Endocrinol. Metab. 64: 1165–1168.

Matsuoka, L. Y., Wortsman, J., Hanifan, N. & Holick, M. F. (1988) Chronic sunscreen use decreases circulating concentrations of 25-hydroxyvitamin D: A preliminary study. Arch. Derm. 124: 1802–1804.

McKenna, M. J., Freaney, R., Meade, A. & Muldowney, F. P. (1985) Hypovitaminosis D and elevated serum alkaline phosphatase in elderly Irish people. Am. J. Clin. Nutr. 41: 101–109.

Reid, I. R., Gallagher, D. J. A. & Bosworth, J. (1985) Prophylaxis against vitamin D deficiency in the elderly by regular sunlight exposure. Age Ageing 15: 35–40.

Rosen, C. J., Morrison, A., Zhou, H., Storm, D., Hunter, S. J., Musgrave, K., Chen, T., Wen-Wei, L. & Holick, M. F. (1994) Elderly women in northern New England exhibit seasonal changes in bone mineral density and calciotropic hormones. Bone Miner. Res. 25: 83–92.

Sokoloff, L. (1978) Occult osteomalacia in American patients with fracture of the hip. Am. J. Surg. Pathol. 2: 21–30.

Tanner, J. T., Smith, J., Defibaugh, P., Angyal, G., Villalobos, M., Bueno, M. & McGarrahan, E. (1988) Survey of vitamin D content of fortified milk. J. Assoc. Off. Anal. Chem. 71: 607–610.

Thompson, J. N. & Plouffe, L. (1993) Determination of cholecalciferol in meat and fat from livestock fed normal and excessive quantities of vitamin D. Food Chem. 46: 313–318.

Tian, X. Q., Chen, T. C., Matsuoka, L. Y., Wortsman, J. & Holick, M. F. (1993) Kinetic and therodynamic studies of the conversion of previtamin $D_3$ in human skin. J. Biol. Chem. 268: 14888–14892.

Webb, A. R., de Costa, B. R. & Holick, M. F. (1989) Sunlight regulates the cutaneous production of vitamin $D_3$ by causing its photodegradation. J. Clin. Endocrinol. Metab. 68: 882–887.

Webb, A. R., Pilbeam, C., Hanafin, N. & Holick, M. F. (1990) A one-year study to evaluate the roles of exposure to sunlight and diet on the circulating concentrations of 25-OH-D in an elderly population in Boston J. Clin. Nutr. 51: 1075–1081.

 **Article Review Form at end of book.**

# WiseGuide Wrap-Up

- The aging of America will pose a significant challenge to all aspects of our nation's health care system.

- Our elderly can offer wisdom, knowledge, experience, skills, perspective, and patience. The least society can do is to develop nutrition education, recommendations, and strategies to meet the needs of our elderly.

- An individual with Alzheimer's disease may experience significant weight loss and a greater likelihood for infection.

## R.E.A.L. Sites

This list provides a print preview of typical **coursewise** R.E.A.L. sites. (There are over 100 such sites at the **courselinks**™ site.) The danger in printing URLs is that web sites can change overnight. As we went to press, these sites were functional using the URLs provided. If you come across one that isn't, please let us know via email to: webmaster@coursewise.com. Use your Passport to access the most current list of R.E.A.L. sites at the **courselinks**™ site.

**Site name:** Administration on Aging

**URL:** http://www.aoa.dhhs.gov

**Why is it R.E.A.L.?** Material for older individuals and their families. Links are provided so one may access practitioners and other health care professionals.

**Activities:** Describe the nutrition programs for the elderly that have been established.

........................................................................................

**Site name:** Better Eating for Better Aging

**URL:** http://www.realtime.net./anr/eatage/html

**Why is it R.E.A.L.?** With the "graying of America," sound nutrition will become more and more critical.

**Activities:** (1)Do vitamin requirements change as we age? (2)Can exercise and sound nutrition affect longevity?

........................................................................................

**Site name:** Cedars-Sinai Health System

**URL:** http://www.csmc.edu/mktg/whatsnew/WellSAID/F197/

**Why is it R.E.A.L.?** This site gives a great deal of accurate and timely information regarding a wide variety of health issues.

**Activities:** According to this site, what are some common effects of malnutrition?

........................................................................................

# section 5

After studying this section, you will know:

- the significant risk factors for cardiovascular disease.

- that coronary artery disease (atherosclerosis) is reversible with lifestyle changes.

- the American Heart Association's diet plan for healthy Americans.

- common ways of acquiring HIV.

- how diet helps in the management of fatigue, diarrhea, and wasting, which are often associated with AIDS.

- the roles of the following in HIV/AIDS and diet sources for each: antioxidants, phytochemicals, and fiber.

- the importance of food safety for people with AIDS (PWA).

# Nutrition Choices for Your Heart and Your Immune System

 **WiseGuide Intro**

A lot is known, but there is a lot more to be discovered, about the association of nutrition to disease. Not only does it make health sense to understand this association, but it makes economic sense as well. The prevention of disease is much more efficient and cost effective than the treatment and cure of illness.

One of my favorite television programs as a child (most of you know this program through reruns on cable) was the "Andy Griffith Show." Life for Andy, Opie, and Aunt Bea was simple, happy, and peaceful. Deputy Barney Fife made life interesting, to say the least, around Mayberry. Often amusing, sometimes sophomoric, Barney, nevertheless, had a sound outlook on life with his "nip it in the bud" philosophy. Think of your diet choices in the same vein as Barney's "nip it" theory. What you eat now can help you "nip disease in the bud" later.

The World Health Organization states that cardiovascular disease claims 12 million lives in the world annually. Cardiovascular disease causes 50% of all deaths in a number of developed countries. In the United States, approximately 250,000 people die from heart attacks each year before they reach the hospital.

Risk factors for cardiovascular disease are many, and their interaction with this phenomenon is complex. Four risk factors are thought to be most significant in predicting cardiovascular disease:

1. Sedentary lifestyle
2. High blood pressure
3. Smoking
4. Blood lipid profile

A number of diet associations (some preventive, some causative) with cardiovascular disease exist, including saturated fat, total fat, omega 3 fatty acids, cholesterol, soluble fiber, antioxidants, sodium, and alcohol.

Although cardiovascular disease is very costly in terms of loss of life, loss of productivity, and expense, the majority of this condition can be managed with lifestyle choices. What is your choice going to be?

As of January of 1995 there were more than 1 million worldwide AIDS cases in adults and children reported to the World Health Organization. Of these, more than 500,000 were in the United States. AIDS (acquired immune deficiency syndrome) was initially noted in the United States in 1981. AIDS is believed to be caused by a virus known as HIV (human immunodeficiency virus). This virus has a negative consequence on the body's immune system. HIV progressively impairs the body's ability to fight infections and certain cancers. The individual with AIDS is susceptible to a host of conditions referred to as "opportunistic infections."

The most common mode of acquiring HIV is via sexual contact with an infected individual. The most risky sexual behavior is that of unprotected anal intercourse. However, the virus can certainly be transmitted through the lining of the vagina, vulva, penis, or mouth during sex as well.

Individuals who use injected drugs are also at a heightened risk for acquiring HIV. Sharing needles or syringes that may contain small quantities of HIV-infected blood can be passed to another person. Since 1985 blood has been screened for HIV; thus, the likelihood of acquiring HIV from an infected blood transfusion sample is remote.

Another possible mode of HIV transmission is from an infected mother to a child. It is believed that 25 percent to 33 percent of untreated pregnant women who are HIV-positive will pass the virus to their child. Use of the drug known as AZT during pregnancy can significantly reduce the likelihood of mother to baby transmission.

Unfortunately, the epidemic is relatively more common among minority populations and is one of the leading causes of death among African American males. The Centers for Disease Control state that the incidence of AIDS is 600 percent and 300 percent greater in African Americans and Hispanics, respectively, than among whites.

Diet is certainly not the culprit for this condition. However, nutrition therapy is vital in the management of fatigue, diarrhea, and wasting, which frequently are associated with AIDS. Moreover, appropriate diet can help to maintain the function of one's immune system during the course of this syndrome.

# Questions

R22. According to the Bogalusa (LA) Heart Study, more than 50 percent of all children eat too much salt, fat, cholesterol, and sugar. Does this concern you? Why or why not?

R23. Triglyceride levels greater than what resulted in a doubling in the likelihood of heart attack risk, heart attack, or bypass surgery? How does triglyceride level affect blood flow dynamics? Why should alcohol and simple carbohydrate (sugar) intake be monitored in regard to triglycerides? What strategies can be taken to manage triglycerides?

R24. Who initially discovered the possible healthy link between alcohol consumption and heart disease? What are the possible mechanisms of this benefit? What type of alcoholic beverage is most beneficial? How much ethanol is enough? How much is too much?

R25. Would you be willing to try the DASH diet to control blood pressure if you were hypertensive?

R26. Potassium supplementation seems to be effective in the reduction of systolic and diastolic blood pressure. What are the possible mechanisms for this?

R27. How many of the subjects lost weight? What is the significance of lower levels in one's CD4 cells? What happened to CD4 cells in conjunction with weight loss?

R28. How did the researchers come up with the idea of vitamin A supplementation and HIV morbidity?

According to the Bogalusa (LA) Heart Study, more than 50 percent of all children eat too much salt, fat, cholesterol, and sugar. Does this concern you? Why or why not?

# Heart-Healthy Learning Starts Early in the Big Easy

Children in elementary school can learn to spurn junk food and can be motivated to adopt healthy lifestyles, beginning in kindergarten.

These are among the findings from Healthy Ahead/Heart Smart, an NHLBI-funded health education research and demonstration program in New Orleans. A comprehensive health promotion program, Health Ahead/Heart Smart addresses the entire school environment. It also has a broader scope than just cardiovascular health: the program incorporates self-efficacy and responsibility skills to help students prevent negative behaviors such as drug and alcohol abuse, school dropout, teenage pregnancy, and violent behavior.

"We help to change young children's behaviors," says Dr. Carolyn Johnson of Tulane University in New Orleans, who helped develop the program. "The results demonstrate that early intervention can halt destructive diet and lifestyle habits

that lead to heart disease and other life-threatening illnesses."

Health Ahead/Heart Smart was launched after the Bogalusa Heart Study (another NHLBI-funded project in Louisiana) found that early signs of atherosclerosis, hypertension, and even coronary artery disease were showing up in children as young as 5 years old.

Health Ahead/Heart Smart has both in-school and after-school components. The in-school component provides education sessions over the school year for children in kindergarten through grade 6. Beginning in kindergarten, participating students are taught to be responsible for their health, adopting the program's message to "Eat sensibly, be active, and feel good about yourself!" For example, children in the school program learn to choose healthier lunch selections in the school cafeteria, such as foods with lower amounts of fat and salt, than are found on the typical school lunch tray.

Program director Dr. Gerald S. Berenson of Tulane University says that one of the keys to the success of Health Ahead/Heart Smart has been having all school personnel—teachers, cafeteria managers, physical education specialists, and administrators—get involved. "For instance, if the kids are to learn about good nutrition, they have to be able to find healthy foods in the cafeteria." Parents, too, adds Dr. Berenson, are involved in the program through a newsletter, volunteer activities, health fairs, and Heart Smart Week.

The program's in-school curriculum covers five main areas: general health and physiology, nutrition, physical fitness or exercise, coping and decision making skills, and the "It's Me" module that encourages students to take charge of their own cognitive and physical health.

The physical fitness component introduces noncompetitive aerobic games and activities that supplement team sports, which

"Heart-Healthy Learning Starts Early in the Big Easy" as appeared in HEART MEMO Special Edition 1996.

## An Important Message from the Children of Bogalusa

Findings from the landmark Bogalusa Heart Study continue to underscore the importance of reaching children at an early age with heart-healthy messages.

Since 1972, more than 14,000 black and white children ages 5 to 17 in Bogalusa, Louisiana, have participated in this NHLBI-funded epidemiologic study. Results of the longitudinal study confirm that the physiological and behavioral risk factors for heart disease and stroke begin in childhood.

Study findings include the following:

- White males experience a dramatic rise in their ratio of low-density lipoprotein (LDL) to high-density lipoprotein (HDL) cholesterol during adolescence, placing them at increased risk for an early heart attack.
- Hormonal and renal factors among black children combine to increase their susceptibility to high blood pressure, one of the major risk factors for heart disease and the chief risk factor for stroke.
- Among all children, cardiovascular risk factors such as high blood pressure and obesity are interrelated, just as they are in adults.
- More than half of all children eat too much salt, fat, cholesterol, and sugar.
- Families with a history of early heart disease have children with an increased risk of heart disease.

Armed with findings from the Bogalusa Heart Study and others like it, researchers have been able to design effective school-based health promotion programs, such as Health Ahead/Heart Smart.

With help from the children of Bogalusa, youngsters everywhere are learning early how to reduce their risk of heart disease.

---

are so heavily emphasized in most schools. The exercise component, Superkids/Superfit, stresses exercise as fun and rewarding for its own sake.

The training portions use hands-on activities to increase students' interest and participation in the program. Children as well as teachers are urged to pledge that they will make gradual but specific changes in their behavior. Schools are advised to provide feedback to parents about how well children do.

Encouraging students to take charge of their own health also involves helping them overcome social pressures to engage in harmful behaviors, such as using drugs. Dr. Berenson says that the Bogalusa Heart Study shows, for example, that social pressure to smoke and to drink alcohol is a problem as early as third grade.

"We have to address social problems, such as alcohol and drug use, violent behavior, and school dropout," he continues. "If we don't, we're not going to be able to teach children good nutrition."

The self-esteem component, adds Dr. Johnson, "addresses very pertinently the idea of taking responsibility for one's health, being assertive—using psychosocial concepts."

The after-school program, currently in only some schools due to funding restraints, involves teachers and parents. The program keeps parents abreast of what their children were learning in school and teaches them how to make heart-healthy meals. Participants in the after-school program reduced their blood pressure, increased their physical activity, stopped smoking, and significantly expanded their understanding of cardiovascular health. The after-school program also includes community activities, such as health fairs and essay and poster contests. Health Ahead/Heart Smart program coordinator Barbara Katzman believes that the after-school program can make a real difference in the health of the entire community.

Health Ahead/Heart Smart is now in 30 elementary schools in New Orleans and elsewhere in Louisiana. The program has proved so effective in getting kids started toward a heart-healthy life that plans are under way to expand the program to even more schools in New Orleans through the use of telecommunications.

Health Ahead/Heart Smart materials are available for only the cost of printing. For more information, contact Dr. Gerald S. Berenson, Director, Center for Cardiovascular Health, School of Public Health and Tropical Medicine, Tulane University Medical Center, 1501 Canal Street, 14th Floor, New Orleans, LA 70112-2824; telephone 504-585-7197; fax 504-585-7194.

 **Article Review Form at end of book.**

Triglyceride levels greater than what resulted in a doubling in the likelihood of heart attack risk, heart attack, or bypass surgery? How does triglyceride level affect blood flow dynamics? Why should alcohol and simple carbohydrate (sugar) intake be monitored in regard to triglycerides? What strategies can be taken to manage triglycerides?

# Why You Ought to Know Your Triglyceride Level

You've had your total blood cholesterol checked and perhaps even your "good" HDL and "bad" LDL levels, but do you know your triglyceride level? Blood levels of triglycerides are usually measured at the same time as cholesterol, but rarely do doctors discuss them with patients, largely because it is generally thought that triglycerides cannot affect heart health on their own. However, more evidence is coming to light that even high triglycerides by themselves can cause problems. Moreover, what's presently considered "normal" for triglyceride levels may actually be too high.

Both the American Heart Association and the National Heart, Lung, and Blood Institute's National Cholesterol Education Program stipulate that a triglyceride concentration that falls below 200 (milligrams per deciliter of blood) is normal. Levels between 200 and 400 are considered borderline high, while 400 and above is deemed high.

But in assessing the heart health of 460 middle-aged and older adults, researchers at the University of Maryland Medical Center in Baltimore found that those with triglyceride levels greater than 100 had twice the risk of those with lower levels of suffering a heart attack, dying from a heart attack, or requiring bypass surgery or another procedure to treat blocked arteries.

Insight into the potential dangers associated with high triglycerides comes from research at Chicago's Rush Medical Center. The findings there: the presence of triglycerides in the blood at levels of 190 or greater makes blood significantly more viscous. As a result of that viscosity, blood flow becomes sluggish, and less oxygen and nutrients are delivered to the heart muscle.

In addition to their own apparent adverse effects on the heart, high triglycerides often come coupled with low levels of beneficial HDL-cholesterol, which works to remove cholesterol from the bloodstream. Elevated triglycerides also frequently go hand-in-hand with a decrease in the size of LDL-cholesterol particles.

That's significant because the smaller the LDL-cholesterol particles, the more susceptible they are to oxidative processes that turn them into "gunk" on artery walls, which in turn obstructs blood flow.

**The recent surge in consumption of fat-free but high-sugar dessert and snack items is at least partly to blame for elevated triglyceride levels in Americans.**

## Getting Measured, Getting Treated

Triglyceride levels are much more variable than cholesterol levels. While cholesterol is carried through the blood with the help of fats, triglycerides *are* fats—the type in your body as well as the type in foods. Thus, a fat-rich meal is a triglyceride-rich meal and will cause a dramatic short-term jump

"Why You Ought to Know Your Triglyceride Level" reprinted with permission, TUFTS UNIVERSITY HEALTH & NUTRITION LETTER, tel: 1-800-274-7581.

in blood triglyceride levels. That's why it's important to fast for at least 12 hours before having blood drawn to measure triglyceride levels. In addition, it's generally advisable to get a second triglyceride test if the first is above the normal range, says Alice Lichtenstein, DSc, a heart disease researcher at the Jean Mayer USDA Human Nutrition Research Center on Aging at Tufts.

If it does turn out that you have high triglycerides, which are common in obese people as well as in those with diabetes, there are many lifestyle steps you can take to lower them. Better still, experts have noted that triglyceride levels are even more responsive to lifestyle changes than blood cholesterol. Therefore, permanent adoption of triglyceride-lowering habits is likely to produce heart-healthy results.

- **Lose excess weight**, most preferably through a combination of cutting back on calories and increasing the level of physical activity at least three days a week.

- **Avoid alcohol**, or at least cut back to a very occasional drink. Even small amounts of alcohol can cause significant jumps in triglyceride levels.

- **Restrict intake of simple carbohydrates** such as table sugar, honey, molasses, and syrups. It is also important to cut back on products made with these items—cakes, pastries, ice cream, cookies, soft drinks, candy, jams, and jellies. Carbohydrates—simple carbohydrates in particular—get converted to triglycerides in the liver. In fact, nutrition experts believe that the recent surge in consumption of fat-free but high-sugar dessert and snack items is at least partly to blame for elevated blood triglyceride levels in Americans.

People have been led to believe that if they simply cut out fat, they're doing all they can to improve heart health. But fat-free sweets often contain more sugar than their full-fat counterparts, which isn't doing anyone with high triglyceride levels any good. In fact, "they may cause high triglyceride levels in some people," Dr. Lichtenstein suggests.

Even complex carbohydrates such as those found in nutritionally dense whole-grain foods can keep triglycerides elevated in someone who is susceptible. For that reason, practitioners usually say that people trying to lower triglycerides should not go on an extremely low-fat, high-carbohydrate diet in which fat makes up, say, only 20 percent of calories. They should opt for a moderately low-fat plan in which fat makes up about 30 percent of calories, with less than 10 percent of calories coming from saturated fat.

- **Eat more fatty fish** such as bluefish, mackerel, and herring. The omega-3 fatty acids contained in several fatty fish meals a week may help keep triglyceride levels stable.

 **Article Review Form at end of book.**

Who initially discovered the possible healthy link between alcohol consumption and heart disease?  What are the possible mechanisms of this benefit?  What type of alcoholic beverage is most beneficial? How much ethanol is enough? How much is too much?

# The Truth About Women & Wine

## Michael Mason

*Michael Mason is a staff writer.*

By now you've probably heard about the French Paradox. It goes like this: Wine does something fabulous—nobody knows what exactly, but it is fabulous—for your heart. A sip of cabernet, a quaff of fumé blanc, and your arteries are trilling with delight. Just look at the French. Lolling about cafés, eating pâté and cream sauces that ought to leave them dead before dessert, and do they have heart disease? No—that's the paradox. How do they do it? Wine by the bucketful! If Americans drank like the French, we'd be free of heart disease, too. So set up the glasses, dear: It's time to pop the cork on a new era.

If that's your rationale for guzzling zinfandel after work, maybe you'd better think about letting this cup pass. True, the research on drinking and health is promising, even exciting. After two decades of study experts agree that for some people a regular nip can reduce the risk of heart attack by 40 percent. That's a miraculous number. Heart disease is the leading cause of death in this country; 500,000 Americans suffer fatal attacks every year. Only one other measure has been shown to better the odds by so much: stopping smoking. If you don't smoke in the first place, says epidemiologist Curtis Ellison of the Boston University School of Medicine, then no other lifestyle change—not starting a light exercise program, not lowering cholesterol from 240 to 210 or your blood pressure from 140 to 120— wards off heart disease as well.

Despite the impressive statistics, however, drinking for health reasons is a tricky proposition. If you figure, One more glass won't hurt—at least I'm protecting my heart, you could be putting yourself at risk for other serious health problems. A lot depends on how much you drink and when. If you're a woman, especially if you're under 50, the picture is even murkier. The science behind alcohol and death may be achingly clear. But what each of us should do about it . . . well, that story is as tangled as the grapevines of Bordeaux.

The notion that the noon cocktail might somehow benefit the body wasn't always welcomed with open arms. Alcohol has a long, checkered history in this puritanical country, and even some of the first researchers on drinking and heart disease balked at their own findings.

Arthur Klatsky, a cardiologist with the Kaiser Permanente Medical Center in Oakland, California, and his colleague Gary Friedman were among that early crew. Twenty-five years ago they found themselves sitting atop a scientific gold mine: computerized medical histories from hundreds of thousands of enrollees in the Kaiser program. Back then it was unusual to have so many records available in one place. Rarer still, many of the patients had filled out questionnaires on their living habits, including whether they drank alcohol. Seeing a chance to identify new risks for heart disease, Klatsky and Friedman gathered data from 500 heart attack victims and compared them to a similar group of healthy patients.

"We started out looking at things like number of headaches and other symptoms," Klatsky recalls. "But one of the most striking differences was alcohol. Nondrinkers were at higher risk for heart attacks than light drinkers." Klatsky and Friedman published this finding in 1974— to no great fanfare—and subsequently performed more detailed surveys of 130,000 Kaiser patients. To their surprise, the results were the same. Light drinkers were having fewer heart attacks and living longer.

"At first I was sufficiently leery that I tried to attack the finding myself," says Klatsky. After all, doctors had long viewed alcohol as a source of addiction, and in the decades since Prohibition the government had spent tens of millions of dollars warning Americans away from the bottle.

Yet the discovery was no fluke. Over the past 15 years signs of this same relationship between alcohol and mortality have appeared in more than two dozen large population studies in Europe and North America. In a 12-year survey of 85,000 nurses aged 34 to 59, Harvard researchers found that women who drank a few times a week had less chance of death than abstainers. A 13-year study of 12,000 British physicians—all of them men—found that light drinkers were living longer than nondrinkers, primarily because of lower heart disease rates. And after tracking the health of 3,700 women aged 45 to 74 for 13 years, researchers at the Centers for Disease Control and Prevention discovered that women who drank moderately were 39 percent less likely than nondrinkers to suffer from a common form of heart disease.

How it works, no one is sure. Drinking raises blood levels of good cholesterol (high-density lipoprotein, or HDL), which may slow the formation of dangerous plaques in the arteries. And immediately after it's consumed, alcohol seems to make certain blood-clotting cells less sticky, which may prevent blockages. Whatever the mechanism, the evidence for alcohol's heart protection is so overwhelming that what once seemed bunkum is fast gaining legitimacy.

Last year both the U.S. government and the American Heart Association acknowledged, if grudgingly, that moderate drinking might help adults live a little longer. At the insistence of Congress, the National Institute on Alcohol Abuse and Alcoholism awarded $2 million in grants for research into the potential benefits of alcohol. A conservative Washington think tank sued the U.S. Bureau of Alcohol, Tobacco, and Firearms to lift a rule forbidding health claims on wine bottles. And the American College of Cardiology encouraged everyone to hoist a glass by citing abstinence from alcohol as a probable risk for heart disease.

"It takes a long time for an idea like this to be accepted, because people are used to thinking about alcohol as evil," says Meir Stampfer, an epidemiologist at the Harvard School of Public Health. "But if you aren't drinking, you really ought to consider it."

Maybe, maybe not. For many of us, all the hoopla about drinking has raised more questions than it has answered. Anne-Catherine Vinickas, a marketing

**No one actually knows if drinking in your thirties can keep you from getting a heart attack in your sixties.**

official with a San Diego transit agency, first heard about the French Paradox from a television newscast. It made an impression: These days Vinickas often throws together a smashing pine-nut risotto for dinner, and she likes nothing better that to coax it down with a glass of wine.

But the news also left Vinickas with the impression that only red wine benefits the heart. "It's too bad," she says. "I drink white and probably not as much as they were talking about, so it's not doing me a bit of good."

The boom in the red wine industry suggests Vinickas isn't the only one who got the message. Last year consumer sales reached a record $726 million amid strong consumer demand for zinfandels (up 41 percent), merlots (29 percent), pinot noirs (21 percent), and cabernets (10 percent). In 1993 three of four California wineries were losing money; now three in four are profitable.

Yet wine-makers are simply riding the tailwind of a misleading media campaign. Despite the televised transformation of merlot into medicine, most scientists believe that *any* alcoholic beverage will protect the heart.

What matters most is ethanol, the kind of alcohol in hard liquor and beer as well as wine. Wine also contains antioxidants and other compounds that may turn out to be especially useful someday. But ethanol is what buttresses good cholesterol levels and keeps sticky blood clots from forming. And it provides this type of insurance against heart disease whatever form it takes. Studies have shown that Japanese

## Should Americans Really Be Encouraged to Drink?

The heart benefits of alcohol may be compelling—for some of us, at least. But even if the prescription is right, ours may be the wrong society for it. Though we drink less per capita than most other nations, our alcoholism rate is among the highest in the world.

If we were talking about pills, not beer or wine, the dangers would be obvious, says Michael Criqui, an epidemiologist at the University of California at San Diego. "Suppose alcohol were brought before the Food and Drug Administration for approval as a heart drug. Trials would show some cardiac protection, but they would also show that 10 percent of users would develop lifelong addiction. The potential for harm is just too high."

Part of the problem is that most Americans have a love/hate relationship with the bottle. We are a nation of bingers and teetotalers, surrendering ourselves to Saturday night benders, then swearing on Sunday we'll never touch another drop.

Still, some segments of our society manage to drink moderately, even to get drunk on occasion, without disaster. Psychiatrist George Vaillant of Harvard Medical School tracked the health of 400 men from the Boston area for more than 50 years. The men from Italian American families were seven times less likely to become alcoholics than those from Irish American families.

Some experts speculate that genetics may play a role in explaining why certain cultures are more vulnerable to alcoholism than others. But attitude may be more important, Vaillant says. While Italians viewed drinking as a matter-of-fact part of their daily lives, the Irish stigmatized it as a sin—in church, at least. In the bars, Vaillant found, Irish men were far more accepting of drunkenness than their Italian neighbors and even admired one another's capacity to overindulge.

If we could emulate our Italian fellow citizens, experts say, it would make sense for health watchdogs to push the light-drinking message. But given our current ambivalence, alcohol could prove one of the riskiest remedies we've ever tried.   —M. M.

---

American men in Honolulu, for instance, earn the same cardiac benefits from sake that the French do from wine.

"The wine industry just loves the health message and tries to promote it," say Mary Jane Ashley, an epidemiologist at the University of Toronto. "But the active ingredient is ethanol. If wine-drinkers seem healthier, it's probably just because they tend to be well-to-do."

Still, that's no reason to breathe a sigh of relief if vodka is your drink of choice. The reduction in heart disease risk attributed to drinking has been observed in broad surveys of large populations. That doesn't mean every individual benefits from a daily nip. Martini or merlot, alcohol is fickle medicine—especially for women.

In Harvard's nurse study, one of the largest groups of women ever examined, moderate drinking helped only those over age 50. Several other studies have produced the same finding, and for women like Vinickas that presents something of a conundrum. For one thing, she's only 43. She also gets plenty of exercise and has no apparent risk for heart disease. So here's the question that experts have a hard time answering: Do women like her benefit from drinking?

The fact is, among pre-menopausal women, the risk of heart disease is vanishingly small. In 1993, the most recent year for which statistics are available, 240,000 women died from heart attacks, but only 6,200 of them were under 55. Estrogen seems to play a pivotal role in protect-ing younger women, though researchers aren't sure how.

But it's clear regular tippling won't improve the odds for most of these women. It's simple: You can't protect yourself from a disease there's virtually no chance you'll get. Perhaps more important, no one knows whether drinking in your thirties keeps you from getting heart attacks in your sixties.

"I wouldn't advise a young woman not to drink," says Klatsky. "But if she had no risks for heart disease, I'd have to say that having a drink each day probably wouldn't do her much good." The same logic applies to men under 40, the age at which their heart disease rates begin to rise.

For young women who *do* have risk factors for heart disease—obesity, mildly elevated blood pressure, or a parent who had a heart attack before turning 60—light drinking may be helpful, as long as they have no other reasons to avoid alcohol. And alcohol can work magic for women once they pass menopause and their estrogen levels decline. Modest amounts of alcohol seem to shore up the body's natural production of this key hormone, improve the balance of good and bad cholesterol, and keep arteries open. For women in their sixties and seventies, the age range at which *their* heart disease rates rise, a little alcohol may make a lot of sense.

With one possible exception: women on estrogen replacement therapy. Studies show that those little pills help prevent clogged arteries, and it's not clear that alcohol provide much additional benefit. Not only that, drinking seems to accelerate the estrogen's absorption into the bloodstream, which may raise the chances of breast cancer. Still, three-quarters of postmenopausal women are not on hormone therapy, and for them a martini, say, might be just the right heart prescription.

Even if you fall into one of the alcohol-friendly groups, you have one more reason to be wary: The good effects of ethanol decline sharply if you drink too much. By and large, experts in this country now agree that one drink a day for women, and two for men, is the optimal amount. But researchers at the University of Western Australia recently came up with even lower numbers. Analyzing 148 studies of mortality among drinkers and nondrinkers, they found that women who had less than one drink daily were the least likely to die of any cause, outliving women who abstained from alcohol. At one drink or slightly more daily, a woman's change of death began to parallel that of an abstainer; at just two drinks, her chance of death was 13 percent higher than a nondrinker's. The researchers concluded that the best "dose" for women was "approximately two standard drinks per day less than in men."

Which is to say, hardly any at all. Women who lived longest were having not quite half a drink a day. The Australians consider a standard drink to be ten grams of pure ethanol, while the typical American drink holds 12 grams. Factor in the difference, and the ideal amount for women is hardly enough to last through a plate of Vinickas's risotto.

"One drink a day is the maximum amount for women," says Ashley. "You can get most of the heart benefit from less." In the Harvard Nurses study, for instance, researchers found that just one to three drinks a week

brought about a 17 percent drop in chances of death for middle-aged women, compared to non-drinkers.

That may sound like good news. Even abstemious Aunt Tilly should be able to manage a measly five ounces for her heart's sake. But how practical is this prescription? Committed teetotalers aren't likely to change their ways, no matter how sweet the carrot that researchers are dangling. And what moderate drinker is going to stop happily at half a drink? Even wine-lovers, the most temperate of imbibers, tend to consumer more than one glass at an average sitting. Two drinks are de rigueur for those who prefer beer or spirits. Sipping just a smidge seems pointless somehow, like ordering a hot fudge sundae just to take one bite.

Besides, when experts talk about an average drink, they mean five ounces of wine, 12 ounces of beer, or one and a half ounces of 80-proof liquor.

**A woman who has two or more drinks a day may raise her risk of breast cancer by as much as 40 percent.**

Which is a whole lot less than what those stemware diri-gibles you get at fancy housewares stores can hold. And at restaurants, if the bartender's generous, watch out.

Countless Americans may unknowingly drink more than they need to gladden their hearts. And that's what worries some experts, because at higher amounts—not that much higher than the one-drink guideline—alcohol carries health risks that may outweigh its benefits. When plotted on a graph, the death rates among drinkers form a J-shaped curve: The chances of dying dip if women drink just a little more than not-at-all but begin to rise

again if they take as few as two drinks a day. The heaviest drinkers—those who have more than six servings a day—not only lose the heart benefits of alcohol but also die from other events such as accident or cancer at extraordinarily high rates.

In fact, here's something you don't hear much about the French Paradox: While heart disease rates are low in France, the French don't live much longer than we do. They just die differently—often from cirrhosis, accidents, and other problems related to alcohol use and abuse.

Among American women, the most frightening "other problem" may be a greater risk of breast cancer. According to the Harvard School of Public Health, two drinks a day may raise a woman's odds of getting this deadly disease by 25 percent. That may be a conservative estimate. Some epidemiologists believe the risk rises as much as 40 percent.

In either case, however, the likelihood of breast cancer remains small, especially compared to the chances of de-veloping heart disease. About 43,000 women lose their lives to breast cancer annually, while some 240,000 die of heart attacks. But in real life, figuring the probabilities can be a difficult and nerve-racking calculus.

Remember our risotto-loving friend? Vinickas's maternal grandmother died of breast cancer in 1945 at age 53, and Vinickas's doctor has already warned her to have annual mammograms. Family history puts her at risk for breast cancer. Conceivably, a daily chardonnay might make matters worse.

"It's a big worry," says Vinickas. "I certainly don't want to increase the chances of it happening." But how can she know whether a drink here and there matters? She can't.

Believe it or not, the picture gets still more complicated: *When* women drink may be as important as how much they drink. Epidemiologist Maurizio Trevisan of the University of Buffalo recently collected survey data from 8,000 male and 6,000 female drinkers in Italy. Those who drank apart from meals, he found, tended to have more overall than those who enjoyed their drinks with food. And the alcohol consumed away from the dinner table provided no additional cardiovascular benefits.

Worse, after accounting for other risk factors, Trevisan found that women who drank apart from meals had an 80 percent greater chance of dying from noncardiovascular causes than those who paired food and drink.

The reason? Not only is drinking while you eat a hedge against drinking too much—which may keep your cancer risk steady—but there seems to be a healthy synergy between what's on the plate and what's in the glass. For starters, food slows the absorption of ethanol into the bloodstream. That's particularly useful for women because the enzyme that breaks down alcohol in the stomach is four times less active on women than in men (barroom Don Juans have depended on this quirk for generations). Drink while you eat and you're less apt to get sloshed and end up in a fatal car crash. Also, ethanol may be even more effective at inhibiting the blood clotting caused by dietary fat if you drink and eat at the same time.

Feeling woozy yourself? No surprise: Getting a grasp on the drinking debate isn't easy. So here's some advice. If alcohol is to be your weapon against heart disease, the program should include not more than one drink a day,

preferably less, taken at meals. That's not quite as glamorous as sucking down a bottle of burgundy with a stranger at a Paris café. And even in relatively small amounts, the risks of drinking may well exceed the benefits.

Already some experts are questioning whether a health strategy that requires so much hairsplitting can be worth the trouble. "There are easier ways to avoid heart attacks," says psychologist Tom Greenfield of the Alcohol Research Group in Berkeley, California. "Exercise. Reduce the stress in your job. These behaviors carry a lot less risk."

Greenfield isn't the only one who thinks so. Despite America's incessant rhapsodizing about drinking habits in France, the French themselves are choosing to drink less and less. We're reaching for the cabernet; they're reaching for the Perrier.

Now *there's* a paradox.

 **Article Review Form at end of book.**

Would you be willing to try the DASH diet to control blood pressure if you were hypertensive?

# Beyond the Salt Shaker

## A New Look at Diet and Blood Pressure

For years health professionals have echoed the same blood-pressure-lowering mantra: cut back on sodium and alcohol and lose weight. That may change, however, given the results of a new study that took place at 6 major medical centers around the country.

Researchers from the centers put more than 450 people on 1 of 3 diets, none of which involved rigid sodium or alcohol restriction or even weight loss. One group followed an eating plan that included nearly 10 servings of fruits and vegetables a day plus low-fat dairy foods. The plan was also low in saturated and total fat. Fat comprised 26 percent of total calories—well below the 30-percent benchmark health experts recommend.

A second group ate a diet that was also heavy on produce, with 8-plus servings a day on average. But this was a high-fat plan, containing 36 percent of calories as fat. The third group followed a typical American diet: fewer than 4 servings of fruits and vegetables daily and 36 percent of calories as fat.

## The DASH Diet

Scientists don't know what it is about the high-fruit-and-vegetable, low-fat DASH diet that may help lower blood pressure. Some point to the fact that the eating plan is richer than the typical American diet in minerals such as potassium, magnesium, and calcium, which preliminary research suggests may be involved in keeping blood pressure down.

One thing is for sure. The eating plan is a particularly produce-rich version of the kind of healthful eating pattern experts urge all Americans to adopt to lower the risk of chronic diseases like heart disease and cancer.

The plan here shows how many servings of various foods a person on a 2,000-calorie diet would have to eat to adhere to a DASH regimen.

For sample menus, an excellent overview on the roles of sodium, alcohol, and weight in blood pressure, and other information related to hypertension, people with Internet access can visit the DASH Diet Web site at http://dash.bwh.harvard.edu. Or, to learn more about blood pressure, call the National Heart, Lung, and Blood Institute at 1-800-575-9355.

| Food Group | Daily Number of Servings | 1 Serving |
|---|---|---|
| Grains and grain products | 7–8 | 1 slice bread<br>½ cup dry cereal<br>½ cup cooked rice, pasta, or cereal |
| Vegetables | 4–5 | 1 cup raw leafy vegetable<br>½ cup cooked vegetable<br>6 oz. vegetable juice |
| Fruits | 4–5 | 1 medium fruit<br>½ cup fresh, frozen, or canned fruit<br>¼ cup dried fruit<br>6 oz. fruit juice |
| Low-fat or non-fat dairy foods | 2–3 | 8 oz. milk<br>1 cup yogurt<br>1.5 oz. cheese |
| Lean meats, poultry, or fish | 2 or less | 3 oz. cooked meats, skinless poultry, or fish |
| Nuts and other alternatives to meat | ½ | 1.5 oz. or ⅓ cup nuts<br>2 Tbsp. seeds<br>½ cup cooked legumes |

After 8 weeks, people who followed the higher-fat, fruit-and-vegetable-rich diet experienced reductions in blood pressure. But those on the low-fat, high-produce plan checked in with blood pressure readings that had fallen the most. Specifically, systolic pressure (the first number in a reading) had dropped 5.5 millimeters more than in the group following the typical American diet. Diastolic pressure (the second number) had come down by 3 millimeters more. Those on that plan who started out with hypertension generally ended up with particularly significant reductions in blood pressure—reductions similar in magnitude to those often seen in patients who begin drug therapy.

**Those following the low-fat, high-fruit-and-vegetable plan had blood pressure readings that fell the most.**

The findings have created a buzz among medical experts for a number of reasons. For one, all 3 groups took in at least 2,800 milligrams of sodium daily—17 percent more than the 2,400-milligram limit recommended by the National Academy of Sciences. Furthermore, none of the participants was told to abstain from alcohol or follow a reduced-calorie plan for weight loss. Thus, the new eating plan, dubbed the DASH diet for Dietary Approaches to Stop Hypertension, allows far more flexibility and therefore is the kind of healthful diet a person can live with for the long haul (although experts speculate that combining established interventions with the low-fat, high-produce eating plan might promote even greater drops in blood pressure).

 **Article Review Form at end of book.**

Potassium supplementation seems to be effective in the reduction of systolic and diastolic blood pressure. What are the possible mechanisms for this?

# Effects of Oral Potassium on Blood Pressure

## Meta-analysis of randomized controlled clinical tests

Paul K. Whelton, MD, MSc; Jiang He, MD, PhD; Jeffrey A. Cutler, MD, MPH; Frederick L. Brancati, MD, MHS; Lawrence J. Appel, MD, MPH; Dean Follmann, PhD; Michael J. Klag, MD, MPH

*From the Welch Center for Prevention, Epidemiology and Clinical Research, The Johns Hopkins University School of Hygiene and Public Health and School of Medicine, Baltimore, Md (Drs Whelton, He, Brancati, Appel, and Klag), and Division of Epidemiology and Clinical Applications, National Heart, Lung, and Blood Institute, National Institutes of Health, Bethesda, Md (Drs Cutler and Follmann). Dr Whelton is now with School of Public Health, Tulane University, New Orleans, La.*

*Reprints: Paul K. Whelton, MD, MSc, Office of the Dean, 17th Floor, 1501 Canal St, New Orleans, LA 70112.*

**Objective**—To assess the effects of supplementation with oral potassium on blood pressure in humans.

**Design**—Meta-analysis of randomized controlled trials.

**Data Sources**—English-language articles published before July 1995.

**Study Selection**—Thirty-three randomized controlled trials (2609 participants) in which potassium supplementation was the only difference between the intervention and control conditions.

**Data Extraction**—Using a standardized protocol, 2 of us independently abstracted information on sample size, duration, study design, potassium dose, participant characteristics, and treatment results.

**Results**—By means of a random-effects model, findings from individual trials were pooled, after results for each trial were weighted by the inverse of its variance. An extreme effect of potassium in lowering blood pressure was noted in 1 trial. After exclusion of this trial, potassium supplementation was associated with a significant reduction in mean (95% confidence interval) systolic and diastolic blood pressure of –3.11 mm Hg (–1.91 to –4.31 mm Hg) and –1.97 mm Hg (–.52 to –3.42 mm Hg), respectively. Effects of treatment appeared to be enhanced in studies in which participants were concurrently exposed to a high intake of sodium.

**Conclusions**—Our results support the premise that low potassium intake may play an important role in the genesis of high blood pressure. Increased potassium intake should be considered as a recommendation for prevention and treatment of hypertension, especially in those who are unable to reduce their intake of sodium.

*JAMA. 1997;277:1624–1632*

High blood pressure (BP) is an important modifiable risk factor for cardiovascular disease.[1] Interpopulation,[2]intrapopulation,[2–5] and migrant[6–12] studies suggest that several factors play a role in age-related increases in BP and hypertension. Overweight, excessive sodium chloride intake, and alcohol consumption are established causes of hypertension[10–11]

Observational studies have demonstrated an inverse relationship between potassium and BP[12-18] but also associations between BP and nutritional variables, some of which are highly correlated with one another.[18] In 1928, a clinical trial of potassium supplementation in hypertension was reported.[19] Since then, almost 60 reports of the BP-lowering effects of potassium in humans have been published,[20-79] about half randomized controlled clinical trials, and most too small for definitive results. Pooling of results allows more precise estimates of intervention effect and exploration of the basis for outcome heterogeneity.

## Methods

### Selection of Studies

The English-language literature was searched for all reports on the effects of potassium supplementation in humans published before July 1995. This included (1) a MEDLINE search with "blood pressure," "dietary potassium," "potassium," and "potassium chloride" used as search terms, (2) a review of reference lists from original research articles and review articles[10,80-82]; and (3) a review of our reference files. Sixty-two reports were identified[19-79] and independently reviewed by 2 of us (P. K. W. and J. H.) to determine whether they met predetermined criteria for inclusion in our analysis. Areas of disagreement or uncertainty were adjudicated by other authors. For inclusion, a study had to have (1) been used on human experimentation, (2) included a treatment (potassium supplementation) intervention and concurrent control group (using either parallel or crossover design),

(3) included no intervention difference between treatment and control conditions other than potassium supplementation (concurrent treatment with antihypertensive medications or sodium restriction had to have been applied equally to treatment and control groups or periods); (4) used randomly allocated study participants to treatment or control groups; and (5) reported mean BP changes (systolic and/or diastolic) after both active and control treatment. Inclusion criteria did not include requirement for success of intervention or duration of therapy, but the impact of these factors was explored.

Thirty-three trials met inclusion criteria in this analysis.[50-79] Major reasons for exclusion were (1) nonrandomized treatment allocation,[24,33] (2) lack of concurrent control group or balanced crossover comparison period,* (3) antihypertensive drug therapy in control but not treatment group,[46,47] (4) comparison of treatment with potassium chloride vs treatment with sodium chloride,[22,25-28] (5) comparison of treatment with combined potassium supplementation and sodium reduction intervention vs control treatment with a normal diet,[40,43,44] (6) differences in other dietary nutrients between treatment and control groups,[49] and (7) absence of data to calculate the net mean change in BP from baseline to end of follow-up.[34,48]

### Data Abstraction

Information was abstracted independently by 2 of us (P. K. W. and J. H.) who were blinded to each other's coding but not to treat-

*References 21, 23, 29–32, 35, 36, 38, 39, 41, 42

ment group. Interrater agreement was greater than 95% for initial coding of data related to BP results. Study characteristics recorded were as follows: (1) first author's name, publication year, and country of origin; (2) number of participants; (3) mean age, age range, and race and sex distributions of participants; (4) design details, including whether parallel or crossover and open, single blind, or double blind; (5) study duration; (6) presence or absence of hypertension and use of antihypertensive medications; (7) methods of BP measurement (automatic or manual); (8) dose and formulation of potassium supplementation, placebo, and other treatment intervention; (9) average pretreatment BP; (10) average pretreatment 24-hour urinary excretion of sodium and potassium; (11) net change from pretreatment to end of follow-up in urinary excretion of sodium and potassium, body weight, and BP (systolic and diastolic) for treatment and control conditions; and (12) mean 24-hour urinary sodium excretion during follow-up, recorded at the trial's end, this being the only time point when such data were consistently available in all studies.

### Statistical Analysis

For each trial we calculated mean baseline BP and urinary electrolyte excretion by pooling average values for the potassium supplementation and control groups. For parallel trials, net changes in blood pressure, urinary electrolyte excretion, and weight were calculated as the difference (potassium supplementation minus control) of the changes (baseline minus follow-up) in these mean values. For crossover trials, net changes were calculated as the mean difference in values at the end of the potassium supplementation and control periods. In a few instances, these values had to be estimated from illustrations.[53,59,61,75]

To calculate pooled effect size, each study was assigned weights consisting of the reciprocal of the total variance for BP change (1 weight for systolic and 1 weight for diastolic). Because variances for BP net changes were not reported directly for most studies, they were calculated from confidence intervals, $t$ statistics, $P$ values, or individual variances for intervention and control groups (parallel trials) or intervention or control periods (crossover trials). For parallel trials in which variance for paired differences was reported separately for each group, we calculated a pooled variance for net change by standard methods.[83] When the variance for paired differences was not reported, we calculated it from variances at baseline and at the end of follow-up. On the basis of the method of Follmann et al,[84] we assumed a correlation coefficient of 0.5 between initial and final BPs. We assumed equal variances during the trial and between intervention and control groups.

Estimates of the mean effect of potassium supplementation on BP and corresponding 95% confidence intervals were calculated by means of fixed-effects and random-effects models,[85,86] which yielded similar patterns but different effect estimates. Homogeneity of effect size across studies was tested by Q statistics.[87] Because of significant variation in effect size across the 33 trials (see the "Results" section), we present re-

sults from the random-effects model used as described.[87] Assumption of heterogeneity implied by use of the random-effects model is plausible, because the trials were conducted in subgroups that differed in hypertensive status, race, and other covariables.

To explore influence of covariables on net exchanges in BP, a series of prestated subgroup analyses were performed. Subgroups were selected on the basis of biological plausibility and our knowledge of the literature. Continuous variables (e.g., sample size) were categorized by tertile. For each subgroup, pooled effects were calculated by the random-effects model and statistical significance was tested by analysis of variance. Univariate and multivariate linear regression models were used to explore the influence of a series of prestated covariates on net BP change. The linear regression models were weighted by the inverse of variance for change in BP in each trial. For each trial, the covariates were calculated as average values at baseline or during the study, or average change from baseline. Where information on mean age was missing (7 trials), we used an average of minimum and maximum values. Where information on race was not reported but the trial was conducted in Europe, we assumed all participants were white. For crossover trials, we used mean BP and 24-hour urinary electrolyte excretion information during the control period as baseline values. For the 2 trials in which no urinary electrolyte excretion information was available,[64,65] we used an average of values for the remaining 31 trials. Covariables for multiple linear regression analyses were selected

on the basis of results of our univariate analyses and previous biological knowledge.

## Results

Participant and study design characteristics for the 33 clinical trials included in our meta-analysis are presented in Table 1. The trials, conducted between 1981 and 1995, varied from 10 to 484 participants, with a median of 32. Total number of participants was 2609, but data for 44 subjects were evaluated twice in separate protocols. All trials were conducted in adults, with ages ranging from 18 to 79 years. Twenty-one trials included women, but men were the majority or sole participants in 24. Blacks were represented in 14 of 16 trials with available information on race and were the majority or sole participants in 6. Whites were the sole or majority participants in 10 trials. Twenty-one trials were conducted in hypertensive subjects (1560 participants) and 12 in normotensive subjects (1005 participants). Antihypertensive medications were concurrently administered in 4 of 21 trials conducted in hypertensive patients. In 3 of these trials,[55,57,65] all study participants were treated with thiazide or thiazidelike diuretics (no concurrent administration of potassium-sparing medications). In the fourth trial, 84% of study participants received potassium-wasting diuretics (chlorthalidone or hydrochlorothiazide [no concurrent potassium-sparing medication]) and 43% were treated with a β-blocker; a small percentage of the subjects was taking other medications, eg, reserpine (6%), hydralazine (6%), and methyldopa (5%).[66] Underlying renal disease was excluded in all 33 trials, and hyperkalemia was an exclusion in 11 studies.[51,53,56,58,64,68,71,72] Hypokalemia was an exclusion in 1 trial,[63] and 2 trials were restricted to hypokalemic participants.[55,57]

A crossover design was used in 21 trials and a parallel-arm design in 12. Treatment was double blind in 23 trials, single blind in 3, and open in 7. In 2 of the single-blind trials, observers were unaware of treatment assignment,[58,75] whereas participants were masked in the third.[65] Trials varied from 4 days to 3 years, with a median of 5 weeks. Dosage of potassium prescribed in the intervention arm was 60 mmol/d or more in all but 2 trials and was 100 mmol/d or more in 10 trials (median, 75 mmol/d). In 28 trials (85%) potassium was administered as a pill, and in 24 trials (73%) it was administered as a chloride salt. Twenty-four trials (73%) were placebo controlled. In 4 of the remaining 9 trials, both treatment groups were treated with potassium but the intervention group was given a higher dose than the control group.[50,53,69] In the other 5 trials, intervention and control groups were maintained on a similar diet, but the intervention group was concurrently given potassium supplements.[57,61,65,70] Average pretreatment systolic and diastolic BPs ranged from 105 to 187 mm Hg (median, 147 mm Hg) and 63 to 105 mm Hg (median, 95 mm Hg), respectively. For 27 trials with such information, average pretreatment urinary potassium excretion ranged from 39 to 79 mmol/d (median, 63 mmol/d). Only 3 trials were conducted in participants with a pretreatment

average 24-hour urinary potassium excretion less than 50 mmol/d.[55,60,79] In 26 trials with pretreatment measurement of urinary sodium excretion, values varied from 68 to 196 mmol/d (median, 154 mmol/d), with an average of greater than 160 mmol/d in 11 trials. Average pretreatment serum potassium level varied from 3.0 to 4.7 mmol/L in 19 trials (83%).

In 31 trials with available urinary electrolyte excretion estimates, average net change in urinary potassium excretion for intervention vs control varied from 0 to 129 mmol/d (median, 50 mmol/d) and was 40 mmol/d or more in 21 trials (68%) (Table 2). Weighted net change in urinary potassium excretion was 53 mmol/d. Net change in urinary sodium excretion for intervention vs control group ranged from –55 to 44 mmol/d, with a median of 7 mmol/d. Average urinary sodium excretion during follow-up in 31 trials in which it was measured ranged from 28 to 221 mmol/d (median, 150 mmol/d); in 12 trials the average was greater than 160 mmol/d and in 4, 80 mmol/d or less. Net mean change in body weight for intervention vs control group was available for 19 trials (58%) and showed a range of –0.9 to 1.2 kg (median, –0.1 kg).

Possibility of publication bias was examined by plotting sample size against corresponding change in systolic or diastolic BP, resulting in a funnel-shaped pattern with broader spread of net change in BP for smaller studies and a progressively decreasing spread as sample size increased. After an outlier trial was removed,[68] funnel plots were symmetrical about the mean net change in BP. A rank correlation

test between sample size and standardized effect size based on Kendall τ showed rank correlation coefficients of 0.08 ($P$>.50) for systolic and 0.22 ($P$>.05) for diastolic BP. Thus, no evidence that publication bias was a factor in our meta-analysis emerged.

Compared with control, intervention was associated with an average net change in BP ranging from –41.0 to 2.8 mm Hg for systolic BP and –17.0 to 4.8 mm Hg for diastolic BP (Table 2). There was an intervention-related trend toward a reduction in systolic BP in 26 (81%) of the 32 trials with the requisite information, and in 11 trials (34%) BP reduction was statistically significant (Figure 1). For diastolic BP, a trend toward intervention-related reduction in BP was noted in 24 (73%) of 33 trials, and in 11 (30%), BP reduction was statistically significant (Figure 2).

Overall pooled estimates of effect of potassium supplementation on systolic and diastolic BP were –4.4 and –2.4 mm Hg, respectively ($P$<.001 for both values; Table 3). Exclusion of an outlier trial[68] reduced overall pooled effect size estimates, which were still significant ($P$<.001) for systolic (–3.1 mm Hg) and diastolic (–1.97 mm Hg) BP. Effect estimates were higher for systolic (–4.9 mm Hg) and diastolic (–2.7 mm Hg) BP when analyses were restricted to 29 trials with a documented intervention-related net change in urinary potassium excretion of 20 mmol/d or more. Effect estimates for systolic (–4.9 mm Hg) and diastolic (–2.7 mm Hg) BP were also higher when analyses were restricted to 29 trials in which no antihypertensive medications were administered.

**Table 1** Participant and Study Design Characteristics in 33 Potassium Supplementation Trials

| Source, y | No. of Subjects | Age, y Mean | Age, y Range | % Male | % White | % Hypertensive | Antihypertensive Medication | Study Design* | Study Duration, wk |
|---|---|---|---|---|---|---|---|---|---|
| Skrabal et al,[50] 1981 | | | | | | | | | |
| (a) | 20 | ... | 21–25 | 100 | ... | 0 | No | XO | 2 |
| (b) | 20 | ... | 21–25 | 100 | ... | 0 | No | XO | 2 |
| MacGregor et al,[51] 1982 | 23 | 45 | 26–66 | 52 | 78 | 100 | No | XD | 4 |
| Khaw and Thom,[52] 1982 | 20 | ... | 22–35 | 100 | ... | 0 | No | XD | 2 |
| Richards et al,[53] 1984 | 12 | ... | 19–52 | 67 | ... | 100 | No | XO | 4–6 |
| Smith et al,[54] 1985 | 20 | 53 | 30–66 | 55 | 90 | 100 | No | XD | 4 |
| Kaplan et al,[55] 1985 | 16 | 49 | 35–66 | 38 | 19 | 100 | Yes‡ | XD | 6 |
| Zoccali et al,[56] 1985 | 19 | 38 | 26–53 | 53 | 100 | 100 | No | XD | 2 |
| Bulpitt et al,[57] | 33 | 55 | ... | 45 | ... | 100 | Yes‡ | PO | 12 |
| Matlou et al,[58] 1986 | 32 | 51 | 34–62 | 0 | 0 | 100 | No | XS | 6 |
| Barden et al,[59] 1986 | 44 | 32 | 18–55 | 0 | ... | 0 | No | XD | 4 |
| Poulter and Sever,[60] 1986 | 19 | ... | 18–47 | 100 | 0 | 0 | No | XD | 2 |
| Chalmers et al,[61] 1986 | | | | | | | | | |
| (a) | 107 | 52 | ... | 85 | ... | 100 | No | PO | 12 |
| (b) | 105 | 52 | ... | 86 | ... | 100 | No | PO | 12 |
| Grobbee et al,[62] 1987 | 40 | 24 | 18–28 | 85 | ... | 100 | No | XD | 6 |
| Siani et al,[63] 1987 | 37 | 45 | 21–61 | 62 | ... | 100 | No | PD | 15 |
| Svetkey et al,[64] 1987 | 101 | 51 | ... | 74 | 88 | 100 | No | PD | 8 |
| Medical Research Council,[65] 1987 | 484 | ... | 35–64 | 56 | ... | 100 | Yes‡ | PS | 24 |
| Grimm et al,[66] 1988 | 312 | 58 | 45–68 | 100 | ... | 100 | Yes‡ | PD | 12 |
| Cushman and Langford,[67] 1988 | 58 | 54 | 26–69 | 100 | 47 | 100 | No | PD | 10 |
| Obel[68] 1989 | 48 | 41 | 23–56 | 44 | 0 | 100 | No | PD | 16 |
| Krishna et al,[69] 1989 | 10 | ... | 20–40 | 100 | 100 | 0 | No | XD | 10 d |
| Hypertension Prevention Trial,[70] 1990 | 391 | 39 | 25–49 | 64 | 83 | 0 | No | PO | 3 y |
| Mullen and O'Connor,[71] 1990 | | | | | | | | | |
| (a) | 24 | 25 | 22–31 | 100 | 92 | 0 | No | XD | 2 |
| (b) | 24 | 25 | 22–31 | 100 | 92 | 0 | No | XD | 2 |
| Patki et al,[72] 1990 | 37 | 50 | ... | 22 | ... | 100 | No | XD | 8 |
| Valdes et al,[73] 1991 | 24 | 50 | ... | 54 | ... | 100 | No | XD | 4 |
| Barden et al,[74] 1991 | 37 | 32 | ... | 0 | ... | 0 | No | XD | 4 d |
| Overlack et al,[75] 1991 | 12 | 37 | 25–59 | 67 | ... | 100 | No | XS | 8 |
| Smith et al,[76] 1992 | 22 | 67 | ≥60 | 57 | 71 | 100 | No | XD | 4 d |
| Fotherby and Potter,[77] 1992 | 18 | 75 | 66–79 | 28 | ... | 100 | No | XD | 4 |
| Whelton et al,[78] 1995 | 353 | 43 | 30–54 | 72 | 86 | 0 | No | PD | 24 |
| Brancati et al,[79] 1996 | 87 | 48 | 27–65 | 36 | 0 | 0 | No | PD | 3 |

*XO indicates crossover open; XS, crossover single blind; XD, crossover double blind; PO, parallel open; PS, parallel single blind; PD, parallel double blind; and ellipses, no data.

†BP indicates blood pressure; SBP systolic BP; and DBP diastolic BP. Sitting BP was used in the studies by Khaw and Thom,[52] Matlou et al,[58] Poulter and Sever,[60] Chalmers et al,[61] Svetkey et al,[64] Grimm et al,[66] Hypertension Prevention Trial,[70] Barden et al,[74] and Overlack et al.[75]

| Intervention | Control | Pretreatment Supine BP, mm Hg† | | Pretreatment Urinary Electrolytes, mmol/d | | Pretreatment Serun Potassium, mmol/L |
|---|---|---|---|---|---|---|
| | | SBP | DBP | K | Na | |
| 200 mmol K from diet, 200 mmol from NaCl | 80 mmol KCl, 200 mmol NaCl | . . . | . . . | . . . | . . . | 4.7 |
| 200 mmol K from diet, 50 mmol NaCl | 80 mmol KCl, 50 mmol NaCl | . . . | . . . | . . . | . . . | 4.6 |
| 64 mmol KCl | Placebo | 154 | 99 | 68 | 152 | 4.0 |
| 64 mmol KCl | Placebo | 118 | 74 | 73 | 138 | . . . |
| 200 mmol K from diet, 180 mmol NaCl | 60 mmol KCl, 180 mmol NaCl | 140–180 | 90–105 | . . . | . . . | 3.8 |
| 64 mmol KCl, 70 mmol NaCl | Placebo, 70 mmol NaCl | 163 | 103 | 72 | 68 | 3.9 |
| 60 mmol KCl | Placebo | 131 | 96 | 46 | 166 | 3.0 |
| 100 mmol KCl Placebo | 154 | 96 | | . . . | . . . | 3.8 |
| 64 mmol KCl | Usual care | 150 | 95 | 66 | . . . | 3.7 |
| 65 mmol KCl | Placebo | 154 | 105 | 62 | 172 | 3.8 |
| 80 mmol KCl | Placebo | 118 | 71 | 50 | 131 | . . . |
| 64 mmol KCl | Placebo | 113 | 69 | 39 | 123 | . . . |
| ≥100 mmol K from diet | Normal diet | 150 | 95 | 71 | 155 | . . . |
| ≥100 mmol K from diet, low Na | Low Na | 152 | 95 | 68 | 148 | . . . |
| 72 mmol KCl, low Na | Placebo, low Na | 143 | 78 | 71 | 141 | 3.8 |
| 48 mmol KCl | Placebo | 145 | 92 | 60 | 190 | 4.4 |
| 120 mmol KCl | Placebo | 145 | 95 | . . . | . . . | 4.4 |
| 17–34 mmol KCl | Usual care | 161 | 98 | . . . | . . . | 4.2 |
| 96 mmol KCl, low Na | Placebo, low Na | 124 | 80 | 79 | 166 | 4.2 |
| 80 mmol KCl | Placebo | 150 | 95 | 52 | 176 | . . . |
| 64 mmol KCl | Placebo | 174 | 100 | 59 | 171 | 4.0 |
| 90 mmol KCl | 10 mmol KCl | 120 | 77 | 70 | 164 | 3.2 |
| 100 mmol K from diet, low Na | Low Na | 124 | 82 | 64 | 161 | . . . |
| 75 mmol KCl | Placebo | 117 | 69 | 77 | 153 | 4.2 |
| 75 mmol K citrate | Placebo | 117 | 69 | 77 | 153 | 4.2 |
| 60 mmol KCl | Placebo | 155 | 100 | 62 | 196 | 3.6 |
| 64 mmol KCl | Placebo | 147 | 96 | 57 | 155 | 3.8 |
| 80 mmol KCl | Placebo | 105 | 63 | 53 | 105 | . . . |
| 120 mmol K citrate and bicarbonate | Placebo | 150 | 100 | 62 | 169 | 4.4 |
| 120 mmol KCl | Placebo | 152 | 87 | 70 | 192 | 3.9 |
| 60 mmol KCl | Placebo | 187 | 96 | 63 | 115 | 4.2 |
| 60 mmol KCl | Placebo | 122 | 81 | 59 | 153 | . . . |
| 80 mmol KCl | Placebo | 125 | 78 | 47 | 147 | . . . |

‡Study participants were treated with thiazide or thiazidelike diuretics (hydrochlorothiazide [25–75 mg/d] or chlorthalidone [50 mg/d] and in addition, clonidine [0.1 mg twice daily] in 1 subject [Kaplan et al[55]]; bendrofluazide [2.5–10 mg/d] cyclopenthiazide [25–50 mg/d], hydrochlorothiazide [25 mg/d], furosemide [40–80 mg/d], and chlorthalidone [50–100 mg/d] [Bulpitt et al[57]] ); bendrofluazide [5–10 mg/d] [Medical Research Council[65]]; chlorthalidone or hydrochlorothiazide [84%], b-blockers [43%], other medications, eg, reserpine [6%], hydralazine [6%], and methyldopa [5%] [doses not specified] [Grimm et al[66]] ).

Table 2

Urinary Electrolyte Excretion, Body Weight, and Blood Pressure During Follow-up in 33 Potassium Supplementation Trials*

| Source, y | Mean Net Change in Urinary Electrolytes, mmol/d | | Urinary Sodium Excretion During Follow-up, mmol/d | Mean Net Change in Body Weight, kg | Mean Net Change in Blood Pressure, mm Hg | |
|---|---|---|---|---|---|---|
| | K | Na | | | Systolic | Diastolic |
| Skrabal et al,[50] 1981 | | | | | | |
| (a) | 44 | −55 | 155 | −0.9 | −1.7 | −4.5 |
| (b) | 107 | −12 | 28 | −0.2 | 0.4 | −0.5 |
| MacGregor et al,[51] 1982 | 56 | 29 | 169 | −0.2 | −7.0 | −4.0 |
| Khaw and Thom,[52] 1982 | 52 | 9 | 164 | . . . | −1.1 | −2.4 |
| Richards et al,[53] 1984 | 129 | 5 | 200 | 0.8 | −1.9 | −1.0 |
| Smith et al,[54] 1985 | 50 | 7 | 80 | 0.1 | −2.0 | 0 |
| Kaplan et al,[55] 1985 | 46 | 1 | 168 | 0.8 | −5.6 | −5.8 |
| Zoccali et al,[56] 1985 | 81 | 13 | 195 | . . . | −1.0 | −3.0 |
| Bulpitt et al,[57] 1985 | 40 | 10 | 149 | 1.2 | 2.3 | 4.8 |
| Matlou et al,[58] 1986 | 62 | 35 | 165 | −0.4 | −7.0 | −3.0 |
| Barden et al,[59] 1986 | 68 | 5 | 130 | . . . | −1.4 | −1.4 |
| Poulter and Sever,[60] 1986 | 38 | 1 | 114 | −0.1 | −1.2 | 2.0 |
| Chalmers et al,[61] 1986 | | | | | | |
| (a) | 22 | 7 | 150 | . . . | −3.9 | −3.1 |
| (b) | 12 | 25 | 79 | . . . | 1.0 | 1.6 |
| Grobbee et al,[62] 1987 | 57 | 12 | 69 | 0.4 | −2.5 | −0.6 |
| Siani et al,[63] 1987 | 30 | 6 | 189 | . . . | −14.0 | −10.5 |
| Svetkey et al,[64] 1987 | . . . | . . . | . . . | . . . | −6.3 | −2.5 |
| Medical Research Council,[65] 1987 | . . . | . . . | . . . | . . . | −0.8 | −0.7 |
| Grimm et al,[66] 1988 | 80 | −9 | 114 | . . . | 0.7 | 1.4 |
| Cushman and Langford,[67] 1988 | 77 | 36 | 177 | . . . | . . . | −0.1 |
| Obel[68] 1989 | 39 | . . . | 172 | . . . | −41.0 | −17.0 |
| Krishna et al,[69] 1989 | 47 | 44 | 144 | −0.6 | −5.5 | −7.4 |
| Hypertension Prevention Trial,[70] 1990 | 0 | −6 | 155 | 0.2 | −1.3 | −0.9 |
| Mullen and O'Connor,[71] 1990 | | | | | | |
| (a) | 23 | −12 | 141 | −0.1 | 0 | 3.0 |
| (b) | 34 | −15 | 138 | −0.2 | −2.0 | 2.0 |
| Patki et al,[72] 1990 | 22 | −14 | 184 | . . . | −12.1 | −13.1 |
| Valdes et al,[73] 1991 | 68 | 19 | 166 | −1 | −6.3 | −3.0 |
| Barden et al,[74] 1991 | 72 | 15 | 120 | . . . | −1.7 | −0.6 |
| Overlack et al,[75] 1991 | 105 | −13 | 156 | 0 | 2.8 | 3.0 |
| Smith et al,[76] 1992 | 109 | 29 | 221 | 0.2 | −4.3 | −1.7 |
| Fotherby and Potter,[77] 1992 | 39 | 13 | 136 | −0.7 | −10.0 | −6.0 |
| Whelton et al,[78] 1995 | 42 | 6 | 144 | . . . | −0.3 | 0.1 |
| Brancati et al,[79] 1996 | 70 | 20 | 141 | −0.1 | −6.9 | −2.5 |

*Ellipses indicate no data.

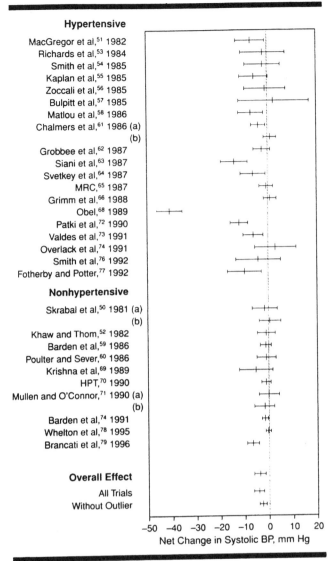

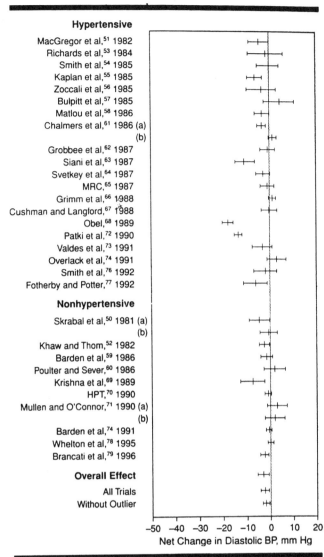

**Figure 1.** Average net change in systolic blood pressure (BP) and corresponding 95% confidence interval after treatment with oral potassium supplementation in 32 randomized controlled trials (data on systolic BP were not available in 1 trial[67]). Net change was calculated as the difference of the baseline minus follow-up levels of BP for the intervention and control groups (parallel trials) or the difference in BP levels at the end of the intervention and control treatment periods (crossover trials). The overall effect represents a pooled estimate obtained by summing the average net change for each trial, weighed by the inverse of its variance. "All trials" represents results from all 32 randomized trials; "without outlier" represents results after exclusion of an outlier trial.[80] MRC indicates Medical Research Council; and HPT, Hypertension Prevention Trial.

**Figure 2.** Average net change in diastolic blood pressure (BP) and corresponding 95% confidence interval after treatment with oral potassium supplementation in 33 randomized controlled trials. Net change was calculated as the difference of the baseline minus follow-up levels of BP for the intervention and control groups (parallel trials) or the difference in BP levels at the end of the intervention and control treatment periods (crossover trials). The overall effect represents a pooled estimate obtained by summing the average net change for each trial, weighted by the inverse of its variance. "All trials" represents results from all 33 randomized trials; "without outlier" represents results after exclusion of an outlier trial.[80] MRC indicates Medical Research Council; and HPT, Hypertension Prevention Trial.

For systolic and diastolic BP, there was significant (P<.001) variation across the 33 trials in the estimate of intervention-related average net change in BP. Even after the outlier trial was removed,[80] effect sizes for systolic and diastolic BP varied significantly by study (P<.001). Table 4 summarizes pooled estimates of treatment effect in subgroups of trials defined according to participant characteristics and study design features. Given the disproportionate effect of outlier estimates on results derived from subgroup analysis, the outlier trial[68] was excluded from these analyses. The most notable finding was a trend toward greater treatment-related reductions in systolic and diastolic BP at progressively higher levels of urinary sodium excretion during follow-up

**Table 3** Mean Net Systolic Blood Pressure Changes in Trials Using Different Exclusion Criteria*

| | SBP | | | | DBP | | |
| | No. | Net Change (95% CI) | P | | No. | Net Change (95% CI) | P |
|---|---|---|---|---|---|---|---|
| All trials | 32 | −4.44 (−2.53 to −6.36) | <.001 | | 33 | −2.45 (−0.74 to −4.16) | <.01 |
| All trials without outlier† | 31 | −3.11 (−1.91 to −4.31) | <.001 | | 32 | −1.97 (−0.52 to −3.42) | <.01 |
| Trials with net change in urinary K ≥20 mmol/d‡ | 28 | −4.91 (−2.69 to −7.12) | <.001 | | 29 | −2.71 (−0.71 to −4.71) | <.01 |
| Trials in which no antihypertensive medications were administered§ | 28 | −4.85 (−2.74 to −6.95) | <.001 | | 29 | −2.71 (−0.80 to −4.61) | <.01 |

*SBP indicates systolic blood pressure; DBP, diastolic blood pressure; and CI, confidence interval.
†Trial of Obel[68] excluded.
‡Trials of Chalmers et al[61] (b), Svetkey et al,[64] Medical Research Council,[65] and Hypertension Prevention Trial[70] excluded.
§Trials of Kaplan et al,[55] Bulpitt et al,[57] Medical Research Council,[65] and Grimm et al[66] excluded.

($P$<.001). As illustrated in Figure 3, the relationship did not appear to result from our choice of cut-points for the 3 categories of urinary sodium excretion identified in Table 4. Treatment-related systolic BP effect size was also significantly ($P$=.03) greater for the 6 trials with more than 80% black participants compared with 25 trials with more than 80% white participants. A similar, but statistically nonsignificant, trend for diastolic BP was seen. A nonsignificant trend toward larger systolic ($P$=.07) and diastolic ($P$=.10) treatment effect for 20 trials conducted in hypertensive patients compared with 12 trials conducted in normotensive subjects was also seen. A nonsignificant trend toward a greater effect size in midsized than in smaller and larger studies was shown, as was greater reduction in systolic ($P$=.02) and diastolic ($P$=.006) BP in studies conducted over 4 to 11 weeks compared with those with longer or shorter follow-up. Treatment effect size did not vary statistically significantly across trial subgroups categorized according to tertiles of change in 24-hour urinary excretion of sodium or potassium.

Linear regression analysis identified a significant, independent positive relationship between average 24-hour urinary sodium excretion during follow-up in each trial and corresponding net reduction in systolic ($P$=.004) and diastolic ($P$=.003) BP (Table 5). There was also a significant inverse relationship between sample size and corresponding treatment-related effect size for systolic ($P$<.001) and diastolic ($P$=.05) BP, and a significant direct relationship between average pretreatment diastolic BP and corresponding average treatment-related effect size for systolic BP ($P$=.02). There was a nonsignificant trend ($P$=.06) toward association between percentage of participants in each trial who were black and the corresponding systolic BP treatment-related effect size. There was no relationship between study duration or treatment-related change in urinary potassium excretion and corresponding net change in systolic or diastolic BP. Approximately 62% of variance in systolic BP- and 58% of variance in systolic BP-related treatment effect size could be explained by 6 variables included in the multivariate model (Table 5), virtually all re-

sulting from combined effects of urinary sodium excretion during follow-up, sample size, percentage of participants who were black, and average level of pretreatment BP. There was no evidence of a relationship between effect size and age, sex, method of BP measurement (manual vs automatic), study design (crossover vs parallel arm), or change in body weight (data not shown).

Although there was no overall association between 24-hour urinary potassium excretion and change in systolic or diastolic BP, this relationship was statistically significantly modified by corresponding level of 24-hour urinary sodium excretion. Specifically, at higher levels of baseline 24-hour urinary sodium excretion and of change in 24-hour urinary sodium excretion, change in 24-hour potassium excretion showed a dose-response relationship with effect size for both systolic and diastolic BP ($P$<.01). A similar graded relationship between change in 24-hour urinary potassium excretion and effect size was observed at higher levels of 24-hour urinary sodium excretion during follow-up for systolic ($P$<.01) but not for diastolic ($P$=.20) BP.

# Table 4

**Mean Net Systolic and Diastolic Blood Pressure Changes in Subgroups of Trials Defined by Participant and Study Design Characters***

| Characteristics | No. of Studies | No. of Subjects† | Systolic Blood Pressure, mm Hg | | | Diastolic Blood Pressure, mm Hg | | |
|---|---|---|---|---|---|---|---|---|
| | | | Effect Size | 95% Confidence Interval | P‡ | Effect Size | 95% Confidence Interval | P‡ |
| Hypertension status | | | | | | | | |
| Hypertensive | 20 | 1512 | −4.4 | −2.2 to −6.6 | | −2.5 | −0.1 to −4.9 | |
| Normotensive | 12 | 1049 | −1.8 | −0.6 to −2.9 | .07 | −1.0 | 0.0 to −2.1 | .11 |
| Race§ | | | | | | | | |
| Black | 6 | 197 | −5.6 | −2.4 to −8.7 | | −3.0 | −0.7 to −5.3 | |
| White | 25 | 2282 | −2.0 | −0.9 to −3.0 | .03 | −1.1 | −0.1 to −2.1 | .19 |
| Sample size | | | | | | | | |
| <22 | 11 | 186 | −2.2 | −0.4 to −3.9 | | −2.4 | −0.5 to −4.3 | |
| 22–43 | 11 | 333 | −5.3 | −2.5 to −8.1 | .20 | −2.6 | 1.3 to −6.5 | .06 |
| ≥44 | 10 | 2042 | −1.9 | −0.2 to −3.5 | | −0.7 | 0.3 to −1.7 | |
| Study duration, wk | | | | | | | | |
| <4 | 11 | 302 | −2.3 | −0.7 to −3.8 | | −1.3 | 0.1 to −2.7 | |
| 4–11 | 13 | 437 | −5.2 | −2.7 to −7.6 | .02 | −3.0 | 0.2 to −6.2 | .006 |
| ≥12 | 8 | 1822 | −1.8 | 0.2 to −3.8 | | −1.0 | 0.8 to −2.7 | |
| Net change in urinary K, mmol/d | | | | | | | | |
| <42 | 10 | 795 | −4.3 | −1.2 to −7.4 | | −2.2 | 1.9 to −6.3 | |
| 42–67 | 9 | 534 | −2.9 | −1.0 to −4.9 | .46 | −2.8 | −1.1 to −4.5 | .27 |
| ≥68 | 11 | 674 | −2.2 | −0.3 to −4.1 | | −0.7 | 0.3 to −1.8 | |
| Net change in urinary Na, mmol/d | | | | | | | | |
| <5 | 10 | 875 | −2.1 | 0.4 to −4.6 | | −1.4 | 2.7 to −5.6 | |
| 5–12 | 9 | 666 | −2.8 | −0.6 to −5.0 | .52 | −1.9 | 0.0 to −3.8 | .55 |
| ≥13 | 11 | 435 | −4.6 | −2.2 to −6.9 | | −2.2 | −0.7 to −3.6 | |
| Urinary Na during follow-up, mmol/d | | | | | | | | |
| <140 | 10 | 639 | −1.2 | 0.0 to −2.4 | | 0.1 | 1.1 to −1.0 | |
| 140–164 | 10 | 1057 | −2.1 | −0.3 to −4.0 | <.001 | −1.4 | 0.0 to −2.8 | <.001 |
| ≥165 | 10 | 280 | −7.3 | −4.6 to −10.1 | | −4.7 | −1.1 to −8.3 | |

*Trial of Obel[68] excluded from analysis.
†Forty-four subjects were included in 2 independent studies.
‡From analysis of variance.
§More than 80% of trial participants were in stated ethnic group.

Oral potassium supplementation appeared to be well tolerated in all studies included in our meta-analysis, although only 2 reports provided specific accounting of type and frequency of treatment-related adverse effects.[64,66] Adverse effects in these 2 trials were fairly inconsequential and primarily consisted of abdominal pain, belching, and flatulence (although only 1 individual stopped taking potassium because of gastrointestinal tract symptoms[64]); symptoms reported by Grimm et al[66] included stomach pains (4.4%), bright-red blood in stool (2.3%), nausea or vomiting (3.0%), and diarrhea (9.7%). There was no difference in compliance, as assessed by pill count, between treatment and control groups in Svetkey et al[64]; compliance was assessed by capsule counts in Grimm et al[66] and described as "excellent." Regarding compliance, change in urinary potassium secretion (considered the optimal measure of compliance) was available for all but 2 trials (see Table 2), 1 of which[64] used pill count to assess compliance. The Medical Research Council study[65] did not

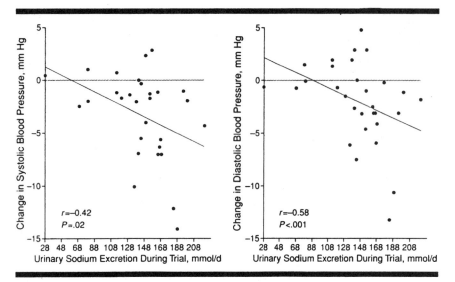

**Figure 3.** Net change in systolic and diastolic blood pressure as a function of 24-hour urinary sodium excretion. A significant inverse relationship was identified for both systolic (*P*=.02) and diastolic (*P*<.001) blood pressure.

## Comment

It has been suggested that potassium supplementation results in reduction of systolic and diastolic BP,[10,11,58,80–82,88,89] yet the role of potassium supplementation in treating and preventing high BP remains controversial.[10,11,90] In part, this may be because some large and rigorously designed trials in hypertensive[45,65] and non-hypertensive[78] subjects are among those yielding the least impressive results. The current meta-analysis was conducted to take advantage of recently published randomized controlled trials. Previous reports by Whelton et al[88,90] and Cappuccio and MacGregor[82] were based on pooling of results from 22 and 19 trials, respectively. Only 12 of 19 studies in one of the analyses[82] were randomized controlled trials. To ensure that our meta-analysis was based on high-quality studies, we used a standardized protocol for selection of studies, requiring them to be randomized controlled trials; in our analysis, study results were weighted by reciprocal of variance. Methodological issues in assessment of treatment effects have been addressed by Schulz et al.[91]

Our overall mean effect size estimates of –3.11 mm Hg for systolic and –1.97 mm Hg for diastolic BP (after exclusion of the outlier trial) were close to previous estimates of –2.7 and –2.0 mm Hg[90] and –5.9 and –3.8 mm Hg.[82] Overall effect size estimates in our meta-analysis were identified in the context of mean change in urinary potassium excretion of 55 mmol/d, similar to corresponding effect size estimates predicted from Intersalt.[2] After correction for reliability of urinary potassium excretion estimates and adjustment for age, sex, and other potential confounders, pooled regression coefficients for the relationship between urinary potassium excretion and systolic and diastolic BP in Intersalt were –0.0446 and –0.0289 mm Hg per 1 mmol of change in urinary potassium excretion, respectively. Thus, our 53-mmol/d-higher excretion of urinary potassium, given these INTERSALT coefficients, would be expected to show a 2.4- and 1.5-mm Hg-lower level of systolic and diastolic BP, respectively.

A causal relationship between potassium supplementation and reduced BP is suggested by the strength of the association, narrow 95% confidence intervals around mean effect size estimates, temporal sequence in prospective, observational studies and clinical trials, dose-response relationship between potassium and BP in observational and experimental studies (although apparently dependent on concurrent sodium intake in the latter), replication of the relationship in varying settings and study designs, and biological plausibility.

The average effect size noted in 20 trials conducted in hypertensive subjects (excluding the outlier trial) was of sufficient magnitude (–4.4 and –2.5 mm Hg for systolic and diastolic BP, respectively) to suggest that potassium supplementation may have a role in treatment of patients with hypertension.[92] Although effect size was smaller in trials in normotensive subjects (–1.8 and –1.0 mm Hg for systolic and diastolic BP, respectively), its magnitude was consistent with a role for potassium supplementation in prevention of hypertension.[93–95]

Race-related findings in the current analysis must be interpreted with caution because of the ecologic nature of the analysis and because racial characteristics in several studies were unclear. Although the number of trials (n=6) in which blacks were a majority of the participants was

assess change in urinary potassium excretion or other measures of compliance. Quality of life scores were not reported for any of the 33 trials.

Table 5

Multiple Linear Regression Analysis* of Average Net Reduction in Blood Pressure as a Function of the Study Characteristics

| Characteristics | Systolic Blood Pressure, mm Hg ($R^2$=0.622) | | | | Diastolic Blood Pressure, mm Hg ($R^2$=0.576) | | | |
|---|---|---|---|---|---|---|---|---|
| | Regression Coefficient | SE | Partial $R^2$ | P | Regression Coefficient | SE | Partial $R^2$ | P |
| Pretreatment blood pressure, mm Hg | 0.056 | 0.023 | 0.125 | .02 | 0.062 | 0.049 | 0.169 | .2 |
| % Black | 0.026 | 0.014 | 0.130 | .06 | −0.005 | 0.018 | 0.012 | .8 |
| Sample size | −0.010 | 0.003 | 0.190 | .001 | −0.009 | 0.004 | 0.152 | .05 |
| Study duration, wk | 0.007 | 0.015 | 0.013 | .6 | −0.015 | 0.021 | 0.018 | .5 |
| Change in urinary K, mmol/d | 0.003 | 0.021 | 0.001 | .9 | −0.039 | 0.026 | 0.036 | .2 |
| Urinary Na during study, mmol/d | 0.045 | 0.014 | 0.163 | .004 | 0.060 | 0.018 | 0.190 | .003 |

*Weighted by inverse of variance of effect size; trial by Obel[68] excluded from analysis.

small,[55,58,60,67,68,79] relatively large effect sizes were common in these trials.[55,58,68,79] A large effect size in blacks has also been noted in subgroup analysis in a trial[64] in which average reduction in systolic and diastolic BP was 20.0 and 13.0 mm Hg among the 13 African-American participants compared with 6.5 and 2.5 mm Hg for the entire group of 101 participants.[64]

Our finding of a greater effect size in trials with a higher level of urinary sodium excretion during the trial is consistent with previous reports[50,54,76] and observational investigations where ratio of urinary sodium-potassium excretion has appeared to be more closely related to BP than either urinary sodium or potassium excretion individually,[16] consistent with 2 possible mechanisms for BP-lowering effects of potassium supplementation.[95–97]

A majority of trials excluded from the meta-analysis support the hypothesis that potassium administration reduces BP. Three randomized controlled trials deserve comment. In a large (n=287), rigorously controlled, 2-year potassium supplementation trial,[45] there was no apparent benefit of supplementation on BP control, but all participants were concurrently placed on a sodium-reduced diet, which may have diminished the effect. In contrast, a treatment-related reduction in the need for antihypertensive drug therapy was noted in a dietary supplementation trial,[47] and findings were also positive for potassium in a clinical trial of potassium supplementation vs bendrofluazide conducted in 84 untreated hypertensive Kenyans.[46] Although we recognize the need for additional information, the existing body of evidence from experimental and observational investigations is consistent and favors the notion that potassium supplementation should be considered as part of recommendations for prevention and treatment of hypertension. Potassium supplementation may be especially useful for blacks and those with difficulty in reducing their dietary intake of sodium. Although most of the clinical trial experience to date emanates from studies in which potassium was administered in pill form as a chloride salt, there is little reason to suspect a different outcome after dietary supplementation and/or administration of other potassium salts provided potassium itself is sufficiently increased.

This study was supported in part by Outpatient General Clinical Research Center grant 5 MO1 RR00722 from the National Institutes of Health (National Center for Research Resources), Bethesda, Md. Computational assistance was supported by National Institutes of Health grant RR0035. Dr Appel is supported by Clinician Investigator Award 5 KO8 HL02642 from the National Institutes of Health. Dr Klag is an Established Investigator of the American Heart Association.

## References

1. Whelton, PK. Epidemiology of hypertension. *Lancet.* 1994;344:101–106.
2. Intersalt Cooperative Research Group. Intersalt: an international study of electrolyte excretion and blood pressure: results for 24 hour urinary sodium and potassium excretion. *BMJ.* 1988;297:319–328.
3. Shaper AG, Pocock SJ, Walker M, Cohen NM, Wale CJ, Thomson AG. British Regional Heart Study: cardiovascular risk factors in middle-aged men in 24 towns. *BMJ.* 1981;283:179–186.
4. Bruce N, Wannamethee G, Shaper AG. Lifestyle factors associated with geographic blood pressure variations among men and women in the UK. *J Hum Hypertens.* 1993;7:229–238.
5. Smith WC, Crombie IK, Tavendale RT, Gulland SK, Tunstall-Pedoe H. Urinary electrolyte excretion, alcohol consumption, and blood pressure in the Scottish Heart Health Study. *BMJ.* 1988;297:329–330.
6. Prior IAM, Stanhope JM, Evans JG, Salmond CE. The Tokelau Island

Migrant Study. *Int J Epidemiol.* 1974;3:225–232.

7. Sever PS, Gordon D, Peart WS, Beighton P. Blood pressure and its correlates in urban and tribal Africa. *Lancet.* 1980;2:60–64.

8. Poulter NR, Khaw KT, Hopwood BE, et al. The Kenyan Luo migration study: observations on the initiation of rise in blood pressure. *BMJ.* 1990;300:967–972.

9. He J, Klag MJ, Whelton PK, et al. Migration, blood pressure pattern, and hypertension. *Am J Epidemiol.* 1991;134:1085–1101.

10. Working Group on Primary Prevention of Hypertension. Report of the National High Blood Pressure Education Program Working Group on Primary Prevention of Hypertension. *Arch Intern Med.* 1993;153:186–208.

11. Beilin LJ. Diet and hypertension: critical concepts and controversies. *J Hypertens.* 1987;5(suppl 5):S447–S457.

12. Walker WG, Whelton PK, Saito H, Russell RP, Hermann J. Relation between blood pressure and renin, renin substrate, angiotensin II, aldosterone and urinary sodium and potassium in 574 ambulatory subjects. *Hypertension.* 1979; 1:287–291.

13. Lever AF, Beretta-Piccoli C, Brown JJ, Davies DL, Fraser R, Robertson JS. Sodium and potassium in essential hypertension. *BMJ.* 1981;283:463–468.

14. Khaw KT, Rose G. Population study of blood pressure and associated factors in St. Lucia, West Indies. *Int J Epidemiol.* 1982; 11:372–377.

15. Langford HG. Dietary potassium and hypertension: epidemiologic data. *Ann Intern Med.* 1983;98:770–772.

16. Dai WS, Kuller LH, Miller G. Arterial blood pressure and urinary electrolytes. *J Chronic Dis.* 1984; 37:75–84.

17. Simpson FO. Monovalent and divalent cations in hypertension. *Prev Med.* 1985;14:436–450.

18. Reed D, McGee D, Yano K, Hankin J. Diet, blood pressure, and multicollinearity. *Hypertension.* 1985;7:405–410.

19. Addison WLT. The use of sodium chloride, potassium chloride, sodium bromide and potassium bromide in cases of arterial hypertension which are amenable to potassium chloride. *Can Med Assoc J.* 1928;18:281–285.

20. Priddle WW. Observations on the management of hypertension. *Can Med Assoc J.* 1931;25:5–8.

21. McQuarrie I, Thompson WH, Anderson JA. Effects of excessive ingestion of sodium and potassium salts on carbohydrate metabolism and blood pressure in diabetic children. *J Nutr.* 1936;11:77–101.

22. Gros G, Weller JM, Hoobler SW. Relationship of sodium and potassium intake to blood pressure. *Am J Clin Nutr.* 1971;24:605–608.

23. Mickelson O, Makdani D, Gill JL, Frank RL. Sodium and potassium intakes and excretions of normal men consuming sodium chloride or a 1:1 mixture of sodium and potassium chlorides. *Am J Clin Nutr.* 1977;30:2033–2040.

24. Burstyn P, Hornall D, Watchorn C. Sodium and potassium intake and blood pressure. *BMJ.* 1980; 2:537–539.

25. Iimura O, Kijima T, Kikuchi K, et al. Studies on the hypotensive effect of high potassium intake in patients with essential hypertension. *Clin Sci.* 1981; 61(suppl 7):77s–80s.

26. Parfrey PS, Wright P, Holly JMP, et al. Blood pressure and hormonal changes following alteration in dietary sodium and potassium in young men with and without a familial predisposition to hypertension. *Lancet.* 1981; 1:113–117.

27. Parfrey PS, Wright P, Goodwin FJ, et al. Blood pressure and hormonal changes following alteration in dietary sodium and potassium in mild essential hypertension. *Lancet.* 1981;1:59–63.

28. Holly JMP, Goodwin FJ, Evans SJW, Vandenburg MJ, Ledingham JM. Re-analysis of data in two *Lancet* papers on the effect of dietary sodium and potassium on blood pressure. *Lancet.* 1981;2:1384–1386.

29. Gillum RF, Prineas RJ, Kebede J. Independent effects of Na reduction and K supplementation on blood pressure. *Am Heart J.* 1982;103:449.

30. Morgan TO. The effect of potassium and bicarbonate ions on the rise in blood pressure caused by sodium chloride. *Clin Sci.* 1982;63:407s–409s.

31. Smith SJ, Markandu ND, Sagnella GA, Poston L, Hilton PJ, MacGregor GA. Does potassium lower blood pressure by increasing sodium excretion? a metabolic study in patients with mild to moderate essential hypertension. *J Hypertens.* 1983;1:27–30.

32. Overlack A, Muller H-M, Kolloch R, et al. Long-term antihypertensive effect of oral potassium in essential hypertension. *J Hypertens.* 1983; 1(suppl 2):165–167.

33. Fujita T, Ando K. Hemodynamic and endocrine changes associated with potassium supplementation in sodium-loaded hypertensive. *Hypertension.* 1984;6:184–192.

34. Jeffery RW, Pirie PL, Elmer PJ, et al. Low-sodium, high-potassium diet: feasibility and acceptability in a normotensive population. *Am J Public Health.* 1984;74:492–494.

 **Article Review Form at end of book.**

How many of the subjects lost weight?  What is the significance of lower levels in one's CD4 cells?  What happened to CD4 cells in conjunction with weight loss?

# Assessment of Nutritional, Clinical, and Immunologic Status of HIV-Infected, Inner-City Patients with Multiple Risk Factors

**Elisabeth Luder, PhD; Emilie Godfrey, MS, RD; James Godbold, PhD; David M. Simpson, MD**

*E. Luder is an associate professor in the Department of Pediatrics, J. Godbold is an associate professor in the Department of Community Medicine, D.M. Simpson is an associate professor in the Department of Neurology, and, at the time of the study, E. Godfrey was a research nutritionist, Mt Sinai School of Medicine, New York, NY. Presently, E. Godfrey is a research scientist at the New York City Department of Health, New York, NY.*

## Abstract

**Objective** To evaluate the nutritional, clinical, and immunologic factors associated with human immunodeficiency virus (HIV)-infected, inner-city patients with multiple risk factors.

**Design** Prospective cross-sectional nutrition evaluation of patients with HIV infection.

**Setting** Patients were interviewed at the outpatient clinic at Mt. Sinai Medical Center, New York City, NY.

**Subjects** Our subjects were men and women older than 18 years of age and at all stages of HIV infection (n=56).

**Outcome measures** Anthropometric measurements, history of weight changes (maintenance of preillness body weight or decrease from preillness weight status), 3-day food records, and clinical laboratory tests.

**Statistical analyses** $t$ Tests were used to compare patients who were at a stable weight with patients who had lost weight with regard to the anthropometric, dietary, and clinical variables. Spearman's rank correlation coefficient and $X^2$ tests were applied to examine correlations between pairs and differences in proportions, respectively.

**Results** Patients were classified into groups according to whether they were at a stable weight (n=25) or had lost weight (n=31). All anthropometric, measurements, CD4 lymphocytes, and CD8 lymphocytes were significantly lower in the patients who had lost weight. No differences were observed between the groups for absolute lymphocyte count or transferrin, hemoglobin, and albumin levels. The mean energy intake of the 56 patients was 74% of the Recommended Dietary Allowance (RDA). Forty-seven patients (84%) took vitamin and/or mineral supplements within a range of 2% to 50,000% of the RDA. No significant positive correlations were observed between nutrient intake, CD4 cells, and absolute lymphocyte count.

**Conclusions/applications** All anthropometric measurements, CD4 lymphocytes, and CD8 lymphocytes were notably lower in patients with weight loss. The mean energy intake of the subjects was only 74% of the RDA. Megadoses of vitamin supplements were taken by a large number of patients, but no significant positive effects were observed for absolute lymphocyte count and CD4 cells. Although supplementation of micronutrients may influence the progression of HIV infection, a balanced, nutritious diet may be more beneficial in maintaining or improving the physiologic status of the patients. However, members of a high-risk population may benefit less from HIV-related social services and food or nutrition resources. With the growing number of injection-drug users in the acquired immunodeficiency syndrome population, it will be essential to develop comprehensive strategies to address the interconnected needs for medical and nutrition care. Ensuring that patients have adequate meals during an extended course of treatment in the outpatient clinic or that dietitians have meals available in group settings or through home-delivery service may be the most appropriate nutrition intervention in these high-risk patients. *J Am Diet Assoc. 1995; 95: 655-660.*

Progressive body mass depletion, loss of appetite, and reduced energy and nutrient intake are major characteristics of chronic infection with human immunodeficiency virus type I (HIV-I). Weight loss and malnutrition may involve de-

creased nutrient intake or absorption and altered metabolism, perhaps caused by overproduction of cytokines (1–3). Although antiretroviral therapies are presently available, other treatment modalities are often sought out by persons infected with the human immunodeficiency virus (HIV) to halt the progression of the disease (4). Patients may modify their diet and often view nutrition therapy as being as important as drug therapy in maintaining their immune function. They may assume that without adequate nutrient and lean body mass stores, medical therapies are less effective and may fail (5,6). Studies that evaluated the nutritional status, dietary intake, and vitamin and mineral supplementation in well-educated, homosexual men indicated that nutritional manipulation may help to maintain physiologic and functional integrity of the systems affected by HIV (6,7). It is not clear whether these findings can be extrapolated to inner-city, high-risk groups because multiple factors may influence the nutritional status in these patients (8). We have found no systematic studies that have performed nutrition evaluation in groups with multiple risk factors. The objective of this study is to evaluate the nutritional, clinical, and immunologic factors associated with HIV infection in inner-city patients with multiple risk factors.

## Methods

A cross-sectional, nutrition evaluation of patients with HIV was performed between January 1991 and January 1993. Subjects were prospectively recruited from the AIDS Center and the Neuro-AIDS Research Center at Mt Sinai Medical Center, New York City, NY. All studies performed were approved by the Institutional

Review Board at Mt Sinai School of Medicine.

## Subjects

Men and women older than 18 years and at all stages of HIV infection (asymptomatic through acquired immunodeficiency syndrome [AIDS] were eligible for the study. Subjects who were alcoholics were excluded because of the confounding effect of alcohol on nutritional status. Fifty-six HIV-infected patients participated in the nutrition evaluation study. The HIV/AIDS status of the patients was defined according to the criteria of the Centers for Disease Control and Prevention (CDC) (9). On the basis of history and neurologic examination, 30 subjects (53%) were diagnosed with HIV-associated myopathy (muscle weakness). Approximately 35% of HIV-infected subjects have HIV-1–related neurologic signs and symptoms (10). Nutrition counseling by a nutritionist or dietitian was not provided to any of the patients before the interview. Patients were referred to social services as needed.

## Clinical Measurements

The Mt Sinai Hospital Clinical Laboratories performed studies including serum HIV antibody testing by enzyme-linked immunosorbent assay (ELISA) with confirmation by Western blot assay (DuPont, Wilmington, Del), complete blood counts and studies of lymphocyte subgroups. Tumor necrosis factor-alpha (TNFα) levels were measured by ELISA.

## Anthropometric Measurements

All of the anthropometric measurements were obtained by a nutritionist (E.G.) according to standard published procedures

(11). Height was recorded to the nearest centimeter and weight to the nearest 100 g. Height and weight measurements were used to calculate body mass index (BMI) using the formula kg/m² The midarm circumference (MAC) of the right arm was measured with a tape measure to the nearest 0.1 cm with the other arm hanging relaxed. The measurement was taken midway between the tip of the acromion and olecranon process. The triceps skinfold (TSF) was measured to the nearest millimeter with a Lange skinfold caliper (Cambridge Scientific Industries, Cambridge, Mass). The measurement was taken over the triceps muscle halfway between the elbow and the acromial process of the scapula, with the skinfold parallel to the longitudinal axis of the upper arm. All anthropometric measurements were taken three times; the mean value of the measurements was used to determine the midarm muscle circumference (MAMC) using the formula MAC-πTSF.

## Dietary Intake

All subjects completed a 3-day dietary intake record. Patients were directed to eat "as usual" and received instructions from a nutritionist (E.G.) on recording food and beverage intake for 2 weekdays and 1 weekend day. Data on generic and brand names, methods of food preparation, and portion size of each reported food were collected. In addition, patients were given written instructions and encouraged to contact the nutritionist by telephone on the first day of the 3-day food record. Subjects were instructed either to bring all vitamin or mineral supplements for evaluation to the interview or to transcribe the brand name, frequency, and amount of every nutritional supplement taken on the 3-day food

| Table 1 | Demographic Characteristics of Subjects with Human Immunodeficiency Virus (HIV) at Time of Nutrition Assessment |

| Characteristics | No. of Patients |
| --- | --- |
| **Sex** | |
| Men | 47 |
| Women | 9 |
| **Ethnicity** | |
| Black | 15 |
| Hispanic | 23 |
| White | 16 |
| Unknown | 2 |
| **Risk factors** | |
| Homosexual | 31 |
| Intravenous drug abuser | 14 |
| Partner of HIV-infected person | 8 |
| Blood transfusion | 1 |
| Unknown | 2 |
| **HIV stage** | |
| HIV-1 positive | 16 |
| Acquired immunodeficiency syndrome (AIDS)-related complex | 23 |
| AIDS | 17 |

record form. The records were subsequently reviewed with the patient by the nutritionist using three-dimensional food models for accurate assessment of portion size. The 3-day food records were analyzed for energy and macronutrients and micronutrients, with Nutritionist III nutrient analysis software (version 6.0, 1990, N-Squared Computing, Salem, Ore). For descriptive purposes, reported nutrient intake from food and supplements alone and total nutrient intake from food and supplements combined were expressed as a percentage of the Recommended Dietary Allowances (RDAs) (12). Additionally, appetite level, food intolerance, gastrointestinal symptoms, diarrhea, and history of weight changes were recorded.

## Statistical Analysis

t tests were used to compare patients with stable weights with patients who had lost weight with regard to BMI; TSF; MAC; MAMC; energy per kilogram body weight; CD4 and CD8 lymphocyte count; absolute lymphocyte count (ALC); and transferrin, hemoglobin, and albumin levels. Spearman's rank correlation coefficient ($r_s$) was used to examine the correlation between pairs of continuous variates; $r_s$ was tested for significance with a t test. $X^2$ Tests were used to test for differences in proportions. All analyses were carried out using SAS statistical software (SAS User's Guide, version 5, 1985, SAS Institute Inc. Cary, NC.)

## Results

The subjects' demographic and clinical characteristics are presented in Table 1. Anthropometric, laboratory, and dietary data are presented in Table 2. Patients were classified into two groups

**Table 2** Anthropometric, Laboratory, and Dietary Data (mean ± standard deviation) at Time of Nutrition Assessment

| Variable | Patients with stable weight[a] n = 25 | Patients who had lost weight[b] n = 31 | P |
|---|---|---|---|
| Age (yr) | 40 ± 8 | 42 ± 10 | NS[c] |
| Weight loss (kg) | ... | 9.2 ± 6.2 | ... |
| Body mass index (calculated as kg/m$^2$) | 25.5 ± 5.2 | 21.2 ± 2.4 | .0001 |
| Triceps skinfold (mm) | 18.3 ± 10.5 | 10.5 ± 3.4 | .0001 |
| Midarm circumference (cm) | 31.6 ± 4.4 | 27.1 ± 2.9 | .0001 |
| Midarm muscle circumference (cm) | 26.0 ± 2.6 | 23.7 ± 2.7 | .005 |
| CD4 cells × 10$^6$/L | 250 ± 264 | 150 ± 181 | .05 |
| CD8 cells × 10$^6$/L | 897 ± 500 | 756 ± 695 | .02 |
| Absolute lymphocyte count (cells × 10$^6$/L) | 1,426 ± 708 | 1,237 ± 1,028 | NS |
| Transferrin[d] (g/L) | 1.68 ± 0.41 | 1.60 ± 0.46 | NS |
| Albumin (g/L) | 42 ± 4 | 40 ± 5 | NS |
| Hemoglobin (g/L) | 127 ± 19 | 125 ± 18 | NS |
| Energy (kcal) | 1,933 ± 587 | 2,041 ± 574 | NS |
| Energy (kcal/kg) | 26 ± 8 | 32 ± 10 | .02 |
| Protein (g) | 80 ± 32 | 83 ± 29 | NS |
| Protein (g/kg) | 1.1 ± 0.4 | 1.3 ± 0.5 | .02 |
| Carbohydrate (g) | 236 ± 71 | 257 ± 81 | NS |
| Fat (g) | 73 ± 32 | 77 ± 25 | NS |
| Zidovudine (mg) cumulative exposure | 282,882 ± 193,148 | 320,250 ± 223,681 | NS |

[a]Able to maintain usual weight (preillness body weight)
[b]Lost weight from preillness weight status
[c]NS=not significant
[d]Derived from (TIBC × .8) - 43

according to the weight history. *Stable weight* was defined as the ability to maintain usual preillness weight or gain weight; *weight loss* was defined as a loss of more than 2% of usual preillness weight. Among the 56 patients, 31 (55%) had lost weight; 17 (30%) of these had wasting syndrome according to the CDC criteria (profound involuntary weight loss > 10% of preillness body weight) (9).

We used *t* tests to compare nutritional status indicators in patients with stable weight to patients who had lost weight. Statistically significant differences are presented in Table 2. No significant differences between pa-

tients with stable weight and those who had lost weight were observed for ALC and transferrin, hemoglobin, and albumin levels. Serum level of TNFα was undetectable in most subjects and varied over a wide range in patients with stable weight and patients who had lost weight. Therefore, TNFα was graded as negative or positive. Only 3 of 56 patients were TNF-positive.

Eighteen of the 25 patients with stable weight (72%) and 12 of the 31 patients who had lost weight (39%) reported good appetite. Dietary intake of nutrients from food and vitamin/mineral supplements of the 56 patients are presented in Table 3. The mean

level of nutrients from food and supplement intake was similar in the patients who had maintained a stable weight and those who had lost weight. The mean energy intake was 74% of the RDA specific for age and sex. Fat contributed 34% of the energy intake. Nutrient intake (from food) below 90% of the RDA was recorded for vitamin B-6 (79%), magnesium (80%), zinc (66%), and copper (59%). Forty-seven patients (84%) took vitamin and/or mineral supplements with a range of 2% of the RDA to greater than 10,000% of the RDA for some of the B-complex vitamins. Consumption of vitamin B-12 reached the highest level, 50,000% or 500 times the

**Table 3** Vitamin and Mineral Intake from Food and Supplements

| Macronutrient and Micronutrient | Food Intake | Food % RDAa | Supplement | Supplement (% RDA) | Total Intake | Total (% RDA) |
|---|---|---|---|---|---|---|
| **Vitamin A (RE)** | | | | | | |
| Mean± SDb | 1,793±4,030 | 187±407 | 1,977±2,439 | 205±244 | 3,770±5,868 | 392±590.2 |
| Range | 171-29,816 | 17-2,982 | 0-12,000 | 0-1,200 | 171-41,816 | 17-4,182 |
| **Vitamin D (mg)** | | | | | | |
| Mean± SD | 3.6±2.8 | 73±55 | 6.5±8.1 | 126±163 | 10.1±8 | 201±161.7 |
| Range | .02-13 | 5-258 | 0-50 | 0-1,000 | 0.3-51 | 5-1,050 |
| **Vitamin E (mg)** | | | | | | |
| Mean± SD | 17±11.3 | 173±114 | 137±244 | 1,400±2,457 | 154±248 | 1,573±2,485 |
| Range | 1-48 | 13-477 | 0-1,210 | 0-12.100 | 4-1,251 | 17-12,512 |
| **Vitamin C (mg)** | | | | | | |
| Mean±SD | 151±140 | 215±233 | 752±1,628 | 1,253±2,714 | 903±1,707 | 1,504±2,845 |
| Range | 8-768 | 13-1,280 | 0-10,800 | 0-18.000 | 18-11,568 | 30-19,280 |
| **Thiamin (mg)** | | | | | | |
| Mean±SD | 1.8±1.0 | 129±71 | 26.1±48.1 | 1,855±3,361 | 27.9±48.3 | 1,984±3.369 |
| Range | 0.7-7 | 43-467 | 0-225 | 0-15,000 | 0.8-226 | 43-15,087 |
| **Riboflavin (mg)** | | | | | | |
| Mean±SD | 1.7±0.7 | 112±45 | 24.0±44.8 | 1,488±2,721 | 25.7±44.9 | 1,600±2,727 |
| Range | 0.8-5 | 49-300 | 0-225 | 0-13,235 | 0.8-227 | 50-13,324 |
| **Niacin (mg)** | | | | | | |
| Mean±SD | 19±9 | 110±51 | 52±115 | 285±608 | 71±119 | 395±626 |
| Range | 4-51 | 24-269 | 0-800 | 0-4,210 | 8-842 | 24-4,431 |
| **Vitamin B-6 (mg)** | | | | | | |
| Mean±SD | 1.5±1.0 | 79±48 | 26.2±45.4 | 1,345±2,312 | 27.7±45.6 | 1,426±2,321 |
| Range | 0.4-6 | 21-300 | 0-225 | 0-11,250 | 0.5-225 | 21-11,550 |
| **Folate (µg)** | | | | | | |
| Mean±SD | 288±301 | 146±151 | 283±279 | 131±139 | 571±416 | 277±208 |
| Range | 67-2,180 | 34-1,090 | 0-1,400 | 0-700 | 67-2,880 | 34-1,790 |
| **Vitamin B-12 (µg)** | | | | | | |
| Mean±SD | 3.8±2.4 | 192±122 | 77.0±177.6 | 3,849±8,881 | 80.8±178.3 | 4,041±8,913 |
| Range | 0.3-15 | 19-750 | 0-1,000 | 0-50,000 | 0.3-1,015 | 19-50,750 |
| **Calcium (mg)** | | | | | | |
| Mean±SD | 770±384 | 96±48 | 296±444 | 37±116 | 1,066±676 | 127±84.5 |
| Range | 181-2,285 | 23-286 | 10-2,000 | 0-800 | 247-4,285 | 23-800 |
| **Phosphorus (mg)** | | | | | | |
| Mean±SD | 1,134±372 | 142±47 | 120±305 | 15±38 | 1,254±470 | 157±59 |
| Range | 515-2,230 | 64-279 | 0-1,600 | 0-200 | 515-2,726 | 64-341 |
| **Magnesuim (mg)** | | | | | | |
| Mean±SD | 274±410 | 80±117 | 136±213 | 42±65 | 409±564 | 122±160 |
| Range | 84-3,226 | 27-922 | 0-1,030 | 0-294 | 84-4,256 | 27-1,216 |
| **Zinc (mg)** | | | | | | |
| Mean±SD | 9.7±6.0 | 66±4.0 | 16.5±30.8 | 112±206 | 26.2±33.4 | 178±222 |
| Range | 3-35 | 19-235 | 0211 | 10-1,407 | 4-235 | 29-1,642 |
| **Iron (mg)** | | | | | | |
| Mean±SD | 13.4±5.4 | 130±55 | 15.5±24.6 | 151±247 | 28.9±28.0 | 281±282 |
| Range | 3-35 | 20-350 | 0-142 | 0-1,420 | 8-177 | 20-1,770 |
| **Copper (mg)** | | | | | | |
| Mean±SD | 1.3±0.7 | 59±30 | 1.2±1.9 | 55±84 | 2.6±2.1 | 114±93.9 |
| Range | 0.3-4 | 15-178 | 0-11 | 0-489 | 0.3-13 | 15-667 |
| **Selenium (µg)** | | | | | | |
| Mean±SD | 89±38 | 132±57 | 33±49 | 48±71 | 122±68 | 180±99.0 |
| Range | 3-153 | 5-267 | 0-200 | 0-286 | 3-353 | 5-553 |

aFood and Nutrition Board. *Recommended Dietary Allowances.* 10th ed. Washington, DC: National Academy Press; 1989.

bStandard deviation.

RDA. As evaluated by $X^2$ tests, no difference was found in the amount and type of vitamin supplementation taken by patients at different stages of the HIV infection or by patients with or without myopathy.

To evaluate the relationship between the level of nutrient intake from food alone, food and supplements combined (as shown in Table 3), and measurements of ALC, CD4, and transferrin levels, we calculated and evaluated $r_s$ for significance. Positive correlations of borderline significance were observed in patients with a stable weight between energy intake and ALC ($r_s = 37$; $P = .07$); zinc intake from food and ALC ($r_s = .38$; $P = .07$); and zinc intake from food and CD4 levels ($r_s = 391$ $P = .06$). Significant negative correlations were observed between total intake (food and supplements) from the vitamins A, C, E, B-6, and B-12 and riboflavin; the minerals zinc and iron; and grams of protein per kilogram body weight and ALC and CD4 levels. No significant correlations were observed between nutrients and transferrin levels. At the time of assessment, severe diarrhea (three loose stools/day for >2 weeks) was not reported by any of the patients.

## Discussion

This cross-sectional study describes the nutritional, clinical, and immunologic factors in 56 HIV-infected subjects from the inner city, of multiple ethnicities, and with numerous risk factors for HIV infection. Twenty-five subjects (45%) were able to maintain their usual, preillness weight status, whereas 31 patients (55%) experienced weight loss from their preillness status. Furthermore, 17 of the patients who lost weight lost greater than 10% of body weight, thus fulfilling the CDC criteria for wasting syndrome. Previous studies that examined weight changes in patients with HIV and AIDS described that major, involuntary weight losses occurred only when CD4 levels were below 100 cells $\times$ $10^6$/L (13,14). Some of our 7 subjects with myopathy (muscle weakness) experienced a 13% weight loss at CD4 levels greater than 100 cells $\times$ $10^6$/L (mean = 350), and at CD4 counts less than 100. However, patients without myopathy had a notable weight loss (>10%) only at CD4 levels less than 100 cells $\times$ $10^6$/L.

An initial study (15) reported increased levels of TNF in patients with AIDS, and it was proposed that TNF (ie, cachectin) was responsible for the cachexia of AIDS. However, only 3 of our 56 patients showed TNF$\alpha$-positive levels. Other studies have found that TNF levels likely increase episodically in AIDS patients with acute secondary infections such as *Pneumocystis carinii* pneumonia (2,3). Recent evidence suggests that TNF$\alpha$ may be a key player in AIDS. A growing body of data indicate that a state of chronic inflammation may be necessary to maintain HIV infection (16).

The patients in this study had reduced mean levels of ALC and transferrin associated with a mild degree of visceral protein malnutrition, although infections and immunosuppressant drugs (six patients were on prednisone) may have altered these measures. No significant difference was found between patients with stable weight and those who had lost weight for these measurements and for albumin and hemoglobin levels. Mean values for albumin and hemoglobin were within normal ranges in both groups. Studies (17–20) showed that albumin, hemoglobin, and hematocrit levels were prognostically associated with survival, specifically in AIDS patients with very low CD4 counts.

Some of the patients were defined as maintaining a stable weight had previously lost weight during opportunistic infections, but fluctuations of weight were maintained above usual weight or subjects were at their usual weight at time of assessment. Weight recovery was not complete in all patients. In some subjects who had lost weight, efforts to gain weight were terminated by a new episode of acute secondary infection (2,18,21,22). The patients who had lost weight had significantly lower anthropometric measurements—lower BMI, decreased fat stores (eg, TSF), reduced muscle mass (eg, MAC, MAMC), and lower CD4 levels—than patients with stable weight.

The amount of wasting, rather than the specific cause of weight loss, is the primary determinant of death in AIDS and other chronic conditions (23–26). Our patients understood the importance of weight status and made an effort to maintain or improve their dietary intake. Nevertheless, the mean energy intake of the patients was 74% of the RDA, lower than that reported in other studies (7,14,27). Several patients placed great importance on the efficacy of specific vitamin supplements and consumed megadose levels to preserve their immune function (4). Some subjects consumed extremely high levels of B-12 in the belief that a low plasma vitamin B-12 status could cause or worsen neurologic complications in HIV infection (28).

Abrams et al (7) prospectively studied the relationship between dietary intake at baseline and the development of AIDS during the course of 6 years in HIV-1 seropositive men and documented that the hazard of AIDS decreased as consumption of micronutrients increased. When supplements were included, median intakes for most micronutrients reached 300% to 350% of the RDA. In the prospective study by Tang et al (29), high intakes of vitamin C (>715 mg/day) and niacin (>61 mg/day) at baseline were associated with a slower progression from HIV to AIDS. But vitamin A may have a U-shaped relation with risk of AIDS, and increasing zinc intake (>1.3 times the RDA) was associated with more rapid disease progression.

Beach et al (6) reported that when dietary intake of the vitamins B-6, B-12, A, and E and the mineral zinc were high (for example, 2 to 25 times the RDA in some patients), there was little evidence of biochemical inadequacy in HIV-1-positive men during the early stages of the disease. In most patients, the level of dietary intake was closely associated with plasma levels of the nutrient. Moreover, at a subsequent evaluation when patients were receiving zidovudine treatment, significant correlations between dietary and plasma levels of nutrients were generally not observed, suggesting that the therapeutic regimen with zidovudine may play an important role in the nutritional abnormalities associated with treatment (30). Theses findings are supported by those of Coodley et al (31) who documented that decreased serum micronutrient concentrations are common in HIV infection and occur more frequently in patients with wasting syndrome than in patients with comparable CD4 cell counts who are not suffering from wasting syndrome.

We did not perform serum biochemical tests to evaluate vitamin deficiencies or toxicity in our patients. However, the fact that positive correlations between nutrient intake and CD4 and ALC levels were only observed for intakes from food, and not from megadoses of supplements, may indicate an upper and lower threshold of nutrient intake for optimum immune function and the threshold might be altered with the progression of the disease (29,31–34).

A survey (5) documented that 80% of asymptomatic HIV-infected patients changed their diet at the time of or subsequent to their HIV diagnosis. The patients in the survey decreased their intake of animal products but increased their intake of vegetable and seafood. The majority of participants (87%), viewed vitamin and mineral supplements of key importance in influencing their immune function. Similarly, 47 of our 56 subjects (84%) were taking vitamins and/or mineral supplements. Some patients followed strict dietary regimens such as drinking a quart of freshly pressed orange or carrot juice every day, or following a "fruit juice day" (ie, a day in which only fruit juice is consumed) every week. Patients often restricted the intake of fat, cholesterol, and salt on the advice given by a friend, but very few had discussed the importance of nutrition and the dietary modifications with their primary care physicians or with a dietitian or nutritionist. Several patients stated that they did not eat regular meals because of the severity of the disease and frequent extensive clinic appointments; their food records confirmed these statements. These patients need help for both shopping and cooking because of chronic fatigue that interferes with normal activity.

## Applications

The mechanism of weight loss in the progression of HIV has not been clearly elucidated. The etiology is likely to be multifactorial, including interactions among decreased energy and nutrient intake, malabsorption, and altered energy use or expenditure secondary to infection, hormonal, and/or metabolic abnormalities (2,3,21,22). All anthropometric measurements and CD4 and CD8 lymphocyte counts were significantly lower in our patients who had lost weight. Mean values for albumin and hemoglobin were within normal ranges for stable weight and weight loss patients. Twenty-one subjects (45%) took vitamin supplements at levels >200% of the RDA, but no significant positive effects were observed for ALC and CD4 cells. Although supplementation of micronutrients can influence the progression of HIV, nutrition intervention and nutrition counseling starting at the time of diagnosis and emphasizing a balanced, nutritious diet could be more beneficial in maintaining or improving the physiologic status of patients (6,29,35,36).

It might be difficult to achieve the objective of a nutritious diet in an inner-city population that has multiple risk factors. The mean energy intake of our patients was only 74% of the RDA. Active drug users may be less likely than others to receive primary medical-care services and thus benefit from HIV-related social services and interventions such as food and/or nutrition resources (8). With the growing number of injection-drug users in the AIDS population, it will be essential to develop comprehensive strategies to address their interconnected needs for medical and nutrition care and social services. To provide patients with a meal during extensive clinic visits (patients receive a meal ticket for the hospital cafeteria), having meals available in group settings or through home-delivery service may be the most appropriated nutrition intervention in this high-risk population.

Nutritional status, whether measured by hemoglobin level, serum albumin concentration, or magnitude of body cell depletion, predicts survival in adults with HIV infection (1,16–19). Our findings suggest that preventing or slowing the development of severe wasting may prolong survival of AIDS patients. Aggressive nutrition counseling and intervention, adapted to the needs of the patient, during all phases of HIV infection and in conjunction with treatment of primary and secondary complications, may be the appropriate recommendation at our present understanding nutrition's role in HIV infection.

## References

1. Kotler DP, Wang J, Pierson RN. Body composition studies in patients with the acquired immunodeficiency syndrome. *Am J Clin Nutr.* 1985; 42:1255–1265.
2. Grunfeld C, Feingold KR. Metabolic disturbances and wasting in the acquired immunodeficiency syndrome. *N. Engl J Med.* 1992; 327:329–337.
3. Tracey KJ, Vlassara H, Cerami A. Cachectin/tumor necrosis factor. *Lancet.* 1989; 1:1122–1126.
4. Greenberg J. An alternative treatment activist manifesto. *Gay Men's Health Crisis Treatment Issues.* 1993; 7:1–31.
5. Mantero-Atienza E, Baum MK, Javier JJ, Shor-Posner G. Millon CM, Szapocznik J, Eisdorf C, Beach RS. Nutritional knowledge, beliefs and practices in the HIV infected patient. *Nutr Res.* 1991; 11:33–40.
6. Beach RS, Mantero-Atienza E, Shor-Posner G, Javier JJ, Szapocnik J, Morgan R, Sauberlich HE, Cornwell PE, Eisdorf C, Baum MK. Specific nutrient abnormalities in asymptomatic HIV infection. *AIDS.* 1992; 6:701–708.
7. Abrams B, Duncan D, Hertz-Picciotto I. A prospective study of dietary intake and acquired immunodeficiency syndrome in HIV-seropositive homosexual men. *J Acquir Immune Defic Syndr.* 1993; 6:949–958.
8. Selwyn PA, Alcabes P, Hartel D, Buono D, Schoenbaum EE, Klein RS, Davenny K, Friedland GH. Clinical manifestations and predictors of disease progression in drug users with human immunodeficiency virus infection. *N Engl J Med.* 1992; 327:1697–1703.
9. Revision of the CDC case surveillance definition for acquired immunodeficiency syndrome. *MMWR.* 1987; 36(suppl 1S):3S–14S.
10. Schmid P, Conrad A, Syndulko K, Singer EJ, Handley D, Li X, Tao G, Fahy-Chandon B, Toutelotte W. Quantifying HIV-1 proviral DNA using the polymerase chain reaction on cerebrospinal fluid and blood of seropositive individuals with and without neurologic abnormalities. *J Acquir Immune Defic Syndr.* 1994; 7:777–788.
11. Lohman TG, Roche AF, Martorell R. *Anthropometric Standardization Reference Manual.* Champaign, Ill: Human Kinetics Book; 1988.
12. Food and Nutrition Board. *Recommended Dietary Allowances.* 10th ed. Washington, DC: National Academy Press; 1989.
13. Graham NMH, Munoz A, Bacellar H, Kingsley LA, Visscher BR, Phair JP. Clinical factors associated with weight loss related to infection with human immunodeficiency virus type 1 in the multicenter AIDS cohort study. *Am J Epidemiol.* 1993; 137:439–446.
14. Sharkey SJ, Sharkey KA, Sutherland LR, Church DL. Nutritional status and food intake in human immunodeficiency virus infection. *J Acquir Immune Defic Syndr.* 1992; 5:1091–1098.
15. Lahdevirta J, Maury CPJ, Teppo AM, Repo H. Elevated levels of circulating cachectin/tumor necrosis factor in patients with acquired immunodeficiency syndrome. *Am J Med.* 1988; 85:289–291.
16. Balter M. Cytokines move from the margins into the spotlight. *Science.* 1995; 268:205–206.
17. Chlebowski RT, Grosvenor MB, Bernard NH, Morales LS, Bulcavage LM. Nutritional status, gastrointestinal dysfunction, and survival in patients with AIDS. *Am J Gastroenterol.* 1989; 84:1288–1293.
18. Guenter P, Muuarahainen N, Simons G, Kosok A, Cohan GR. Rudenstein R, Turner JL. Relationships among nutrition status, disease progression, and survival in HIV infection. *J Acquir Immune Defic Syndr.* 1993; 6:1130–1138.
19. Saah AJ, Hoover DR, He Y, Kingsley LA, Phair JP. Factors influencing survival after AIDS: Report from the Multicenter AIDS Cohort Study. *J Acquir Immune Defic Syndr.* 1994; 7:287–295.
20. Colford JM, Long N, Tager I. Factors associated with survival in human immunodeficiency virus-infected patients with very low CD counts. *Am J Epidermiol, 1994; 139:206–218.*
21. Grunfeld C, Pang M, Simizu L, Shigenaga JK, Jensen P, Feingold KR. Resting energy expenditure, caloric intake, and short-term weight change in human immunodeficiency virus infection and the acquired immunodeficiency syndrome. *Am J Clin Nutr.* 1992; 55:455–460.
22. Macallan DC, Noble C, Baldwin C, Foskett M, McManus T. Prospective analysis of patterns of weight change in stage IV human immunodeficiency virus infection. *Am J Clin Nutr.* 1993; 58:417–424.
23. Kotler DP, Tierney AR, Wang J, Pierson RN Jr. Magnitude of body-cell-mass depletion and the timing of death from wasting in AIDS. *Am J Clin Nutr.* 1989; 50:444–447.
24. Heymsfield SSB, McManus C, Smith J, Stevens V, Nixon DW. Anthropometric measurement of muscle mass: Revised equations for calculating bone-free arm muscle area. *Am J Clin Nutr.* 1982; 36:680–690.
25. Stein Z, Susser M, Saenger G, Marolla F. *Famine and Human Development: The Dutch Hunger Winter of 1944–45.* London, England: Oxford University Press; 1975.

26. Scrimshaw NS. The phenomenon of famine. Ann Rev Nutr. 1982; 36:680–690.

27. Dworkin BM, Wormser GP, Axelrod F, Pierre N, Schwarz E, Schwartz E, Seaton T. Dietary intake in patients with acquired immunodeficiency syndrome (AIDS), patients with AIDS-related complex, and serologically positive human immunodeficiency virus patients: correlative with nutritional status. *JPEN*. 1990; 14:605–609.

28. Beach RS, Morgan R, Wilkie F, Mantero-Atienza E, Blaney N, Shor-Posner G, Lu Y, Eisdorfer C, Baum MK. Plasma Vitamin $B_{12}$ level as a potential cofactor in studies of human immunodeficiency virus type 1 related cognitive changes. *Arch Neurol,* 1992; 49:501–506.

29. Tang AM, Graham NMH, Kirby AJ, McCall LD, Willett WC, Saah AJ. Dietary micronutrient intake and risk of progression to acquired immunodeficiency syndrome (AIDS) in human immunodeficiency virus type 1 (HIV-1)-infected homosexual men. *Am J Epidermiol.* 1993; 138:937–951.

30. Baum MK, Javier JJ, Mantero-Atienza E, Beach RS, Fletcher MA, Sauberlich HE,Feaster D, Shor-Posner G. Zidovudine-associated adverse reactions in a longitudinal study of asymptomatic HIV-1-infected homosexual males. *J Acquir Immune Defic Syndr.* 1991; 4:1218–1226.

31. Coodley GO, Coodley MK, Nelson HD, Loveless MO. Micronutrient concentrations in the HIV wasting syndrome. *AIDS*. 1993; 7:1595–1600.

32. Graham NMH, Sorensen D, Odaka N, Brookmeyer R, Chan D, Willett WC, Morris JS, Saah AJ. Relationship of serum copper and zinc levels to HIV-1 seropositivity and progressive to AIDS. *J Acquir Immune Defic Syndr.* 1991; 4:976–980.

33. Sembra RD, Graham NMH, Caiaffa WT, Margolick JB, Clement L, Vlahov D. Increased mortality associated with vitamin A deficiency during human immunodeficiency virus type 1 infection. *Arch Intern Med.* 1993; 153:2149–2154.

34. Chandra RK. 1990 McCollum Award Lecture. Nutrition and immunity: lessons from the past and new insights into the future. *Am J Clin Nutr.* 1991; 53:1087–1102.

35. Kotler DP, Tierney AR, Culpepper-Morgan JA,Wang J, Pierson RN. Effect of home total parenteral nutrition on body composition in patients with acquired immunodeficiency syndrome. *JPEN.* 1990; 14:454–458.

36. Kotler DP, Tierney AR, Ferraro R, Cuff P, Wang J, Pierson RN, Heymsfield SB. Enteral alimentation and repletion of body cell mass in malnourished patients with acquired immunodeficiency syndrome. *Am J Clin Nutr.* 1991; 53:149–154.

 **Article Review Form at end of book.**

How did the researchers come up with the idea of vitamin A supplementation and HIV morbidity?

# The Effects of Vitamin A Supplementation on the Morbidity of Children Born to HIV-Infected Women

**Anna Coutsoudis, PhD, Raziya A. Bobat, MBChB, Hoosen M. Coovadia, MD, Louise Kuhn, PhD, Wei-Yann Tsai, PhD, and Zena A. Stein, MBChB**

*Anna Coutsoudis, Raziya A. Bobat, and Hoosen M. Coovadia are with the Department of Paediatrics and Child Health, University of Natal, Durban, South Africa. Louise Kuhn and Zena A. Stein are with the Division of Epidemiology and the Gertude H. Sergievsky Center, Columbia University, New York, NY, and the HIV Center for Clinical and Behavioral Studies, New York State Psychiatric Institute, New York, NY. Wei-Yann Tsai is with the Division of Biostatistics, Columbia University.*

## Abstract

**Objective.** The effects of vitamin A supplementation on morbidity of children born to human immunodefiency virus (HIV)-infected women were evaluated in a population where vitamin A deficiency is not endemic.

**Methods.** A randomized, placebo-controlled trial of vitamin A supplementation was carried out in 118 offspring of HIV-infected women in Durban, South Africa. Those assigned to receive a supplement were given 50,000 IU of vitamin A at 1 and 3 months of age; 100,000 IU at 6 and 9 months; and 200,000 IU at 12 and 15 months. Morbidity in the past month was then recalled at each follow-up visit. Analysis was based on 806 child-months.

**Results.** Among all children, the supplemented group had lower overall morbidity than the placebo group (OR = 0.69; 95% confidence interval [CI] = 0.48, 0.99). Among the 85 children of known HIV status (28 infected, 57 uninfected), morbidity associated with diarrhea was significantly reduced in the supplemented infected children (OR = 0.51; 95% CI = 0.27, 0.99), whereas no effect of supplementation on diarrheal morbidity was noted among the uninfected children.

**Conclusion.** In a population not generally vitamin A deficient, vitamin A supplementation for children of HIV-infected women appeared to be beneficial, reducing morbidity. The benefit was observed particularly for diarrhea among HIV-infected children. (Am J Public Health 1995;85: 1076-1081)

## Introduction

This article reports a test of the hypothesis that vitamin A supplementation for children of human immunodeficiency virus (HIV)-infected women will reduce morbidity even in a population where vitamin A deficiency is not endemic.

Administration of vitamin A to children with overt and marginal vitamin A deficiency has been shown to reduce mortality.[1,2] Morbidity in infants and children has also been reduced, although less consistently.[3] In one African example, in Ghana,[4] a country with borderline vitamin A deficiency by World Health Organization criteria, those infants receiving supplements had fewer hospital admissions and clinic attendances, although total episodes of diarrhea and acute respiratory infections were not significantly reduced. In Brazil, vitamin A supplementation reduced the prevalence of severe diarrhea when the supplemented and placebo groups of children were compared.[5]

In two controlled trials of vitamin A in measles (one, like the present trial, conducted in Durban, South Africa), morbidity and mortality were reduced with supplementation, even though neither study population was initially vitamin A deficient[6,7] Measles infection may result in a depletion of vitamin A reserves, which can be remedied with supplementation. Supplementation strengthens humoral immune responses and increases numbers of lymphocytes.[8]

It therefore seemed reasonable to propose a trial of vitamin A supplementation for children born to HIV-infected women, also in Durban, South Africa. These children might be vitamin A deficient at birth because of vitamin A deficiency in the mother, or infected children might develop vitamin A deficiency associated with their own HIV infection. On the assumption that strengthening immune responses could be beneficial, intravenous administration of immunoglobulin has been investigated in the United States as a therapeutic intervention in HIV-infected infants in the hope of improving resistance to other infections.[9] Developing countries are unlikely to encourage the use of intravenous im-

munoglobulin, given the costs and logistics of its use, nor are they likely to be able to afford antiretroviral drugs such as zidovudine. Vitamin A supplementation, on the other hand, would be inexpensive and simple to administer, might strengthen immune responses, might reduce the severity of infectious-disease episodes, and perhaps prolong life.

In this article, we describe the methods and results of a double-blind, randomized, controlled trial of vitamin A supplementation for children born to HIV-infected women in Durban, South Africa.

## Subjects and Methods

### Subjects

Subjects were recruited from among HIV-infected women who had attended the prenatal clinic and who delivered infants at King Edward VIII Hospital, Durban, from April 1991 through November 1993. The hospital, a long-established teaching unit of Natal University, has a large prenatal care service and maternity unit, with about 15,000 deliveries per annum. Most of the patients are Zulu, and many are referred to the hospital from peripheral and rural clinics. For this study, only women living within 10 miles of the hospital were included. Eligible mothers in the trial all had attended the prenatal clinic, and after pretest counseling, all had chosen to be tested for HIV (all but 5% of the prenatal attendees agree to testing). At that time, about 10% of all women tested through the clinic were HIV positive. The study was approved by the Ethics Committee, Faculty of Medicine, University of Natal. All women gave their written informed consent to participate in the trial.

At delivery, all mothers recruited into a related study of maternal-infant HIV transmission who had, over the period of this study, delivered full-term infants were asked to attend a follow-up clinic after 1 month. The 118 mothers who did so were invited to take part in the vitamin A intervention trial. All accepted and joined the trial. (This high acceptance rate is the usual experience in the department. The promise of medical supervision is highly valued by the mothers.) Preterm infants, often given vitamin A routinely, were not included in the trial.

For lack of statistical power, a study of the effects on mortality was never contemplated. We calculated, however, that a sample size of 120 had sufficient power to detect a reduction in morbidity from 50% to less than 25%. In practice, the analytic method applied here permits every visit to be used in the analysis, and it accretes greater statistical power than initially calculated for individuals in the sample.

### Follow-Up

Mothers were asked to attend a follow-up clinic when their infants reached 2 months and 3 months of age and thereafter at 3-month intervals up to 18 months on days prespecified by the protocol. Mothers were also encouraged to attend the clinic during the intervening period if they had problems. Their traveling costs were reimbursed, and home visits were made to follow-up defaulters.

### Measurement of Morbidity

The morbidity data reported here reflect the current condition of the child at each scheduled clinic visit and a 1-month morbidity recall. The mother was given a card on which to record illnesses experienced by the child. At each scheduled clinic visit, the child received a full clinical examination, and all morbidity in the past month was recorded. The mother was closely questioned about any reported illness episode to ensure that it met the definition for each condition. The incidence, duration (more than 7 days), and severity (hospital admission) of the following were recorded: diarrhea (four or more loose watery stools a day); upper-respiratory-tract infection (presence of one or more of the following: rhinitis, throat infection, ear infection, or cough); lower-respiratory-tract infection (presence of cough with one or more of the following: rapid breathing, chest in-drawing, crackles, or wheezing); isolated fever; thrush; and rash. Special attention was also paid to possible side effects arising from vitamin A treatment. Weight and height were recorded at 3-month intervals, with the National Center for Health Statistics growth charts as the reference standard.

Over 95% of the study infants were initially breast-fed. About half were exclusively breast-fed for 6 months. No significant differences in breast-feeding were found by treatment group.

## Randomization and Treatment Regimen

Identifier numbers indicating vitamin A treatment or placebo were randomly allocated from a table of random numbers. All investigators and participants were blind as to the treatment group of the children. At 1 and 3 months the children received orally 50,000 IU of water-miscible vitamin A (retinyl palmitate, Arovit Drops, Roche, Basel, Switzerland) or an equal volume of placebo, and at 6 and 9 months they received a similar preparation of 100,000 IU of vitamin A or placebo. Both the

placebo and vitamin A were administered in an amber-colored syringe that had been filled and appropriately numbered by the person holding the trial code. At 12 and 15 months, the children were given orally the contents of an amber-colored gelatin capsule containing either 200,000 IU of retinyl palmitate in arachis oil and 40 IU of vitamin E as an antioxidant (Roche, Basel, Switzerland) or a placebo with arachis oil and 20 IU of vitamin E. The capsules looked identical and were placed in number-coded envelopes from which they were removed when appropriate. In November 1993, after recruitment into the trial had been stopped, the vitamin A drops and capsules were analyzed for potency by the local Roche laboratory (Isando, South Africa), which was unaware of their contents. The mean concentration of the Arovit Drops was 142,500 IU/mL, which represent 95% potency, and the mean concentration of the capsules was 191,000 IU/capsule, which represents 95.5% potency.

## Diagnosis of HIV Infection in the Children

The diagnosis of HIV infection in the children was made on the basis of a positive HIV antibody test at 15 months (enzyme-linked immunosorbent assay [ELISA], Abbott, N Chicago, Ill). Children who had lost maternal antibody by 15 months or sooner were diagnosed as uninfected. Among the 11 deaths in children younger than 15 months, 9 were diagnosed as HIV infected on the basis of criteria laid down at the Ghent workshop[10] (i.e., at least one HIV-related sign or symptom when last seen and death from severe infection or persistent diarrhea beyond the first 4 weeks of life). Infection status could not be es-

tablished for the remaining two deaths, nor for 33 children lost to follow-up before 15 months of age who had neither lost antibody nor developed clinical disease when last seen. At the time the analysis reported here was undertaken, all surviving children were 15 months or older.

## Vitamin A Concentrations

Vitamin A concentration was measured in a subsample of 36 infants, tested at 1 month and 9 months. These assays were to establish comparability of the supplemented and placebo groups at baseline and to validate the increase of vitamin A levels with supplementation. Sera were collected from alternate infants at baseline. Out of a necessary economy, the analysis was limited to the first 36 infants who had visited the clinic at 9 months and who had been tested at 1 month.

One milliliter of venous blood was obtained and centrifuged within 5 hours. The serum was separated and stored at −70°C until analysis. Precautions were taken to protect the serum from light during separation, storage, and analysis. Vitamin A (serum retinol) was measured by normal-phase high-pressure liquid chromatography with fluorescence detection. The method used was a modification of a previously reported method.[11] The instrument used was a Hewlett-Packard HP 1090, which was attached to a programmable fluorescence detector (HP 1046). The column was a normal-phase microbore column (Spherisorb S3W; Phase Sep, Queensferry, Wales, United Kingdom). The method was validated by using standard reference material for retinol (SRM 968a) from the National Institute of Standards and Technology (Gaithersburg, Md).

The technician was blind to the treatment regimen.

## Statistical Methods

In accord with the a priori hypothesis, the primary intention-to-treat analysis compared the supplemented and placebo groups overall with respect to all morbidity. The components were diarrhea, diarrhea lasting 7 or more days, thrush, lower- and upper-respiratory-tract infections, rash, and hospitalization for diarrhea and for lower-respiratory-tract infections. The occurrence of each condition separately and of all morbidity combined was expressed as incidence density morbidity rates. These were calculated by dividing the number of episodes of the condition (multiple episodes of the same condition in a single month were counted as one episode), and for all morbidity the number of months in which any of the conditions had occurred, by the child-months of observation.

Odds ratios (ORs) and standard errors to compare morbidity between groups were estimated from logistic regression models with repeated measurement that make use of generalized estimating equations. This method, which can take into account within-individual correlation, was specifically developed for the analysis of longitudinal data sets comprised of repeated observations of an outcome in the same individuals over time.[12-14] For the primary analysis, the logit transformation of the outcome (occurrence of each condition coded dichotomously as either absent or present) was modeled as a function of the treatment status (vitamin A or placebo). The independent working correlation structure and robust standard errors were used.

Analyses were conducted with a macro written for SAS software by M. Rezaul Karim.[15]

A prespecified corollary to the primary hypothesis tested whether supplementation was particularly effective for HIV-infected infants. At the time and place this study was carried out, the diagnosis of HIV infection in the offspring of infected mothers had to rely on clinical features and the persistence of antibody to the age of 15 months. The necessary delay precluded randomization of HIV-infected infants at entry. Therefore, this question was examined by comparing treated and untreated children within infected and uninfected subgroups. Morbidity rates and odds ratios were calculated within the HIV status strata. Children whose infection status was not established were excluded (20 in the vitamin A group, 13 in the placebo group). To investigate the sensitivity of the analysis to the exclusion of children for whom HIV status was not established, further analyses were conducted in which children of unknown HIV status were either all included with the infected subgroup or all included with the uninfected subgroup.

Each condition was analyzed separately with multivariate logistic models based on generalized estimating equations. Odds ratios and confidence intervals (CIs) were determined for the effect of the treatment on HIV-infected and uninfected infants. Outcome was dichotomous, recorded as the presence (coded as 1) or absence (coded as 0) of the condition in the preceding month. Covariates were treatment status (supplemented [1] vs placebo [0]), HIV status (infected [1] vs uninfected [0]), and interaction between HIV status, and treatment, and the child's age (as a continuous covariate).

## Results

*Table 1.* Of 118 children who entered in the trial, 11 died, all before 6 months of age: 5 of 60 in the supplemented group and 6 of 58 in the placebo group. (For two deaths in the supplemented group, the infection status could not be established.) In a life-table analysis, survival time did not differ by treatment. The numbers of HIV-infected children in the supplemented and placebo groups were similar (13 vs 15, respectively). The groups fared equally in terms of follow-up.

*Table 2.* Randomization produced comparable groups in terms of baseline characteristics at the 1-month visit, before randomization. No statistically significant differences by treatment assignment in sex, maternal age or parity, nutritional parameters, and reported morbidity in the previous month were observed. There were no significant differences (data not shown) between supplemented and placebo groups in terms of sociodemographic characteristics (education, previous sibling loss, availability of domestic water and electricity, and household crowding). These data were not available for the whole sample.

The vitamin A concentrations were examined by treatment status at 1 month and 9 months of age in the subsample of 36 infants selected as described in "Vitamin A Concentrations." At assignment, when the first vitamin A level was assessed, the treatment groups did not differ (mean concentrations of 29.6 µg/dL in the supplemented group and 27.7 µg/dL in the placebo group). As expected, however, at 9 months, the supplemented group had significantly higher levels of vitamin A than the placebo group (mean concentrations of 38.4 µg/dL and 30.0 µg/dL, respectively; $P < .001$).

## Table 1: Numbers of Children Enrolled in Study, Mortality, HIV Status, and Follow-Up in Vitamin A and Placebo Groups

| | Treatment Assignment | |
| --- | --- | --- |
| | Vitamin A | Placebo |
| No. enrolled | 60 | 58 |
| No. deaths by end of study | | |
|   HIV infected | 3 | 6 |
|   Infection status not established | 2 | 0 |
| No. alive | | |
|   HIV infected | 10 | 9 |
|   Uninfected | 27 | 30 |
|   Infection status not established | 18 | 13 |
| Total no. child-months of follow-up | 416 | 390 |
| % followed to | | |
|   6 mo | 83 | 75 |
|   12 mo | 64 | 67 |
|   18 mo | 42 | 37 |
| Based on total duration of follow-up: | | |
|   % children attending all treatment or placebo visits | 96 | 98 |
|   % children attending every month until 18 mo. | 69 | 71 |

## Table 2: Baseline Characteristics of Vitamin A and Placebo Groups: Sex, Maternal Age and Parity, Nutritional Parameters, and Morbidity

| | Treatment Assignment | | |
| --- | --- | --- | --- |
| | Vitamin A | Placebo | $P^a$ |
| % male | 50.0 | 56.9 | .453 |
| Mean maternal age, (y) | 25.0 | 24.8 | .855 |
| Mean parity | 2.2 | 2.4 | .379 |
| Nutritional parameters | | | |
|   % with weight for age below 2 standard deviations of the standard | 0 | 3.4 | .239 |
|   % with height for age below 2 standard deviations of the standard | 6.7 | 5.2 | 1.000 |
| Pretreatment morbidity,[b] % | | | |
|   Diarrhea | 6.7 | 5.2 | 1.000 |
|   Thrush | 18.3 | 31.0 | .109 |
|   Lower-respiratory-tract infection | 8.3 | 1.7 | .207 |
|   Upper-respiratory-tract infection | 21.7 | 20.7 | .897 |
|   Rash | 3.3 | 8.8 | .268 |

[a]P values were calculated with the chi-square test for categorical variables, except for comparisons with any cell sizes less than 5, in which case Fisher's exact test was used. The t test was used for continuous variables.

[b]At least one occurrence of the condition in the first month.

*Table 3.* Overall morbidity was significantly lower among the children receiving supplementation (OR = 0.69; 95% CI =0.48, 0.99). For almost every condition, assessed separately, rates with supplementation were lower, but the upper confidence limit was greater than 1. In the supplemented group, incidence was reduced for all diarrhea by 29%, for diarrhea lasting 7 or more days by 38%, and for hospital admissions for diarrhea by 77%. Smaller differences were seen for thrush and for respiratory infections. There were no differences in the frequency of rashes or in weight gain between the two groups. Mean weight gain from 1 to 9 months was 4.42 kg (95% CI = 4.15, 4.70) and 4.84 kg (95% CI = 4.37, 5.31) in the vitamin A group and the placebo group, respectively.

*Table 4.* Among HIV-infected children, the reduction associated with vitamin A supplementation (controlling for age) was estimated to be 49% for all diarrhea (a significant reduction; $P < .05$) and 56% for diarrhea lasting 7 or more days. For children known to be uninfected, effects of supplementation were smaller for all diarrhea and for severe diarrhea (the interaction term in the model is not statistically significant). For hospital admissions for diarrhea (all were among infected children), the estimated reduction with supplementation was 77%.

Separate analyses of morbidity occurring below 6 months of age, at 7 through 12 months, and at 13 through 18 months (data not shown) found similar effects of treatment across the age strata.

## Discussion

The women attending the King Edward VIII Hospital maternity service are not, in general, a vitamin A–deficient population. Thus,

| | Incidence Density per 100 Child-Months (No. Episodes) | | |
|---|---|---|---|
| Morbidity | Vitamin A (n = 416 mo) | Placebo (n = 390 mo) | Model Odds Ratio (95% CI) |
| Diarrhea | 19.7(82) | 25.6(100) | 0.71 (0.47, 1.08) |
| Diarrhea lasting ≥7 days | 6.3 (26) | 9.7 (38) | 0.62 (0.32, 1.20) |
| Hospitalized for diarrhea | 0.5 (2) | 3.1 (8) | 0.23 (0.04, 1.20) |
| Thrush | 5.0 (21) | 7.2 (28) | 0.69 (0.37, 1.28) |
| Lower-respiratory-tract infection | 7.7 (32) | 11.0 (43) | 0.67 (0.37, 1.21) |
| Hospitalized for lower-respiratory-tract infection | 1.7 (7) | 1.8 (7) | 0.94 (0.37, 2.70) |
| Upper-respiratory-tract infection | 40.1 (167) | 46.7 (182) | 0.77 (0.53, 1.10) |
| Rash | 11.1 (46) | 10.0 (39) | 1.12 (0.63, 1.98) |
| All morbidity | 36.5 (152) | 45.4 (177) | 0.69 (0.48, 0.99) |

**Table 3** Morbidity for All Infants in the Trial (Infected, Uninfected and Status Not Established Combined): Vitamin A vs Placebo Groups

it is notable, if not very surprising, that the offspring of HIV-infected women were not vitamin A deficient at 1 month of age. Nevertheless, in accord with the primary a priori hypotheses, this study suggests that in this population vitamin A administered orally to the offspring of HIV-infected women in regular moderate to high doses beginning at 1 month of age reduces morbidity, at least through the first 18 months of life covered by this trial. The magnitude of the reduction in overall morbidity appears to be quite substantial. For specific conditions, the effects are generally in the same direction but do not reach significance.

As anticipated with sample sizes calculated for a hypothesis of reduced morbidity, we were unable to show a reduction in mortality. Loss to follow-up was considerable. Given randomization, the strict maintenance of blinding of both investigators and participants throughout the study, and an analysis that included all participants in the denominators, however, the results are unlikely to overestimate the effect of vitamin A supplementation.

The second a priori hypothesis was that the reduction in morbidity associated with vitamin A supplementation would be particular to HIV-infected children. The multivariate analyses support the hypothesis in that the effect appears to be strengthened in such children. This result is more vulnerable than the result for the primary hypothesis because a diagnosis of HIV infection could not be established in the almost one third lost to death or follow-up before 15 months of age. Nevertheless, the results are unchanged whether those for whom an HIV diagnosis was not established are excluded, included with the infected subgroup, or included with the uninfected subgroup. Thus, among supplemented children, those infected had a significant reduction in episodes of diarrhea compared with children receiving placebo who were infected, whereas no comparable treatment effect was observed among the uninfected children.

Treatment and placebo groups had similar nutritional and health indicators at baseline. However, no interim measures of characteristics that may have influenced morbidity in the two groups are available, nor are there laboratory measures of HIV viral load or of immune status in the children in the trial. In this respect, the study is not proof against all confounders (i.e., we did not estimate conditional treatment effects with adjustment for these variables), nor can it illuminate biological processes. Nevertheless, given the initial randomization, unbiased exposure, unbiased observation of outcomes, and no exclusions after randomization, the results remain valid within the appropriate limits of the statistical tests (i.e., the unadjusted treatment effect estimates are unbiased estimates of the conditional parameters).

The findings are consistent with biological knowledge, although they are to some degree tentative because of relatively small numbers. Human immunodeficiency virus infection is accompanied by multiple nutritional deficiencies including vitamin A deficiency.[16,17] In HIV-infected adults, vitamin A deficiency has been found in association with immunoparesis, accelerated progression to the acquired immunodeficiency syndrome (AIDS), and reduction in life span.[18] Among offspring of HIV-infected women, vitamin A deficiency has been associated with increased infant and perinatal mortality.[19,20] Whether this increase results from increased transmission of the virus, from accelerated progress of the infection in the infants, or from other causes is still unclear.

The likely mechanisms through which vitamin A reduces

**Table 4** Observed Morbidity Rates per 100 Child-Months of Follow-Up among Known HIV-Infected Children and Uninfected Children: Vitamin A vs Placebo

| | HIV Infected Children | | | Uninfected Children | | |
|---|---|---|---|---|---|---|
| | Morbidity Rate (No. Episodes) | | | Morbidity Rate (No. Episodes) | | |
| Morbidity | Vitamin A | Placebo | Treatment OR (95% CI[a]) | Vitamin A | Placebo | Treatment OR (95% CI[a]) |
| Diarrhea | 21.6 (21) | 35.1 (34) | 0.51 (0.27, 0.99) | 21.1 (56) | 23.1 (63) | 0.89 (0.37, 2.10) |
| Diarrhea lasting ≥ 7 days | 10.3 (10) | 20.6 (20) | 0.44 (0.17, 1.18) | 5.7 (15) | 6.6 (18) | 0.84 (0.23, 3.13) |
| Hospitalized for diarrhea | 2.1 (2) | 8.3 (8) | 0.23 (0.05, 1.19) | 0 | 0 | |
| Thrush | 9.3 (9) | 13.4 (13) | 0.66 (0.25, 1.73) | 3.4 (9) | 4.4 (12) | 0.77 (0.20, 2.94) |
| Lower-respiratory-tract infection | 11.3 (11) | 17.5 (17) | 0.60 (0.29, 1.24) | 6.4 (17) | 8.5 (23) | 0.75 (0.24, 2.38) |
| Hospitalized for lower-respiratory-tract infection | 3.1 (3) | 5.2 (5) | 0.59 (0.13, 2.65) | 1.1 (3) | 0.7 (2) | 1.57 (0.16, 15.9) |
| Upper-respiratory-tract infection | 47.4 (46) | 46.4 (45) | 1.04 (0.48, 2.24) | 38.5 (102) | 45.1 (123) | 0.76 (0.31, 1.87) |
| Rash | 17.5 (17) | 9.4 (9) | 2.07 (0.61, 7.08) | 8.7 (23) | 10.3 (28) | 0.83 (0.21, 3.35) |
| All morbidity | 45.5 (46) | 54.8 (51) | 0.69 (0.36, 1.31) | 44.6 (90) | 52.1 (175) | 0.74 (0.34, 1.61) |
| No. follow-up months | 97 | 97 | | 265 | 273 | |

*Note.* Children whose infection status was not established were excluded. Results were not different when these children were included either with the infected or the uninfected subgroup.
[a]Confidence intervals (CIs) for odds ratios (ORs) for the treatment effect were calculated from a multivariate model based on generalized estimating equations, specifying as the outcome the occurrence of the condition (1 or 0) and as the covariates treatment status (vitamin A [1] placebo [0]), HIV status (infected [1] uninfected [0]), and interaction between HIV status, treatment, and child's age (continuous).

morbidity are rehabilitation of mucosal integrity and boosting of the immune response.[21,22] Both these protective barriers are known to be breached in HIV infection. Specifically, a decline in the number of CD4+ T lymphocytes[23] correlates with the risk and severity of HIV-related clinical syndromes.[24] In humans and experimental animals deficient in vitamin A, vitamin A therapy corrects abnormalities and enhances impaired cellular and humoral immunity. Vitamin A works both in prior nutritional deficiency states[25] and in deficiency states (diminished blood levels) caused by the body's excessive consumption of vitamin A during severe disease.[6,7]

Vitamin A supplementation plausibly has an effect on morbidity in cases of HIV infection similar to that in cases of measles.[6,7] Measles virus affects CD4+ lymphocytes,[26] with lymphopenia being an important indicator of the severity of measles[27]; conversely, vitamin A supplementation increases lymphocyte numbers and antibody response.[8] Serum levels of vitamin A in this study were similar to those among measles patients in whom large doses improved their clinical condition.[28]

In this study, vitamin A supplementation, administered to full-term infants in the postnatal period, did appear to raise vitamin A levels. An alternative procedure might have been to supplement the mothers at delivery.[29]

Vitamin A supplementation appeared to reduce morbidity associated with diarrhea. Associations were stronger with increasing severity of the diarrhea. In keeping with results from other studies,[3,5] this finding suggests that benefits of supplementation are owed to reduced severity of illness, rather than reduced numbers of episodes of illness. In HIV-infected children, diarrhea is among the prime causes of morbidity[30] and use of health services and, in Africa, an important cause of death.[31] Although a notable consequence of protracted diarrhea in HIV-infected children is growth retardation, we detected no differences in weight gain and length between treated and placebo groups. Growth velocity determinations might be more revealing.

The dose and schedule regimens of vitamin A used here seem to have been appropriate and well tolerated. No unforeseen difficulties were experienced with its use. Side effects (vomiting and bulging fontanelle) were monitored by history and, when possible, by clinical examination.

A reasonable inference, which will need to be examined in subsequent trials, is that vitamin A is beneficial for HIV-infected children, even if begun postnatally and even in a population not normally vitamin A deficient. Vitamin A is inexpensive and can be expected to benefit infected children by reducing the incidence and severity of diarrhea and the burden on health services and, not least, by improving the quality of life for the children and their caretakers.

## References

1. Glasziou PP, Mackerras DEM.Vitamin A supplementation in infectious diseases: a meta-analysis. *BMJ*. 1993; 306:366–370.
2. Fawzi WW, Chalmers TC, Herrera MG, Mosteller R. Vitamin A supplementation and child mortality: a meta-analysis. *JAMA*. 1993; 269:898–903.
3. Beaton GH, Martorell R, L'Abbe KA, et al. *Effectiveness of Vitamin A Supplementation in the Control of Young Child Morbidity and Mortality in Developing Countries*. Toronto, Canada: University of Toronto; 1993. Final report to CIDA.
4. Ghana VAST Study Team. Vitamin A supplementation in northern Ghana: effects on clinic attendances, hospital admissions, and child mortality. *Lancet*. 1993; 342:7–12.
5. Barreto ML, Santos LMP, Assis AMO, et al. Effect of vitamin A supplementation on diarrhoea and acute lower-respiratory-tract infections in young children in Brazil. *Lancet*. 1994; 344:228–231.
6. Coutsoudis A, Brouhton M. Coovadia HM. Vitamin A supplementation reduces measles morbidity in young African children: a randomized, placebo controlled, double blind trial. *Am J Clin Nutr*. 1991; 54:890–895.
7. Hussey GD, Klein M. A randomized controlled trial of vitamin A in children with severe measles. *N Engl J Med*. 1990; 323:160–164.
8. Coutsoudis A, Kiepiela P, Coovadia HM, Broughton M. Vitamin A supplementation enhances specific IgG antibody levels and total lymphocyte numbers while improving morbidity in measles. *Pediatr Infect Dis J*. 1992; 11:203–209.
9. The National Institute of Child Health and Human Development Intravenous Immunoglobulin Study Group. Intravenous immune globulin for the prevention of bacterial infections in children with sympotomac human immunodeficiency virus infection. *N Engl J Med*. 1991; 325:73–80.
10. Dabis F, Msellati P, Dunn D, et al. Estimating the rate of mother-to-child transmission of HIV. Report of a workshop on methodological issues. Ghent (Belgium), 17–20 February 1992. *AIDS*. 1993; 7:1139–1148.
11. Rhys Williams AT. Simultaneous determination of serum vitamin A and E by liquid chromatography with fluorescence detection. *J Chromatogr*. 1985; 341:198–201.
12. Zeger SL, Liang KY. Longtidunal data analysis for discrete and continuous outcomes. *Biometrics*. 1986; 42:121–130.
13. Zeger SL, Liang KY. An overview of methods for the analysis of longitudinal data. *Stat Med*. 1992; 11:1825–1839.
14. Liang KY, Hanfelt J. On the use of the quasi-likelihood method in teratology experiments. *Biometrics*. 1994; 50:872–880.
15. Karim MR. SAS macro. Baltimore, Md: Department of Biostatistics, The Johns Hopkins University; 1989.
16. Beach RS, Mantero-Atienza E, Shor-Posner G, et al. Specific nutrient abnormalities in symptomatic HIV-1 infection. *AIDS*. 1992; 6:701–708.
17. Baum MK, Shor-Posner G, Bonvehi P, et al. Influence of HIV infections on vitamin status and requirements. *Ann NY Acad Sci*. 1992; 669:165–174.
18. Semba RD, Graham NMH, Caiaffa WT, Margolick JB, Clement L, Vlahov D. Increased mortality associated with vitamin A deficiency during human immunodeficiency virus type 1 infection. *Arch Intern Med*. 1993; 153:2149–2154.
19. Dushimimana A, Graham NMH, Humphrey JH, et al. Maternal vitamin A levels and HIV-related birth outcome in Rwanda. Presented at the 8th International Conference on AIDS; July 19–24, 1992; Amsterdam, The Netherlands. Abstract.
20. Semba RD, Miotti PG, Chiphangwi JD, et al. Maternal vitamin A deficiency and mother-to-child transmission of HIV-1. *Lancet*. 1994; 343:1593–1597.
21. Chandra RK, Vyas D. Vitamin A, immuno-competence and infection. *Food Nutr Bull*. 1989; 11(September):12–19.
22. Semba RD, Muhilal, Ward BJ, et al. Abnormal T-cell subset proportions in vitamin A-deficient children. *Lancet*. 1993; 341:5–8.
23. Ho DD, Pomerantz RJ, Kaplan JC. Pathogenesis of infection with human immunodeficiency virus. *N Engl J Med*. 1987; 317:278–286.
24. Wade N. Immunological considerations in pediatric HIV infection. *J Pediatr*. 1991; 119(suppl):5–7.
25. Daulaire NMP, Starbuck ES, Houston RM, Church MS, Stukel TA, Pandey MR. Childhood mortality after a high dose of vitamin A in a high risk population. *BMJ*. 1992; 304:207–210.
26. Kiepiela P, Coovadia HM, Coward P. T helper cell defect related to severity in measles. *Scan J Infect Dis*. 1987; 19:185–192.
27. Coovadia HM, Wesley A, Brian P. Immunological events in acute measles influencing outcome. *Arch Dis Child*. 1978; 53:2177–2181.
28. Coutsoudis A, Coovadia HM, Broughton M, Salisbury RT, Elson I. Micronutrient utilisation during measles treated with vitamin A or placebo. *Int J Nutr Res*. 1991; 61:199–204.
29. Stoltzfus RJ, Hakimi M, Miller KW, et al. High dose vitamin A supplementation of breast-feeding Indonesian mothers: effects on the vitamin A status of mother and infant. *J Nutr*. 1993; 123:666–675.
30. Kotloff KL, Johnson JP, Nair P, et al. Diarrheal morbidity during the first 2 years of life among HIV-infected infants. *JAMA*. 1994; 271:448–452.
31. Thea DM, St Louis ME, Atido U, et al. A prospective study of diarrhea and HIV-infection among 429 Zairian infants. *N Engl J Med*. 1993; 329:1696–1702.

**Article Review Form at end of book.**

# WiseGuide Wrap-Up

- A number of diet links with cardiovascular disease exist, including saturated fat, total fat, cholesterol, omega-3 fatty acids, soluble fiber, antioxidants, sodium, and alcohol.

- With strict dietary, stress-management, and exercise lifestyle choices, atherosclerosis (the progressive narrowing of an artery) can be reversed.

- Nutrition therapy is vital in the management of fatigue, diarrhea, and wasting, which are frequently associated with AIDS.

## R.E.A.L. Sites

This list provides a print preview of typical **coursewise** R.E.A.L. sites. (There are over 100 such sites at the **courselinks**™ site.) The danger in printing URLs is that web sites can change overnight. As we went to press, these sites were functional using the URLs provided. If you come across one that isn't, please let us know via email to: webmaster@coursewise.com. Use your Passport to access the most current list of R.E.A.L. sites at the **courselinks**™ site.

**Site name:** The American Heart Association

**URL:** http://www.amhrt.org

**Why is it R.E.A.L.?** An excellent resource to discover how to live healthy, including diet and fitness. Data are from health-care professionals, and the page provides links to these individuals.

**Activities:** (1)Assess your risk for heart disease. Are you concerned with the results? Why or why not? (2)What is the American Heart Association's diet/eating plan for healthy Americans?

**Site name:** AIDSNYC

**URL:** http://www.aidsnyc.org

**Why is it R.E.A.L.?** This page provides a number of links to additional AIDS projects. Many of the linked pages are from community-based organizations in New York City.

**Activities:** (1)Why is nutrition important to people living with HIV/AIDS? (2)What are the roles of antioxidant nutrients, phytochemicals, and fiber in individuals who are HIV-positive?

**Site name:** Arbor Nutrition Guide

**URL:** http://arborcom.com

**Why is it R.E.A.L.?** This site provides a large number of cross-references. Even though there is a great deal of information available here, the page format makes simple work of accessing the material.

**Activities:** (1)Explain how to interpret serum cholesterol values. (2)Assume that your recent blood lipid analysis revealed the following:

 Total cholesterol = 200 mg/dl
 HDL-cholesterol = 35 mg/dl

Is this anything to worry about? Why or why not? (3)How are antioxidant nutrients protective in terms of heart disease?

# section 6

## Learning Objectives

After studying this section, you will know:

- what each of the following are, how they affect cancer risk, and the diet sources for: fat, alcohol, nitrites, aflatoxins, antioxidants, insoluble fiber, cruciferous vegetables, phytochemicals, and lycopene.

- eight diet strategies to lower cancer risk.

- what free radicals are, and how they are supposedly linked to cancer.

- associated health concerns of individuals with diabetes mellitus.

- signs of diabetes mellitus.

- causes and consequences of ketoacidosis.

- diet and exercise strategies to help manage diabetes mellitus.

# Diets to Avoid Cancer and Diabetes Mellitus

**WiseGuide Intro**

Approximately 25 percent of us will die from cancer, while 75 percent of all families will have or have had a member with cancer. Cancer, and its treatment, strikes fear in many Americans. The phenomenon is characterized by an abnormal and uncontrollable growth of cells. Often, this growth manifests itself in the form of a tumor. These tumors may be benign (not cancerous) or malignant (cancerous). It is these malignant tumors which are capable of moving (metastasizing) to another locale. The key to successfully combating this disease is early detection.

Dissemination of cancer health education is paramount. Individuals should be informed regarding risk factors, warning signs, and suggestions for early detection. The statement "An ounce of prevention is worth a pound of cure" could not be more true concerning cancer.

Cancer Warning Signs:

C = change in bowel or bladder habits
A = a sore that will not heal
U = unusual bleeding or discharge
T = thickening or lump in the breast or elsewhere
I = indigestion or difficulty in swallowing
O = obvious change in wart or mole
N = nagging cough or hoarseness

Science is far from complete concerning cancer causes. Often, environment, genetics, and lifestyle choices work together in determining one's risk for cancer. Diets which are high in fat, alcohol, nitrites (preservatives for meats), and aflatoxins (poisons from moldy peanuts and seeds) seem to be contributors to cancer. Conversely, beta-carotene, vitamin C, vitamin E, selenium, fiber, and cruciferous vegetables (broccoli, kale, cauliflower) are dietary protectors.

How can you reduce the likelihood of developing cancer? Try modifying your diet to

- Eat a wide variety of foods.

- Eat more high-fiber foods, including vegetables, fruits, and whole grain products.

- Eat dark green and deep yellow fruits and vegetables.

- Eat cruciferous vegetables such as cabbage, broccoli, Brussels sprouts, and cauliflower.

- Moderate your consumption of salt-cured, smoked, and nitrite-cured foods.

- Reduce your intake of fat and saturated fat.

**R29.** What are antioxidants, and how are they protective in terms of cancer? The American Cancer Society Guidelines on Diet, Nutrition and Cancer are noted in the article. Do you presently follow these suggestions? Why or why not? If not, would you be willing to make a lifestyle change and heed these suggestions?

**R30.** How does an antioxidant work? What are some good food sources for selenium? Might one receive too much selenium? If so, what might occur?

**R31.** Might some of the recent results regarding selenium's possible antioxidant role be exaggerated?

**R32.** List and briefly explain the dietary factors that may promote cancer.

**R33.** What is in tomatoes that may be protective in terms of prostate cancer? Can the preparation of the food affect the amount of lycopene available in tomatoes?

**R34.** What are the benefits of emphasizing soy foods?

**R35.** Differentiate between Type I and Type II diabetes mellitus. What are the symptoms of hypoglycemia? What is ketoacidosis?

**R36.** Summarize the characteristics of the two diets administered during the study. The high-carbohydrate diet increased fasting levels of what two variables?

- Maintain a healthy body weight.

- Be moderate in your consumption of alcohol.

Each individual has the opportunity to make lifestyle choices that will help prevent, and help to detect cancer. What will be your choice?

Another common disease in America is diabetes mellitus. Nearly 16 million individuals in the United States have diabetes mellitus. Of this number, 50 percent do not even realize that they have the condition. Approximately 1,800 new cases are discovered daily.

There are two types of diabetes mellitus: Type I and Type II. These are sometimes referred to as insulin dependent diabetes mellitus (IDDM) and non-insulin dependent diabetes mellitus (NIDDM), respectively. This phenomenon is characterized by the body's inability to move blood glucose (sugar) into the cells. Typically, glucose accumulates in the blood, resulting in the condition hyperglycemia. Hyperglycemia results in thirst (polydipsia) and frequent urination (polyuria), and the excess glucose will spill over into the urine (glucosuria).

Normally, insulin, a hormone made in the pancreas, moves glucose from the blood into the cells. Diabetics either do not produce insulin (IDDM) or cannot effectively use the insulin that is produced (NIDDM). Both types of diabetes mellitus deprive body cells of energy. The cells consequently mobilize protein and fat supplies. However, without an adequate supply of glucose available, the fat is not properly metabolized. This incomplete fat metabolism causes the production of ketone bodies, which accumulate in the blood (ketonemia). This phenomenon may be diagnosed in an individual who has a fruity smell to their breath (acetone breath). The ketone bodies in the blood ultimately lower the body's pH (ketones are acidic). In an attempt to respond, the ketones become present in the urine. However, while eliminating the ketone bodies in the urine, sodium and potassium (base-forming electrolytes) are lost as well. This exacerbates the acidic condition and if not treated may lead to the potentially fatal condition of diabetic coma.

Chronic hyperglycemia can cause a number of additional complications in the body, including

- circulatory disruption, sometimes leading to amputations

- heart disease

- kidney disease

- loss of vision due to retinal degeneration

Fortunately, diabetes mellitus and the aforementioned complications can be managed by keeping a reign on one's blood glucose level.

What are antioxidants, and how are they protective in terms of cancer? The American Cancer Society Guidelines on Diet, Nutrition and Cancer are noted in the article. Do you presently follow these suggestions? Why or why not? If not, would you be willing to make a lifestyle change and heed these suggestions?

# New Perspectives on Diet and Cancer

Interview with American Cancer Society's Daniel Nixon, M.D.

*When not at the Pentagon or on active duty in the Naval Reserves, Daniel W. Nixon, M.D. serves as vice president of professional education for the American Cancer Society in Atlanta. Prior to his current position, Dr. Nixon spent the majority of his career in medical oncology at Emory University School of Medicine, with more than 15 years of specialized research in diet-related manuscripts in books and journals. He currently serves on several nutrition committees for the National Cancer Institute and is co-editor in chief of the internationally recognized journal, Cancer Prevention.*

**How do the new dietary guidelines recently issued by the American Cancer Society differ from the previous version?**

The American Cancer Society (ACS) first published nutritional guidelines in 1982, and they have evolved over time. Today, ACS guidelines are not materially different from the dietary recommendations of the National Cancer Institute and the American Heart Association. All three organizations stress the importance of eating a low-fat, high-fiber diet and plenty of fruits and vegetables.

The new ACS guidelines emphasize eating a variety of foods. It seemed that some people were eating only cruciferous vegetables to the exclusion of other foods. Thus, we stress the need to eat a varied diet, rather than any one particular food or group of foods.

Our new guidelines also emphasize the need to limit or control obesity, not only through decreased caloric intake, but through exercise as well. The leading ACS recommendation is to avoid being overweight.

**Why aren't there any quantitative recommendations in the new guidelines?**

We feel the data are not solid enough to quantify how many grams of fiber it takes to prevent colon cancer, for example, or how few grams of fat will reduce risk of breast cancer. We give a general range for dietary fat, which is 30 percent of calories or less.

**Is it the percent of calories from fat or the total number of calories in the diet that increases cancer risk?**

Fat intake and total calories are both important. It's clear from animal studies that both fat itself and calories, whether from fat or from other foods, play a role, probably not as cancer initiators but as cancer promoters.

**What is the current evidence on polyunsaturated fat and cancer?**

The polyunsaturate story is still very cloudy as far as cancer is concerned. At this point, we would advise people to watch their total fat intake rather than worry about the type of fat they're consuming.

"New Perspectives on Diet and Cancer" by Dr. Daniel Nixon as appeared in FOOD INSIGHT March/April 1992. Reprinted by permission.

• Maintain a desirable body weight.

• Eat a varied diet.

• Include a variety of both vegetables and
fruits in the daily diet.

• Eat more high-fiber foods, such as whole-
grained cereals, legumes, vegetables and
fruits.

• Cut down on total fat intake.

• Limit consumption of alcoholic beverages,
if you drink at all.

• Limit consumption of salt-cured, smoked
and nitrite-preserved foods.

**Why does being overweight increase the risk of cancer?**

There are two phenomena going on. When people consume excess calories, it stimulates the metabolic overdrive into making cells divide faster. This increases the risk that something can go awry, resulting in cancerous cells. Then too, fat people have more cells, so there is an increased statistical chance that some of those cells might become cancerous.

**What role do antioxidants play in preventing cancer?**

Vitamins A, C and E are known to have certain antioxidant properties. It's believed that these antioxidants work by stopping damage to the DNA; or if the DNA is already damaged, they help in its repair.

But there are also other properties in vitamins that work to prevent cancer. For example, vitamin A retinoids seem to be able to take cells that are on the way to becoming malignant and help restore them to normal activity. This has been shown in studies of pre-malignant regions of the head and neck; doses of synthetic retinoids

have been able to reverse that condition. So there's more than one possible good effect of vitamins.

**Do so-called "designer foods" hold great potential in cancer prevention?**

We're just beginning to understand what characteristics to design into foods. Foods, including fruits and vegetables, have many more useful substances in them besides vitamins. In designing anti-cancer foods like the 'super carrot,' we don't want to inadvertently eliminate other essential components at the same time. For example, there are potentially beneficial chemicals in foods that are not nutrients as we understand them. The compound beta-glycyrrhetinic acid gives licorice its distinctive taste, but is also a potent chemo-preventive agent in laboratory animals. It's not a nutrient in the standard sense.

That's also why ACS's nutritional guidelines don't include the recommendation to take vitamin supplements. It's not just the benefits of certain vitamins in food, but rather the combination of vitamins and these compounds that can help reduce cancer risk.

**Are people who consume more fruits and vegetables at increased cancer risk from pesticide residues?**

The consensus of our work study group on diet, nutrition and cancer was that the benefits of eating fruits and vegetables far outweigh any potential risk from pesticide residues.

Most pesticide residues are reduced through food processing and by washing fruits and vegetables. Nonetheless, the committee will continue to monitor data in this area.

**Should parents be concerned about the pesticide risks to infants and children?**

The ACS dietary guidelines apply to children over the age of two years. But in terms of nutritional guidelines for young children, I think parents should be more concerned about the overall eating patterns they're setting for their lifetimes, rather than focusing on any specific food risks like pesticide residues.

**What kinds of cancer affect children? Are they related to diet in any way?**

The common types of pediatric cancers are bone tumors, leukemias, brain tumors and lymphomas such as Hodgkin's lymphoma. But in the childhood group, I'm not aware of any increase in tumors that are thought to be linked to diet. That's why it's important that good eating habits are set for a lifetime, because the diet-related tumors are those that affect adults—breast cancer, colon cancer and prostate cancer, for example.

**What about the natural carcinogens that are present in food?**

One thing that has confused the public is the difference between a mutagen and a carcinogen; they're not the same thing. Just because something is a mutagen, which means it can change bacteria on the Ames test, does not mean it will cause cancer in humans.

The fact that food mutagens are present is not proof that food carcinogens are present. Nonetheless, the liver has developed a sophisticated detoxification system to ward off these compounds fairly efficiently.

## Keeping in Shape

How likely are you to lose weight on a Mediterranean cruise? Not very, unless the only meals available are prepared according to the new American Cancer Society dietary guidelines. To put those guidelines to the test, ACS tried them out on an entire U.S. Navy crew that was shipped to the Mediterranean for a six-month deployment in 1990. Before they went to sea, the ship's cooks were instructed on how to prepare menus designed to conform to the new guidelines and crew members were educated about them as well as the importance of exercise.

Before and after the mission, the 350 crew members on the USS Scott underwent tests to determine their overall health. For comparison, similar data were collected from crew members on a separate ship on which standard Navy menus were served. Preliminary results show immediate health benefits for the USS Scott crew.

USS Scott crew members lost an average of 10 pounds and took nearly two inches off their waists. Crew members on the other ship gained an average of seven pounds and their waist sizes grew one to two inches.

In addition, of those USS Scott members who weighed 200 pounds or more at the start of the mission, 74 percent lost weight. Only 26 percent of the similar group lost weight on the other ship, and 74 percent of the 200 pound-plus group gained weight.

For meals, sailors were served foods like oven-roasted lean meats and baked potatoes in place of fried steaks and mashed potatoes with gravy. Low-fat frozen yogurt and low-fat cookies were offered in place of other higher-fat desserts.

The USS Scott commander was concerned that a change of diet not adversely affect the crew's morale, so he insisted that the ship's commissary continue to sell candies and other snacks. It appears those occasional foods did not interfere with the overall benefits of the ACS diet.

As it turns out, many sailors on the USS Scott preferred the new diet and 44 percent said they would maintain similar eating habits on land.

---

**What kinds of dietary research is ACS currently funding?**

We've just completed field-testing the new ACS dietary guidelines with a healthy population to determine if they accomplished what we intended (see above). With the success of that project, we're now moving into the next phase of our research plan, which aims to develop cancer-specific nutritional guidelines.

We're funding two studies: one limits dietary fat intake in patients with breast cancer and the other prescribes a high-fiber cereal for persons with abnormal polyps of the colon.

 **Article Review Form at end of book.**

How does an antioxidant work? What are some good food sources for selenium? Might one receive too much selenium? If so, what might occur?

# The New Nutritional Superstar

## Nancy Snyderman, M.D.

First came beta-carotene, then vitamin E. Now, it's selenium's turn in the diet and disease-prevention spotlight—thanks to new research that suggests that taking high doses of the mineral can prevent certain cancers.

A just-completed ten-year study conducted by the Arizona Cancer Center, involved 1,312 men and women with a history of skin cancer (either basal cell or squamous-cell carcinoma). Half were given a supplement of 200 micrograms (mcg) a day, and half took a placebo. Neither the patients nor the doctors and nurses following them knew who was taking what.

While selenium didn't keep subjects from getting new skin cancers, it did protect them from other types of cancer. People who took selenium had 63 percent fewer prostate cancers, 58 percent fewer colorectal cancers, and 46 percent fewer lung cancers than patients in the placebo group. In fact, these findings were so promising that researchers felt confident enough to halt the trial two years short of its planned completion.

Scientists have long suspected that high doses of selenium may play a role in cancer prevention. Geographical surveys have shown that in areas of the United States where the soil is poor in selenium, cancer rates are 10 percent higher than in areas with selenium-rich soil. (The Arizona study involved patients from the eastern United States, where the soil's selenium levels are low.) A number of laboratory studies have shown that high doses can protect animals against cancer.

But the Arizona study's findings were surprising, nonetheless, given that other recent research on humans has failed to find a connection between selenium and cancer protection. In particular, a 1995 study of 62,000 female nurses showed that women with the highest levels of selenium were no less likely to get cancer than women with lower levels. However, some experts criticized this study, saying the results were inconclusive. Many believed that the method used to measure the selenium levels was unreliable.

## How Does Selenium Work?

Scientists believe the mineral acts as an antioxidant, blocking the cell damage that can eventually lead to cancer and other diseases. There is also speculation that selenium may boost the immune system by altering the body's metabolism.

Meanwhile, there's also evidence that even low-dose supplements of selenium can lift your spirits and make you feel more energetic. Researchers as the U.S. Department of Agriculture recently tested various levels of selenium supplements in women in New Zealand (in an area with selenium-poor soil) for six months and found that those who took just 40 mcg a day showed a significant improvement in their moods and energy levels, compared with women taking either no or lower amounts of the mineral.

## How Much Do You Need?

Selenium is known as a trace mineral, meaning only a small amount is necessary for the body to work properly. Most Americans have no trouble meeting the Recommended Dietary Allowance (for women: 55 mcg; for men: 70 mcg) in their normal diets. In fact, it's estimated that the average American consumes more than 100 mcg per day. The best sources are seafood and liver, as well as grains and nuts (especially brazil nuts sold in their shells) that are grown in selenium-rich soil.

More is not necessarily better. Although no one in the Arizona study suffered any toxic effects taking 200 mcg a day, more than that can cause skin rashes, hair and nail breakage, fatigue, and stomach upset. Excessively large doses (more than 1000 mcg a day) can lead to serious side effects, including liver damage and potentially fatal heart problems.

So, should you run out and start taking selenium now? Though these most recent findings are exciting, researchers caution that it's still too early to make general recommendations that everyone—or even those with cancer—should be stocking up. One reason for caution is that those enrolled in the Arizona study were known to be at a higher risk for cancer because they had previously diagnosed skin cancers. So it may be that this patient population was predisposed to having a more dramatic response than a healthy person whose immune system is working properly would have. If these same results can be achieved in a study of healthy people, we may then see new public health recommendations regarding selenium supplementation.

If you already have cancer of the colon, lung, or prostate, I believe it probably won't hurt you to take up to 200 mcg of selenium a day. But you should *never* take a nutritional supplement instead of undergoing conventional treatment. And always make sure your doctor knows exactly what and how much you're taking.

 **Article Review Form at end of book.**

Might some of the recent results regarding selenium's possible antioxidant role be exaggerated?

# The Selenium Shocker

In December we reviewed the research on selenium and concluded that none of the benefits claimed for this very interesting and popular mineral had been proven. Then on Christmas day a major study appeared in the *Journal of the American Medical Association.* The newspaper headlines said it all: "Selenium pills prevent cancer." The director of the Selenium Research Group went this far: "We now have an opportunity to eliminate up to 50% of the top three cancer killers in our lifetime. This is like the discovery of penicillin or the polio vaccine." We certainly hope this turns out to be true, but this statement goes way beyond the facts in this study, about which there are still lots of questions.

The new study involved 1,300 people who had been treated for skin cancer, half of whom were given 200 micrograms of selenium a day (about three times the RDA), the other half a placebo. The goal was to see if selenium, taken for 10 years, would reduce the chances of a recurrence of skin cancer. (In fact, the subjects took selenium—and were subsequently observed—for widely varying lengths of time, since they joined the study and stopped taking the pills at different times over the course of nine years. The largest group took the pills for four to five years.) The pills did *not* prevent skin cancer recurrence. The selenium takers actually had a slightly higher incidence of skin cancer. But, surprise, the selenium group has a 45 to 63% lower risk of developing three other cancers—prostate, colon, and lung—and 50% fewer cancer deaths than the placebo group.

These benefits were so great that the researchers halted the study two years earlier than planned, presumably so that all the subjects could take selenium if they wished. The data show that the protective effect occurred very quickly—and almost exclusively during the first five years. Selenium seemed to stop cancer in its tracks. The researchers suggested it did this by inhibiting tumor growth and killing early cancer cells at the "promotion" stage.

## Why You Should Wait and See

- This was only one study, and a small and short one as cancer studies go.

- The subjects were a very special population. They all had had skin cancer. And they were chosen because they came from parts of the U.S. (mostly in the Southeast) where the soil has low selenium levels. They had blood levels of selenium far below the American average. It can't be assumed that the same effects would occur in the general population.

- Earlier studies on selenium yielded inconsistent results. Some found it protective against certain cancers, but not always against the same cancers, and usually only in regions of the world (notably parts of China) where people have extremely low blood levels of selenium. Other studies found no protective effect. And still others found that the mineral can *increase* the risk of some cancers.

- By the way, selenium did *not* protect against heart disease in this study, as is often claimed. And there was no effect on breast cancer. But since there were relatively few women in the study (only 25% of the subjects), it's uncertain whether *any* of the study's findings apply to them.

- The researchers themselves cautioned that these remarkable results need to be confirmed by other studies.

## Best Selenium Sources

It's much too soon for everyone to start taking selenium pills. Few Americans need to worry about getting enough of the mineral. In fact, many Americans already get as much selenium from their food as these subjects got from both their food and pills. While it's hard to say exactly how much we get because the mineral content of the soil varies from region to region, selenium intake no longer depends totally on local soil conditions. Food, especially grains, are shipped from all over the country. Meats, chicken, and seafood are excellent sources of selenium. Three ounces of red snapper, for instance, supplies 150 micrograms; three ounces of beef, 33 micrograms. Grains and some nuts are also good sources (vegetables to a lesser extent), but this depends on the selenium content of the soil they're grown in.

If you opt for selenium pills, take no more than 200 micrograms a day. The difference between the daily requirement for selenium and a toxic dose is very small. Your best bet would be to take a multi-vitamin/mineral pill that contains selenium.

**Words to the wise:** Vitamin E greatly increases the effectiveness of selenium in the body, so if you're taking E pills, as we've recommended, it's even likelier that you don't need selenium supplements.

 **Article Review Form at end of book.**

List and briefly explain the dietary factors that may promote cancer.

# How to Lower Your Cancer Risk

The newspapers and other media are rife with reports that this or that food or chemical or environmental factor—everything from canaries to toasters—causes cancer. But most reports are given out of context, and it's easy to lose sight of the big picture and of the scientific progress that's been made in understanding and preventing cancer. Scare tactics often get more publicity than growing knowledge or common sense.

See if the answers to any of these questions surprise you:

1. What are the first and second leading causes of cancer? (**a**) air and water pollution, (**b**) tobacco, (**c**) pesticides in food, (**d**) diet, or (**e**) exposure to synthetic chemicals.

2. What other factors are linked to cancer? (**a**) intense sun exposure, (**b**) overeating and obesity, (**c**) chronic inflammation and infection, or (**d**) human hormones.

3. *True or false:* Vegetable grown organically contain no cancer-promoting substances.

The answers: (**1**) b and d; (**2**) all; (**3**) false.

## New Insights

Cancer does not kill as many people as heart disease, but it still claims 530,000 American lives a year. Four major cancers (lung, colorectal, breast, and prostate) account for slightly more than half of these deaths. Some kinds of cancer (stomach, cervical, and uterine) have dramatically declined in this country, both in incidence and as a cause of death, while others are rising, or seem to be rising. For example, breast and prostate cancer may be occurring more often, or may simply be accurately diagnosed more frequently. (In fact, the number of new cases of prostate cancer has begun to drop, at least for white Americans.) Some other cancers appear to be occurring more frequently because the population is aging.

People often wonder when the "cancer breakthrough" will occur: when will researchers unlock the secret and find the cure? The dramatic breakthroughs we all yearn for—a cancer vaccine, perhaps, or a miraculous cure for all kinds of cancer—may or may not materialize. But enormous progress has been made, and in-sight into the origins and causes of cancer is growing.

Many of us worry too much about possible cancer promoters that are actually negligible. And at the same time, we may pay too little attention to simple but effective measures we can take to protect ourselves. Important measures for preventing cancer are already at hand.

## How Does Cancer Occur?

Genetics has something to do with cancer, though the picture is far from clear. Genes control every aspect of our body chemistry and the growth of cells; some genes may promote cancer, others may protect against it. There is a puzzling interplay of environmental, life-style, and genetic factors, and it's still uncertain where environmental and life-style influences actually come in. Generating energy, which is the basic process of all life, produces unstable molecules known as free radicals that can damage genetic material. This is a normal, everyday process, and most damage is immediately repaired. But sometimes the repair process fails. Exposure to our

## How Fruits and Vegetables Prevent Cancer

Fruits and vegetables contain large amounts of antioxidant vitamins (C and E), as well as folacin, carotenoids, and dietary fiber, which are all important in preventing cancer. One carotenoid, beta carotene, is converted by the body into vitamin A; both beta carotene and vitamin A may help protect against cancer. Readers of this newsletter will already have encountered such terms as indoles, sulforaphane, and flavones—just a few of the recently identified chemicals in foods from plants that may also be protective. For example, an indole found in vegetables like broccoli and Brussels sprouts has been shown to slow the growth of mammary cancer in rats. Substances in soybeans help reduce the risk of certain cancers in lab animals. These protective chemicals seem to "mop up" toxins that promote cancer. There are hundreds of natural chemicals in foods that protect against cancer—many still waiting to be discovered.

own hormones, to infectious organisms that have penetrated our immune defenses, and to environmental toxins can also create free radicals that scramble genetic codes and eventually damage cells. If cells are damaged, cell growth may produce tumors rather than copies of healthy cells. According to the *Report on Cancer Prevention* (November 1996) from the Harvard Center for Cancer Prevention, *three-quarters of all cancers occur largely because of external influences, not our genes.*

## What Are the External Causes?

- **Tobacco use** causes more cancer here and in the rest of the world than anything else. It is also a factor in millions of deaths from heart disease. The age at which a person begins to smoke and how much he/she smokes is important, too. The longer you smoke, the likelier it is to be lethal. Besides lung cancer, smoking increases the risk of cancer of the bladder, cervix, mouth, throat, pancreas, kidney, and stomach. It may also promote colon and even breast cancer. About 3 million people die of smoking-related causes every year around the world, and that number will rise to 10 million in the next century if the number of smokers continues to increase. Passive smoking (inhaling other people's smoke) causes thousands of deaths a year. But the evidence that passive smoking causes cancer is still not as strong as that linking smoking itself and cancer.

  If all tobacco users in this country suddenly quit—and no new customers were recruited—total deaths from cancer would eventually drop by at least one-third. Lung cancer would become a rare disease, rather than the major cancer killer of both American men and women that it now is.

- **Diet** causes about one-third of all cancer cases, almost as many as tobacco use. Having a diet that consists predominantly of fruits, vegetables, and grains (the current recommendation is at least five servings of fruits and vegetables a day) is the most important factor currently identified in the prevention of cancer through diet. The evidence for this is overwhelming: study after study has confirmed that people who have the highest intakes of fruit and vegetables have the lowest rates of most cancers. It's not certain yet to what extent diet affects the risk of breast and prostate cancer, which are influenced by hormones. Diet may well be a major factor even in such cancers.

## Dietary Factors That May Promote Cancer

- **Animal fat.** A diet high in animal fat, especially from red meat, has shown up in several studies as a risk factor for prostate and colon cancer. A high-fat diet is also suspected of being a factor in breast cancer, although recent research suggests there is no link. Countries with high-fat diets do have the highest rates of breast and prostate cancer, but other factors could be at work.

- **Cooking.** Cooking meats at very high temperatures, especially over an open flame, creates compounds known to promote certain cancers—for example, polycyclic aromatic hydrocarbons (PAHs), which form when meats are charcoal-broiled. Little is known, however, about how often you have to eat such foods to increase your cancer risk. An occasional barbecue is probably not harmful. As a rule, you're better off to steam, braise, bake, poach, stew, or microwave than to barbecue.

- **Nitrites, molds, salt.** Certain nitrogen compounds added to foods to preserve them can promote cancer, because they turn into nitrosamines in the digestive tract. (In China and Japan, the high consumption of nitrites and nitrates is thought to be responsible for the high rates of esophageal and stomach cancers.) Molds that grow on foods can promote cancer. Specifically, aflatoxin, which forms on foods like peanuts and corn, is a powerful promoter of liver cancer. (This is not a problem in this country because foods are inspected for aflatoxin, and contaminated items cannot be marketed or processed.) But it's never been demonstrated that any single food, such as bacon, mushrooms, or peanuts, is a cancer promoter. Regularly eating foods preserved in salt also promotes stomach and esophageal cancer, but only in countries where fish preserved in salt is a dietary staple. Nitrites, salt-preserved foods, and aflatoxin are not significant causes of cancer in the U.S. or most other developed countries.

- **Alcohol.** The government recently endorsed the idea that moderate alcohol intake can help prevent heart disease. ("Moderate" means no more than one drink daily for women, two for men, with a drink defined as 12 ounces of beer, 4 to 5 ounces of wine, or 1.5 ounces of 80-proof liquor, which all supply about half an ounce of pure alcohol.) But too much alcohol can cause cirrhosis of the liver and liver cancer. Especially when combined with smoking, heavy drinking also contributes to cancers of the mouth, throat, and esophagus, for example. No health authority recommends exceeding "moderation," and some still say that drinking no alcohol is best. The *Wellness Letter* will discuss the pro's and con's of alcohol in an upcoming issue.

## Other Known and Suspected Causes of Cancer

- **Being sedentary.** In the past ten years, several studies have suggested that exercise helps prevent breast and prostate cancer, and there's solid evidence it can prevent colon cancer. It's hard to say what level of activity is needed; but moderate activity starting early in a woman's life seems to protect against breast cancer.

- **The sun and other forms of radiation.** Cumulative sun exposure is responsible for most skin cancers, which account for about 2% of cancer deaths. Radiation also comes from radon, a colorless, odorless gas that the earth emits naturally in some regions. High exposure to radon has been pinpointed as a cause of lung cancer, but this is a problem chiefly among those who work in mines. Very high does of X-rays can also cause cancer. There's no evidence, from surveys done in countries with nuclear power plants, that there's any cancer risk associated with living near such facilities.

- **Workplace exposure to chemicals.** For people who work with cancer-causing chemicals, such as asbestos, benzene, and formaldehyde, this is a serious problem. However, extensive exposure to such chemicals is uncommon among the population at large. According to the Harvard report, less than 5% of all cancer cases are caused by workplace exposure.

- **Air pollution,** such as ozone, diesel exhaust, and nitrogen oxide, contains carcinogens that may affect many people. So far, it has been difficult to pinpoint the impact of pollution on cancer risk.

- **Hormones.** The causes of breast and prostate cancer, as well as other cancers of the reproductive system, remain unknown, but there is good evidence that these cancers are influenced by sex hormones. Hormones may variously protect against cancer or promote it. (For information about the risks and benefits of hormone replacement therapy, including the risk of cancer, see *Wellness Letter,* October 1995.)

- **Pesticides.** Food is a complex mixture of natural ingredients, not all of them benign. Plans themselves produce pesticides to ward off attack from animals and microorganisms. Our bodies are equipped to defend themselves against most of the potentially harmful elements in foods, just as we have chemical defenses against other kinds of low-level toxins. But it's man-made pesticides that cause the most worry. Humans have been consuming natural pesticides for thousands of years, and we may have ways of protecting ourselves from them, whereas we might be less able to fend off synthetic chemicals. Much remains to be learned about pesticide residues in foods. As yet, there's no evidence that they are a significant cause of cancer.

- **Microorganisms and chronic infection.** Worldwide, infections may be responsible for one-third of all cancers. In China and other parts of Asia, as well as Africa, millions of people suffer from infections that can eventually lead to liver, bladder, and colon cancer. In the industrialized world, these chronic infections are less prevalent, and some are nonexistent. Hepatitis B, which can lead to liver cancer, can now be prevented by vaccination (recommended for all children). The bacterial infection that is now known to cause most stomach ulcers and that may also lead to stomach cancer can be treated successfully with antibiotics. Infection with certain types of human papilloma viruses has been linked with both cervical and rectal cancer, but the former is now a curable disease in countries where women get regular Pap tests. People with HIV (the virus that causes AIDS) are at increased risk for certain cancers. However, most of the cancers related to chronic infections occur in developing countries.

- **Obesity.** Being significantly overweight puts you at risk for such diseases as stroke and heart disease, and probably also for some cancers (uterine and postmenopausal breast cancer in women; colon and prostate cancer in men). No one is sure why obesity might boost the risk of cancer. Nevertheless, this is still another reason to maintain a healthy weight.

- **Poverty.** Rates for many cancers, including lung, stomach, and cervical, are higher among the poor and underprivileged. This may be partly because the poor are more likely to smoke, eat a poor diet, and be exposed to infection, and less likely to get preventive medical care. But other factors may also come into play.

 **Article Review Form at end of book.**

What is in tomatoes that may be protective in terms of prostate cancer? Can the preparation of the food affect the amount of lycopene available in tomatoes?

# Prostate Protector

## Tomatoes may topple prostate-cancer risk

**Matthew Klein**

"Bachelor-gourmet" cuisine—you know, pizza and spaghetti—might do more than keep the local take-out palace in business. It might keep the prostate in business, too.

A five-year study of 47,849 men found that guys who ate the most cooked tomato products were the ones with the lowest risk of prostate cancer (*Journal of the National Cancer Institute,* December 6, 1995).

Tomatoes weren't an on-again/off-again thing for guys with the healthiest prostates. Men who got 10 servings a week had a third of the risk that men getting 1½ servings a week had. One-third amounts to a big cut, considering that prostate cancer is the most frequently occurring cancer for men.

If 10 servings sounds like a lot, consider this: One serving is only ½ cup of tomato sauce or one slice of pizza. If that still sounds

like a lot, consider that while more was better in this study, even four servings per week was associated with a 22 percent reduction in risk, says study leader Edward Giovannucci, M.D., Sc.D., in the department of medicine at Harvard Medical School, Boston.

What's believed to be so special about tomatoes is that they're high in a vitamin A cousin called *lycopene,* one of the carotenoids. It may prevent cancer from happening by mopping up free radicals that are thought to beat up innocent cells and turn them into cancerous ones. Lycopene may be one of the strongest mops known yet—it may be twice as potent as betacarotene, says Dr. Giovannucci. There's some evidence from other studies that lycopene may protect against other cancers, too, such as those of the colon, stomach and esophagus.

Right off the vine is a great way to get your tomatoes, but it seems that cooking might provide more of this carotenoid. Cooked

in a little bit of oil (a *little,* we said) might be even better. "Probably what's happening is that the lycopene in tomatoes is in the cell walls, and it's hard to get at. If you just eat a tomato, a lot of the lycopene passes through, somewhat like fiber passes through," says Dr. Giovannucci. "But if you cook tomatoes in a little oil, then the cell walls break down with the heat, and the lycopene gets absorbed into the oil."

For protection from prostate cancer, he says, it makes sense to include some tomato sauce in the diet. Just don't make it your one and only veggie. "We don't want people to avoid other vegetables. Things in other vegetables may be beneficial for fighting other cancers and conditions." And, of course, don't load up on a lot of high-fat pizza on account of the sauce.

 **Article Review Form at end of book.**

What are the benefits of emphasizing soy foods?

# Where's the Meat?

## Some new soy options may be worth a try

You know they're a healthful alternative to meat. You know they may help fight cancer. And you're probably seeing a lot more of them in the supermarket. So what's keeping you from trying foods made with soy? As research on the possible health benefits of soybeans fills the media, an array of soy-based products have cropped up on supermarket shelves. Maybe now's the time to taste test some of these nutritious foods.

### What the Scientists Say

Although research has not yet firmly established the health benefits associated with eating soy foods, population studies show low rates of certain cancers in countries where soy is a regular part of the diet—such as many areas in Asia. This may be because soy contains several naturally-occurring compounds—phytochemicals like isoflavones, protease inhibitors and saponins—which seem to protect against the development of cancer. For instance, studies suggest that isoflavones may inhibit enzymes necessary for the growth and spread of many types of cancer.

Other research indicates that daily use of soy foods may help protect against heart disease by significantly lowering "bad" LDL cholesterol without reducing "good" HDL levels.

### Soy Many Options

If you are interested in sampling soy products, options abound. Try tofu and tempeh (cooked soybeans formed into cakes) in stir-fries, soups and a variety of other dishes. Spread soynut butter on a sandwich in place of higher-fat peanut butter. Use soymilk in cooking or over cereal. Substitute soy flour for up to one-quarter of the total flour in many recipes for baked goods. You'll find all these products in larger grocery stores, as well as health or natural food stores.

One of the ways many people are introducing soy into their diets is through meat alternatives like soy burgers, hot dogs, sausage, bacon and ground beef replacement like textured soy protein (TSP). Some—such as hot dogs, bacon and some patties—are made to taste like beef, pork or chicken. Others are intended to

replace meat, but not necessarily to taste or look like it.

### Soy Nutritious

Nutritionally, most soy-based meat alternatives are excellent sources of protein, iron and some B vitamins. Fat content varies, but many contain less than half the fat of even the leanest ground beef. Of the fat that is present, cholesterol-raising saturated fat represents a much smaller proportion in soy foods than in meat. Soybeans do have some fat naturally, and added fats may be included in some products, so be sure to check the label.

The isoflavone content of soy products varies depending on the type of soy protein used. Tofu, tempeh and soy milk are high in isoflavones. Isoflavone content in foods made from soy proteins—like soy burgers, hot dogs or sausage—varies depending on the way they are produced. Some are processed in such a way that removes most of the isoflavones, but there is no way of knowing this from the label. Until research confirms the beneficial effects of isoflavones and producers make this information readily available,

"Where's the Meat?" from the American Institute for Cancer Research Newsletter, Fall, 1997. Reprinted with permission of the American Institute for Cancer Research.

it makes the most sense to simply choose a variety of the soy foods you like without worrying about maximizing isoflavone content.

## Tips for Experimenting with Meat Alternatives

If you try to make direct comparisons between soy products and the meat products they replace, you may be disappointed. Many of these foods are good in their own right, so give them a try.

- Soy-based hot dogs, frozen patties and sausage may be found alongside similar meat-based products in the store. Simply follow package instructions to cook on the grill, stove top or even just as you would the meat-containing version.

- Textured soy protein (TSP)—labeled meatless or vegetable burger or chili mix—is usually found with boxed dinner foods like macaroni and cheese. Just pour boiling water over the granules as instructed on the label, let sit five minutes and it's ready to use. Once rehydrated, you can add TSP to chili, spaghetti sauce, Sloppy Joes or anywhere else you might use ground meat.

## Easy Does It

For some people, it's easier to get used to soy when it's mixed into a dish—especially those where the soy product is crumbled and mixed into a sauce rather than standing alone, as with burgers. Here are some other helpful hints:

- If you're not ready to jump right into meatless spaghetti sauce or Sloppy Joes, start by using soy protein for only a quarter of the meat. The same goes for dishes like meatloaf.

- When you make tacos or casseroles, try half meat and half soy protein.

- Rather than trying soy "sausage" on its own, you may be more comfortable mixing it into a soup or casserole.

If you are a cancer patient, always consult with your physician before adding new foods to your diet. But if you are healthy and looking to add variety to your nutritious meals, venture into the world of soy foods.

 **Article Review Form at end of book.**

Differentiate between Type I and Type II diabetes mellitus.
What are the symptoms of hypoglycemia? What is ketoacidosis?

# Understanding Diabetes

You may have diabetes and not even know it. This chronic disease is the fourth-leading cause of death by disease in the U.S. and affects some 16 million Americans. Unfortunately, about half of those don't know they have the disease.

Diabetes education is important because although there's no cure for type I diabetes, it can be controlled. When not controlled, diabetes can lead to life-threatening complications such as blindness, kidney disease, heart disease, stroke and nerve disease (which commonly leads to amputation of a lower limb).

With diabetes, the body doesn't produce or properly use *insulin*, a hormone needed to convert *glucose* (a simple form of sugar) into energy.

## Warning Signs of Diabetes

- sudden weight loss
- frequent urination
- extreme thirst
- skin infections
- tingling or numbing sensations of hands or feet
- urinary tract infections
- blurred vision or a sudden change in vision
- increased appetite
- gum infections
- weakness
- tiredness or exhaustion
- cuts and bruises that are slow to heal
- vaginal infections in women

The American Diabetes Association recommends that adults should have a diabetes test every three years starting at age 45. Those with a higher risk for diabetes—people with a history of diabetes in their family, Asians, Hispanics, African-Americans and American Indians—should be tested more often.

## Types of Diabetes

**Type I (insulin-dependent or juvenile) diabetes mellitus.** People with this type of diabetes produce little or no insulin, so they must take insulin every day to stay alive. This form usually develops in children or young adults, and it is not caused by being overweight.

**Type II (non-insulin-dependent or adult-onset) diabetes mellitus.** With this form of diabetes, the body produces insulin, but isn't able to use it effectively. Type II diabetes often can be controlled with proper diet, weight loss and exercise. However, some diabetics also may require oral hypoglycemic drugs or insulin injections. This type occurs most often in people over 40.

**Gestational diabetes.** Gestational diabetes appears while a woman is pregnant and usually goes away after she gives birth. However, these women have an increased risk of developing type II diabetes later in life.

## Diabetes Treatment and Control

Diabetes requires a constant balancing act to keep the level of sugar (glucose) in the blood as close to normal as possible. Food makes the glucose level rise, and exercise and insulin make the glucose level fall. People with diabetes—regardless of the type—must carefully combine a proper diet, exercise, medication and/or insulin.

"Understanding Diabetes" from YOUR HEALTHSTYLE, September 1997. YOUR HEALTHSTYLE, a health awareness newsletter, 1-800-214-1156. Reprinted by permission.

Keeping the level of insulin as close to normal as possible is important to prevent diabetic emergencies, to help prevent or reverse some of the long-term complications of diabetes and to feel good. Therefore, people with diabetes must monitor their blood sugar frequently. Changes in exercise and diet as well as an increased level of stress can drastically alter blood sugar levels.

## Diet

A doctor, diabetes educator or dietitian will make specific diet recommendations. In general,

weight loss is recommended for diabetics who are overweight

daily calories should be kept close to the same every day:

- 30% from fats, with just 8–10% from saturated fats.

- 10–20% from protein.

- 50–55% from carbohydrates. (Focus on complex carbohydrates such as breads, grains and cereals.)

## Exercise

An individual exercise prescription should be obtained from a doctor, diabetes educator or exercise physiologist.

## Insulin (for type I diabetes)

Some diabetics need a daily dose of insulin; some need multiple injections. Diabetics who need multiple injections of insulin each day must eat at consistent times in conjunction with the time-action of the insulin they use. Wearing an insulin pump 24 hours a day, however, gives these people more flexibility in what and when they eat.

Also, new types of insulin that are absorbed quicker are being developed. These can reduce the number of injections necessary per day.

## Oral Hypoglycemic Drugs (for type II diabetes)

Four classes of oral diabetes drugs are now available.

1. Sulfonylurea (SFZ, such as Glimepiride). Causes the pancreas to produce insulin, the oldest class of oral insulin.

2. Biguanides (such as Metformin). Acts to lower cells' resistance to insulin.

3. Alpha-glucosidase inhibitors (such as Precose and Miglitol). Slows the body's digestion of carbohydrates.

4. Troglitazone (Rezulin). Helps move blood sugar into the body's tissues where it's used as energy. Helps the body use insulin more efficiently, so smaller amounts are needed.

Although drugs can be helpful in treating diabetes, they aren't the ideal solution. Some cause serious side effects. Usually your doctor will try to regulate your blood glucose level with diet and exercise first.

## Diabetic Emergencies

### Hypoglycemia

If a person who must use insulin eats too little food, takes too much insulin or exercises vigorously without planning for the extra sugar that will be burned, *hypoglycemia* will occur. (Hypoglycemia is low blood sugar.) Symptoms of shakiness, increased heart rate and incoherency come on suddenly and must be treated quickly with foods high in sugar or the person

may become unconscious. (Examples of high sugar foods: hard candy, soda, orange juice or other commercial products for this purpose that are available over the counter from a pharmacy.)

### Hyperglycemia

*Hyperglycemia* occurs when there is too much sugar in the blood and not enough insulin. The body can't use the sugar to supply its insulin needs, so it takes energy from the fats stored in the body. Excessive breakdown of fat without sufficient insulin results in the formation of ketone acids. This can lead to *ketoacidosis*, which is a life-threatening condition. A diabetic in this condition may lapse into a coma, which can be fatal.

Hyperglycemia develops gradually, so steps can usually be taken to avert it.

## Diabetes Resources

**American Diabetes Association**
800-DIABETES
(800-342-2383)
http://www.diabetes.org/

Provides information about diabetes and diabetes research, refers to diabetes education programs, publishes a diabetes magazine and other educational materials and offers a diabetes risk test at the web site.

**National Diabetes Information Clearinghouse**
301-654-3327
http://www.niddk.nih.gov/Brochures/NDIC.htm

Publishes a quarterly newsletter and other patient publications, responds to requests for information about diabetes and its complications.

**The National Institute of Diabetes and Digestive and Kidney**

## Questions to Ask Your Doctor About Blood Sugar Control

1. What is my *glycosylated hemoglobin* (a test that measures average blood sugar level over the past two to three months)? What is a normal glycosylated hemoglobin? If mine is abnormal, how can I get it in the normal range?

2. How often and under what conditions should I test my blood sugar? What should I do with the results? What patterns should I try to achieve?

3. What changes should we make in my program as a result of the findings of the Diabetes Control and Complications Trial (DCCT)?

4. Do I have *microalbuminuria* (detection of tiny amounts of albumin in urine indicating early diabetic kidney disease)?

5. What effect has diabetes had on my eyes and kidneys?

6. Should I see a dietitian to review what I eat?

7. What exercises are best for me? What adjustments to my food or insulin should I make if I plan to exercise?

8. What should my family and friends do if my blood sugar goes so low that I need their help?

9. (For women) What should I do about taking care of my diabetes if I plan to become pregnant?

10. How should I take care of my feet?

11. Are there any diabetes groups that I can attend?

—National Institute of Diabetes and Digestive and Kidney Diseases of the National Institute of Health

Diseases of the National Institute of Health
http://www.niddk.nih.gov/NIDDK_HomePage.html

Provides health information for the public. Sponsors the Combined Health Information Database, which is a file of brochures, books, articles, fact sheets, products and other diabetes educational material.

**The Juvenile Diabetes Foundation International**
**The Diabetes Research Foundation**
800-JDF-CURE
(800-533-2873)

Provides information about diabetes and diabetes research.

**Article Review Form at end of book.**

Summarize the characteristics of the two diets administered during the study. The high-carbohydrate diet increased fasting levels of what two variables?

# Effects of Varying Carbohydrate Content of Diet in Patients with Non–Insulin-Dependent Diabetes Mellitus

Abhimanyu Garg, MBBS, MD; John P. Bantle, MD; Robert R. Henry, MD; Ann M. Coulston, RD; Kay A. Griver, RD; Susan K. Raatz, MS, RD; Linda Brinkley, RD; Y-D. Ida Chen, PhD; Scott M. Grundy, MD, PhD; Beverley A. Huet, MS; Gerald M. Reaven MD

From the Center for Human Nutrition and Department of Internal Medicine (Drs Garg and Grundy) and the General Clinical Research Center (Dr. Garg and Mss Brinkley and Huet), University of Texas Southwestern Medical Center at Dallas; Department of Internal Medicine, Stanford (Calif) University School of Medicine (Drs. Chen and Reaven and Ms Coulston); Department of Medicine, University of Minnesota, Minneapolis (Dr. Bantle and Ms. Raatz); Department of Medicine, University of California–San Diego (Dr. Henry); and the Veterans Affairs Medical Center, San Diego, Calif (Dr. Henry and Ms. Griver).

Reprint requests to University of Texas Southwestern Medical Center at Dallas, 5323 harry Hines Blvd, Dallas, TX 75235-9052 (Dr. Garg).

**Objective**—To study effects of variation in carbohydrate content of diet on glycemia and plasma lipoproteins in patients with non–insulin-dependent diabetes mellitus (NIDDM).

**Design**—A four-center randomized crossover trial.

**Setting**—Outpatient and inpatient evaluation in metabolic units.

**Patients**—Forty-two NIDDM patients receiving glipizide therapy.

**Interventions**—A high-carbohydrate diet containing 55% of the total energy as carbohydrates and 30% as fats was compared with a high–monounsaturated-fat diet containing 40% carbohydrates and 45% fats. The amounts of saturated fats, polyunsaturated fats, cholesterol, sucrose, and protein were similar. The study diets, prepared in metabolic kitchens, were provided as the sole nutrients to subjects for 6 weeks each. To assess longer-term effects, a subgroup of 21 patients continued the diet they received second for an additional 8 weeks.

**Main Outcome Measures**—Fasting plasma glucose, insulin, lipoproteins and glycosylated hemoglobin concentrations. Twenty-four-hour profiles of glucose, insulin, and triglyceride levels.

**Results**—The site of study as well as the diet order did not affect the results. Compared with the high–monounsaturated-fat diet, the high-carbohydrate diet increased fasting plasma triglyceride levels and very low-density lipoprotein cholesterol levels by 24% ($P < .001$) and 23% ($P = .0001$), respectively, and increased daylong plasma triglyceride, glucose, and insulin values by 10% ($P = .03$), 12% ($P = .0001$), and 9% ($P = .02$), respectively. Plasma total cholesterol, low-density lipoprotein cholesterol, and high-density lipoprotein cholesterol levels remained unchanged. The effects of both diets on plasma glucose, insulin, and triglyceride levels persisted for 14 weeks.

**Conclusions**—In NIDDM patients, high-carbohydrate diets compared with high–monounsaturated-fat diets caused persistent deterioration of glycemic control and accentuation of hyperinsulinemia, as well as increased plasma triglyceride and very-low-density lipoprotein cholesterol levels, which may not be desirable. (*JAMA*. 1994;271:1421–1428)

Diets high in carbohydrates and low in saturated fats and cholesterol are widely recommended to patients with non–insulin-dependent diabetes mellitus (NIDDM).[1-4] For example, the American Diabetes Association[1] suggests that the dietary carbohydrate intake be increased to between 55% and 60% of total energy and total fat intake be restricted to 30% of total energy. In dyslipidemic patients with NIDDM, a further increase in dietary carbohydrates and restriction of fats to 20% of total energy is advised. Despite these recommendations, there is no consensus about the optimal diet for NIDDM patients, and questions have been raised as to the validity of these dietary recommendations.[5,6] Compared with diets rich in saturated fats, low-fat, high-carbohydrate diets are reported to reduce serum low-density lipoprotein (LDL) cholesterol levels.[7-10] Recent studies, however, suggest that high-carbohydrate diets may accentuate hyper-triglyceridemia, reduce serum high-density lipoprotein (HDL) cholesterol concentrations, and may even worsen hyperglycemia and/or raise plasma insulin lev-

els.[7,11–14] Since dyslipidemia in NIDDM patients often manifests as hypertriglyceridemia and reduced levels of HDL cholesterol, any aggravation of these aspects of dyslipidemia by dietary therapy should be undesirable. Accentuation of hyperglycemia and hyperinsulinemia could also have particularly deleterious consequences in NIDDM.[15,16]

Alternative approaches to diet therapy of NIDDM patients would be to replace saturated fatty acids with either n-6 polyunsaturated fatty acids, such as linoleic acid, or *cis*-monounsaturated fatty acids, such as oleic acid; both types lower LDL cholesterol levels equally.[17,18] However, for lack of epidemiologic evidence of the long-term safety of high intakes of polyunsaturated fatty acids and because of their potential to lower HDL cholesterol levels when consumed in large quantities,[17,19,20] monounsaturated fatty acids may be preferred for replacing saturated fatty acids in the diet of NIDDM patients.[14,21–25] Evidence has been published suggesting that high-monounsaturated-fat diets may be of greater clinical benefit than the use of low-fat, high-carbohydrate diets.[14,21–25] However, acceptance of this alternative approach has been limited, primarily because of questions as to the persistence of the deleterious metabolic changes reported when patients with NIDDM consume high-carbohydrate diets, as well as the universality of these findings. Consequently, the current study was designed in which four different centers used the same protocol to compare the relatively long-term effects of substituting monounsaturated fats for carbohydrates on glucose, insulin, and lipoprotein levels in patients with NIDDM.

## Methods

### Patients

Forty-two patients with NIDDM (33 men and nine women) from four centers participated in this study. Thirty-one patients were white, six were African American, four were Hispanic, and one was Asian. Patients were studied at the metabolic units of the Stanford (Calif) University School of Medicine (10 patients); the University of Texas Southwestern Medical Center at Dallas (10 patients); the University of Minnesota, Minneapolis (11 patients); and the Veterans Affairs Medical Center, San Diego, Calif (11 patients). The protocol for this study was approved by the institutional review board of each center, and all patients gave informed written consent. The patients were 35 to 78 years old (mean [SD], 58 [10] years), and their body mass index (weight in kilograms divided by height in meters, squared) ranged from 23 to 33 (mean [SD], 28.1 [2.9]). All the patients were receiving glipizide therapy, and the doze of glipizide averaged 17 mg per day (SD, 14 mg/d) (Glucotrol, Pfizer Inc, New York, NY). Changes, if any, in the dose of glipizide were made at least 1 month before participating in the study. Fasting plasma glucose and triglyceride concentrations ranged from 5.6 to 11.1 mmol/L (101 to 199 mg/dL) and 0.61 to 4.97 mmol/L (54 to 440 mg/dL), respectively.

### Experimental Design

A randomized crossover study was designed. An independent randomization scheme was prepared for each center to decide the order of the study diets. Patients were randomized in blocks of 10 with equal numbers (five and five) assigned to the two diet orders. All patients underwent a baseline evaluation, which included a detailed history, physical examination, and screening laboratory tests. The daily energy intake needed for weight maintenance was estimated by multiplying the basal energy expenditure calculated according to the Harris-Benedict equations by an activity factor.[26] All patients then received the two study diets, a high-carbohydrate diet and a high-monounsaturated-fat diet, each for a period of 6 weeks during phases 1 and 2. Twenty patients received the high–monounsaturated-fat diet first, and 22 received the high-carbohydrate diet first. There was a median interval of 7 days between the two diet periods when the patients consumed their usual diets. The dose of glipizide was kept constant throughout the study, except if a patient reported symptomatic hypoglycemia when the dose was reduced by 2.5 mg/d.

To assess the longer-term effects of the diets, all patients were invited to consume the second diet for 8 additional weeks (phase 2 extension) without interruption. Considering the total duration of the study, including phase 2 extension (5.5 months), about 50% of the subjects were expected to participate in the extended phase of the study. Twenty-one patients, at least five from each center, chose to do so. The baseline characteristics of these 21 patients were similar to those who did not participate in the phase 2 extension. Of the 21 patients, eight received the high-monounsaturated-fat diet for 14 weeks, and 13 received the high–carbohydrate diet for 14 weeks.

All patients ate at least one meal, ie, breakfast, lunch, or dinner, at the metabolic unit on weekdays. The food for the rest of the day was supplied in packages to be consumed at home. The dietitians monitored compliance by interviewing the patients. The patients were also instructed to bring back any unconsumed food to the metabolic units. Patients were weighed during their visits to the metabolic unit. At weekly intervals, fasting blood samples were obtained for determination of plasma cholesterol, triglyceride, glucose, and insulin levels. During the last 3 days of each phase, the patients were admitted to the metabolic unit, and fasting blood samples were obtained daily for determination of plasma glucose, insulin, and lipoprotein levels. On the last day of each phase, blood specimens were obtained every 2 hours for a period of 24 hours for determination of plasma glucose, insulin, and triglyceride levels. Blood was also drawn for glycosylated hemoglobin determination during the baseline period and at the end of each phase.

## Diets

The nutrient composition of the two study diets is given in Table 1.* Both diets consisted of natural foods. Standard diet menus for each study diet were prepared for an 8.4-MJ (2000-kcal) diet using foods available at all centers. For a different energy level, all food items were proportionately reduced or increased from the standard menu. Recipes and menus of various food items were standardized. A 4-day rotational menu was used. The menus provided similar

*Not included in this publication.

nutrient composition but offered diverse foods. The daily energy intake was distributed among breakfast (22%), lunch (33%), dinner (33%), and bedtime snack (12%).

The high-carbohydrate diet provided 55% of the total energy as carbohydrates and 30% of the total energy as fat. The high–monounsaturated-fat diet provided 45% of the total energy as fat and 40% as carbohydrates. The saturated and polyunsaturated fats (10% of the total energy intake each), protein (15% of the total energy intake), cholesterol (120 mg per 4.2 MJ [1000 kcal]), and sucrose (10% of the total energy intake) contents of the study diets were matched. The content of dietary fiber was kept proportional to the carbohydrate content, and thus the high–monounsaturated-fat diet contained 11 g of dietary fiber per 4.2 MJ, and the high-carbohydrate diet contained 15 g of dietary fiber per 4.2 MJ. The individual food items were weighed daily during meal preparation, and all meals were prepared in metabolic kitchens. Olive oil was used as the main source of fat in the high-monounsaturated-fat diet. The patients were allowed to consume black coffee, black tea, and non-caloric soft drinks. Salt intake was not restricted. The energy intake of each patient was adjusted if needed to maintain constant body weight during the study. The patients were instructed not to change their usual physical activity during the study.

## Biochemical Analyses

Plasma lipids and lipoproteins were analyzed at the Center for Human Nutrition Laboratory at the University of Texas Southwestern Medical Center at

Dallas. Fresh plasma samples from the other three centers were shipped at 4°C on ice by overnight couriers to Dallas and were analyzed within a week. Fasting plasma samples were analyzed for total cholesterol, triglyceride, and lipoprotein cholesterol levels according to the Lipid Research Clinics procedures,[24] except that cholesterol and triglyceride levels were measured enzymatically using kits from Boehringer-Mannheim, Indianapolis, Ind, and Sigma Diagnostics, St. Louis, Mo, respectively. Very low-density lipoproteins (VLDL) (density < 1.006 kg/L) were removed by preparative ultracentrifugation, and cholesterol was measured in the VLDL fraction and the infranatant. Plasma HDL cholesterol was measured in the supernatant after lipoproteins containing apolipoprotein B were precipitated by the addition of heparin manganese.[27] Cholesterol in the LDL fraction was calculated as the difference between the cholesterol contents of the infranatant (density > 1.006 kg/L) and the HDL fraction.

Plasma insulin levels were determined at the radioimmunoassay laboratory, Division of Endocrinology, Gerontology, and Metabolism, Stanford Medical Center, Palo Alto, Calif. Plasma samples for insulin determination from each patient were kept frozen at –20°C until the patient completed the study. Thereafter, the frozen plasma samples from the other centers were shipped on dry ice using overnight delivery service. Plasma insulin samples were analyzed using a radioimmunoassay, according to Hale and Randle.[28]

Plasma glucose concentrations were assayed by the glucose oxidase method at each center. Quantitative analysis of glycosylated hemoglobin was done using high-performance liquid chromatography on a Diamet Glycosylated Hemoglobin Analyzer (Bio-Rad, Hercules, Calif) at the University of Texas Southwestern Medical Center at Dallas and the University of Minnesota and by affinity chromatography kits (Isolab, Akron, Ohio) at Stanford University School of Medicine and the Department of Veterans Affairs Medical Center, San Diego. The results were combined without any correction factor.

## Statistical Analyses

The statistical models included only the measurements made during the two study diet periods. One patient developed a urinary tract infection during the last week of a dietary period; thus, the information obtained during that period was not included in the analyses. In another patient, blood samples were not collected properly during the 24-hour profile, and thus, those data were also excluded from the final analyses. Repeated-measures analysis of variance was used to compare the study diets, to assess the effect of order in which patients received the diets, and to assess the effect of site of study participation.[29] The effects of possible confounding factors, such as age, race, body mass index, and sex, were also evaluated using repeated-measures analysis of variance and covariance models. When analysis of variance revealed significant differences between the three phases, ie, phase 1, 2, and 2 extension, multiple comparisons were performed using two-tailed paired t tests with Bonferroni's correction. To analyze plasma glu-

cose, triglyceride, and insulin profiles during the last day of each phase, areas under the curves were calculated using the trapezoidal rule and compared using repeated-measures analysis of variance with site and order as grouping factors; log-transformed data were used for triglyceride values since the triglyceride area data were slightly skewed. The 24-hour profiles were also compared using analysis of variance models, and subsequently, data at each time point were compared using the two-tailed paired t test without adjustment for multiple testing.

## Results

The compliance to both the study diets was excellent. Only one patient admitted eating small quantities of other food items besides those provided in the metabolic diets occasionally during both the study periods. The data from this patient, however, were not excluded from the analyses. The order in which the patients received the diets and the sites at which the patients were studied did not significantly affect the results. Therefore, combined results from all four centers are presented irrespective of the order of patient randomization.

During the last 3 days of phase 1 and 2, energy intake was similar on the two diets, and no significant difference was noted in the body weights of patients (Table 2*). The mean dose of glipizide was also similar (Table 2). The mean fasting plasma lipid and lipoprotein concentrations on the two diets during the last 3 days of phase 1 and 2 are shown in Table 3.* Compared with the high–monounsaturated-fat diet, the

*Not included in this publication.

high-carbohydrate diet increased fasting plasma triglyceride levels by 24% ($P < .0001$) and VLDL cholesterol levels by 23% ($P = .0001$). The increase of fasting plasma triglyceride levels with the high-carbohydrate diet occurred within the first week and persisted throughout the 6 weeks (Fig 1).* No differences in fasting plasma total cholesterol, LDL cholesterol, and HDL cholesterol levels were observed between the two diets. Generally, the lipoprotein responses of men and women to the two diets were similar except that the high-carbohydrate diet tended to cause greater increases in triglyceride and VLDL cholesterol levels in women than in men (diet and sex interaction, $P = .007$ and $P = .07$, respectively). Age, body mass index, and race, however, were not significant factors affecting the lipoprotein responses to the diets.

The longer-term effects of the study diets on plasma lipid and lipoprotein levels in the subgroup of 21 patients are shown in Tables 4 and 5* and Figs 2 and 3.* Table 4 shows the results in eight patients who received the high–monounsaturated-fat diet for 14 weeks during phase 2 and phase 2 extension. Compared with the high-carbohydrate diet, the high–monounsaturated-fat diet caused a persistent lowering of fasting plasma triglyceride and VLDL cholesterol levels; the week 6 and 14 values of plasma triglycerides were lowered by 23% and 26%, respectively ($P = .03$), and the week 6 and 14 values of plasma VLDL cholesterol were lowered by 24% and 31%, respectively ($P = .23$). Weekly values of fasting plasma triglyc-

*Not included in this publication.

erides also tended to be lower on the high–monounsaturated-fat diet (Fig 2). Table 5 shows the results in the 13 other patients who received the high-carbohydrate diet for 14 weeks during phase 2 and phase 2 extension. The high-carbohydrate diet-induced increases in fasting plasma triglyceride and VLDL cholesterol concentrations also persisted for 14 weeks (Table 5, Fig 3). Plasma total cholesterol, LDL cholesterol, and HDL cholesterol levels during the extended phase of the study did not reveal any significant differences (Tables 4 and 5) except for a difference in plasma total cholesterol values in week 6 and week 14 of the high-carbohydrate diet period (Table 5).

Furthermore, the high-carbohydrate diet, compared with the high–monounsaturated-fat diet, increased the day-long levels of plasma triglycerides by 10% (mean [SD], 67.9 [28.8] mmol·h/L vs 61.5 [21.6] mmol·h/L [area under the curve units], respectively; $P = .03$ [with log-transformed data]; Fig 4*), increased plasma glucose by 12% (mean [SD], 229.1 [57.3] mmol·h/L vs 204.9 [49.0] mmol·h/L, respectively; $P < .0001$; Fig 5*), and increased plasma insulin by 9% (mean [SD], 8467 [3961] pmol·h/L vs 7778 [3831] pmol·h/L, respectively; $P = .02$; Fig 5). The most noticeable differences in plasma triglyceride values on the two diets were during the fasting and preprandial periods compared with the postprandial periods (Fig 4). The high-carbohydrate diet primarily affected the postprandial plasma glucose and insulin values, which were significantly higher at several time points dur-

ing the day-long profile (Fig 5). The fasting plasma glucose and insulin concentrations, however, were not significantly different on the two diets ($P = .10$, and $P = .69$, respectively, Table 2 and Fig 5). Weekly values of fasting plasma glucose and insulin were also not significantly different (data not shown). Glycosylated hemoglobin concentrations remained similar on the two diets (Table 2).

The effects of the high-carbohydrate diet on the daylong glucose profiles tended to persist during the phase 2 extension of the study. In 13 patients, a 7% increase in plasma glucose values was noted with the high-carbohydrate diet by week 6 (mean [SD], 211.2 [43.3] mmol·h/L), and a 12% increase was noted by week 14 (mean [SD], 221.5 [52.3] mmol·h/L) compared with the high–monounsaturated-fat diet (mean [SD], 197.9 [43.9] mmol·h/L) in phase 1 ($P = .08$). In seven patients who followed the other sequence, a persistent improvement in glycemic profile was noted on the high–monounsaturated-fat diet; a lowering of 11% and 10% was observed (mean [SD], 188.0 [36.6] mmol·h/L and 189.8 [32.4] mmol·h/L, respectively [$P = .05$]) by week 6 and 14, respectively, compared with that on the high-carbohydrate diet during phase 1 (mean [SD], 210.7 [33.2] mmol·h/L). Likewise, daylong plasma insulin values tended toward persistent elevation on the high-carbohydrate diet and persistent reduction on the high–monounsaturated-fat diet during the phase 2 extension of the study. The changes, however, were not statistically significant ($P = .15$, and $P = .25$, respectively; data not shown).

## Comment and Conclusions

Results of previous studies have demonstrated that replacement of unsaturated fats with carbohydrates in the diet of NIDDM patients can lead to deterioration of glycemic control, increases in ambient plasma insulin and triglyceride concentrations, and a decrease in HDL cholesterol levels; LDL cholesterol levels, however, do not change.[11-14,21-25] Since the changes noted with high-carbohydrate intakes would tend to increase the risk of vascular complications,[15,16,30-33] questions have been raised as to the wisdom of this particular dietary advice. The current study was initiated in an effort to extend this inquiry, and the protocol was created with two specific goals in mind. The first was to conduct a multicenter study to aid in our ability to generalize from the results. In addition, we wished to extend the dietary periods as long as was practical, within the limits of maintaining control of dietary intake, in an effort to evaluate more chronic effects of dietary manipulations under study. Before addressing the specific changes notes, it must be pointed out that we successfully achieved both of our aims. Forty-two patients with NIDDM were enrolled in four different centers, with each center studying at least 10 patients. The results were similar in each center, making it likely that the conclusions are independent of bias at any given site and that they can be generalized to a considerable degree. Additional evidence has been presented that the effects of dietary changes persisted for at least 14 weeks. Although this is till a short period of time, it seems reasonable to suggest that the burden of proof be shifted to those who contend that the metabolic effects of substituting carbohydrates for unsaturated fats are evanescent.

Another unique aspect of the current study, with respect to the previous investigations comparing metabolic diets rich in carbohydrates and monounsaturated fatty acids,[14,23,24] was that this study was primarily conducted in an outpatient setting whereas previous studies were in patients who were admitted to the metabolic units. The study diets were more practical in composition than those used previously. For example, in the current study, the high–monounsaturated-fat diet contained 45% of the total energy as fat compared with 50% in previous studies,[14,23] and the high-carbohydrate diet contained 55% of the total energy as carbohydrates compared with 60% to 65% in the previous studies.[14,23,24] The selection of the NIDDM patients in the current study was also different because all patients were receiving glipizide therapy whereas in the previous studies they were either receiving insulin therapy[14] or diet therapy alone.[23,24]

Concerning the specific results, the changes noted in this multicenter study are similar to results of previous studies that have addressed this question.[11-14,21-25] The study confirms that high-carbohydrate diets increase plasma triglyceride levels and increase VLDL cholesterol concentrations in NIDDM patients. In this study, the high-carbohydrate diet increased fasting plasma triglyceride levels and VLDL cholesterol concentrations by 24% and 23%, respectively, compared with the high–monounsaturated-fat diet. Furthermore, daylong levels of plasma triglycerides were also increased on the high-carbohydrate diet. Consistent with the results of previous studies,[14,21-24] plasma levels of total cholesterol and LDL cholesterol were not different on the two diets in this study. The study, therefore, further substantiates the fact that high-carbohydrate diets offer no advantage in lowering LDL cholesterol levels in NIDDM patients compared with high-fat diets that are low in saturated fats.

Overall, an insignificant (4%) lowering of HDL cholesterol levels was observed on the high-carbohydrate diet compared with the high–monounsaturated-fat diet. In previous reports, high-carbohydrate diets have caused a 10% to 13% lowering of HDL-cholesterol levels compared with low-carbohydrate, high-fat diets, but in these studies 20% to 25% of the total energy was exchanged between carbohydrates and unsaturated fats.[11,12,14,23] In the current study, only 15% of the total energy was exchanged between carbohydrates and monounsaturated fats. Interestingly, the lowering of HDL cholesterol levels with high-carbohydrate diets is most often noted when the fat content of the diet is less than 30% of the total energy. In the previous investigations showing a decrease in HDL cholesterol levels, the fat content of the high-carbohydrate diets was 20% to 25%,[11,12,14,23] whereas in the current study, the high-carbohydrate diet contained 30% fat. Although the somewhat higher fat intake with the high-carbohydrate diet used in this study may have mitigated lowering of HDL cholesterol levels, it did not prevent a rise in VLDL cholesterol levels. Elevated triglyceride and VLDL levels are being increasingly implicated as independent risk factors for coronary heart disease in NIDDM patients.[31–33] Studies in tissue culture have also suggested that VLDL particles and their remnants from NIDDM patients may be potentially atherogenic.[34] Therefore, increased VLDL levels, as reflected by higher levels of triglyercides and VLDL cholesterol, by a high-carbohydrate diet may be detrimental in NIDDM patients. This is so whether or not there is a concomitant lowering of HDL cholesterol levels.

In addition to the high-carbohydrate diet's adverse effects on plasma lipoproteins, this diet also led to higher daylong glycemic excursions accompanied by higher insulin concentrations. This increase in daylong plasma insulin concentrations on the high-carbohydrate diet probably represents an attempt on the part of pancreatic ß cells to compensate for the additional carbohydrate intake, whereas the higher glucose concentrations suggest that this effect may not have been entirely successful. Glycosylated hemoglobin concentrations were not significantly different on the two diets. Failure to detect a significant increase in glycosylated hemoglobin concentrations corresponding to the 12% increase in glucose levels may be related to insensitivity in the measurement of glycoyslyated hemoglobin.

The observation that the high-carbohydrate diet resulted in higher glucose and insulin concentrations seems to conflict with some previous data; it has been reported that normal healthy subjects and those subjects with impaired glucose tolerance and mild NIDDM improve glucose tolerance and insulin sensitivity after increasingly dietary carbohydrate content.[35–38] The previous studies documenting improvement in glucose and insulin metabolism with high-carbohydrate diets, however, used diets containing 75% to 85% of energy as carbohydrates.[35–38] In our study, the high-carbohydrate diet and a reasonable 55% of total energy as carbohydrates. The results of the current study, however, are in agreement with several other studies that suggested that high-carbohydrate diets worsen glycemic control in NIDDM patients.[11–14,24,39,40] Furthermore, direct measurements of insulin-mediated glucose uptake suggest that increases in carbohydrate intake comparable to this study were associated with either no change[23] or a decrease in insulin sensitivity.[25] Given evidence of a possible link between hyperinsulinemia or insulin resistance and atherogenesis,[15,16,30] the increases in glucose and insulin levels constitute additional potential untoward events that occur when carbohydrates are substituted for monounsaturated fats in the diet of NIDDM patients.

Another important aspect of the current design was its aim to evaluate metabolic effects of the study diets for an extended period in a controlled, randomized manner. A previous report by Antonis and Bersohn[41] on nondiabetic subjects indicated that high-carbohydrate diet–induced hypertriglyceridemia may not persist, and thus some investigators argue that the adverse metabolic effects of high-carbohydrate intakes in NIDDM patients, particularly hypertriglyceridemia, may last for a short time only. Antonis and Bersohn,[41] however, did not use a randomized design, and interestingly, an increase in plasma triglyceride levels was also noted when the subjects switched from a high-carbohydrate diet to a high-fat diet, which was rich in saturated fats. On the contrary, some recent evidence suggests that high-carbohydrate diet–induced huypertriglyceridemia may not be a transitory phenomenon in nondiabetic subjects.[42,43] Epidemiologic studies also support this view.[44,45] These studies indicate that populations consuming low-fat, high-carbohydrate diets have higher plasma triglyceride levels than those with higher fat intakes.[44,45] An advantage of the current study was that longer-term metabolic effects of two dietary regimens were investigated. Although only half the patients participated in the phase 2 extension, the high-carbohydrate diet still induced an increase in plasma triglyceride and VLDL cholesterol levels and caused worsening of glycemic control that persisted for 14 weeks; in contrast, lower levels of plasma triglyceride, VLDL cholesterol, and plasma glucose concentrations during the high–monounsaturated-fat diet also persisted for 14 weeks.

Despite the advantages of the high–monounsaturated-fat diet on lipoprotein and glucose metabolism in NIDDM patients, some investigators may be hesitant to recommend such diets because they believe that diets higher in fat content may promote obesity. This belief is based on results of some cross-sectional observational studies documenting a positive association between fat intake and obesity[46–48] as well as on theoretical considerations of the higher metabolic cost of storing dietary carbohydrates as adipose tissue triglyceride incomparison with dietary fats.[49,50] The direct proof for such a notion, however, is lacking. In short-term and extended-term studies when the energy intake is kept constant, diets rich in fat or carbohydrates have not resulted in any significant weight gain or loss.[11–14,22–24,51] In the current study also, using equal-energy, high-carbohydrate diets and high–monounsaturated-fat diets, no change in body weight was noted during the extended period of 14 weeks. Others may argue that high-fat diets, either due to high energy density or enhanced palatability, may lead to increased energy consumption and thus obesity.[52] On the other hand, well-controlled studies have documents a precise regulation of energy intake in humans despite wide differences in food composition, particularly in the proportion of dietary carbohydrates and fats.[53,54] Also, it has been known since the early 19th century that fat is more satiating and inhibits gastric emptying. Increased palatability of high–monounsaturated-fat diets may in fact mean better patient compliance to the prescribed diets. Despite the controversy, it seems clear that if energy intake is regulated, a high–monounsaturated-fat diet or a high-carbohydrate diet will have similar effects on body weight.

The implications of our study, however, may still be questioned by some because of epidemiologic data from populations, such as the Japanese, the Chinese, and the African, which habitually consume low-fat, high-carbohydrate diets and have low rates of coronary heart disease.[55–57] Furthermore, these populations tend to be lean, have low rates of diabetes mellitus, and have low LDL cholesterol levels. The lower-ing of LDL cholesterol levels in these populations probably is largely due to markedly low intake of saturated fatty acids. On the other hand, low rates of coronary heart disease have also been reported from Mediterranean areas where subjects traditionally eat a high-fat, low-carbohydrate diet; however, most of fat energy is contributed by monounsaturated fatty acids and not by saturated fatty acids.[55,58] These populations also have low LDL cholesterol levels.[59] Therefore, epidemiologic studies support the use of both high-carbohydrate diets and high–monounsaturated-fat diets in nondiabetic healthy subjects. In patients with NIDDM, who often are obese and are prone to hypertriglyceridemia and low HDL cholesterol levels, a high–monounsaturated-fat diet appears to be superior to a high-carbohydrate diet. The final proof, however, will require a direct comparison of the two dietary approaches with the primary outcome variables being cardiovascular morbidity and mortality. Such studies, however, may not be undertaken for economic reasons and because of practical difficulties. In the meantime, it seems appropriate to use the diet that produces the most favorable risk factor profile.

On a practical note, although the current study used olive oil as a source of monounsaturated fatty acids, similar effects can be expected with perhaps less expensive sources of monounsaturated fatty acids, such as canola oil and high-monounsaturated varieties of safflower and sunflower oils. Avocados and nuts, such as pecans, almonds, macadamias, pistachios, hazelnuts, and cashews, as well as mustard seed and peanut oil, are also rich sources of monounsaturated fatty acids. The most important issues inn planning a high-monounsaturated-fat diet are (1) not to exceed the required energy intake and (2) to maintain a low intake of cholesterol-raising saturated fatty acids and *trans*-low fatty acids.

Finally, we conclude that high-carbohydrate diets in NIDDM patients may cause persistent increase in plasma triglyceride and VLDL cholesterol levels, hyperinsulinemia, and deterioration in glycemic control; all of these metabolic changes may be deleterious and have the potential to accelerate atherosclerosis as well as microangriopathy. Since intake of saturated and *trans*-fatty acids should be curtailed and it is not recommended to increase consumption of polyunsaturated fats beyond 10% of total energy intake, *cis*-monounsaturated fats provide a suitable alternative to replace carbohydrates in the diet of NIDDM patients. Diets with higher proportions of *cis*-monounsaturated fats may be advantageous in reducing the long-term complications, particularly coronary heart disease, in NIDDM patients.

This study was supported in part by a grant from Pfizer Inc, New York, NY, the National Institutes of Health grants (M01-RR00633, M01-RR-00400, M01-RR-00827, M01-RR00070, HL-29252, HL-08506, and DK 38949), and the Medical Research Service of the San Diego (Calif) Veterans Affairs Medical Center.

We acknowledge the help of the nursing and dietetic service of the general clinical research centers of the University of Texas Southwestern Medical Center at Dallas, Stanford University (Calif) School of Medicine, and the University of Minnesota, Minneapolis, and the special diagnostic and treatment unit of the Veterans Affairs Medical Center, San Diego, Calif. We thank Keith Lowther, Conrad Augustin, and John Poindexter for data collection, Kathy Schutt and Christopher Clark for lipoprotein analysis and Tamy Wang for technical assistance.

# References

1. American Diabetes Association. Nutritional recommendations and principles for individuals with diabetes mellitus: 1986. *Diabetes Care.* 1987;10:126–132.
2. Special Report Committee of the Canadian Diabetes Association. Guidelines for the nutritional management of diabetes mellitus: 1980: a special report from the Canadian Diabetes Association. *J Can Diet Assoc.* 1981;42:110–118.
3. Diabetes and Nutrition Study Group of the European Association for the Study of Diabetes. Nutritional recommendations for individuals with diabetes mellitus. *Diabetes Nutr Metab.* 1988; 1:145–149.
4. National Heart, Lung, and Blood Institute. Report of the National Cholesterol Education Program Expert Panel on Detection, Evaluation, and Treatment of High Blood Cholesterol in Adults. *Arch Intern Med.* 1988;148:36–39.
5. National Institutes of Health. Consensus development conference on diet and exercise in non–insulin-dependent diabetes mellitus. *Diabetes Care.* 1987; 10:639–644.
6. Reaven GM. Dietary therapy for non–insulin-dependent diabetes mellitus. *N Engl J Med.,* 1988; 319:862–864.
7. Grundy SM. Comparison of monounsaturated fatty acids and carbohydrates for lowering plasma cholesterol. *N Engl J Med.* 1986; 314:745–748.
8. Wolf RN, Grundy SM. Influence of exchanging carbohydrate for saturated fatty acids on plasma lipids and lipoproteins in men. *J Nutr.* 1983;113:1521–1528.
9. Simpson HCR, Simpson RW, Lousley S, et al. A high carbohydrate leguninous fibre diet improves all aspects of diabetic control. *Lancet.* 1981;1:1–5.
10. Abbott WGH, Boyce VL, Grundy SM, Howard BV. Effects of replacing saturated fat with complex carbohydrate in diets of subjects with NIDDM. *Diabetes Care.* 1989;12:102–107.
11. Coulston AM, Hollenbeck CB, Swislocki ALM, Chen Y-DI, Reaven GM. Deleterious metabolic effects of high-carbohydrate, sucrose-containing diets in patients with non–insulin-dependent diabetes mellitus. *Am J Med.* 1987; 82:213–220.
12. Coulston AM, Hollenbeck CB, Swislocki ALM, Reaven GM. Persistence of hypertriglyceridemic effect of low-fat, high-carbohydrate diets in NIDDM patients. *Diabetes Care.* 1989;12:94–101.
13. Riccardi G, Rivellese A, Pacioni D, Genovese S, Mastranzo P, Mancini M. Separate influence of dietary carbohydrate and fibre on the metabolic control in diabetes. *Diabetologia.* 1984;26:116–121.
14. Garg A, Bonanome A, Grundy SM, Zhang ZJ, Unger RH. Comparison of a high-carbohydrate diet with a high-monounsaturated-fat diet in patients with non–insulin-dependent diabetes mellitus. *N Engl J Med.* 1988;319:829–834.
15. Reaven GM. The role of insulin resistance and hyperinsulinemia in coronary heart disease. *Metabolism.* 1992;41:16–19.
16. Stout RW. Insulin and atheroma: 20-year perspective. *Diabetes Care.* 1990;13:631–654.
17. Mattson FH, Grundy SM. Comparison of effects of dietary saturated, monounsaturated, and polyunsaturated fatty acids on plasma lipids and lipoproteins in man. *J Lipid Res.* 1985;26:194–202.
18. Mensink RP, Katan MB. Effect of a diet enriched with monounsaturated or polyunsaturated fatty acids on levels of low-density and high-density lipoprotein cholesterol in healthy women and men. *N Engl J Med.* 1989;321:436–441.
19. Vega GL, Groszek E, Wolf R, Grundy SM. Influence of polyunsaturated fats on composition of plasma lippoproteins and apoliporproteins. *J Lipid Res.* 1982;23:811–822.
20. Shepherd J. Packard CJ, Patsch JR, Gotto AM Jr, Taunton OD. Effect of dietary polyunsaturated and saturated fat on the properties of high density lipoproteins and the metabolism of low density lipoproteins in man. *J Lipid Res.* 1980;21:91–99.
21. Rivellese AA, Giacco R, Genovese S. et al. Effects of changing amount of carbohydrate in diet on plasma lipoproteins and apoliporproteins in type II diabetic patients. *Diabetes Care.* 1990;13:446–448.
22. Bonanome A, Visona A, Lusiana L, et al. Carbohydrate and lipid metabolism in patients with non–insulin-dependent diabetes mellitus: effects of a low-fat, high-carbohydrate diet vs a diet high in monosaturated fatty acids. *Am J Clin Nutr.* 1991;54:586–590.
23. Garg A, Grundy SM, Unger RH. Comparison of effects of high and low carbohydrate diets on plasma lipoproteins and insulin sensitivity in patients with mild NIDDM. *Diabetes.* 1992;41:1278–1285.
24. Garg A, Grundy SM, Koffler M. Effect of high carbohydrate intake on hyperglycemia, islet function, and plasma lipoproteins in NIDDM. *Diabetes Care.* 1992; 15:1572–1580.
25. Parillo M, Rivellese AA, Ciardullo AV, et al. A high–monounsaturated-fat/low-carbohydrate diet improves peripheral insulin sensitivity in non–insulin-dependent diabetic patients. *Metabolism.* 1992; 41:1373–1378.
26. Harris JA, Benedict GG. *A Biometric Study of Basal Metabolism in Man.* Washington, DC: Carnegie Institutes of Washington; 1919. Publication 279.
27. Dept of Health and Human Services, Public Health Service. *Manual of Laboratory Operations: Lipid Research Clinics Program: Lipid and Lipoprotein Analysis.* 2nd ed. Washington, DC: Dept of Health and Human Services; 1982.
28. Hales CN, Randle PJ. Immunoassay of insulin with insulin-antibody precipitate. *Bichem J.* 1963;88:137–146.
29. Neter J. Waserman W, Kutner MH. *Applied Linear Statistical Models.* 2nd ed. Homewood, Ill: Irwin; 1985: 1021–1026.
30. Fontbonne AM, Eschwege EM. Insulin and cardiovascular disease: Paris prospective study. *Diabetes Care.* 1991;14:461–469.
31. West KM, Ahuja MMS, Bennett PH, et al. The role of circulating glucose and triglyceride concentrations and their interactions with other 'risk factors' as determinants of arterial disease in nine diabetic population samples from the WHO multi-national study. *Diabetes Care.* 1983;6:361–369.
32. Hanefeld M, Schmechel H, Julius U, et al. Five-year incidence of coronary heart disease related to major risk factors and metabolic control in newly diagnosed non–insulin-dependent diabetes. *Nutr Metab Cardiovasc Dis.* 1991;1:135–140.

33. Fontbonne A, Eschwege E, Cambien F, et al. Hypertriglyceridemia as a risk factor of coronary heart disease mortality in subjects with impaired glucose tolerance or diabetes: results from the 11-year follow-up of the Paris prospective study. *Diabetologia.* 1989;32:300–304.

34. Klein RL, Lyons TJ, Lopes-Virella MF. Metabolism of very low- and low-density lipoproteins isolated from normolipidaemic type 2 (non–insulin-dependent) diabetic patients by human monocyte-derived macrophages. *Diabetologia.* 1990;33:299–305.

35. Himsworth HP. The dietetic factor determining the glucose tolerance and sensitivity to insulin of healthy men. *Clin Sci.* 1935;2:67–94.

36. Brunzell JD, Lerner RL, Hazzard WR, Porte D Jr, Bierman EL. Improved glucose tolerance with high carbohydrate feeding in mild diabetes. *N Engl J Med.* 1971; 284:521–524.

37. Anderson JW, Herman RH, Zakim D. Effect of high glucose and high sucrose diets on glucose tolerance of normal men. *Am J Clin Nutr.* 1973;26:600–605.

38. Anderson JW. Effect of carbohydrate restriction and high carbohydrate diets on men with chemical diabetes. *Am J Clin Nutr.* 1977;30:402–408.

39. Himsworth HP, Kerr RB. Insulin-sensitive and insulin-insensitive types of diabetes mellitus. *Clin Sci.* 1935;2:119–152.

40. Brunzell JD, Lerner RL, Porte D Jr, Bierman EL. Effect of a fat free, high carbohydrate diet on diabetic subjects with fasting hyperglycemia. *Diabetes.* 1974; 23:138–142.

41. Antonis A, Bershon I. The influence of diet on serum triglycerides in South African white and Bantu prisoners. *Lancet.* 1961;1:3–9.

42. Brussaard JH, Katan MB, Groot PHE, Havekes LM, Hautvast JGAJ. Serum lipoproteins of healthy persons fed a low-fat diet or a polyunsaturated fat diet for three months: a comparison of two cholesterol-lowering diets. *Atherosclerosis.* 1982;42:205–219.

43. Jones DY, Judd JT, Taylor PR, Campbell WS, Nair PP. Influence of caloric contributions and saturation of dietary fat on plasma lipids in premenopausal women. *Am J Clin Nutri.* 1987;45:1451–1456.

44. West CE, Sullivan DR, Katan, MB, Halferkamps IN, van der Torre HW. Boys from populations with high-carbohydrate intake have higher fasting triglyceride levels than boys from populations with high fat intake. *Am J Epidemiol.* 1990;131:271–282.

45. Stern MP, Gonzalez C, Mitchell BD, Villalpando E, Haffner SM, Hazuda HP. Genetic and environmental determinations of type II diabetes in Mexico City and San Antonio. *Diabetes.* 1992;41:484–492.

46. Dreon DM, Frey-Hewitt B, Ellworth N, Williams PT, Terry RB, Wood PD. Dietary fat: carbohydrate ratio and obesity in middle-aged men. *Am J Clin Nutr.* 1988;47:995–1000.

47. Romieu I, Willett WC, Stampfer MJ, et al. Energy intake and other determinants of relative weight. *Am J Clin Nutr.* 1988;47:406–412.

48. Tucker LA, Kano MJ. Dietary fat and body fat: a multivariate study of 205 adult females. *Am J Clin Nutr.* 1992;56:616–622.

49. Bjorntorp P, Sjorstrom L. Carbohydrate storage in man: speculations and some quantitative considerations. *Metabolism.* 1978; 27(suppl 2):1853–1865.

50. Flatt JP. The difference in the storage capacities for carbohydrate and for fat, and its implications in the regulation of body weight. *Ann N Y Acad Sci.* 1987;499:104–123.

51. Berry EM, Eisenberg S, Friendlander T, et al. Effects of diets rich in monounsaturated fatty acids on plasma lipoproteins: the Jerusalem Nutrition Study, II: monounsaturated fatty acids vs carbohydrates. *Am J Clin Nutr.* 1992;56:394–403.

52. Lissner L, Levitsky DA, Strupp BJ, Kalkwarf HJ, Roe DA. Dietary fat and the regulation of energy intake in human subjects. *Am J Clin Nutr.* 1987;46:886–892.

53. Foltin RW, Fischman MW, Moran TH, Rolls BJ, Kelly TH. Caloric compensation for lunches varying in fat and carbohydrate content by humans in a residential laboratory. *Am J Clin Nutr.* 1990;52:969–980.

54. Leibel RL, Hirsch J, Appel BE, Checani G. Energy intake required to maintain body weight is not affected by wide variation in diet composition. *Am J Clin Nutr.* 1992;55:350–355.

55. Keys A, Menotti A, Karvonen MJ, et al. The diet and 15-year death rate in the Seven Countries Study. *Am J Epidemiol.* 1986;124:903–915.

56. Chen Z, Peto R, Collins R, MacMohan S, Lu J, Li W. Serum cholesterol concentration and coronary heart disease in population with low cholesterol concentrations. *BMJ.* 1991; 303:276–282.

57. Bertrand E. Coronary disease in black Africans. *Ann Cardio Angeiol (Paris).* 1993;42:193–198.

58. Menotti A, Keys A, Aravanis C, et al. Seven Countries Study: first 20-year mortality data in 12 cohorts of six countries. *Ann Med.* 1989; 21:175–179.

59. Keys A. Coronary heart disease in seven countries. *Circulation.* 1970; (suppl I):1–211.

 **Article Review Form at end of book.**

# WiseGuide Wrap-Up

- Beta-carotene, vitamin C, vitamin E, selenium, fiber, and cruciferous vegetable (broccoli, cauliflower) are dietary protectors against cancer.

- Diets which are high in fat, alcohol, nitrites (preservatives for meats), and aflatoxins (poisons from moldy peanuts and seeds) seem to be contributors to cancer.

- About 50 percent of people with diabetes mellitus do not even realize that they have the condition.

- A major contributing factor in diabetes mellitus is overweightness.

## R.E.A.L. Sites

This list provides a print preview of typical **coursewise** R.E.A.L. sites. (There are over 100 such sites at the **courselinks**™ site.) The danger in printing URLs is that web sites can change overnight. As we went to press, these sites were functional using the URLs provided. If you come across one that isn't, please let us know via email to: webmaster@coursewise.com. Use your Passport to access the most current list of R.E.A.L. sites at the **courselinks**™ site.

**Site name:** American Cancer Society

**URL:** http://www.cancer.org

**Why is it R.E.A.L.?** You can search this page for a variety of cancer information, including the latest research, prevention strategies, and ways to become involved in the fight against cancer.

**Activities:** What are the major diet and activity factors that affect risks for each of the seven most common cancers? Be sure to summarize each cancer and the best approaches to risk reduction.

**Site name:** Diabetes.com

**URL:** http://www.diabetes.com

**Why is it R.E.A.L.?** Provides opportunities for involvement in support groups, information for children with diabetes mellitus, and information on women's health and pregnancy. This is a very thorough site with a great deal of potential material.

**Activities:** (1)List and describe the typical symptoms of a person with diabetes mellitus. (2)Differentiate between diabetes mellitus and diabetes insipidus.

**Site name:** National Cancer Institute

**URL:** http://www.nci.nih.gov

**Why is it R.E.A.L.?** Allows access to a great deal of reliable cancer information. Your search can be based as a patient, a health professional, or a researcher.

**Site name:** Diabetes Interview World

**URL:** http://www.diabetesworld.com

**Why is it R.E.A.L.?** This page has easy-to-use links to additional sites, in addition to the user asking questions and receiving answers on diabetes-related issues.

**Activities:** This site notes that some therapies used to treat hyperglycemia may result in hypoglycemia; what are the possible mechanisms for this?

# Index

Note: Names in boldface type indicate authors of readings.

# Putting it in *Perspectives*
## -Review Form-

Your name:_____          Date: _____

Reading title: _____

**Summarize:** provide a one sentence summary of this reading: _____

_____

_____

_____

**Follow the Thinking:** how does the author back the main premise of the reading? Are the facts/opinions appropriately supported by research or available data? Is the author's thinking logical?

_____

_____

_____

_____

_____

_____

**Develop a Context:** answer one or both questions: how does this reading contrast or compliment your professor's lecture treatment of the subject matter? How does this reading compare to your textbook's coverage?

_____

_____

_____

_____

_____

_____

**Question Authority:** explain why you agree/disagree with the author's main premise?

_____

_____

_____

_____

_____

_____

**COPY ME!** Copy this form as needed. This form is also available at http://www.coursewise.com Click on: *Perspectives*.